The Journal of
Economic Perspectives

Contents
Volume 18 • Number 2 • Spring 2004

Statement of Purpose

The *Journal of Economic Perspectives* attempts to fill a gap between the general interest press and most other academic economics journals. The journal aims to publish articles that will serve several goals: to synthesize and integrate lessons learned from active lines of economic research; to provide economic analysis of public policy issues; to encourage cross-fertilization of ideas among the fields of economics; to offer readers an accessible source for state-of-the-art economic thinking; to suggest directions for future research; to provide insights and readings for classroom use; and to address issues relating to the economics profession. Articles appearing in the journal are normally solicited by the editors and associate editors. Proposals for topics and authors should be directed to the journal office, at the address inside the front cover.

Policy on Data Availability

It is the policy of the *Journal of Economic Perspectives* to publish papers only if the data used in the analysis are clearly and precisely documented and are readily available to any researcher for purposes of replication. Details of the computations sufficient to permit replication must be provided. The Editor should be notified at the time of submission if the data used in a paper are proprietary or if, for some other reason, the above requirements cannot be met.

Policy on Disclosure

Authors of articles appearing in the *Journal of Economic Perspectives* are expected to disclose any potential conflicts of interest that may arise from their consulting activities, financial interests or other nonacademic activities.

Journal of Economic Perspectives—Volume 18, Number 2—Spring 2004—Pages 3–28

Distinguished Lecture on Economics in Government: Lessons from Past Productivity Booms

Roger W. Ferguson Jr. and William L. Wascher

The U.S. economy has been enjoying substantially faster productivity growth for the past eight years than it did over the preceding two decades. From 1995 to 2003, labor productivity rose at an average annual rate of about 3 percent, up from an average annual rate of around 1.5 percent between 1973 and 1995. In both 2002 and 2003, output per hour increased more than 4 percent. The significance of the improvement since 1995 can hardly be overstated, even after one takes into account the possibility that the increases of the past two years in part reflect cyclical influences and thus overstate the underlying trend. If productivity were to continue to rise at an average annual rate of 3 percent, the standard of living in the United States would double roughly every 24 years. If, on the other hand, productivity growth were to revert to an average annual pace of 1.5 percent, a doubling in the standard of living would occur every 47 years.

A number of observers argue that the present era of robust trend productivity growth will soon come to an end. Others contend that the potential gains to productivity from the technological advances associated with the computer revolution are far from complete.[1] In assessing the likelihood of these alternative outcomes, one should recognize that periods of strong trend productivity growth, although perhaps novel to many of us, are not new to the U.S. economy. In particular, three earlier periods of strong trend productivity growth stand out from

---

[1] For pessimistic views, see Baker (2002) and Madrick (2002). For more optimistic views, see Jorgenson, Ho, and Stiroh (2002) and Oliner and Sichel (2002). For a recent assessment of the new economy in this journal, see Baily's Distinguished Lecture on Economics in Government (Baily, 2002).

■ *Roger W. Ferguson Jr. is Vice Chairman and William L. Wascher is an Assistant Director in the Division of Research and Statistics, Board of Governors of the Federal Reserve System, Washington, D.C.*

the historical record as especially worthy of further scrutiny for the lessons they may offer regarding the current episode: the late 1800s from roughly the end of the Civil War to around 1890; the decade or so between the end of World War I and the onset of the Great Depression; and the period from about 1950 to the early 1970s.[2]

We will start by setting out some facts about these three previous periods of strong productivity growth in the United States. Each period can be associated with particular advances in technology, a connection implying that technological progress is a necessary component of trend productivity growth. But significant technological advances were also evident in periods when productivity growth was less robust. Thus, a natural question to ask is whether complementary factors— including aspects of the labor market, of the business environment or of govern-ment policies like those related to education—combine to render technological change especially potent or help to foster the transmission of technological change into real gains in the efficiency of the production process.

After touching briefly on possible reasons for the end of productivity booms, we will then turn to some of the lessons that can be learned from what, in many ways, are striking similarities across the three previous episodes and the current one. Those lessons suggest that government policies have only a limited role in these periods of elevated productivity growth. The larger share of the credit goes to the private sector, as private agents are generally responsible for creating and exploiting the technologies that drove these previous productivity booms. None-theless, governments can play an important subordinate role by supporting basic research and by fostering an economic environment that is conducive to private sector initiative.

Previous Productivity Booms by the Numbers

Basic facts about economic growth, not to mention the interpretation of those facts, are sometimes subject to considerable debate. Some of these disagreements result from the lack of consistent information on U.S. productivity before data from the Bureau of Labor Statistics (BLS) became available in 1948.[3] For this earlier period, we use data developed by John Kendrick (1961), who constructed estimates

---

[2] Others will undoubtedly disagree with this taxonomy. Gordon (2000a), for example, argues that the historical record of productivity growth in the United States is best seen as one big "wave" that begins its rise in the late 1800s and tapers off in the late 1960s and early 1970s. From a standpoint of technological advance, that characterization may be appropriate. But for assessing the diffusion of technology and the forces that contributed to the speed of the diffusion, a focus on narrower periods of labor productivity booms is arguably more relevant.

[3] Some analysts have also questioned whether the more recent estimates are overstating productivity gains, suggesting that these estimates do not accurately capture increases in hours worked away from the office made possible by the new information technologies. See, for example, Roach (2003). Freeman (2002) mentions this possibility, as well, but he and Gordon (2000b) also note that the availability of the Internet in the workplace may reduce productive work time in the office. To our knowledge, there are no statistical studies that net out these opposing effects.

of GDP going back to the 1870s that were consistent with the prevailing definitions in the National Income and Product Accounts and were, in turn, based on estimates made by Simon Kuznets (1946). These estimates are often cited as the best available measure of U.S. output and productivity growth for that period. Although subsequent researchers—notably Balke and Gordon (1989) and Romer (1989)—have refined these estimates, the additional refinements focus primarily on the cyclical properties of output. A number of economic historians have also estimated U.S. GDP for the period before the Civil War (Gallman, 1966; Rhode, 2002). However, given that these estimates are based on less reliable information than those for the later, more industrialized period, we have elected to focus primarily on the period after 1870.

Table 1 presents average growth rates of productivity over various periods from 1873–2003. The data for labor productivity—defined as output per hour worked in the nonfarm business sector—appear in the first column. The two remaining columns show a breakdown of labor productivity growth into the portion attributable to multifactor productivity (output per unit of labor and capital inputs) and the portion attributable both to capital deepening (capital services per hour multiplied by capital's share of current dollar costs) and the quality (education and work experience) of the workforce. As noted above, we focus mostly on the growth of labor productivity because of its relevance for improvements in the nation's average standard of living. However, the decomposition of labor productivity growth into its major components is also of interest because it provides information on the relative importance of technological progress and efficiency gains (which are included in multifactor productivity growth) versus the diffusion of technological change through investments in fixed and human capital.

For the total period from 1873 to 2003, labor productivity rose at an average rate of 2.2 percent per year, with both multifactor productivity and capital deepening contributing importantly to overall productivity growth. However, the increases in output per hour did not proceed in a steady fashion. Instead, periods of robust growth were interspersed with periods of more modest productivity gains. Recognizing that the choice of periods is subjective, we take as the first episode of strong productivity growth the period from 1873 to 1890. During this period, labor productivity rose 2.6 percent per year, a rate thought to be considerably higher than the average growth experienced over the first 100 years of the United States. Kendrick's (1961) decomposition suggests that labor productivity growth in the late 1800s was fueled in part by capital investment—as indicated by the 1.1 percent annual rate of increase in the last column of the table.[4] From 1890 to 1917, the growth rate of labor productivity slowed to an average pace of only 1.5 percent per

[4] This estimate of productivity growth is the change from Kendrick's estimate of the average level of productivity in the 1870s to the level of productivity in 1890. Decompositions of productivity growth before 1948 are the subject of some debate, and thus estimates of multifactor productivity for these earlier periods should probably be viewed as less reliable than are the estimates of labor productivity.

Table 1
U.S. Productivity Growth, 1873–2003
(average annual percent change, nonfarm business sector)

Period	Labor productivity	Multifactor productivity	Contribution of capital deepening and labor composition
1873–2003	2.2	1.3	.9
Episode I			
1873–1890	2.6	1.5	1.1
1890–1917	1.5	.8	.7
Episode II			
1917–1927	3.8	2.8	1.0
1927–1948	1.8	1.7	.1
Episode III			
1948–1973	2.9	1.9	1.0
1973–1995	1.4	.4	1.0
Episode IV			
1995–2003	3.0	1.0	1.6

Notes: Labor productivity is measured as output per hour worked in the nonfarm business sector. Multifactor productivity is defined as output per unit of combined labor and capital inputs. The contribution of capital deepening to labor productivity growth is the change in capital services per hour weighted by capital's share of nominal output, and the contribution from labor composition is the change in the average quality of the work force (by education and experience); separate estimates for capital deepening and labor composition are available only beginning in 1948. Data from 1873 to 1948 are taken from Kendrick (1961). For the periods after 1948, we use data from the U.S. Bureau of Labor Statistics. Labor productivity data from the BLS are available through 2003, whereas data on multifactor productivity, capital services and labor composition are published only through 2001.

year. The U.S. economy then enjoyed a relatively brief spurt in labor productivity until about 1927, with labor productivity rising 3.8 percent per year and multifactor productivity up 2.8 percent per year. This productivity boom was led by the expansion of the automobile industry and robust productivity gains in manufacturing more generally. Productivity growth was markedly slower during the period that included the Great Depression and World War II (from 1927 to 1948), largely because of a lack of capital deepening. Multifactor productivity rose at a relatively solid pace—albeit not as fast as earlier in the century—despite the weak economy during much of that period.

From 1948 to 1973, a period sometimes referred to as the golden age of productivity growth, labor productivity rose at an annual rate of close to 3 percent. During this period, productivity accelerated across a broad range of industries, and both capital deepening and gains in multifactor productivity contributed to the strong pace of growth. During the productivity slowdown of the 1970s and 1980s, labor productivity growth slowed to an average pace of 1.4 percent per year, while multifactor productivity growth fell to a pace of 0.4 percent, the slowest pace of any of the periods shown in the table. Finally, labor productivity growth averaged 3.0 percent at an annual rate from 1995 to 2003, with higher rates of both capital deepening and multifactor productivity growth contributing to the pickup.

Sources of Past Productivity Booms: Technological Change

Although the productivity booms of the past century and a quarter obviously differed in many respects, each episode can readily be associated with the introduction of one or more prominent new technologies.

The productivity boom after the Civil War, for instance, appears to have had its genesis in a set of technological improvements that increased the flexibility of production and reduced transportation costs, which allowed firms to take advantage of economies of scale in production and distribution. The widespread introduction of steam engines and machinery powered by coal enabled firms to move away from sources of water power and closer to areas where inputs of labor and raw materials were more readily available. The Midwest—where water power was less abundant but coal was more abundant—benefited greatly from this development and, indeed, within a few decades became known as the "industrial heartland" of the United States. As a result of this regional shift in economic activity, the share of personal income generated in the Midwest rose from 20 percent in 1840 to 35 percent in 1880, whereas the share of income generated in the Northeast declined from 43 percent to 31 percent over that period (Easterlin, 1961).

The expansion of railroad transportation also helped raise productivity growth in the second half of the nineteenth century. Improved methods of steel production—notably, the Bessemer process and, later, Siemens's open hearth method—enabled railroads to lay longer-lasting steel track rather than iron track. The growth of telegraphy enabled railroad companies to coordinate the movement of trains over a wider area. As a result, railroads expanded their geographic coverage significantly after the Civil War. From 1860 to 1890, the number of main track miles operated by railroad companies more than quintupled, from 31,000 miles to 167,000 miles, while the number of freight cars in operation jumped from 185,000 to more than 1 million (U.S. Census Bureau, 1997, Series Q321; Fishlow, 1966).

Although the magnitude of the railroad's contribution to productivity growth during this period is the subject of considerable debate (David, 1969; Fishlow, 2000; Fogel, 1979), the expansion of the railroads clearly drove transportation costs sharply lower and resulted in significant increases in the geographic size of product markets. In 1830, the transportation of goods from New York to Chicago occurred mainly by canal and required three weeks even during the warmer months of the year; moreover, canals often did not operate in the winter. In contrast, by 1870 the same goods could be transported between these two cities in three days by railroad any time of the year (Paullin, 1932). In addition, the construction of new rail lines in western states opened those markets to a wide range of east coast and midwestern manufacturers. Subsequently, freight rates fell from $2\frac{1}{4}$ cents per ton-mile in 1860 to less than 1 cent per ton-mile by 1890. As a result, the quantity of goods transported by rail increased sharply, from about 12 billion ton-miles in 1870 to 80 billion ton-miles in 1890.[5]

The advances in transportation were complemented by improved communications, largely as a result of the expansion of the telegraph. As noted above, the telegraph aided the expansion of railroads by improving the coordination of rail traffic. But the ability to send messages rapidly over long distances also proved valuable in many other industries. Initially, sending a telegram was relatively expensive, with rates between New York and San Francisco averaging $7.45 for ten words or less in the late 1860s. By the late 1880s, rates for the same message had fallen to as little as $1.00. As a result, the number of telegraph messages handled by Western Union rose from less than 6 million in 1867 to nearly 56 million in 1890 (U.S. Census Bureau, 1997, Series R48 and R74). The better information flows that accompanied the wider use of telegraphy contributed to better decision making and higher productivity throughout the economy.

Agriculture also was increasingly mechanized in the decades immediately after the Civil War, though the change in agriculture was not as impressive as in the industrial sector. The abundance of land in western states limited the interest among farmers in raising land productivity. However, labor services were often difficult to obtain, so farmers were quite willing to invest in labor-saving machinery. As a result, the better plows, seed drills, reapers and threshers developed by manufacturers were in high demand by farmers, and the amount of labor required to farm an acre of land fell sharply for many crops (Atack, Bateman and Parker, 2000).

In the second productivity boom in the years after World War I, the chief technological innovation was most likely the spread of electrification to the factory floor. The use of electric motors in the production process increased substantially in the first quarter of the century (David, 1990; Mowery and Rosenberg, 2000). For example, the amount of mechanical energy derived from electric motors rose from 475,000 horsepower in 1899 to nearly 34 million horsepower in 1929, and the fraction of overall factory horsepower produced with electricity rose from less than 5 percent to more than 80 percent over that period (U.S. Census Bureau, 1997, Series P70). With electric motors, each machine in a factory could be driven by its own power source. As a result, manufacturing plants could be organized in a way that maximized the efficient movement of materials, rather than the efficient transmission of power. In this regard, electric motors facilitated the spread of

---

[5] Estimates of track construction, freight rates and ton-miles transported are taken from Fishlow (1966, 2000).

continuous processing techniques and assembly lines. As firms moved to reorganize their production processes to take advantage of the increases in efficiency afforded by electric power, factory productivity rose significantly. By one estimate, productivity growth in the manufacturing sector as a whole increased about $5\frac{1}{2}$ percent per year between 1919 and 1929 (Kendrick, 1961, p. 152).

Of course, other technological innovations also contributed to productivity growth during this period. Notable among them were the telephone, which by the 1920s had largely replaced the telegraph; the internal combustion engine, which led to motorized vehicles that brought sizable productivity gains in the transportation and agriculture sectors; and a variety of technological advances in machine tools. In addition, the early 1900s were characterized by the first wave of office automation equipment, including the portable typewriter and adding and duplicating machines. These machines improved the efficiency of a wide range of management and accounting tasks. In real terms, business investment in office equipment increased from about $50 million (in 1929 dollars) in 1899 to nearly $500 million in 1929, with a particularly large jump evident in the 1920s (Cortada, 1993, Figure 3.1).

The productivity gains of the 1950s and 1960s had their roots in a wide range of technological innovations made during the 1930s as well as in research sponsored by the military during World War II. Field (2003), in particular, emphasizes the importance of technological change in the 1930s and points to the array of process and product innovations compiled by Kleinknecht (1987), Schmookler (1966) and Mensch (1979) as evidence.[6] Examples of important innovations during this decade include research advances in polymer chemistry that led to the invention of Plexiglas, Teflon and Nylon; significant advances in civil engineering; and the introduction of the DC-3 aircraft in 1936.

Research aimed at enhancing U.S. military capabilities during World War II also led to new technologies that had important spillovers to commercial applications after the war (Mowery and Rosenberg, 2000). For example, although the major research advances in synthetic polymerization chemistry (most notably, the introduction of catalytic cracking in the processing of crude oil) were made in the 1920s and 1930s, the synthetic rubber program launched during the war resulted in techniques that led to the mass production of the first synthetic polymer from petroleum-based feedstocks. Similarly, production of polyethylene, a petrochemical-based plastic discovered in the 1930s, jumped in the 1940s because of its widespread use in military equipment. The military's need for large stocks of penicillin led to a production process for it that turned out to have applicability to a wide

---

[6] Field also points to the sizable increase in multifactor productivity between 1929 and 1941 as evidence of the extent of technological progress during the 1930s. As he notes, however, Goldin (2000) and Bernanke and Parkinson (1991) offer alternative explanations for the rise in productivity over that decade.

range of pharmaceuticals, while wartime advances in microelectronics subsequently contributed significantly to the development of new commercial electronic products.

The commercialization of these earlier innovations sharply increased the number of products made wholly or partly from newly developed plastic polymers and other synthetic materials. The use of polyethylene, for example, spread quickly after the war, and additional technological advances isolated new forms of synthetics and further reduced production costs for chemicals and pharmaceuticals. Overall, between 1947 and 1970, production in the rubber and plastic products industry rose nearly 7 percent per year, and the output of the chemical products industry rose more than 8 percent per year (Board of Governors of the Federal Reserve System, *Indexes of Industrial Production*). In comparison, over the same period, production in the manufacturing sector as a whole rose about $4\frac{1}{2}$ percent per year.

Other notable contributors to productivity growth during this period include the invention of the transistor in 1947 and the diffusion of earlier technological advances into the transportation sector. Commercial applications of the transistor, initially in solid state consumer electronic products, were stimulated by improvements in the fabrication process (in 1954) and by the introduction of the integrated circuit (in 1958). With the rise in demand, semiconductor production jumped markedly, rising nearly 20 percent per year during the 1960s (Board of Governors of the Federal Reserve System, *Indexes of Industrial Production*).

In transportation, the 1950s and 1960s saw major productivity improvements in all three major segments: air, rail and trucking. Gordon (1992) estimates that labor productivity in the railroad industry rose at an average annual rate of around $4\frac{1}{2}$ percent between 1948 and 1969; contributing importantly to those productivity gains were the replacement of steam locomotives with diesel locomotives and innovations that increased the capacity of the rolling stock (Mansfield, 1965). The use of the jet engine in commercial aircraft—most notably, the introduction of the Boeing 707 in 1958—sharply reduced the time and cost of transporting passengers and freight, and Gordon's estimates place the growth of productivity in the commercial airline industry at more than 7 percent per year during the 1960s, well above the rate of labor productivity growth for the economy as a whole.[7] Finally, while technological improvements in internal combustion engines also found their way into medium and heavy trucks during this period, productivity gains in trucking—estimated by Gordon at about $3\frac{1}{2}$ percent per year in the 1950s and 1960s—were fueled importantly by substantial investment in road improvements,

---

[7] Of course, the invention and commercial use of the airplane was a technological innovation that predated the jet engine, and air travel in the late 1920s represented a substantial improvement over other forms of passenger transportation. The estimates of Gordon (1992) show that productivity in airline transportation rose about 7 percent per year between 1935 and 1959, as well.

most notably the federally funded expansion of the U.S. highway system (Keeler and Ying, 1988).

For purposes of comparison, the technological origins of the more recent productivity boom also bear a brief mention. Obviously, the invention of the transistor and the development of the mainframe computer were precursors of the technological advances that contributed to the current productivity boom. However, the real drivers of the productivity gains in the 1990s were the related high-tech innovations of the 1970s and 1980s, including the personal computer, fiber optics, wireless communications and the Internet. Many of the recent technological innovations have significantly altered the ways in which firms interact with their customers and have raised the productivity of the economy as a result (Brynjolfsson and Hitt, 2000). Nearly all large retail chains have followed the lead of Amazon.com and established an on-line presence; customers now routinely pay bills online; and computerized reservations and e-tickets have become the norm in the travel industry. Moreover, from manufacturing to retailing, innovations in supply-chain management practices made possible by new technologies have substantially reduced inventory-related costs.

Sources of Past Productivity Booms: Organizational Change

In most cases, the principal technologies that stimulated past productivity booms were invented well before the productivity gains were realized. For example, the steam engine was invented in the 1700s, well before it had any measurable effect on the production process in the United States. Similarly, railroads were being built in the 1840s, and the first electric power plant was built in 1882. Computers were introduced in 1945, and the absence of a measurable contribution to productivity was a puzzle to many economists as late as the mid-1990s (Oliner and Sichel, 1994). What delayed the translation of these innovations into gains in productivity? In part, the lags reflected the challenges of developing commercial applications for the new technologies; for example, complementary innovations were frequently required to enable new inventions to be put to practical use. In addition, replacing older machines with equipment that embodied the new technologies was often not immediately profitable, and thus, firms frequently took some time before making the capital investments required to take full advantage of technological progress.

However, substantial changes in business practices and in the organization of firms often were also needed to enable businesses to achieve the potential productivity gains associated with new technologies. In many cases, these organizational changes went hand in hand with the technological advances—the changes both being made possible by the new technologies and being necessary to achieve the additional productivity associated with the use of these technologies. Chandler

(1977), in particular, documents the evolution of the modern business enterprise, pointing out both how new technologies influenced the optimal hierarchical structure of the firm and how the resulting changes in business organization increased productivity.

In the productivity boom of the late nineteenth century, the major organizational changes involved firms growing in size to take advantage of the economies of scale made possible by the new technologies. Before the Civil War, most businesses were either sole proprietorships or partnerships serving local markets, and they consisted of small shops that employed skilled workers involved in each aspect of the production process. As the spread of railroads lowered transportation costs and increased the size and number of potential markets, the greater availability of steam power enabled manufacturers to set up factories to take advantage of economies of scale in production. As a result, the size of firms rose substantially in many industries. In the cotton industry, for example, the median firm size (measured as the annual value of gross production in 1860 dollars) rose from $31,000 in 1850 to nearly $100,000 in 1870; similarly, in the iron industry, the median firm size rose from $24,000 in 1850 to more than $200,000 in 1870 (Atack, 1986). Outside manufacturing, the emergence of large wholesalers (and, later, retailers) to take advantage of increased distributional efficiencies reduced the costs of moving commodities and manufactured goods from the farm or factory to retailers' shelves.

These larger enterprises had to confront communications challenges in both production and distribution. With the telegraph making rapid communication over great distances more feasible, firms were able to monitor activities from a central administrative office. However, processing the increased flow of information required changes in the organizational structure of the firm. In particular, to make effective use of the opportunities presented by better communications, firms often set up hierarchical management systems to control the production process and to coordinate the flow of goods across the distribution system. The more informed decision making associated with this administrative structure enabled firms to match production to orders, shorten delivery times and reduce inventory holdings.

The second major productivity boom, in the years after World War I, required changes in business organization that permitted firms to take advantage of advances in production processes in the early 1900s. These changes involved both the economies of scale associated with the increasingly complex production techniques in the manufacture of goods and also large organizations embracing economies of scope. The diffusion of the electric motor throughout the factory floor increased the use of continuous-process methods and the assembly line and, thus, accelerated the trend toward mass production. In addition, as early as the 1880s, manufacturers had begun to integrate forward into distribution; one noteworthy example was the meatpacking industry, in which firms purchased refrigerated rail cars that allowed the shipment of beef from centralized slaughterhouses to branch houses that served local markets. The advances in mass production techniques and the increasing complexity of many manufactured products led firms in other industries to integrate forward not only into distribution but also into retailing; this vertical integration reduced transactions costs even more and further increased the optimal size of firms. Many of the large corporations that arose at this time—Ford, General Motors and General Electric, for example—are still with us today.

The vertical integration of these large corporations, in turn, led to a greater emphasis on retail, accounting, advertising and other activities not directly related to production (Galambos, 2000). To compete in retail markets, firms needed to understand the latest consumer trends and to encourage consumers to associate specific products with a particular firm; in addition, firms needed to establish accounting systems to keep track of a wider range of activities. As a result, marketing, advertising and accounting departments increased in size and importance within the typical corporation. Also, with their executives now more sensitive to market share and their cost advantage over their competitors, large corporations began to develop applied research departments aimed at providing the firm with a technological edge.

During the third productivity boom, following World War II, firms responded to the myriad of new products made possible by the technological advances of the 1930s and 1940s by making new changes in their organizational structure. In particular, corporate managers increasingly split their firm's activities into separate divisions, each with its own manufacturing and marketing departments. For domestic production, this multidivisional approach was well-suited to the manufacturing of diverse product lines by a single company; DuPont and Monsanto are good examples of this approach (Baskin and Miranti, 1997). This structure also turned out to be an effective method of handling corporate operations in different geographic areas, as seen by the rise of multinational corporations during this period. After World War II, new trade agreements and efforts to revitalize Europe and Japan allowed American firms to make significant inroads into foreign markets. To handle these long-distance operations more easily, corporations often set up foreign subsidiaries that could adapt quickly to changing circumstances in the host country's marketplace. The economic importance of these multinational corporations rose steadily, so that by 1966, the total assets of U.S. multinational firms accounted for nearly 35 percent of U.S. corporate assets (U.S. Bureau of Economic Analysis, 1966).

Organizational structure during the productivity boom of the late 1990s has, in some respects, shifted away from the large corporations that dominated the U.S. economy during much of the twentieth century. To be sure, the marketplace in many industries is still characterized by large, well-established firms. In some industries—the financial services sector comes to mind—recent technological innovations have, if anything, increased the scale of business. But in other industries, intense global competition has motivated many corporations to narrow their focus to core production-related activities and to outsource other functions. Increasingly, these supporting firms are providing their services from overseas, taking advantage both of lower labor costs there and of the revolution in communications. The impact of this outsourcing is already evident in the business community, with some computer-related support for U.S. providers located in India, architectural drawings rendered in the Philippines and some legal functions provided from nations in the Caribbean.

In addition, much of the rapid technological innovation since 1995 or so has occurred outside the large corporate sector, and the success of that innovation has boosted the pace at which new ventures are being created. For example, more than 700,000 new businesses were incorporated each year, on average, in the 1990s, about double the pace of the 1970s (U.S. Census Bureau, 2001). Of course, many of these firms failed. However, many others either grew or were bought by larger firms better able to market and distribute the most promising innovations.

Sources of Past Productivity Booms: Financial Market Change

A third major ingredient in promoting the productivity gains associated with technological innovation has been a complementary set of innovations in the financial sector that have changed the financial landscape in ways that were especially appropriate to the predominant form of business organization in each period.[8]

Before the Civil War, most nonfinancial business investment was financed internally with retained earnings, with capital provided by family or friends or through partnerships formed with other proprietors. The chief exceptions were the canals and railroads, which were issuing stocks and bonds in the 1850s (Chandler, 1977). With the sharp increases in the scale of operations of many firms after the Civil War, however, businesses in other industries perceived a need for greater capital investments and began to look more toward external sources of financing.

The main sources of funding in the decades after the Civil War were debt and preferred stock—that is, stock that promised a certain dividend but had no voting rights. (Railroad companies were an exception to this pattern—they sold sizable amounts of common stock to investors seeking large capital gains after the completion of new construction projects (Fishlow, 2000).) Debt often took the form of secured loans, in large part because investors were concerned about the informational asymmetries they faced in evaluating the bankruptcy risk of particular firms. In addition, the owners of many firms preferred financing with debt rather than common stock because they did not want to see their equity diluted or their control of the enterprise diminished. Similarly, preferred stock, which reduced bankruptcy risk but did not dilute the owners' equity in the firm because it offered no voting rights, was often used when assets were insufficient to secure the loan. Thus, despite the prevalence of information problems, financial intermediaries were able to

---

[8] This section draws from Baskin and Miranti (1997) and White (2000).

provide firms with external sources of funds, making possible the rapid buildup in the capital stock that took place in the late 1800s. Indeed, the total value of bank loans rose from less than $1 billion in 1870 to more than $4 billion in the early 1890s, a notable increase in nominal value during a period when the aggregate price level was falling (U.S. Census Bureau, 1997, Series X581).

Corporate finance in the years after World War I was characterized by an increase in the importance of equity markets. At the New York Stock Exchange alone, the volume of stock sales rose from 186 million shares in 1917 to more than 1 billion shares in 1929 (U.S. Census Bureau, 1997, Series X531), the value of preferred and common stock issuance increased from $455 million to $6.8 billion over the same period (U.S. Census Bureau, 1997, Series X514-515), and the number of individuals holding stock jumped from 500,000 in 1900 to 10 million by 1930 (Hawkins, 1963).

The public's interest in common stock increased for several reasons. First, and probably most important, the profitability of large corporations during the early 1900s was accompanied by expanding middle and upper classes that wanted to take part in the economic gains associated with the introduction of new technologies such as the internal combustion engine and the electric motor. The main way to share in these capital gains was to purchase some ownership in those corporations. About the same time, the informational problems that had constrained interest in common stock through the early 1900s were declining. Rising demand from investors in the late 1800s for information about railroad companies had led to the proliferation of newsletters that reported on developments in that industry, and similar publications soon sprang up to provide information on other traded securities. These newsletters evolved into ratings agencies covering a wide range of individual corporations, with Moody's issuing the first bond ratings in 1909. Although these agencies' ratings focused on corporate bond issues, many also provided economic forecasting services and more detailed information about the relative risk of specific companies. As a result, more public companies recognized a need to address investors' concerns about risk and began to issue regular audited financial statements (Miranti, 2001). Interest in common stock was also fueled by the tendency to imbue them with characteristics similar to those associated with debt, with which investors were more familiar. For example, businesses frequently attempted to establish steady dividend streams in order to boost investors' confidence about the future profitability of the firm and to encourage them to hold their securities (Baskin and Miranti, 1997). Finally, the marketing of securities to the household sector became more aggressive in the 1920s, led by investment trusts—which offered investors a means of diversifying individual portfolios—and retail brokerage firms.

The third productivity boom, in the years after World War II, was accompanied by another rapid increase in bond and equity issuance. Despite significant increases in internal funds, the growth of investment spending over this period outpaced the rise in retained earnings, and the ratio of external financing to overall capital spending rose from an average of around 30 percent in the late 1940s to more than 40 percent in the early 1970s (Board of Governors of the Federal Reserve System, *Flow of Funds Accounts*).

Two specific developments in financial markets during this period bear mentioning. First, the late 1950s and 1960s saw the rise of the Eurodollar market—a market for U.S. dollar deposits and loans outside the United States and, at least initially, in Europe. Although the origin and early development of the Eurodollar market is attributed, in part, to a desire by holders of dollars to avoid U.S. regulations, including the Regulation Q interest rate ceilings, that market subsequently became a useful source of short-term financing—complementary to the commercial paper market—for large corporations seeking alternatives to more costly domestic commercial bank loans (Johnston, 1982; Kindleberger, 1993). Although no direct data on the size of the Eurodollar market are available, Baskin and Miranti (1997) estimate that this market increased from about $9 billion in 1964 to $247 billion by 1976. Second, the 1950s and 1960s were characterized by a sharp rise in the importance of large institutional investors—especially pension funds—in the stock and bond markets. This rise, coupled with the growth of mutual funds and brokerage houses, enabled smaller investors (either explicitly or implicitly) to invest more easily in stocks and bonds and to diversify their portfolios.

In the most recent productivity boom, financial intermediaries have expanded the range of financing alternatives available to businesses in response to the proliferation of start-up businesses and what is, for many firms, a riskier business environment. For larger lower-rated corporations that have significant default risk, the so-called junk bond market has offered the capability to raise funds even when other sources of financing are less available. Such firms' use of this market has increased markedly: Junk bond issuance rose from about $11 billion in 1984 to more than $100 billion in 2001, and the par value of outstanding junk-rated debt has increased from less than $100 billion in the mid-1980s to nearly $700 billion today. For smaller and yet-riskier firms, venture capital and initial public offerings have been important sources of financing. Venture capital investments, which were negligible in the early 1980s, rose to more than $100 billion in 2000, although they have since dropped back. Similarly, initial public offerings for nonfinancial companies (excluding spinoffs and leveraged buyouts) exploded from less than $5 billion per year in the late 1980s to roughly $30 billion in 2000.[9]

In addition, the financial industry has made significant advances in quantifying and managing risk. Many large financial institutions have, over the past decade, increasingly adopted internal credit-risk models to improve their ability to assess the riskiness of their portfolios. Moreover, financial market innovations, including

---

[9] Data on junk bonds in this paragraph are from Thompson Financial Securities Data Corporation and Moody's Investors Service. Data on venture capital investments are from PricewaterhouseCoopers/Thomson Venture Economics/National Venture Capital Association, *MoneyTree Survey*. Data on initial public offerings are from Thompson Financial Securities Data Corporation.

securitizations, credit derivatives and an improved secondary loan market, have allowed these institutions to manage their exposure to such risks better. These improvements in risk management may help to explain why financial institutions weathered the 2001 economic downturn so well relative to their difficulties in previous recessions.

Sources of Past Productivity Booms: Human Capital Accumulation

A fourth ingredient contributing to the productivity booms of the past has been the availability of a workforce capable of bringing to fruition the possibilities opened up by the technological innovations. In the 1800s, the new manufacturing technologies tended to be complementary with unskilled labor, whereas those associated with the distribution of goods tended to require more-skilled workers. In contrast, in the 1900s, technological change tended to increase the demand for skilled workers in both sectors. These shifts in labor demand typically were manifest in changing wage premiums for skilled labor, and workers responded to the incentives in ways that generally provided employers with a mix of workers able to harness the productivity improvements associated with the new technologies.

During the productivity boom in the late nineteenth century, technological change had two disparate effects on the demand for labor. First, the shift in manufacturing production from artisanal shops in the mid-1800s to factories after the Civil War and the subsequent rapid growth in the capital stock led to a substantial increase in the demand for unskilled labor (Engerman and Sokoloff, 2000). The new capital equipment embodying the technological advances of that period, coupled with the use of unskilled labor and the abundance of raw materials, often proved to be an effective substitute for skilled artisans (James and Skinner, 1985), and so firms increasingly looked to hire workers without any specific expertise to operate the new machines. Although such workers—who were often women, children and immigrants—likely reduced the average skill level of the manufacturing workforce, the availability of a large pool of unskilled labor enabled firms to take advantage of the potential organizational efficiencies and economies of scale associated with the new technologies, thus raising productivity for the economy as a whole.

Second, increases in firm size and the growth of businesses in the distribution sector increased the demand for workers who could perform clerical and managerial tasks. For example, the share of employed men who worked in white-collar occupations rose from less than 5 percent in 1850 to nearly 18 percent by 1900 (Margo, 2000). As these jobs typically involved some basic knowledge of reading and mathematics, such workers tended to have more formal education than the average individual. However, the level of competency needed for these jobs generally consisted of bookkeeping and secretarial skills that required, at most, a high school education (Chandler, 1977).

On net, these influences seems to have led to only a slight increase in the wage premium for skilled labor during the 1870 to 1890 period (Margo, 2000), and as a result, there was little impetus for widespread increases in educational attainment among the U.S. population. School enrollment rates among children held steady at about 50 percent over that period, and high-school graduation rates remained below 5 percent (U.S. Census Bureau, 1997, Series H433, H599).

The productivity boom of the early twentieth century was accompanied by a significant rise in the demand for higher-skilled labor. The need for white-collar workers continued to increase with the further growth in corporate size and the new focus on activities not directly related to the manufacture of goods. Moreover, these additional activities required better-educated managers to control and coordinate the diverse functions of the corporation and more-skilled clerical workers to process the increased flow of information associated with vertical integration. The acquisition of these additional skills took place in different ways. Chandler (1977) emphasizes, for example, the inception of the modern business school during this period, with classes on commerce, accounting, marketing, law and finance. Cortada (1993) notes also that vendors of new office machinery often educated clerical workers about the uses and operation of the new equipment.

In contrast to the late 1800s, the use of more-advanced technologies in the manufacturing sector also led to a relative shift in labor demand toward more capable and highly educated blue-collar workers. In particular, the increasing use of continuous processing production techniques made possible by the electrification of factories reduced the demand for unskilled manual workers, while the greater complexity of the newly installed capital equipment increased the demand for workers who could read manuals and blueprints, perform mathematical calculations requiring knowledge of algebra and geometry and had some basic knowledge of science (Goldin and Katz, 1998). In response, enrollment rates in secondary schools increased sharply, and the high school graduation rate rose to more than 25 percent by the late 1920s (U.S. Census Bureau, 1997, Series H599).

The productivity boom of the 1950s and 1960s showed a similar pattern. The new technologies and skilled labor again were complements in production, so that the availability of skilled labor in this episode helped to maintain the returns to technological innovation. As in the early 1900s, the greater cognitive skills possessed by more-educated workers were especially effective in implementing the new technologies (Nelson, Peck and Kalachek, 1967), and in this instance, the demand for workers in professional and technical occupations increased sharply, with especially rapid growth for engineers and technicians (U.S. Census Bureau, 1997, Series D233-D682). With the occupations in highest demand now requiring a college education, the percentage of 18- to 24-year-olds enrolled in college rose from about 14 percent in 1950 to roughly 32 percent in 1970 (U.S. Census Bureau, 1997, Series H701).[10]

The current productivity boom has also been characterized by skill-biased technological change, with the advances in the high-tech sector associated with a sharp increase in the demand for workers with computer-related skills and a further widening in the skill premium for workers with a college degree. As a result, college enrollment rates, which stagnated during the productivity slowdown in the 1970s and 1980s, began to rise again in the 1990s. In addition, the demand for lower-skilled workers has been damped in recent years by the longer-term downtrend in large segments of the manufacturing sector and competitive pressures more generally (Paul and Siegel, 2001). In response, many lesser-skilled adults have moved to retool their skills by returning to school (Kane and Rouse, 1999). Most notably, enrollments at community colleges increased about 30 percent between 1985 and 2000, and the percentage of adults attending an education program rose from 33 percent in 1991 to 45 percent in 1999, with a particularly large increase evident for the unemployed.[11]

Why Do Productivity Booms End?

It is informative not only to identify the sources of past productivity booms, but perhaps also to ask why periods of strong trend productivity growth end. Three possibly overlapping hypotheses have been put forth. First, successful new technologies may eventually lead to financial imbalances and overinvestment associated with excessive optimism. Second, periods of strong productivity growth may eventually run out of steam as the productivity-increasing opportunities associated with new technologies are exhausted. Third, exogenous shocks may bring an end to boom periods. Although elements of these three hypotheses can be seen in the past episodes of productivity booms, no clear pattern emerges.[12]

Some support for the hypothesis that financial imbalances may end productivity booms can be seen in Figure 1. Each of the episodes discussed in this paper

---

[10] The increase in college enrollments during this period was likely also boosted by the use of college deferments during the Vietnam War and by the G.I. bill.

[11] U.S. Department of Education, *Digest of Education Statistics*. Owing to data limitations, this measure includes adults enrolled in personal development programs. In 1999, for which more detailed information is available, roughly one-third of adults were participating in postsecondary education or career-related courses.

[12] We also note that each of the productivity booms we have discussed ended with a severe recession. However, this fact is a feature more of the way we identified the episodes of rapid productivity growth than of the episodes. In particular, we chose to measure our productivity booms between years in which cyclical conditions were roughly comparable precisely because we wanted to avoid contaminating our estimates of longer-run productivity growth with the sharp cyclical decline in productivity that typically accompanies a recession.

Figure 1
S&P Stock Price Index

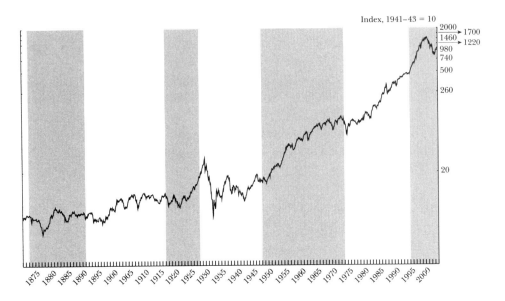

included a period of soaring stock prices: in the late 1870s, the 1920s, the 1960s and the late 1990s. In the late 1920s, the end of the run-up in equity prices was followed by a stock market crash; in the other three cases, after the run-up, stock prices fell substantially, but these declines could perhaps be considered "corrections" rather than "crashes." Did these stock market booms and falls reflect an overbuilding of investment capacity? By the end of the 1920s, certain industries—most notably automobiles and electric utilities—arguably had experienced a significant over-building of capacity. Similarly, in the late 1990s, there does appear to have been an overinvestment in high-tech and telecommunications equipment. But evidence of overinvestment is much harder to find in the late 1800s and in the 1960s. Indeed, one can even argue that the decline in stock prices in the mid-1970s was due largely to the beginning of a recession and the failure of economic policy to control inflation rather than to excessive optimism. Moreover, although the stock market declines of the 1880s and 1920s were both followed by extended economic depressions, modern economic analysis stresses that serious monetary policy mistakes were necessary for these depressions to occur (Rockoff, 2000; Bernanke, 1995). Also, although there likely was overinvestment in the high-tech sector in the late 1990s, the recent productivity data do not suggest that the current productivity boom has ended.

The second hypothesis—that productivity booms end when innovation and technical change levels off—surfaced to explain the productivity slowdown of the 1970s, with proponents pointing to a deceleration in the growth of research and development spending in the late 1960s as evidence of a decline in innovation.

Griliches (1988) has argued convincingly that this shortfall in R&D spending was not of sufficient magnitude to contribute much to that productivity slowdown, and the absence of data on R&D spending in earlier periods makes this hypothesis difficult to evaluate more generally. However, even if technological advances are eventually exhausted, we have no evidence that this possibility is as yet a significant risk to the current productivity boom. Both industrial R&D and patent applications have risen rapidly in recent years, suggesting that innovation—and the potential productivity gains associated with technological progress—will likely remain an important source of economic growth in the United States in coming years.

The third hypothesis—that exogenous shocks may contribute to the end of productivity booms—is also evident in some, but not all, past productivity booms. The 1973 oil shock is perhaps the most convincing example of an adverse shock that came at the end of a productivity boom, although the question of whether the "golden era" of productivity growth had actually ended a few years earlier is still the subject of much discussion. In addition, the severe bank panic of 1893 is viewed by some as an important contributor to the depression of the 1890s; however, whether this event was an exogenous shock or an indication of earlier economic excess (as in 1929) is debatable. Of course, the U.S. economy has also experienced significant exogenous shocks in recent years: for example, the terrorist attacks of September 11, 2001, the Iraq conflict and a variety of corporate scandals. It is encouraging that the economy seems to have successfully weathered these shocks with no significant harm to productivity growth.

With so few episodes to examine, we cannot definitively identify the reasons that productivity booms come to an end, as no clear pattern emerges among the four productivity booms discussed in this paper. Of course, we have no reason to expect that all productivity booms should end because of the same circumstances. Thus, our sense is that focusing on the conditions that are most conducive to fostering extended periods of strong productivity growth will be a more fruitful line of research.

Lessons from Past Productivity Booms

Productivity booms seem to involve four key ingredients: technological innovation; the willingness and ability of owners and corporate managers to reengineer the internal organization of their firms to take maximum advantage of those innovations; financial sector innovations tailored to the forms of business organization predominating at the time; and a skilled and flexible workforce. We undoubtedly can learn many valuable lessons from these similarities, but we will touch on a few that seem particularly important.

First, many of the technological innovations associated with past productivity booms were "general purpose technologies" with widespread applicability. Such technologies often operate through various channels—through improvements in energy, transportation or communications, for example—raising productivity not only in production but also in distribution and business practices. In many cases— railroads and computers being notable examples—the productivity improvements were initially most pronounced in the production of the capital equipment embodying the new technologies. Fishlow (1966) estimates that multifactor productivity in the railroad industry rose nearly 4 percent per year, on average, between 1840 and 1900, compared with increases of around 1 percent per year for the economy as a whole. Similarly, Oliner and Sichel (2002) estimate that, since 1990, efficiency gains in the production of high-tech equipment have accounted for about half of overall multifactor productivity growth in the nonfarm business sector.

In addition, general purpose technologies tend to attract substantial new investment capital. Fishlow (2000) points out that in the 1870s, investment in transportation facilities (mainly railroads) amounted to more than 15 percent of capital formation. Similarly, in 2003, investment in high-tech equipment as a share of overall business fixed investment stood at 34 percent, up from 13 percent in 1980. Moreover, the development of these new technologies often had important intersectoral linkages to other industries (Fishlow, 2000; Mowery and Rosenberg, 2000). In the nineteenth century, for example, the construction of railroads had backward linkages to the coal, iron and steel, and machinery industries and forward linkages to the distribution sector. Likewise, in the twentieth century, the innovations in electricity, chemistry and the development of the internal combustion engine led both to widespread productivity improvements in mature industries (like steel and railroads) and the creation of new industries (like plastics and commercial air transportation).

The importance of general purpose technologies raises the question of whether governments should attempt to stimulate the development of these technologies. To be sure, government intervention has, at times, made valuable contributions to technological progress. At a general level, state and federal governments have been an important source of funding for basic research, often in research universities or federal laboratories. In addition, the legal system provides incentives for innovation through the protection of intellectual property rights; in this regard, patent laws in the United States have attempted to strike a balance— allowing the inventors of new technologies to reap the benefits of their innovations, while encouraging the timely diffusion of new technologies and limiting the damage from monopoly power (Engerman and Sokoloff, 2000).[13] In some cases, government has supported certain new technologies more directly. In the 1850s

---

[13] For a discussion of patent policy tradeoffs in this journal, see Gallini (2002). For a discussion of patent policy in the context of financial market innovations, see Ferguson (2003). Some observers have also emphasized that technological diffusion can be effectively achieved through the sharing of information or collective invention. See Meyer (2003), who points to the technological improvements in steel production in the 1800s and in personal computers in the 1970s as examples of such networking gains.

and after the Civil War, for example, federal land grants and state and local aid were a source of financing for railway construction. Military support for chemical research that focused on developing new materials during World War II contributed to subsequent productivity gains in the private sector. The federal government funded the building of the interstate highway system during the 1950s and 1960s, while the Department of Defense supported the development in the 1960s of the ARPANET, the precursor of the Internet.[14]

Without downplaying the role of government in encouraging invention, however, the private sector seems better equipped to identify the most promising technologies and to work out the most effective way to use these new technologies. Indeed, general purpose technologies such as the steam engine, the electric motor and the computer were developed and diffused through the economy primarily because of the profit opportunities they afforded the private sector. And even for the nineteenth-century railroads, external financing came mainly from private domestic or foreign sources; the proportion of government-funded investment by railroad companies was less than 10 percent after the Civil War (Fishlow, 2000).

In this regard, the government can arguably contribute most effectively to technological change by promoting an economic, financial and legal environment that is conducive to innovation and to the diffusion of new technologies—and then allowing businesses the flexibility to reorganize their operations in ways that permit them to take maximum advantage of new technologies. Of course, some government regulation of business and labor markets is essential for consumer and worker protection. But in retrospect, the deregulation in the 1970s and 1980s of pricing in a number of industries, such as airlines, trucking, financial services and natural gas, seems to have boosted productivity growth by allowing businesses in those industries to operate with fewer constraints and more flexibility.[15] For example, Winston (1998) cites evidence that unit operating costs have fallen 25 percent in the airline

---

[14] Also, each of the historical productivity booms followed the end of a major war. This sequence raises the question of whether these postwar booms reflected either a combination of new technologies and pent-up demand developed during the war or a war-related breakdown of factors previously restraining long-run growth (for example, the special interest groups emphasized by Olson, 1982). We have already noted the importance of war-related technological advances in the post–World War II productivity boom. However, it is more difficult to see such factors playing an important role in the booms that followed the Civil War and World War I. Moreover, other major wars were not followed by productivity booms, nor did the post-1995 productivity boom follow the end of a war.

[15] There has been an ongoing debate about whether protectionist measures—such as tariffs and quotas—might also be helpful in raising long-run productivity growth by encouraging the diffusion of new technologies into the domestic capital stock. Lipsey (2000) summarizes the debate for the nineteenth century, reviewing the argument that tariffs, which protected domestic markets from foreign competition, provided U.S. manufacturers the opportunity to expand more rapidly. However, even if one can build a case for targeted protectionism of "infant industries" in low-income countries, the experience of the United States in the twentieth century suggests that protectionist measures are not an effective means of promoting the diffusion of technology in an industrialized economy. Indeed, the United States has, over time, consistently and successfully responded to competitive pressures from abroad, often through technological innovations that create new markets and opportunities.

industry since deregulation, between 35 percent and 75 percent in trucking and roughly 35 percent in the natural gas industry.

Another lesson from past productivity booms is that investors must be willing to hold securities if firms are to raise the working capital they need to take advantage of the productivity potential of new technologies. As noted above, the information problems of the late 1800s and early 1900s constrained interest in common stock, and this reluctance by investors to hold equity presumably raised the overall cost of capital until methods of reducing these information problems were in place. Similarly, unless the corporate governance issues of the past few years are aggressively addressed, the damage to the financial intermediation process will undoubtedly result in a higher cost of capital. In this regard, prudent regulation of financial markets is particularly important, starting with the requirement that firms provide financial information that is extensive, accurate and interpretable in a straightforward manner.

Efforts by policymakers to provide broad access to education has also helped to stimulate economic growth by improving the ability of the workforce to adapt to technological change. In the past, a basic facility in reading, mathematics and science has been essential to workers in a wide range of occupational settings; in the future, the educational requirements of the population will likely be even greater. As a result, continued public recognition of the value of education as well as ongoing efforts to ensure widespread access to effective schooling at all levels will be indispensable.

Finally, sound macroeconomic policies have also been essential in promoting long-run economic growth. Although identifying a strong causal relationship between a healthy economy and productivity growth is difficult, several empirical observations suggest such a link. First, some evidence points to a correlation between low inflation and strong productivity growth (Fischer, 1993; Rudebusch and Wilcox, 1994).[16] Second, the number of patent applications tends to be higher in good economic times than during recessions.[17] If patenting is a valid measure of technological change, such a correlation suggests that innovation is stimulated by healthy economic conditions. Third, business fixed investment—and thus the diffusion of new technologies through renewal of the capital stock—is likely to be better maintained in an economic environment characterized by sustainable economic growth and low inflation.

---

[16] However, the direction of causation associated with this correlation is difficult to assess. For example, in the United States, it is sometimes argued that strong productivity growth reduced inflation in the late 1990s (Ball and Mankiw, 2002). In addition, Bruno and Easterly (1998), in a cross-country study, find evidence only of a correlation between inflation and productivity growth at high rates of inflation.

[17] Engerman and Sokoloff (2000) point out that the growth in patenting was especially high in the 1850s and 1880s, both periods of rapid economic growth. Similarly, Griliches (1990) finds a positive coefficient on real GDP growth in a regression relating the growth in patent applications to changes in real GDP and gross private domestic investment for the period 1880 to 1987. Geroski and Walters (1995) find a similar result for the United Kingdom.

Conclusion

Productivity improvements are the building blocks for increases in the standard of living. The experience in the United States suggests that extended periods of strong productivity growth are characterized by innovations in technology that are accompanied by changes in organizational structure and in business financing arrangements and by investments in human capital. Underlying these determinants of productivity growth, however, is a more fundamental factor: the willingness of society to transform itself dramatically, with the confidence that technological progress and the economic opportunities attending that progress will enable people to improve their lives. In such a society, economic growth is best fostered in an environment of economic and personal freedom and government policies that are focused on erecting sound and stable macroeconomic conditions most conducive to private-sector initiative.

■ *This paper is an edited version of a lecture delivered by Roger W. Ferguson Jr. to a joint session of the Society of Government Economists and the American Economic Association at the meetings of the Allied Social Science Associations in San Diego, California, on January 4, 2004. We are grateful to William English, Paul Harrison, Daniel Sichel and David Wilcox for their valuable insights on many of the historical examples discussed in the paper; to James Hines, Michael Palumbo, Lawrence Slifman, Charles Struckmeyer, Timothy Taylor, Mike Waldman and Joyce Zickler for helpful comments on earlier drafts; and to Jennifer Gregory for excellent research assistance. The views expressed are those of the authors and do not necessarily represent the views of other members of the Board of Governors or staff of the Federal Reserve System.*

References

Atack, Jeremy. 1986. "Firm Size and Industrial Structure in the United States during the Nineteenth Century." *Journal of Economic History.* June, 46:2, pp. 463–75.

Atack, Jeremy, Fred Bateman and William N. Parker. 2000. "The Farm, the Farmer, and the Market," in *The Cambridge Economic History of the United States, Volume 2.* Stanley Engerman and Robert Gallman, eds. New York: Cambridge University Press, pp. 245–84.

Baily, Martin Neil. 2002. "The New Economy: Post Mortem or Second Wind?" *Journal of Economic Perspectives.* Spring, 16:2, pp. 3–22.

Baker, Dean. 2002. "Is the New Economy Wearing Out?" *Challenge.* January/February, 45:1, pp. 117–21.

Balke, Nathan S. and Robert J. Gordon. 1989. "The Estimation of Prewar Gross National Product: Methodology and New Evidence." *Journal of Political Economy.* February, 97:1, pp. 38–92.

Ball, Lawrence and N. Gregory Mankiw. 2002. "The NAIRU in Theory and Practice." *Journal of Economic Perspectives.* Fall, 16:4, pp. 115–36.

Baskin, Jonathan Barron and Paul J. Miranti Jr. 1997. *A History of Corporate Finance.* New York: Cambridge University Press.

Beniger, James R. 1986. *The Control Revolution: Technological and Economic Origins of the Information Society.* Cambridge, Mass.: Harvard University Press.

Bernanke, Ben S. 1995. "The Macroeconomics of the Great Depression: A Comparative Approach." *Journal of Money, Credit, and Banking.* February, 27:1, pp. 1–28.

Bernanke, Ben S. and Martin L. Parkinson. 1991. "Procyclical Labor Productivity and Competing Theories of the Business Cycle: Some Evidence from Interwar U.S. Manufacturing Industries." *Journal of Political Economy.* June, 99:3, pp. 439–59.

Board of Governors of the Federal Reserve System. Various years. *Flow of Funds Accounts.* Washington, D.C.: Federal Reserve Board.

Board of Governors of the Federal Reserve System. Various years. *Indexes of Industrial Production.* Washington, D.C.: Federal Reserve Board.

Bruno, Michael and Michael Easterly. 1998. "Inflation Crises and Long-Run Growth." *Journal of Monetary Economics.* February, 41:1, pp. 3–26.

Brynjolfsson, Erik and Lorin M. Hitt. 2000. "Beyond Computation: Information Technology, Organizational Transformation and Business Performance." *Journal of Economic Perspectives.* Fall, 14:4, pp. 23–48.

Chandler, Alfred D. 1977. *The Visible Hand: The Managerial Revolution in American Business.* Cambridge, Mass.: Belknap Press of Harvard University Press.

Cortada, James W. 1993. *Before the Computer: IBM, NCR, Burroughs, & Remington Rand & the Industry They Created, 1865–1956.* Princeton, N.J.: Princeton University Press.

David, Paul A. 1969. "Transportation Economics and Economic Growth: Professor Fogel On and Off the Rails." *Economic History Review.* December, 22:3, pp. 506–25.

David, Paul A. 1990. "The Dynamo and the Computer: An Historical Perspective on the Modern Productivity Paradox." *American Economic Review.* May, 80:2, pp. 355–61.

Easterlin, Richard A. 1961. "Regional Income Trends, 1840–1950," in *American Economic History.* Seymour E. Harris, ed. New York: McGraw-Hill Press, pp. 525–47.

Engerman, Stanley and Kenneth L. Sokoloff. 2000. "Technology and Industrialization 1790–1914," in *Cambridge Economic History of the United States, Volume 2.* Stanley Engerman and Robert Gallman, eds. Cambridge: Cambridge University Press, pp. 367–401.

Ferguson, Roger W. Jr. 2003. "Patent Policy in a Broader Context." Remarks at the 2003 Financial Markets Conference of the Federal Reserve Bank of Atlanta, April.

Field, Alexander J. 2003. "The Most Technologically Progressive Decade of the Century." *American Economic Review.* September, 93:4, pp. 1399–413.

Fischer, Stanley. 1993. "The Role of Macroeconomic Factors in Growth." *Journal of Monetary Economics.* December, 32:3, pp. 485–512.

Fishlow, Albert. 1966. "Productivity and Technological Change in the Railroad Sector, 1840–1910," in *Output, Employment, and Productivity in the United States after 1800.* Dorothy S. Brady, ed. New York: National Bureau of Economic Research, pp. 583–646.

Fishlow, Albert. 2000. "Internal Transportation in the Nineteenth and Early Twentieth Centuries," in *Cambridge Economic History of the United States, Volume 2.* Stanley Engerman and Robert Gallman, eds. Cambridge: Cambridge University Press, pp. 543–642.

Fogel, Robert W. 1979. "Notes on the Social Saving Controversy." *Journal of Economic History.* March, 39:1, pp. 1–50.

Freeman, Richard B. 2002. "The Labour Market in the New Information Economy." *Oxford Review of Economic Policy.* Autumn, 18:3, pp. 288–305.

Galambos, Louis. 2000. "The U.S. Corporate Economy in the Twentieth Century," in *Cambridge Economic History of the United States, Volume 3.* Stanley Engerman and Robert Gallman, eds. Cambridge: Cambridge University Press, pp. 927–67.

Gallini, Nancy T. 2002. "The Economics of Patents: Lessons from Recent U.S. Patent Reforms." *Journal of Economic Perspectives.* Spring, 16:2, pp. 131–54.

Gallman, Robert E. 1966. "Gross National Product in the United States, 1834–1909," in *Output, Employment, and Productivity in the United States after 1800.* Dorothy S. Brady, ed. New York: National Bureau of Economic Research, pp. 3–76.

Geroski, P. A. and C. F. Walters. 1995. "Innovative Activity Over the Business Cycle." *Economic Journal.* July, 105:431, pp. 916–28.

Goldin, Claudia. 2000. "Labor Markets in the Twentieth Century," in *Cambridge Economic History of the United States, Volume 3.* Stanley Engerman and Robert Gallman, eds. Cambridge: Cambridge University Press, pp. 549–623.

Goldin, Claudia and Lawrence F. Katz. 1998. "The Origins of Technology-Skill Complementarity." *Quarterly Journal of Economics.* August, 113:3, pp. 693–732.

Gordon, Robert J. 1992. "Productivity in the Transportation Sector," in *Output Measurement in the Service Sectors.* National Bureau of Economic Research Studies in Income and Wealth. Zvi Griliches, ed. Chicago: University of Chicago Press, pp. 371–422.

Gordon, Robert J. 2000a. "Interpreting the 'One Big Wave' in U.S. Long-Term Productivity Growth," in *Productivity, Technology, and Economic Growth.* Bart van Ark, Simon Kuipers and Gerard Kuper, eds. New York: Kluwer Publishers, pp. 19–65.

Gordon, Robert J. 2000b. "Does the 'New Economy' Measure Up to the Great Inventions of the Past?" *Journal of Economic Perspectives.* Fall, 14:4, pp. 49–74.

Griliches, Zvi. 1988. "Productivity Puzzles and R&D: Another Nonexplanation." *Journal of Economic Perspectives.* Fall, 2:4, pp. 9–21.

Griliches, Zvi. 1990. "Patent Statistics as Economic Indicators: A Survey." *Journal of Economic Literature.* December, 28:4, pp. 1661–707.

Hawkins, David F. 1963. "The Development of Modern Financial Reporting Practices among American Manufacturing Companies." *Business History Review.* Winter, 37:1, pp. 135–68.

James, John A. and Jonathan S. Skinner. 1985. "The Resolution of the Labor-Scarcity Paradox." *Journal of Economic History.* September, 45:3, pp. 513–40.

Johnston, R. B. 1982. *The Economics of the Euro-Market.* New York: St. Martin's Press.

Jorgenson, Dale W., Mun S. Ho and Kevin Stiroh. 2002. "Projecting Productivity Growth: Lessons from the U.S. Growth Resurgence." *Federal Reserve Bank of Atlanta Economic Review.* Third Quarter, 87:3, pp. 1–13.

Kane, Thomas J. and Cecilia Elena Rouse. 1999. "The Community College: Educating Students at the Margin Between College and Work." *Journal of Economic Perspectives.* Winter, 13:1, pp. 63–84.

Keeler, Theodore E. and John S. Ying. 1988. "Measuring the Benefits of a Large Public Investment: The Case of the U.S. Federal-Aid Highway System." *Journal of Public Economics.* June, 36:1, pp. 69–85.

Kendrick, John W. 1961. *Productivity Trends in the United States.* Princeton, N.J.: Princeton University Press.

Kindleberger, Charles P. 1993. *A Financial History of Western Europe.* New York: Oxford University Press.

Kleinknecht, Alfred. 1987. *Innovation Patterns in Crisis and Prosperity: Schumpeter's Long Cycle Reconsidered.* New York: St. Martin's Press.

Kuznets, Simon S. 1946. *National Product Since 1869.* New York: National Bureau of Economic Research.

Lipsey, Robert E. 2000. "U.S. Foreign Trade and the Balance of Payments 1800–1913," in *Cambridge Economic History of the United States, Volume 2.* Stanley Engerman and Robert Gallman, eds. Cambridge: Cambridge University Press, pp. 685–732.

Madrick, Jeffrey. 2002. "Optimism Needs a Warning Label When It Comes to Forecasting Productivity." *New York Times.* January 24, p. C2.

Mansfield, Edwin. 1965. "Innovation and Technical Change in the Railroad Industry," in *Transportation Economics.* New York: National Bureau of Economic Research, pp. 169–97.

Margo, Robert A. 2000. "The Labor Force in the Nineteenth Century," in *Cambridge Economic History of the United States, Volume 2.* Stanley Engerman and Robert Gallman, eds. Cambridge: Cambridge University Press, pp. 207–43.

Mensch, Gerhard. 1979. *Stalemate in Technology: Innovations Overcome the Depression.* Cambridge, Mass.: Ballinger.

Meyer, Peter B. 2003. "Episodes of Collective Invention." Bureau of Labor Statistics Working paper, Washington, D.C., August.

Miranti, Paul J. Jr. 2001 "U.S. Financial Reporting Standardization: 1840–2000." *World Development Report 2002: Institutions for Markets.* Washington, D.C.: World Bank.

Mowery, David and Nathan Rosenberg. 2000. "Twentieth-Century Technological Change," in *Cambridge Economic History of the United States, Volume 3.* Stanley Engerman and Robert Gallman eds. Cambridge: Cambridge University Press, pp. 803–925.

Nelson, Richard R., Merton J. Peck and Edward D. Kalachek. 1967. *Technology, Economic Growth, and Public Policy.* Washington, D.C.: The Brookings Institution.

Oliner, Stephen D. and Daniel E. Sichel. 1994. "Computers and Output Growth Revisited: How Big is the Puzzle?" *Brookings Papers on Economic Activity.* 2, pp. 273–317.

Oliner, Stephen D. and Daniel E. Sichel. 2002. "Information Technology and Productivity: Where are We Now and Where are We Going?" *Federal Reserve Bank of Atlanta Economic Review.* Third Quarter, 87:3, pp. 15–44.

Olson, Mancur. 1982. *The Rise and Decline of Nations.* New Haven: Yale University Press.

Paul, Catherine J. Morrison and Donald S. Siegel. 2001. "The Impacts of Technology, Trade and Outsourcing on Employment and Labor Composition." *Scandinavian Journal of Economics.* 103:2, pp. 241–64.

Paullin, Charles O. 1932. *Atlas of the Historical Geography of the United States.* Washington, D.C.: Carnegie Institute and American Geographical Society.

PricewaterhouseCoopers/Thompson Venture Economics/National Venture Capital Association. Various years. *MoneyTree Survey.*

Rhode, Paul W. 2002. "Gallman's Annual Output Series for the United States, 1834–1909." National Bureau of Economic Research Working Paper No. 8860, Cambridge, Mass., April.

Roach, Stephen. 2003. "Clueless on Productivity." *Global Economic Forum.* Morgan Stanley; Available at ⟨http://www.morganstanley.com/GEFdata/digests/20030905-fri.html⟩.

Rockoff, Hugh. 2000. "Banking and Finance, 1789–1914," in *Cambridge Economic History of the United States, Volume 2.* Stanley Engerman and Robert Gallman, eds. Cambridge: Cambridge University Press, pp. 643–84.

Romer, Christina D. 1989. "The Prewar Business Cycle Reconsidered: New Estimates of Gross National Product, 1869–1908." *Journal of Political Economy.* February, 97:1, pp. 1–37.

Rudebusch, Glenn D. and David W. Wilcox. 1994. "Productivity and Inflation: Evidence and Interpretations." Unpublished manuscript, Board of Governors of the Federal Reserve System.

Schmookler, Jacob. 1966. *Invention and Economic Growth.* Cambridge, Mass.: Harvard University Press.

Sichel, Daniel E. 1997. *The Computer Revolution: An Economic Perspective.* Washington, D.C.: The Brookings Institution.

Spitz, P. H. 1988. *Petrochemicals: The Rise of an Industry.* New York: John Wiley.

U.S. Bureau of Economic Analysis. 1966. *U.S. Direct Investment Abroad, 1966.* Washington, D.C.: BEA.

U.S. Census Bureau. 1997. *Historical Statistics of the United States on CD-ROM: Colonial Times to the Present.* Susan Carter, Scott Gartner, Michael Haines, Alan Olmstead, Richard Sutch and Gavin Wright, eds. New York, N.Y: Cambridge University Press.

U.S. Census Bureau. 2001. *Statistical Abstract of the United States.* Austin, Tex.: Reference Press.

U.S. Department of Education, National Center for Education Statistics. Various years. *Digest of Education Statistics.* Washington, D.C.: Government Printing Office.

U.S. Patent and Trademark Office. 2002. *U.S. Patent Activity, 1790–Present.* Washington, D.C.: USPTO.

Vernon, Raymond. 1971. *Sovereignty at Bay: The Multinational Spread of U.S. Enterprises.* New York: Basic Books.

White, Eugene N. 2000. "Banking and Finance in the Twentieth Century," in *Cambridge Economic History of the United States, Volume 3.* Stanley Engerman and Robert Gallman, eds. Cambridge: Cambridge University Press, pp. 743–802.

Winston, Clifford. 1998. "U.S. Industry Adjustment to Economic Deregulation." *Journal of Economic Perspectives.* Summer, 12:3, pp. 89–110.

Journal of Economic Perspectives—Volume 18, Number 2—Spring 2004—Pages 29–50

Consumer Confidence and Consumer Spending

Sydney C. Ludvigson

At least since the work of John Maynard Keynes, economists have pondered the ways in which consumer and investor sentiment—what Keynes (1936, Chapter 12) referred to as "animal spirits"—might influence the real economy. Today, the outcome of monthly consumer confidence surveys provides steady fodder for the business and financial press and is treated as an important piece of economic information. In the *New York Times* alone, more than 15 articles about consumer confidence and its potential impact on the economy appeared between July 2002 and June 2003. Consumer confidence is often cited by Federal Reserve Chairman Alan Greenspan as a key determinant of near-term economic growth (for example, Greenspan, 2002).

Despite the widespread attention given to surveys of consumer confidence, the mechanisms by which household attitudes influence the real economy are less well understood. Do consumer confidence surveys contain meaningful independent information about the economy, or do they simply repackage information already captured in other economic indicators? Do the surveys provide information about the future path of household spending, or do they reflect current or past events? Finally, do the surveys correspond neatly to any well-defined economic concept, or do they furnish only a nebulous barometer of household disposition?

This paper begins with an overview of how consumer confidence is measured and reported. It then evaluates what is known about the relationship between consumer attitudes and the real economy. The evidence suggests that the most popular survey measures do contain some information about the future path of

■ *Sydney C. Ludvigson is Assistant Professor of Economics, New York University, New York, New York, and Faculty Research Fellow, National Bureau of Economic Research, Cambridge, Massachusetts.*

aggregate consumer expenditure growth. However, much of that information can be found in other popular economic and financial indicators, and the independent information provided by consumer confidence predicts a relatively modest amount of additional variation in future consumer spending. Moreover, there is some evidence that consumer confidence surveys reflect expectations of income and non–stock market wealth growth, but evidence on the connection between these surveys and precautionary saving motives is mixed.

Measuring Consumer Attitudes: Survey Questions and Survey Components

The University of Michigan's Consumer Sentiment Index and the Conference Board's Consumer Confidence Index are the most widely followed measures of U.S. consumer confidence.[1] Although the financial markets and the business community closely follow both indexes, much published academic research focuses on the Michigan index—most likely because of its longer time series. The Michigan index began as an annual survey in the late 1940s. In 1952, it was converted to a quarterly survey and in 1978 to a monthly survey. The Conference Board launched its index on a bimonthly basis in 1967 and expanded it to a monthly series in 1977. Figure 1 presents the basic time series of the two indices, with periods of recession shown by shaded areas. The two indexes broadly measure the same concept—public confidence in the economy—but they are based on different questions and sometimes give conflicting signals. To interpret movements in these two series, it is important to understand some key differences in the specific questions that are asked as well as in sample size, survey methodology and index formulation.

Both the Conference Board and the University of Michigan base their overall index of consumer confidence on five questions that are part of a broader survey of consumer attitudes and expectations, shown in Exhibit 1. In both of the surveys, each of the five questions is given equal weight in the overall consumer confidence index. In addition to the overall index, both organizations report two component indexes: a present situation component and an expectations component.

Present Situation Component

On each survey, two of the five questions ask respondents to assess present economic conditions. The Conference Board's present situation component takes a "snapshot" approach, asking respondents to evaluate current business conditions and job availability. Notice that the Conference Board survey asks specifically about

---

[1] The material in this section closely reflects the discussion in Bram and Ludvigson (1998).

Figure 1
Two Indexes of Consumer Attitudes

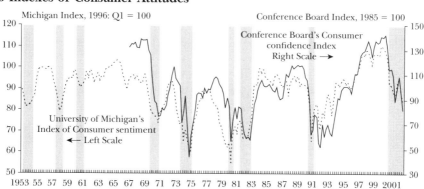

Sources: Conference Board; University of Michigan Survey Research Center.
Note: Shaded areas denote periods designated recessions by the National Bureau of Economic Research.

job prospects in the respondent's area. As a result, the Conference Board's present situation component closely tracks labor market conditions like the nation's unemployment rate and the growth in payroll employment. Michigan asks respondents to comment on the advisability of big-ticket household purchases and to assess changes in their own financial situation. Although this latter question is about the personal financial situation of the respondent, it does not directly ask about changes in the employment outlook. Thus, Michigan's present conditions component is less closely tied to labor market conditions and tends to reflect recent changes in the economy rather than the level of economic activity.

These differences are reflected in the cyclical behavior of the two component indexes. As shown in Figure 2, Michigan's present conditions component generally peaks in the early stages of economic recovery, when growth is high. By contrast, the Conference Board's present situation component generally peaks in the late stages of economic expansion, when unemployment is low and the level of economic activity is high. The present conditions components of the two indexes are not closely correlated.

Expectations Component

The three questions that ask about consumers' expectations are fairly comparable in the two surveys. The Conference Board survey asks about expected changes in business conditions, job availability and respondents' income over the next six months. Because the Conference Board index includes a question about nominal income, it may overstate "confidence" during periods of high inflation. Michigan's poses questions on expected business conditions—both over the next year and over the next five years—and expected changes in the respondent's financial situation

Exhibit 1

Component Questions of Consumer Confidence

Five questions make up the confidence indexes reported by the University of Michigan and the Conference Board. Each set of questions is part of a broader monthly survey of consumer attitudes. The questions have been renumbered and reordered here, compared to the way in which they are asked, to facilitate comparisons between the surveys. Also, the two surveys use slightly different terminology for the index component based on the first two questions; the discussion here will adopt the term *present conditions* for both organizations.

Michigan Survey	*Conference Board Survey*
PRESENT CONDITIONS QUESTIONS	PRESENT CONDITIONS QUESTIONS
Q1) Do you think now is a good or bad time for people to buy major household items? [good time to buy/uncertain, depends/bad time to buy]	Q1) How would you rate present general business conditions in your area? [good/normal/bad]
Q2) Would you say that you (and your family living there) are better off or worse off financially than you were a year ago? [better/same/worse]	Q2) What would you say about available jobs in your area right now? [plentiful/not so many/hard to get]
EXPECTATIONS QUESTIONS	EXPECTATIONS QUESTIONS
Q3) Now turning to business conditions in the country as a whole—do you think that during the next twelve months, we'll have good times financially or bad times or what? [good times/uncertain/bad times]	Q3) Six months from now, do you think business conditions in your area will be [better/same/worse]?
Q4) Looking ahead, which would you say is more likely—that in the country as a whole we'll have continuous good times during the next five years or so or that we'll have periods of widespread unemployment or depression, or what? [good times/uncertain/bad times]	Q4) Six months from now, do you think there will be [more/same/fewer] jobs available in your area?
Q5) Now looking ahead—do you think that a year from now, you (and your family living there) will be better off financially, or worse off, or just about the same as now? [better/same/worse]	Q5) How would you guess your total family income to be six months from now? [higher/same/lower]

over the next year. This difference in time horizons appears to have little effect on response patterns and hence on index results.

The expectations components in the two surveys are highly correlated with each other, as shown in Figure 3. Moreover, Michigan's present conditions and expectations components are much more closely correlated than are the Conference Board's: the former exhibit a correlation of 0.82; the latter, a correlation of 0.40.

Figure 2

Present Conditions of Consumer Attitudes

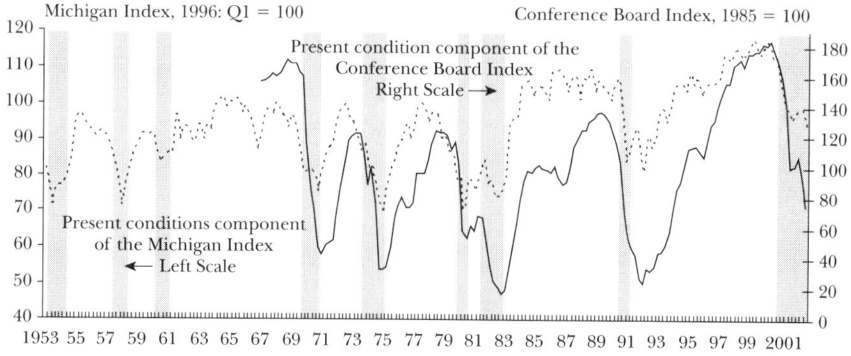

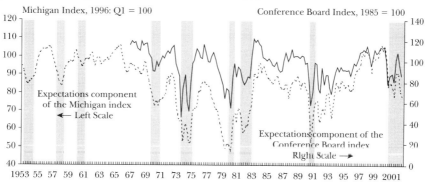

Sources: Conference Board; University of Michigan Survey Research Center.
Note: Shaded areas denote periods designated recessions by the National Bureau of Economic Research.

Figure 3

Expectations Component of Consumer Attitudes

Sources: Conference Board; University of Michigan Survey Research Center.
Note: Shaded areas denote periods designated recessions by the National Bureau of Economic Research.

Sample Size and Survey Procedures

The most important methodological differences between the two surveys concern sample size, which affects sampling error and, thus, reliability, and index construction, which affects the range of movement in the indexes. The survey timing and release schedules also differ, which is an especially relevant consideration when conducting real-time analysis.

Michigan conducts its survey by phone throughout most of the month. Its sample size is approximately 500; a preliminary mid-month release is based on about two-thirds of the full sample phone interviews conducted early in the month. Final figures for the full sample are subsequently made available at the end of the month and are not subject to further revision. The Conference Board sends out a mail survey at the end of the prior month, and responses flow in throughout the survey month. The effective sample size is roughly 3,500 (of a total mailing of 5,000). This sample of 5,000 is drawn from an original sample in which respondents agree to do the interviews. On the last Tuesday of the survey month, the Conference Board formally releases its preliminary figures based on about 2,500 responses. Final, revised data based on the full monthly sample are released with the next month's preliminary figures and are not subject to further revision. Thus, Michigan's preliminary figures are available earlier than the Conference Board's.

Both surveys may be affected by sampling problems. The Michigan index is based on a relatively small sample size of roughly 500, with the preliminary mid-month release only two-thirds of that. This small sample size undoubtedly leads to noisy estimates of the population values. The larger the sample size the smaller the sampling error and therefore the narrower the statistical confidence interval for the estimated consumer confidence index. Curtin (2002) computes quantitative estimates of how much sampling error could be reduced by increasing the sample size of the Michigan survey. He concludes that tripling the sample from 500 interviews to 1,500 would reduce the 95 percent confidence interval for the Index of Consumer Sentiment from $\pm$ 3.3 index points to $\pm$ 1.9 index points, which is a sizable reduction. On the other hand, Curtin (2002) also reports that the preliminary survey results based on two-thirds of the full Michigan sample are very accurate, having a correlation of 0.99 with the final estimate.

The Conference Board survey has a larger sample, but—unlike the Michigan index—the overall response rate is unknown because only the response rate of households that previously agreed to participate in the survey is reported. This procedure makes it difficult to assess the representativeness of the Conference Board sample. A representative sample requires assigning each sample element a known probability of selection and on the absence of nonresponse bias. For the Michigan survey, Curtin, Presser and Singer (2000) report that the response rate ranged from a high of 72 percent to a low of 67 percent between 1979 and 1996, averaging about 70 percent; Curtin, Presser and Singer (2003) find that since 1996, the Michigan index has experienced much more substantial reductions in the response rate. The authors note that access to technology designed to screen unwanted calls has skyrocketed in recent years, a factor that has likely increased the nonresponse error in both surveys. Both surveys are also subject to nonsampling sources of error including reporting, editing and processing errors.

Constructing the Indexes

The University of Michigan and the Conference Board use different methodologies to construct their indexes from the raw response data. The example in Table 1 illustrates how the Conference Board and Michigan would construct an index for one question using the same raw response data. For each index, the responses to the question can be categorized as positive, negative or neutral.

Table 1

Calculating the Two Indexes

(example: calculating index levels from raw response data)

	Base period	Prior month	Current month
Percentages of responses			
Positive	25	30	24
Neutral	60	60	64
Negative	15	10	12
Indicator level			
Michigan diffusion measure	110.0	120	112.0
Michigan index	100.0	109.1	101.8
Conference Board			
Diffusion measure	62.5	75.0	66.7
Conference Board index	100.0	120.0	106.7

Hypothetical figures are shown for two months along with the base-period levels against which the indexes are benchmarked.

Michigan would first calculate a "diffusion measure" by adding the difference between the positive and negative percentages, plus 100. Thus, for example, the current month's value is 112 (100 + 24 – 12), and the prior month's level is 120 (100 + 30 – 10). Next, an index is constructed by dividing the level of diffusion measure by the base-period level of 110 and then multiplying by 100. In the example below, this calculation yields a value of 101.8 (112 ÷ 110 × 100) for the current month, down from the prior month's level of 109.1 (120 ÷ 110 × 100).

Using the same raw responses, the Conference Board would calculate its diffusion measure by dividing the positive response percentage by the sum of the positive and negative response percentages. This procedure gives a value of 66.7 (24 ÷ (24 + 12) × 100) for the current month and 75 (30 ÷ (30 + 10) × 100) for the prior month. Next, the index is calculated to be 106.7 (66.7 ÷ 62.5 × 100) in the current month, down from a level of 120 (75.0 ÷ 62.5 × 100) in the prior month—a drop of 13.3 points.

How are the question-level indexes aggregated to obtain an overall index? Michigan first averages the diffusion indexes into a composite diffusion index and then converts the results to a base-period index. Conversely, the Conference Board converts each diffusion index to a base-year index and then averages the indexes together.[2] Because the Conference Board and Michigan use different base periods—1985 and 1966:Q1, respectively—the response patterns on which the indexes

---

[2] Because the Conference Board's diffusion measures are converted into base-year indexes before they are averaged arithmetically, a given question's effective weight in the index is influenced by the selection of the base year. In theory, the choice of the base year could affect the magnitude and even the direction of change in the index. (The resulting problems are similar to those associated with the old fixed-base-year GDP deflator.) In practice, however, this feature has no discernible effect on the Conference

are based may differ. As a result, the index *levels* of the two surveys are not comparable.

As a result of these methodological differences, the Conference Board's overall index and component measures have a wider range of movement than Michigan's; as the hypothetical example illustrates, identical shifts in the underlying responses tend to produce significantly larger moves in the Conference Board's indexes than in Michigan's. A good rule of thumb is that a one-point move in Michigan's index is comparable to a two-point move in the Conference Board index. Because of differences in survey methodology, index construction and base year, index levels are not comparable; monthly changes must be compared on a standardized basis rather than in absolute terms. On a standardized basis, the Conference Board's index is significantly less volatile than Michigan's index.

Interpretation of the Indexes

Two of the most common dilemmas in relying on consumer confidence as an economic indicator are whether to focus on index-level or month-to-month changes and whether to focus on the present conditions or the expectations component. For the Conference Board index, it is particularly useful to examine the present condition and expectations components individually. The level of the present conditions component serves as a good proxy for the *level* of economic activity, while the expectations component is more closely correlated with the *rate* of economic growth. For example, the present conditions component has a negative correlation of 0.88 with the unemployment rate, whereas the expectations component has a correlation with a four-quarter percent change in GDP growth of almost 0.60. On Michigan's survey, both components are closely correlated and in general serve as an indicator of the pace of economic growth.

Do Consumer Confidence Surveys Predict Consumption?

It would hardly be surprising to find that confidence surveys reflect the *current* state of the economy. After all, most households should be aware of recent changes in their own economic situation. A more interesting question is whether the surveys provide information about the *future* path of household spending that is not already contained in other popular economic indicators. We begin by presenting regressions that forecast consumer expenditure using consumer confidence, a baseline set of economic indicators, and then combin-

---

Board's index. Also, the Conference Board's responses are seasonally adjusted, while Michigan's are not. However, the seasonal adjustment has little effect, because neither index exhibits much seasonality.

ing the two. We then discuss other research drawing connections between consumer confidence and consumption.

Regressions with Consumer Confidence and Consumption

Table 2 presents how well the consumer confidence surveys can forecast the growth of various categories of personal consumption expenditure. Following Bram and Ludvigson (1998), Table 2 measures the effect of consumer attitudes on five categories of household personal consumption expenditure: total expenditure, motor vehicle expenditure, expenditure on all goods (excluding motor vehicles), expenditure on services and expenditure on durable goods excluding motor vehicles. The data, from the Bureau of Economic Analysis, span the period from the first quarter of 1968 to the fourth quarter of 2002; that is, the largest possible sample for which both indexes are available.

The independent variables included lags of consumer confidence over the previous four quarters. I do not report results for the present situation component because preliminary tests indicated that the expectations component of both indexes typically exhibited greater forecasting power. Previous research suggests that consumer sentiment may be linked to economic indicators largely because of unusually volatile movements in consumer attitudes during the Persian Gulf War and the 1990–1991 recession (for example, Leeper, 1992). To control for this possibility, we also included a dummy variable set equal to one in the quarters corresponding to the 1990–1991 recession.

For each category of consumption, Table 2 presents the adjusted R-squared statistic from a regression of consumption growth on the confidence measures. The p-values for the joint marginal significance of the lags of each variable, which appear in parentheses, give the probability that the explanatory variable can be excluded from the forecasting equation.[3] When the p-values are very low, the variables are statistically significant predictors of consumption growth.

Table 2 shows that measures of consumer attitudes on their own have both statistically and economically significant predictive power for quarterly consumption growth, in a variety of expenditure categories. Lagged values of both the Conference Board and Michigan overall index explain about 15 percent of the one-quarter-ahead variation in total personal consumption expenditure growth. The probability that this explanatory power was generated by chance is very small,

---

[3] The growth in spending on durable goods may be positively autocorrelated, with the error term following a first-order moving-average process (Mankiw, 1982). Such first-order autocorrelation in the error term could cause the error term to be correlated with the one-period-lagged endogenous variable, a condition that could skew in-sample statistical tests of the joint marginal significance of the explanatory variables (the reported p-values). To address this problem, I explicitly model the error term, as an MA(1) process in the in-sample regressions.

Table 2

Forecasts of Consumption Growth by Consumer Confidence Indicators

Real personal consumption expenditure	Michigan index	Conference Board index	Both
		Overall index	
Total	0.147	0.150	0.197
Conference Board	—	(0.008)	(0.082)
Michigan	(0.002)	—	(0.040)
Motor vehicles	0.021	0.036	0.052
Conference Board	—	(0.109)	(0.036)
Michigan	(0.066)	—	(0.067)
Goods, excluding motor vehicles	0.196	0.133	0.211
Conference Board	—	(0.011)	(0.208)
Michigan	(0.001)	—	(0.003)
Services	0.096	0.137	0.137
Conference Board	—	(0.007)	(0.008)
Michigan	(0.010)	—	(0.150)
Durables, excluding motor vehicles	0.174	0.084	0.231
Conference Board	—	(0.016)	(0.002)
Michigan	(0.000)	—	(0.000)
		Expectations component	
Total	0.158	0.211	0.200
Conference Board	—	(0.000)	(0.069)
Michigan	(0.002)	—	(0.593)
Motor vehicles	0.023	0.057	0.040
Conference Board	—	(0.006)	(0.054)
Michigan	(0.040)	—	(0.453)
Goods, excluding motor vehicles	0.193	0.157	0.186
Conference Board	—	(0.024)	(0.817)
Michigan	(0.002)	—	(0.016)
Services	0.098	0.207	0.197
Conference Board	—	(0.000)	(0.000)
Michigan	(0.006)	—	(0.709)
Durables, excluding motor vehicles	0.153	0.081	0.146
Conference Board	—	(0.138)	(0.526)
Michigan	(0.001)	—	(0.006)

Source: Author's calculation.

Notes: The table reports the adjusted R^2 statistic from the forecast of consumption growth with four lags of the confidence measures and a dummy variable for the 1990–1991 recession; p-values for the joint marginal significance of the lags of the confidence measures appear in parentheses. Hypothesis tests were conducted using a heteroskedasticity and serial correlation robust covariance matrix. The sample covers the period from the first quarter of 1968 to the fourth quarter of 2002.

less than 1 percent. The expectations component of each index exhibits even more predictive power. For example, the Conference Board's expectations component explains more than 20 percent of the variation in next quarter's total consumer expenditure growth; similarly, Michigan's expectation's component explains 19 percent of the variation in next quarter's expenditures on goods (excluding motor vehicles). Thus, the evidence from in-sample regressions suggests that measures of consumer confidence—taken alone—have important predictive power for quarterly consumer expenditure growth. The next question is whether confidence measures contain predictive information that is not already contained in a standard set of baseline economic indicators.

Here, I use the same baseline indicators that are common in previous work on the predictive power of consumer confidence surveys, like Carroll, Fuhrer and Wilcox (1994) and Bram and Ludvigson (1998). The baseline indicators are lagged values of the dependent variable, labor income growth, the (log) first difference of the real stock price and the first difference of the three-month Treasury bill rate. Labor income is defined as wages and salaries plus transfers minus personal contributions for social insurance, as it appears in the quarterly components from the Department of Commerce's National Income and Product Accounts. Stock prices are quarterly averages based on the Standard and Poor's 500. The interest rate is the quarterly average based on the three-month Treasury bill rate, reported monthly by the Board of Governors of the Federal Reserve System. Nominal labor income and the Standard and Poor's 500 index are deflated by the personal consumption expenditure implicit price deflator, as reported quarterly in the National Income and Product Accounts. Four lags of each of these variables are used in the benchmark regression.

The stock price and Treasury bill rate data are included because other researchers have argued that the information contained in consumer survey indicators should be assessed relative to that contained in financial indicators. For example, Leeper (1992) argues that consumer sentiment may have predictive power for spending because consumer surveys are made available on a more timely basis than other economic indicators such as income and consumption data. However, he notes that financial market indicators are available on an almost continuous basis and may contain much of the same information captured by consumer sentiment. Indeed, Leeper finds that consumer attitudes are only weakly correlated with variables such as unemployment and industrial production once financial indicators are included.

Table 3 reports the results of this baseline model, without consumer confidence indicators. For each category of consumption, the table presents the sum of the coefficients on the lags of each baseline variable and *p*-values for the joint marginal significance of the lags of each variable in parentheses. The sum of the coefficients on the four lags of each variable estimates the long-run effect of the variable on consumption growth. The long-run impact of most variables has the expected sign. Consumption growth is positively related to lagged consumption growth in every category of consumer expenditure studied, while lagged interest rates have a small negative effect on future consumption. Interestingly, the inclusion of the consumption and interest rate variables appears to reduce the statistical significance of the income and stock market variables in forecasting consumer expenditure growth on services, durable goods, excluding motor vehicles, and all goods, excluding motor vehicles.

To determine whether consumer sentiment contains additional information about future consumer spending, a measure of consumer confidence can be added

Table 3
Baseline Forecast of Consumption Growth

Predicted variables	Four lags of consumption	Four lags of income	Four lags of Treasury Bill rate	Four lags of S&P 500	$\bar{R}^2$
Total	0.76	0.02	−0.003	0.002	0.31
	(0.000)	(0.37)	(0.002)	(0.01)	
Motor vehicles	0.56	0.15	−0.021	0.008	0.26
	(0.02)	(0.62)	(0.022)	(0.007)	
Goods, excluding motor vehicles	0.55	0.15	−0.004	0.015	0.23
	(0.003)	(0.66)	(0.027)	(0.37)	
Services	0.97	0.01	−0.0004	−0.004	0.40
	(0.000)	(0.047)	(0.000)	(0.21)	
Durable goods, excluding motor vehicles	0.79	0.21	−0.007	0.02	0.25
	(0.000)	(0.86)	(0.000)	(0.24)	

Source: Author's calculations.
Notes: The table reports the sum of the coefficients on the lags of the variable indicated; the probability that the variable can be excluded from the prediction equation appears in parentheses. Hypothesis tests were conducted using a heteroskedasticity and serial correlation robust covariance matrix. The column labeled "$\bar{R}^2$" reports the adjusted R^2 statistic for each regression. The sample covers the period from the first quarter of 1968 to the fourth quarter of 2002. S&P = Standard and Poor's.

to the baseline regression in Table 3. Consumer confidence is measured by either the Michigan or the Conference Board overall index, or the expectations component of each overall index. As before, I do not report results for the present situation component, but a dummy variable for the 1990–1991 recession is included in the regression. Table 4 presents forecasting results from adding four lags of one of these consumer confidence measures to the baseline set of predictive variables for consumption growth. The table reports the *increment* to the adjusted R^2 that results from augmenting the baseline regression to include each of the attitudinal indicators. For example, if the increment to the adjusted R^2 from adding the four lags of some measure of confidence is X percent, the confidence augmented regression predicts about X percent more of the variation in the next quarter's consumption growth than do the baseline predictive indicators. Again, the probability that the confidence indexes can be excluded from the forecasting equation appears in parentheses.

The results indicate that both the Michigan and Conference Board overall indexes have modest incremental forecasting power for total personal consumer expenditure growth. For the Michigan survey, the lagged values of consumer sentiment increase the adjusted R^2 index by 5 percent, while adding the last four quarters of data from the Conference Board's overall confidence index to the baseline equation predicts an additional 7 percent of the variation in the next quarter's consumption growth. Including both indexes in the set of baseline indicators allows the regression to explain an additional 10 percent of the variation

Table 4

Forecast of Consumption Growth, Augmented by Consumer Confidence Indicators

Real personal consumption expenditure	Michigan index	Conference Board index	Both
		Overall index	
Total	0.05	0.07	0.10
Conference Board	—	(0.004)	(0.013)
Michigan	(0.012)	—	(0.026)
Motor vehicles	−0.05	−0.06	0.09
Conference Board	—	(0.114)	(0.001)
Michigan	(0.008)	—	(0.007)
Goods, excluding motor vehicles	0.03	0.05	0.05
Conference Board	—	(0.028)	(0.046)
Michigan	(0.106)	—	(0.284)
Services	−0.10	−0.08	0.01
Conference Board	—	(0.242)	(0.000)
Michigan	(0.082)	—	(0.000)
Durables, excluding motor vehicles	0.02	0.04	0.03
Conference Board	—	(0.146)	(0.109)
Michigan	(0.092)	—	(0.462)
		Expectations component	
Total	0.03	0.05	0.06
Conference Board	—	(0.087)	(0.047)
Michigan	(0.046)	—	(0.201)
Motor vehicles	0.04	0.04	0.05
Conference Board	—	(0.044)	(0.102)
Michigan	(0.018)	—	(0.055)
Goods, excluding motor vehicles	0.01	0.06	0.06
Conference Board	—	(0.038)	(0.013)
Michigan	(0.257)	—	(0.177)
Services	−0.10	−0.09	0.02
Conference Board	—	(0.143)	(0.000)
Michigan	(0.117)	—	(0.001)
Durables, excluding motor vehicles	0.01	0.11	0.10
Conference Board	—	(0.233)	(0.024)
Michigan	(0.172)	—	(0.359)

Source: Author's calculations.

Notes: The table reports the increment to the adjusted R^2 statistic from adding four lags of the confidence measures; p-values for the joint marginal significance of the lags of the confidence measures appear in parentheses. Hypothesis tests were conducted using a heteroskedasticity and serial correlation robust covariance matrix. The sample covers the period from the first quarter of 1968 to the fourth quarter of 2002.

in next period's total personal consumer expenditure growth.[4] The bottom half of Table 4 shows the predictive power of each index's measure of consumer expectations. Interestingly, the expectations index of each survey appears to have less forecasting power for total expenditure growth than does the overall index.

The results from the components of consumer spending are also mixed. For motor vehicle spending, the overall indexes taken individually actually weaken the predictive power of the baseline equation, but when *both* overall indexes are included, however, or when only the expectations component of either index is included, measures of consumer confidence have forecasting power for spending on motor vehicles. For spending on services and durable goods (excluding motor vehicles), lagged values of either Michigan's or the Conference Board's overall index or their expectations component generally add little explanatory power to the consumption growth regressions. For services spending growth, the incremental adjusted R^2 is negative when either the Michigan or the Conference Board overall index is included, suggesting that including lagged measures of consumer attitudes in the baseline model weakens its predictive capacity. The Conference Board index does help to forecast growth in the goods (excluding motor vehicles) category, but again the improvement is quite modest, although statistically significant. Neither the Michigan expectations component nor the Michigan overall index is a statistically significant marginal predictor of expenditure on goods (excluding motor vehicles), but when both the Michigan and Conference Board expectations component are included as predictive variables, the fraction of next quarter's expenditure growth that is explained rises by a fairly large 10 percent, with the Conference Board variables strongly statistically significant.

In summary, the results on the predictability of consumer attitudes for consumer spending are somewhat mixed. For total consumer expenditures, there is modest incremental information about the future path of spending in both the Michigan and Conference Board indexes, and including both surveys' measure of expectations delivers fairly strong predictability of expenditure growth on goods (excluding motor vehicles). For other expenditure categories, however, the results are generally weaker, and for some categories of expenditure the inclusion of confidence indicators actually weakens the statistical relation between contemporaneous indicators and future consumer spending.

Other Empirical Connections from Consumer Confidence to Consumption

The analysis above uses historical data on consumption and income. Historical data on consumption and income become available as advanced estimates only with

---

[4] Although these regressions are the same as those carried out and reported in Bram and Ludvigson (1998), the results reported here differ because of the inclusion of new data. In a sample that ended in the third quarter of 1996, Bram and Ludvigson found that the Conference Board Index substantially outperformed the Michigan index in forecasting total consumer expenditures. Here, in data ending in the fourth quarter of 2002, the difference between the two indicators is found to be much more modest.

a one-month delay, and are subsequently revised twice over the following two months, with occasional "benchmark revisions" done approximately every five years. It thus leaves open questions about whether consumer confidence might be useful as a real-time predictor.[5]

Some researchers have used historical data to explore the possibility that consumer confidence measures may improve forecasts because observations on sentiment for the first month of the quarter are available to predict the advanced estimate of the full-quarter value of consumption. Howrey (2001) and Slacalek (2003) recognize that this timing advantage of consumer confidence data is a benefit to real-time forecasters who are often charged with predicting the actual releases of consumer spending data. For example, if one wanted to forecast the advanced quarterly estimate of consumer expenditure growth from the Bureau of Economic Analysis, available with a one-month delay, one could use the *contemporaneous* value of consumer confidence as a predictive variable, since it is available within the month. Slacalek (2003) finds that both measures of consumer confidence have statistically significant out-of-sample forecasting power for three-month consumption growth. Howrey (2001) also finds that the first-month value of Michigan's Index of Consumer Sentiment is a statistically significant predictor of the full-quarter value of several categories of consumption growth, but once the values of personal consumption expenditure and disposable income for the first month of the current quarter are known, the statistical significance of the sentiment index disappears. Although this approach explicitly takes into account the timing advantage of consumer confidence indexes over other indicators in real-time-forecasting exercises, it still relies on historical data that has been revised, rather than real-time data.

To assess the real-time forecasting power of consumer surveys for consumption would require the construction of a real-time data set, a laborious task demanding tedious amalgamation of thousands of data points from the historical archives of data collection agencies. A real-time data set of several macroeconomic series has been amassed by researchers at the Federal Reserve Bank of Philadelphia and by Dean Croushore at the University of Virginia, but no formal statistical study of the real-time forecasting power of consumer confidence indexes has yet been completed.[6]

It is natural to ask if surveys of consumer attitudes forecast the spending of households actually surveyed, rather than merely capturing the broad economic trends in aggregate consumption data. To address this question, Souleles (2003)

---

[5] One can simulate the real-time forecasting process using historical data by performing out-of-sample forecasts of consumer expenditure growth. For example, one could estimate the forecasting model on an initial subset of the whole sample and then perform a series of one-step-ahead forecasts. Such out-of-sample procedures are subject to caveats, however, because they are known to be considerably less powerful than in-sample procedures at detecting true predictability (Inoue and Kilian, 2002).

[6] However, Lovell (2001) points out that the preliminary data errors have likely decreased over time, implying that the historical gap between real time data and the most recent revisions will overstate the errors in future preliminary observations.

analyzed the household-level data that underlies the Michigan Index of Consumer Sentiment, a data set called the Michigan Survey of Consumer Attitudes and Behavior. The CAB contains the answers each household gave to the five questions that comprise the Michigan Index of Consumer Sentiment. To study how sentiment is related to spending, Souleles uses the most comprehensive household-level data set on consumer expenditures, the Consumer Expenditure Survey, which also contains a rich set of household demographic indicators. Souleles links the household-level sentiment data with consumer spending by imputing the sentiment levels of households who participated in the Consumer Expenditure Survey from demographically similar households who participated in the survey of Consumer Attitudes and Behavior. Using the imputed values of sentiment, Souleles finds that consumer confidence is useful in forecasting the one-quarter-ahead consumption of individual households, even controlling for lagged consumption growth, other household characteristics and several macroeconomic variables.

Finally, other consumer survey questions may play a role in forecasting household expenditure. Carroll and Dunn (1997) study the University of Michigan's Unemployment Expectations Index, constructed by forming the fraction of consumers surveyed who thought unemployment would rise over the next twelve months minus the fraction who thought unemployment would fall. Carroll and Dunn find that higher unemployment expectations predict lower consumer spending, even controlling for the movement in consumption that could be attributed to predictable movements in labor earnings.

What Economic Concept Does Consumer Confidence Measure?

Does the output of consumer confidence surveys correspond to any well-defined economic concept that would help explain the modest predictive power of consumer attitudes? This section considers two possible economic interpretations: that the indexes reflect precautionary savings motives or that the indexes capture household expectations of future income or wealth.

Consumer Confidence and Precautionary Saving

If higher consumer confidence levels capture reduced uncertainty about the future and therefore diminished the precautionary motive for saving, then higher consumer confidence should be associated with a higher level of consumption today, relative to tomorrow. All else equal, this means lower consumption *growth* going forward. Thus, if precautionary motives drive consumer sentiment, consumption growth measured from today to tomorrow should be negatively correlated with consumer sentiment today. This result is not what is found here, nor in previous studies like Carroll, Fuhrer and Wilcox (1994) or Bram and Ludvigson (1998). Instead, the sum of coefficients on the lagged consumer confidence measures in the forecasting regressions reported above is almost always greater than zero, indicating a positive rather than negative correlation between sentiment and future spending growth. Thus, a simple model of precautionary saving cannot explain the sentiment-spending correlation documented above.

Interestingly, one empirical study using micro data finds the opposite result. Using the Michigan Survey of Consumer Attitudes and Behavior (CAB), the household-level data that underlies the Michigan Index of Consumer Sentiment, Souleles (2003) reports that higher confidence is correlated with less saving (lower consumption growth), consistent with precautionary motives. It's possible that the discrepancy between the micro-level and macro-level results is attributable to some sort of aggregation bias, but without a detailed study of the relation between the individual and aggregate survey responses, the possibility remains speculative.

Confidence and Expectations of Future Income or Wealth

Another interpretation of consumer confidence surveys is that they primarily capture household expectations of future income or wealth. Of course, under the general version of the permanent income hypothesis, consumption should change because of unexpected rises in permanent income. However, higher confidence levels could be related to future consumption growth if households are liquidity constrained so that greater income is closely tracked by greater consumption, or if some households follow a "rule-of-thumb" of consuming some fraction of their current income every period (Campbell and Mankiw, 1989).

To assess this interpretation, we should first investigate the possibility that confidence surveys forecast quarterly income and wealth growth. Table 5 reports the results of several forecasting regressions. The dependent variables are labor income growth (defined in the same way as in Table 2), the growth of wealth as measured by Federal Reserve data on stock market wealth or nonstock wealth;[7] and the excess return on the Standard and Poor's 500 stock market index, measured as returns to the Standard and Poor's 500 index minus the three-month Treasury bill rate. The explanatory variables were four lags of either the Conference Board or Michigan measure of consumer confidence or consumer expectations, in each case controlling for lags in the dependent variable. Four lags each of the dependent variable were included in each regression.

As above, the table reports the increment to the adjusted R^2 statistic from

---

[7] A complete description of the Federal Reserve wealth data may be found at ⟨http://www.federalreserve.gov/release/Z1/Current/⟩. Briefly, total wealth is household net worth in billions of current dollars, measured at the end of the period. Stock market wealth includes direct household holdings, mutual fund holdings, holdings of private and public pension plans, personal trusts and insurance companies. Nonstock wealth includes tangible/real estate wealth, nonstock financial assets (all deposits, open market paper, U.S. Treasuries and Agency securities, municipal securities, corporate and foreign bonds and mortgages) and also includes ownership of privately traded companies in noncorporate equity and other. Subtracted off are liabilities, including mortgage loans and loans made under home equity lines of credit and secured by junior liens, installment consumer debt and other.

Table 5

Forecast of Income Growth, Wealth Growth and Excess Return Augmented by Consumer Confidence Indicators

Predicted variable	Michigan index	Conference Board index	Both	$\bar{R}^2$
		Overall index		
Income growth	0.07	0.07	0.06	0.11
Conference Board	—	(0.004)	(0.445)	
Michigan	(0.002)	—	(0.410)	
Stock wealth	0.004	0.03	0.04	−0.03
Conference Board	—	(0.175)	(0.071)	
Michigan	(0.302)	—	(0.337)	
Nonstock wealth	0.05	0.03	0.04	0.24
Conference Board	—	(0.050)	(0.413)	
Michigan	(0.081)	—	(0.300)	
Excess return	0.004	0.05	0.07	−0.01
Conference Board	—	(0.211)	(0.047)	
Michigan	(0.465)	—	(0.308)	
Excess return	0.01	0.03	0.04	0.07
Conference Board	—	(0.422)	(0.135)	
Michigan	(0.384)	—	(0.257)	
CAY	(0.000)	(0.001)	(0.001)	
		Expectation component		
Income growth	0.07	0.12	0.10	0.11
Conference Board	—	(0.000)	(0.027)	
Michigan	(0.001)	—	(0.687)	
Stock wealth	0.02	0.01	0.02	−0.03
Conference Board	—	(0.132)	(0.108)	
Michigan	(0.163)	—	(0.120)	
Nonstock wealth	0.05	0.05	0.07	0.24
Conference Board	—	(0.006)	(0.240)	
Michigan	(0.035)	—	(0.183)	
Excess return	0.02	0.03	0.05	−0.01
Conference Board	—	(0.097)	(0.061)	
Michigan	(0.313)	—	(0.126)	
Excess return	0.01	0.02	0.04	0.07
Conference Board	—	(0.303)	(0.116)	
Michigan	(0.311)	—	(0.102)	
CAY	(0.001)	(0.002)	(0.001)	

Source: Author's calculation.

Notes: The table reports the increment to the adjusted R^2 statistic from adding four lags of the confidence measures for income growth, stock and nonstock wealth growth and excess return; p-values for the joint marginal significance of the lags of the confidence measures and CAY appear in parentheses. Hypothesis tests were conducted using a heteroskedasticity and serial correlation robust covariance matrix. The column labeled "$\bar{R}^2$" reports the adjusted R^2 statistic for the predictive regression excluding consumer confidence. The sample covers the period from the first quarter of 1968 to the fourth quarter of 2002.

including the lagged confidence measures to a regression of future income or wealth on lagged values of the dependent variable. The *p*-values for the joint marginal significance of the lags of each variable, which appear in parentheses, give the probability that the confidence measure can be excluded from the forecasting equation for income or wealth growth.

The results from Table 5 suggest that consumer confidence has some forecasting power for future labor income growth. The lagged values of both Michigan's measure of consumer sentiment and the Conference Board's measure of consumer confidence increase the adjusted R^2 index by 7 percent, and the statistical probability that these variables have no predictive power for labor income growth is estimated to be less than 1 percent. By contrast, neither measure on its own has statistically significant predictive power for stock market wealth growth. Nevertheless, some evidence exists that consumer attitudes lead the stock market. When both the Michigan and Conference Board index are included in a predictive regression for the one-quarter-ahead excess return on the Standard and Poor's 500 stock market index, the measures together explain about 7 percent of next quarter's stock return and lags of the Conference Board measure are jointly statistically significant at better than the 5 percent level.

This result is not, however, robust to the inclusion of a proxy for the log consumption-wealth ratio, denoted CAY, shown in the last row of each panel.[8] CAY is equal to the log of nondurables and services consumption minus a linear combination of the log of labor income and the log of household asset wealth. This variable can be thought of as a proxy for the log consumption-aggregate wealth ratio, where aggregate wealth includes human capital. Labor income is included as a proxy for the trend movements in unobservable human capital, and the linear combination of log labor income and log asset wealth serves as a proxy for the trend movements in log aggregate wealth. CAY has been found to be a strong forecaster of quarterly excess returns on the aggregate stock market (Lettau and Ludvigson, 2001). In this regression, CAY drives out the sentiment variables, implying that whatever information is in sentiment about future stock returns is better captured by the consumption-wealth proxy CAY.

Finally, both measures of consumer attitudes have some forecasting power for non–stock market wealth (primarily housing and nonstock financial wealth). The Conference Board and the Michigan expectations component, for example, predict about 5 percent more of next quarter's fluctuations in non–stock market wealth growth.

In summary, the results from Table 5 suggest that consumer confidence has

---

[8] The coefficients of the linear combination of log labor income and log asset wealth in CAY are estimated using a dynamic least squares procedure. See Lettau and Ludvigson (2001, 2004) for details. CAY is not included as a control in the nonstock wealth regressions because it is has no forecasting power for future nonstock wealth (Lettau and Ludvigson, 2004).

modest but statistically significant predictive power for future labor income growth and non–stock market wealth growth. Can this predictive power explain the fore-castability of consumption growth by measures of consumer attitudes? In other words, does consumer confidence matter for future consumption only because it predicts future income and wealth growth, which in turn determine future consumer spending growth?

For labor income, this question was addressed by Carroll, Fuhrer and Wilcox (1994). They used a two-stage approach. In the first stage, income and/or nonstock wealth growth can be predicted by lags of consumption growth, labor income growth, the Standard and Poor's 500 price index return, a Treasury bill rate *and* one of the consumer confidence measures studied above. The forecasted values of labor income and nonstock wealth growth are saved. In the second stage, measures of consumption growth are regressed on the forecasted values of labor income growth and/or nonstock wealth growth, as well as the same lagged values of consumer confidence that were used in the first stage. If the consumer confidence measures only matter for future consumption because they forecast future labor income or wealth growth, they should display no incremental predictive power for consumption growth in the second stage regression.

However, Carroll, Fuhrer and Wilcox find that the forecasting power of consumer confidence cannot be entirely attributed to its predictive power for labor income growth. I updated their data on labor income to the present, carried out their calculations and also carried out a parallel exercise using data on nonstock wealth. The general pattern is that consumer sentiment again has predictive power for consumption growth above and beyond its ability to forecast labor income and/or nonstock wealth. In short, the information about expenditures in consumer attitudes is largely independent of the information in the predictable movements of household's resources.

In summary, to the extent that measures of consumer attitudes have genuine forecasting power for consumption, the explanation for such a relation remains unclear. Measures of consumer confidence do forecast future changes in labor earnings and non–stock market wealth, but measures of consumer attitudes appear to be directly related to future consumption growth, not just indirectly through their predictive power for household income or wealth. Carroll, Fuhrer and Wilcox (1994) rule out other explanations for why sentiment forecasts aggregate spending growth, including a simple model of habit formation. The question of why consumer attitudes help predict future consumption growth remains a puzzle.

Concluding Remarks

The preceding investigation has focused only on the consumer spending-consumer confidence relation, but other researchers have explored the relation between consumer confidence and broader measures of economic activity. Mishkin (1978) focuses on the interrelation between household investment and consumer sentiment. Matsusaka and Sbordone (1995) find a relation between the Michigan Index of Consumer Sentiment and GDP growth. Of course, the results in these papers and those presented here raise the question of whether confidence measures serve mainly as proxies for some other fundamental variable that contributes to business cycle fluctuations. The difficulty with assessing this concern is that we don't know what those other fundamentals might be. In assessing the incremental predictive power of consumer confidence measures, the best researchers can do is to rely on including, as control variables, those determinants of household spending that are both suggested by economic theory and empirically observable.

The discussion above has also focused on the question of whether consumer confidence forecasts consumption; much less research has been done on what causes movements in consumer confidence itself. For example, Fuhrer (1993) finds that 70 percent of the variation in Michigan's Index of Consumer Sentiment can be explained by variation in national income, the unemployment rate, inflation and real interest rates. Nevertheless, Fuhrer also finds that some of the movement in consumer attitudes cannot be explained with broad economic aggregates. It is possible that there are more complex, possibly nonlinear, interactions between consumer confidence and economic variables, such as the stock market or unemployment. More work, both theoretical and empirical, is needed to understand the simultaneous relation between household attitudes and household spending.

■ *I am grateful to the Alfred P. Sloan Foundation, the National Science Foundation and the C.V. Starr Center for Applied Economics (NYU) for financial support, to Jason Bram, Richard Curtin and Alan Krueger for helpful comments and to Jinyong Kim for excellent research assistance.*

References

Bram, Jason and Sydney C. Ludvigson. 1998. "Does Consumer Confidence Forecast Household Expenditure? A Sentiment Index Horse Race." *Federal Reserve Bank of New York: Economic Policy Review.* June, 4:2, pp. 59–78.

Campbell, John Y. and N. Gregory Mankiw. 1989. "Consumption, Income, and Interest Rates: Reinterpreting the Time Series Evidence," in *NBER Macroeconomics Annual.* Oliver Blanchard and Stanly Fischer, eds. Cambridge: MIT Press, pp. 185–216.

Carroll, Christopher D. and Wendy E. Dunn. 1997. "Unemployment Expectations, Jumping (S,s) Triggers, and Household Expectations," in *NBER Macroeconomics Annual.* Benjamin S. Bernanke and Julio Rotemberg, eds. Cambridge: MIT Press, pp. 165–229.

Carroll, Christopher D., Jeffrey C. Fuhrer and David W. Wilcox. 1994. "Does Consumer Sentiment Forecast Household Spending? If So Why?" *American Economic Review.* December, 84:5, pp. 1397–408.

Curtin, Richard. 2002. "Surveys of Consumers: Theory, Methods, and Interpretation." Paper written for the NABE 44th Annual Meeting, September 30.

Curtin, Richard, Stanley Presser and Eleanor Singer. 2000. "The Effects of Response Rate

Changes on the Index of Consumer Sentiment." *Public Opinion Quarterly.* 64:4, pp. 413–28.

Curtin, Richard, Stanley Presser and Eleanor Singer. 2003. "Recent Response Rate Changes on the Michigan Survey of Consumer Attitudes." Working paper, Survey Research Center, University of Michigan.

Fuhrer, Jeffrey C. 1993. "What Role Does Consumer Sentiment Play in the U.S. Macroeconomy?" *New England Economic Review.* January/February, pp. 32–44.

Greenspan, Alan. 2002. "Remarks to the Bay Area Council Conference." San Francisco, California, January 11; Available at ⟨http://www.federalreserve.gov/boarddocs/speeches/2002/20020111/default.htm⟩.

Howrey, E. Philip. 2001. "The Predictive Power of the Index of Consumer Sentiment." *Brookings Papers on Economic Activity.* 1, pp. 175–216.

Inoue, Atsushi and Lutz Kilian. 2002 "In-Sample or Out-of-Sample Tests of Predictability: Which One Should We Use?" Working paper, University of Michigan.

Keynes, John Maynard. 1936. *The General Theory of Employment, Interest, and Money.* New York: Hartcourt, Brace.

Leeper, Eric M. 1992. "Consumer Attitudes: King for a Day." *Federal Reserve Bank of Atlanta Economic Review.* July/August, 77:3, pp. 1–16.

Lettau, Martin and Sydney C. Ludvigson. 2001. "Consumption, Aggregate Wealth, and Expected Stock Returns." *Journal of Finance.* 56:3, pp. 815–49.

Lettau, Martin and Sydney C. Ludvigson. 2004. "Understanding Trend and Cycle in Asset Values: Reevaluating the Wealth Effect on Consumption." *American Economic Review.* Forthcoming.

Lovell, Michael C. 2001. "Discussion of 'The Predictive Power of the Index of Consumer Sentiment.'" *Brookings Papers on Economic Activity.* 1, pp. 208–13.

Mankiw, Gregory. 1982. "Hall's Consumption Hypothesis and Durable Goods." *Journal of Monetary Economics.* 10:3, pp. 417–25.

Matsusaka, John G. and Argia M. Sbordone. 1995. "Consumer Confidence and Economic Fluctuations." *Economic Enquiry.* 33:2, pp. 296–318.

Mishkin, Frederic S. 1978. "Consumer Sentiment and Spending on Durable Goods." *Brookings Papers on Economic Activity.* 1, pp. 217–32.

Slacalek, Jiri. 2003. "Forecasting Consumption." Working paper, Johns Hopkins University.

Souleles, Nicholas. 2003. "Expectations, Heterogeneous Forecast Errors, and Consumption: Micro Evidence From the Michigan Consumer Sentiment Surveys." *Journal of Money, Credit, and Banking.* Forthcoming.

Journal of Economic Perspectives—Volume 18, Number 2—Spring 2004—Pages 51–66

How Should We Measure Consumer Confidence?

Jeff Dominitz and Charles F. Manski

In April 2001, concern about the U. S. economy was evident in a *New York Times* headline declaring "Confidence of Consumers at 8-Year Low" (Leonhardt, 2001) and in an *Economist* story reporting, "Consumer confidence is now down to the same level as when America went into recession in 1990" ("The Kiss of Life," 2001). Two years later, in February 2003, *Reuters* reported "Consumer Sentiment Hits 9-Year Low" (2003). The *Times, Economist* and *Reuters* reports stated that their conclusions were based on an index issued monthly by the University of Michigan, but did not describe the index. Apparently, the meaning and measurement of "consumer confidence" were considered sufficiently well-known so as not to require explanation. Indeed, the Michigan Index of Consumer Sentiment is reported regularly in the media, along with commentary on its significance for the economy. So is another measure, the Consumer Confidence Index issued monthly by the Conference Board.

The Michigan index was developed a half-century ago by George Katona and colleagues at the Survey Research Center of the University of Michigan (Curtin, 1982). The Conference Board index has been issued since 1967 (Linden, 1982). Notwithstanding their prominence in public discussions of the economy, the Michigan and Conference Board indices have little presence in modern economic research. Neither "consumer confidence" nor "consumer sentiment" appear in the *Journal of Economic Literature* Subject Index of Journal Articles. A search for the two terms in *EconLit* revealed 78 occurrences in the abstracts of articles and discussion

■ *Jeff Dominitz is Assistant Professor of Economics and Public Policy, H. John Heinz III School of Public Policy and Management, Carnegie Mellon University, Pittsburgh, Pennsylvania. Charles F. Manski is Board of Trustees Professor of Economics and a Faculty Fellow, Institute for Policy Research, Northwestern University, Evanston, Illinois. Their e-mail addresses are ⟨dominitz@andrew.cmu.edu⟩ and ⟨cfmanski@northwestern.edu⟩, respectively.*

papers published from 1969 through February 2003, but relatively few of these were in "mainstream" economics journals.

Despite the sparsity of modern research, economists of an earlier period scrutinized in some depth the methods and data used to produce consumer confidence indices. In the 1940s, the U.S. Federal Reserve Board began to fund an annual Survey of Consumer Finances, conducted by the University of Michigan Survey Research Center (SRC), that posed qualitative questions of the type used to form the Index of Consumer Sentiment. The idea was that the responses to these questions might be useful in predicting consumer spending and other economic variables. This proposition was controversial, and the Federal Reserve Board appointed a committee to assess the value of the SRC data. The Federal Reserve Consultant Committee on Consumer Survey Statistics (1955), known informally as the Smithies committee for its chair, Harvard economics professor Arthur Smithies, issued findings that questioned the predictive power of the SRC data. The negative findings of the committee were challenged by SRC researchers, notably Katona (1957). A contentious conference followed (National Bureau of Economic Research, 1960). Then Juster (1964) reported an intensive study, drawing largely negative conclusions, on the predictive usefulness of qualitative approaches to elicitation of consumer expectations. By the mid-1960s, opinion among mainstream economists was firmly negative. However, the SRC continued to perform its consumer surveys and to publish aggregated findings in its Index of Consumer Sentiment. Moreover, the Conference Board initiated its own index shortly thereafter.

The Index of Consumer Sentiment (ICS) is currently formed from the responses to five questions asked in the Michigan Survey of Consumers, a monthly nationwide telephone survey. These five questions concern two assessments of current outcomes—family finances and "buying conditions"—and three assessments of future outcomes—family finances in the year ahead, business conditions in the year ahead and aggregate economic conditions over the next five years. The monthly sample size includes approximately 500 adult men and women who live in the coterminous United States. Michigan has adopted a rotating panel design for this survey, in which the majority of individuals (approximately 300) are first-time respondents from whom re-interviews will be attempted six months thereafter. The re-interview response rate is typically about 70 percent.

Research on consumer confidence has mainly sought to evaluate the power of consumer confidence data to predict economic outcomes. Following Katona (1957) and Mueller (1957), researchers by and large have sought to evaluate the power of consumer confidence indices to predict aggregate consumption and other macroeconomic variables. Sydney Ludvigson discusses some recent evidence in a companion paper in this issue. The Smithies committee, as well as Tobin (1959) and Juster (1964), recommended that consumer confidence data be evaluated by the ability of individual survey responses to predict subsequent individual outcomes, like those on durable goods expenditures, reported later in re-interviews.

This article takes a different approach. Rather than use existing consumer confidence data to predict aggregate or individual economic outcomes, we consider how best to measure consumer confidence. In particular, we analyze the responses to eight expectations questions, each with a 12-month horizon, that have appeared on the Michigan Survey of Consumers in the period June 2002 through May 2003.[1] These questions are shown in Exhibits A and B.

The four questions in Exhibit A elicit micro- and macroeconomic expectations in the traditional qualitative manner. The first two questions are components of the Index of Consumer Sentiment, but the last two are not. (All questions have three response options, except for the first. Throughout this article we treat the first question about business conditions as a three-response question as well, by aggregating the "good" and "qualified good" responses and likewise aggregating the "bad" and "qualified bad" responses.)

The four questions in Exhibit B use a newer "percent chance" format designed to elicit interpersonally comparable expectations of well-defined events. These expectations are elicited in the form called for by modern economic theory: that is, in the form of subjective probabilities. Versions of these questions have previously appeared in our own Survey of Economic Expectations.[2] Examination of the responses to these eight questions suggests three practical implications for consumer confidence surveys. First, it makes more sense to ask for expectations of events directly relevant to individual economic decisions than for predictions of general "business conditions." Second, confidence surveys should shift away from using qualitative questions in favor of questions that elicit specific subjective probability judgments. Third, while aggregating the answers to many questions given by all sample members into a single index may provide simple summary statistics, the results of confidence surveys should also be presented on a question-by-question basis for different subgroups of the population. We think that modifying data collection and analysis in these ways would lead to improved measurement of consumer confidence. Although our analysis pertains specifically to the Michigan survey, our conclusions apply with similar force to the Conference Board and similar surveys as well.

Temporal Fluctuations in Expectations

The main use of the Index of Consumer Sentiment has been to measure temporal fluctuations in consumer confidence. However, this is problematic because the index aggregates responses to disparate questions with qualitative

---

[1] A more detailed presentation of our analysis is available in Dominitz and Manski (2003).

[2] With the exception of the mutual fund question, these questions were asked in the Survey of Economic Expectations (SEE) from 1994 to 2002. We discuss the origins of these SEE questions in Dominitz and Manski (1997a, b). A set of mutual fund expectations questions, similar to those asked in the Michigan survey, were asked in SEE from 1999 through 2001.

Exhibit A

Qualitative Expectations Questions on the Survey of Consumers

BUS12 (ICS question): Now turning to business conditions in the country as a whole—do you think that during the next 12 months we'll have good times financially, or bad times, or what?

1. Good times
2. Good with qualifications
3. Pro-con
4. Bad with qualifications
5. Bad times

PEXP (ICS question): Now looking ahead—do you think that a year from now you (and your family living there) will be better off financially, or worse off, or just about the same as now?

1. Will be better off
3. Same
5. Will be worse off

BEXP: And how about a year from now, do you expect that in the country as a whole business conditions will be better, or worse than they are at present, or just about the same?

1. Better a year from now
3. About the same
5. Worse a year from now

INEXQ1: During the next 12 months, do you expect your (family) income to be higher or lower than during the past year?

1. Higher
3. Same
5. Lower

Exhibit B

"Percent Chance" Expectations Questions on the Survey of Consumers

V250: The next question is about investing in the stock market. Please think about the type of mutual fund known as a diversified stock fund. This type of mutual fund holds stock in many different companies engaged in a wide variety of business activities. Suppose that tomorrow someone were to invest one thousand dollars in such a mutual fund. Please think about how much money this investment would be worth one year from now. What do you think is the percent chance that this one thousand dollar investment will increase in value in the year ahead, so that it is worth more than one thousand dollars one year from now?

V252: Next I would like to ask you about your OWN (personal) income prospects in the next twelve months. What do you think is the percent chance that your income in the next twelve months will be higher than your income in the past twelve months?

V255: What do you think is the percent chance that you will lose your job during the next twelve months?

V256: If you were to lose your job during the next twelve months, what do you think is the percent chance that the job you eventually find and accept would be at least as good as your current job in terms of wages and benefits?

---

response categories. Specifically, the ICS is constructed as follows: For each of the five questions in the index, the *relative score* is calculated as the difference between the percentage of respondents giving "favorable" responses and the percentage giving "unfavorable" responses, plus the value 100. Then, the index equals a) the sum of the five relative scores divided by 6.7558 (the sum of the relative scores in

1966), plus b) a constant to "correct for" changes in sample design over the history of the survey. Notice that the five components are given equal weight. With this methodology, there is no clear meaning to the magnitude of changes over time in the index. Indeed, even the direction of change in the ICS is not clearly interpretable if responses to the component questions move in different directions.

To obtain a sense of temporal fluctuations, we examined the month-to-month variation in responses to each question, one at a time. We also compared the responses to related qualitative and percent-chance questions.

Higher Volatility in National Business Questions

In a pattern that recurred throughout our analysis of qualitative expectations, we found much greater month-to-month volatility in responses to the macroeconomic expectations question concerning national business conditions (BUS12) than to the personal expectations question concerning family finances (PEXP). In Table 1, we show the range of frequencies (as a percentage of the sample) giving favorable or unfavorable responses and the difference in these percentages plus 100 (that is, the Index of Consumer Sentiment relative score) during the 12 months from June 2002 to May 2003.

The relative score for the national business conditions question BUS12 rose from a 12-month minimum of 65.5 in March 2003 to a 12-month maximum of 118.4 in May 2003, just two months later. In contrast, the relative score for personal expectations of family finances PEXP varied only between 125.4 and 137.1 during the entire 12-month period. We also found greater nonresponse to BUS12 (9 percent) than to PEXP (3 percent).

The greater time series volatility of responses to the question about national business conditions and the higher nonresponse rate could have several explanations. It could be that the macroeconomic and personal financial outcomes are equally variable, but that respondents are less informed about the economy than about personal finances and, hence, have expectations that fluctuate more over time and are less willing to answer. Or the economy may really be more volatile than are personal finances. Or the volatility of responses and higher nonresponse rate to the business conditions question may arise from the vagueness of the wording, which asks whether "business conditions" are "good" or "bad."

The result of this variation, whatever its cause, is that fluctuation in the Index of Consumer Sentiment is more strongly determined by changing expectations about national business conditions than by changing expectations about personal finances. Historical evidence shows that this is a longstanding feature of the ICS. The Survey of Consumers website at ⟨http://www.sca.isr.umich.edu/⟩ makes available quarterly reports of the relative score for each component of the ICS since 1960. Over the past 42 years, the personal finances PEXP relative score varied from a minimum of 92 to a maximum of 141, with a standard deviation of 9.9. The national business conditions BUS12 relative score varied from 35 to 168, with a standard deviation of 31.7.

Table 1

Range of Responses to Two Questions from the Index of Consumer Sentiment

		Minimum	(Month)	Maximum	(Month)
(BUS12) Now turning to business conditions in the country as a whole—do you think that	% good	26.6	Feb 2003	54.4	May 2003
during the next 12 months we'll have good times financially, or bad times, or what?	% bad	34.7	Jun 2002	62.1	Mar 2003
1. Good times 2. Good with qualifications 3. Pro-con 4. Bad with qualifications 5. Bad times	% good − % bad + 100	65.5	Mar 2003	118.4	May 2003
(PEXP): Now looking ahead—do you think that a year from now	% better	37.9	Jan 2003	43.8	May 2003
you (and your family living there) will be better off financially, or worse off, or just	% worse	5.6	Jun 2002	12.6	Jan 2003
about the same as now? 1. Will be better off 3. Same 5. Will be worse off	% better − % worse + 100	125.4	Jan 2003	137.1	Jun 2002

We next considered responses to two other qualitative questions from the Survey of Consumers that may help identify why responses to the question on business conditions fluctuate more. Another question about national business conditions, BEXP, seeks a "better" versus "worse" response rather than the "good" versus "bad" response sought in BUS12. The survey also asks another question, INEXQ1, which focuses on family income rather than personal finances in general. Questions BEXP and INEXQ1 do not suffer from as much vagueness in wording as do BUS12 and PEXP. Hence, their responses may be somewhat more interpretable. Table 2 shows the peaks and troughs for these questions from June 2002 to May 2003. Nonresponse for both of these questions was very low: the national business question BEXP was 2 percent overall, and the family income question INEXQ1 was 1 percent overall.

These results indicate again that expectations for national business conditions are more volatile than are those for personal outcomes. However, the "better/ worse" responses to this business conditions question BEXP are considerably less volatile than are the "good/bad" responses to the previous question BUS12. Noting that nonresponse to the better/worse question BEXP is much less common than to the good/bad question BUS12, we conjecture that ambiguous wording is the primary explanation for the greater volatility of responses to the latter question. However, it is also logically possible that beliefs about the level of economic activity are more volatile than are beliefs about changes in the level of activity.

Table 2

Range of Responses in Comparable Qualitative Questions

		Minimum	(Month)	Maximum	(Month)
BEXP: And how about a year from now, do you expect that in the country as a whole business conditions will be better, or worse than they are at present, or just about the same?	% better	28.3	Jan 2003	45.2	May 2003
	% worse	12.4	Jun 2002	26.2	Mar 2003
1. Better a year from now 3. About the same 5. Worse a year from now	% better − % worse + 100	102.8	Jan 2003	132.2	May 2003
INEXQ1: During the next 12 months, do you expect your (family) income to	% higher	58.8	Apr/May 2003	63.5	Sep 2002
be higher or lower than during the past year?	% lower	12.0	Sep 2002	17.0	Jan 2003
1. Higher 3. Same 5. Lower	% higher − % lower + 100	142.7	Jan 2003	151.5	Sep 2002

Finally, compare the two questions asking about personal events, family finances PEXP or family income INEXQ1. The responses to both of these questions exhibit much less time series variation than do the responses to either of the business conditions questions; the minimum and maximum values of the relative score for INEXQ1 (PEXP) varied by only 8.8 (11.7) points during the 12-month period. Again, it appears that expectations for national business conditions actually are more volatile than are expectations for personal finances.

Qualitative versus Probabilistic Questions

Unlike the qualitative questions, the "percent chance" questions concern relatively well-specified events and have consistent wording across these events. The discussion in this section focuses on two probabilistic questions that are related to the Michigan qualitative questions. The full text of the questions was given earlier in Exhibit B. Question V250, which asks about the percent chance that an investment in a diversified stock mutual fund will increase in the next year, can be viewed as a more concrete question about business conditions. V252, which asks for the percent chance that personal income in the next 12 months will be higher than in the previous 12 months, is a more concrete question about personal finances.

Analyzing these probabilistic questions, we did not find the wide range of response that was evident in the responses to the qualitative questions over the 12-month period from June 2002 to May 2003. The mean likelihood of a positive return to a mutual fund investment ranged from a 39.3 percent chance in October 2002 to 45.3 in June 2002. The mean likelihood of an increase in personal income ranged from 47.9 percent in May 2003 to 54.2 percent in December 2002. The median chance of mutual fund growth varied from 40 to 50 percent over the 12-month period, whereas the median chance of personal income growth remained constant at 50 percent each month. We did find more nonresponse to the mutual fund question (8 percent) than to the personal finance question (4 percent). We conjecture that respondents are less informed about the stock market than about personal income and, hence, less likely to respond.[3]

We compared the monthly mean percent chance of mutual fund growth reported in the Survey of Consumers question against the monthly time series of the Standard and Poor's 500.[4] The two series clearly move together. The Spearman rank correlation, which measures the ordinal covariation of the two monthly time series, is 0.80. We think it premature with only one year of data to attempt to assess whether expectations of mutual fund growth lead, coincide with or lag the Standard and Poor's realizations. However, it may become possible to assess this relationship when a longer time series becomes available.

Other Personal Economic Experience: Job Expectations

The five questions that make up the Index of Consumer Sentiment ask qualitative questions about family finances (present and future), "buying conditions," business conditions and aggregate economic conditions. They do not ask about other economic information that people can report based on their personal experience, like job expectations.

Respondents to the Survey of Consumers who are currently working were posed two probabilistic questions about job prospects. Question V255 asks for the percent chance that the respondent will lose his or her current job in the next 12 months. Question V256 asks the respondent for the percent chance, should the current job be lost, that a new job would provide at least the same level of wages and benefits.

---

[3] An equivalent mutual fund question was asked on three waves of the Survey of Economic Expectations conducted in the period 1999–2001, also by telephone with a national sample of respondents. The results from that survey indicate that investment expectations in the period June 2002 to May 2003 were sharply lower than they were in the earlier period July 1999 to March 2001. However, this comparison does not demonstrate that stock market expectations typically have a much wider range of response than other questions. After all, broad stock market indexes dropped after 2000, so it is not surprising that expectations of returns dropped as well. Also, comparisons should be made with care because the nonresponse rate to the Survey of Economic Expectations question was 27 percent, considerably higher than the 8 percent experienced when a similar question has been administered on the Survey of Consumers.

[4] For the monthly value of the Standard and Poor's 500, we use the mean closing value across the trading days in the month.

We found that these expectations vary little month-to-month.[5] The mean percent chance of job loss ranged from 19.0 in September 2002 to 24.7 in February 2003, and the median ranged from 5 to 10 percent. The mean likelihood of finding and accepting a job "at least as good" as the current one ranged from 45.2 percent in April 2003 to 49.6 percent in August 2002, and the median remained constant at 50 percent. Nonresponse was minimal: 1 percent for job loss and 3 percent for the re-employment question. These results provide further evidence that personal expectations are not very volatile.

Covariation Among Expectations

We also examined how the various time series covaried over the 12-month period. The Spearman rank correlation describes the ordinal covariation between each pair of time series. For the qualitative questions, we used the relative scores to summarize the responses and ranked the monthly relative scores from the minimum of 1 to the maximum of 12 during the 12 months from June 2002 to May 2003. For the probabilistic questions, we used the mean percent chance to summarize the responses and again ranked the monthly scores from 1 to 12. The Spearman calculations presented in Table 3 show the extent to which the rankings of the responses to the questions, from lowest to highest, are correlated with each other.

We found that the monthly responses to the qualitative questions covaried very strongly with each other, as shown in the upper left portion of Table 3. The rank correlations of all pairs of the qualitative variables lie in the range [0.72, 0.93]. Thus, from an ordinal perspective, the four qualitative questions provide largely overlapping information on consumers' expectations. In contrast, the responses to the four probabilistic questions covaried weakly, if at all, with one another, as shown by the bottom right portion of Table 3. The rank correlations of all pairs of the probabilistic variables lie in the range [−0.12, 0.23]. Thus, each of these four questions appears to provide distinct information on consumers' expectations.

Finally, consider the covariation of responses to the qualitative and probabilistic questions, shown in the bottom left portion of Table 3. Responses to the qualitative macroeconomic questions—the business conditions question BUS12 and the personal finances question BEXP—covaried moderately with responses to the mutual-fund investment question (V250); the rank correlations are 0.58 and 0.46, respectively. However, responses to the two qualitative questions BUS12 and

---

[5] The composition of employment changes over time for various reasons: regular seasonal variation in employment, business-cycle fluctuations and long-term changes associated with changes in the demographic composition of the population. For these reasons, care needs to be taken in interpretation of the time series variation in responses to the job questions. Volatility in the responses could reflect changes in the composition of the respondents. To remove a particularly important source of cyclical fluctuation in composition, we assigned to the currently unemployed a 100 percent chance of job loss, as we did in the Dominitz and Manski (1997b) analysis of SEE data on job expectations.

Table 3

Spearman Rank Correlations Among Aggregated Expectations

		Relative score (monthly)				Mean response (monthly)			
		BUS12	PEXP	BEXP	INEXQ1	v250	v252	v255	v256
Relative	BUS12	1.00							
score	PEXP	0.78	1.00						
(monthly)	BEXP	0.93	0.78	1.00					
	INEXQ1	0.74	0.73	0.72	1.00				
Mean	V250	0.58	0.50	0.46	0.32	1.00			
response	V252	0.23	0.49	0.16	0.65	0.08	1.00		
(monthly)	V255	−0.41	−0.25	−0.29	−0.21	0.20	−0.12	1.00	
	V256	0.25	0.60	0.39	0.40	0.23	0.18	0.03	1.00

BEXP covaried only weakly with responses to the probabilistic question about personal income growth (V252); these rank correlations are 0.23 and 0.16. The responses to the probability question V252 on personal income growth covaried more strongly with those to the two qualitative personal finance questions. Viewed in their entirety, these findings make good sense; the highest rank correlations occur between variables that inquire about the most closely related events.

Temporal Fluctuations in Individual Expectations

The above analysis has examined how the monthly distribution of expectations changes over time. Another perspective on temporal fluctuations can be obtained from analysis of changes over time in individual expectations. Although the Michigan survey does not sample all of the same individuals month after month, it does sample some individuals twice, at six-month intervals. In this section, we restrict attention to those who completed both an initial interview during the period June 2002 through November 2002 and a re-interview during the period December 2002 through May 2003. These data enable study of fluctuations in individual expectations.

Considering the percent chance questions, we performed linear autoregressions of individual expectations on the same expectations lagged six months. We found that all autoregressions have substantial predictive power, lagged expectations being a strongly positive predictor of expectations six months later. Thus, we found considerable stability over time in individual expectations. The slopes of the autoregressions of expectations for personal events were steeper than those for investment outcomes. This finding suggests greater volatility in the latter expectations.

Table 4 shows transition matrices for responses to the two questions from the Index of Consumer Sentiment, question BUS12 on business conditions and question PEXP on personal financial situation. Each matrix presents the probability that a person gives each of the three possible responses in the re-interview conducted

Table 4A

Transition Probabilities for Index of Consumer Sentiment Qualitative Expectations for Business Conditions (BUS12)

Initial response	Re-interview response (six months later)			
	Good	Pro-con	Bad	All
Good	0.58	0.05	0.36	1.00
Pro-con	0.32	0.09	0.59	1.00
Bad	0.21	0.04	0.75	1.00

Note: Transition probabilities for the 1084 individuals who gave positive (470), neutral (66) or negative (548) responses in the initial interview and such a response in the re-interview.

Table 4B

Transition Probabilities for Index of Consumer Sentiment Qualitative Expectations for Family Finances (PEXP)

Initial response	Re-interview response (six months later)			
	Better off	Same	Worse off	All
Better off	0.60	0.35	0.05	1.00
Same	0.26	0.65	0.09	1.00
Worse off	0.16	0.47	0.37	1.00

Note: Transition probabilities for the 1202 individuals who gave positive (469), neutral (598) or negative (135) responses in the initial interview and such a response in the re-interview.

between December 2002 and May 2003, conditional on that person's response six months earlier. We find that the probability of repeating the same response exceeds one-half in all cases except two rarely chosen options—"pro-con" for the business conditions question BUS12 and "worse" for the personal finance question PEXP.

Observe that the transition probabilities between positive and negative assessments of the future are much higher for responses to the business conditions question BUS12 than to the personal finances question PEXP. In particular, 36 percent of those who initially foresaw "good" business conditions subsequently reported "bad," and 21 percent of those who initially foresaw "bad" conditions subsequently reported "good." In contrast, just 5 percent of those who initially thought their family finances will improve subsequently expected them to worsen, and just 16 percent with an initial report of "worse" later said "better." These results add yet further evidence that the qualitative expectations of macroeconomic events elicited in the Survey of Consumers are more volatile than the expectations of personal events.

Cross-Sectional Variation in Expectations

The Index of Consumer Sentiment, which presents an aggregated population-wide view of consumer confidence, obscures the fact that confidence actually varies substantially across the population. We have found that, in each month, a substantial fraction of respondents answering the qualitative questions in the Survey of Consumers reported that conditions, be they microeconomic or macroeconomic, will improve, whereas a substantial fraction reported that conditions will worsen. Similarly, probabilistic expectations varied substantially across respondents.

This section examines how expectations varied with respondent attributes. Our analysis pools the samples of initial interviews from June 2002 through May 2003, leaving out anyone who is being re-interviewed from any earlier survey. The initial interviews are independent random samples of the population.

Cross-sectional variation may reflect differences in the way that persons interpret the questions posed, rather than differences in their expectations, per se. This possibility seems most acute for the qualitative questions, as respondents may reasonably differ in how they interpret the term "business conditions" or "better off financially." We focus primarily on the percent chance questions, which should be less susceptible to variation in interpretation.

Investment Expectations

Table 5 shows the cross-sectional variation in investment and income expectations with each of several personal attributes. The results on investment expectations elicited in question V250 about expectations of mutual fund returns are particularly intriguing. We conjecture that most people have no meaningful private information about diversified stock mutual funds. If so, then the observed variation in expectations mainly reflects differences in the way people access or process the available public information. The mean answer to question V250 is that there is a 42.0 percent chance of an increase in the value of a mutual fund, but the standard deviation of the responses is 28.6. The empirical existence of such strong heterogeneity in investment expectations runs counter to the conventional rational expectations assumption that all persons access and process public information in the same way.

Some of this heterogeneity is systematic, in the sense that persons with different demographic attributes have different distributions of expectations. Males tended to be more optimistic than females. Optimism increased with schooling. Younger persons were more optimistic than older ones, and most of this decline occurs at the highest age group (65 and older). We also found variation by marital status, which we conjecture to reflect variation by age. Most optimistic were the never-married, who tend to be young, and least optimistic were the widowed, who tend to be old. Finally, we found that nonresponse was highest in the parts of the population that tended to be least optimistic.

These findings raise important behavioral questions: Why do investment expectations vary so sharply and so systematically across the population? How does the

Table 5

Variation in Expectations with Personal Attributes

| Group | A. Percent chance of mutual fund investment increase, by attributes (V250) | | | | B. Percent chance of personal income increase, by attributes (V252) | | | |
	N respondents	Mean	Std dev	N nonrespondents	N respondents	Mean	Std dev	N nonrespondents
All	3257	42.0	28.6	286	3394	50.9	37.0	139
Male	1480	45.4	29.3	74	1507	55.7	36.2	47
Female	1777	39.1	27.7	212	1887	47.1	37.2	92
Non-Hispanic white	2633	42.5	28.5	196	2736	51.4	37.5	86
Non-Hispanic black	260	39.2	28.6	43	282	52.9	34.4	20
Hispanic	183	40.9	29.7	27	187	41.9	32.2	22
American Indian	25	30.4	25.6	0	24	47.4	33.6	1
Asian	65	43.3	31.4	5	68	52.6	37.2	1
Married	1910	42.9	28.7	122	1969	52.2	36.7	55
Divorced	488	40.8	29.1	40	513	50.6	36.8	14
Widowed	241	31.1	29.4	74	273	25.4	33.3	42
Never married	609	44.4	26.5	47	630	58.4	34.9	25
Age 18–34	808	46.3	26.1	48	835	62.3	33.1	20
Age 35–49	1151	43.2	27.9	59	1184	57.4	35.0	21
Age 50–64	788	41.1	30.4	55	814	47.1	37.3	26
Age 65+	510	33.5	29.4	124	561	26.0	33.6	72
Schooling 0–12	1113	38.4	27.8	174	1195	41.8	35.9	86
Schooling 13–15	878	41.9	28.4	61	910	51.4	37.0	26
Schooling 16+	1251	45.3	29.1	51	1273	59.3	36.1	27

observed variation in expectations affect investment behavior? The data available in the Survey of Consumers do not enable us to answer these questions here, but we think them important subjects for future research.

Other Findings

Much of the variation in income expectations described in Table 5 resembles that found in investment expectations. Males tended to be more optimistic than females, the young were more optimistic than the old, and optimism increased with schooling. Unlike the case of a mutual fund investment, income realizations actually do vary cross-sectionally. Moreover, income growth does tend to be higher for males, the young and the better educated. Thus, the findings on income expectations broadly conform to the observed variation in realizations.[6]

We also examined the cross-sectional variation in responses to qualitative questions. For example, the responses to question BEXP, the more precisely

[6] Evidence from the Survey of Economic Expectations has also found that differences in expectations of personal economic events match the probable occurrence of those events. See, for example, Manski and Straub (2000) on job expectations and Dominitz (2001) on income expectations.

worded of the two qualitative questions on national business conditions, showed the same ordinal patterns as the responses to investment question V250. Males were more optimistic than females. Whites were more optimistic than others. Younger persons were more optimistic than older ones. Optimism increased with schooling. Similarly, the variation in family income expectations (INEXQ1) resembled that found for probabilistic expectations of personal income growth.

To describe how expectations vary jointly with multiple personal attributes and over time, we computed best linear predictors under square loss of the probabilistic responses to the investment and income questions. All but one of the ordinal patterns found in our univariate analysis remained intact in this multivariate analysis. The one ordinal pattern that notably waned was the substantial variation in expectations with marital status, which corroborates our conjecture that the univariate marital status pattern actually reflects a pattern of variation with age.

Conclusion

Almost 50 years ago, one of the principal investigators of the Index of Consumer Sentiment called for careful reconsideration of the index in the concluding paragraph of her article: "The index of consumer attitudes which was related here to individual purchases is still in an experimental stage. Ahead is the challenging problem of seeing whether closer correlations with purchases can be established by improving the index—by adding new series, revising the weighting of components, and refining the attitudinal measures themselves" (Mueller, 1957, p. 965). Yet except for eliminating a question on price expectations, the questions in the index and how they are aggregated have been essentially unchanged. The findings reported in this article suggest that improvement is feasible along three main dimensions.

First, we do not see an obvious rationale for asking consumers about such distant, ambiguous phenomena as "business conditions." The respondents are not expert economic forecasters, as in the Livingston panel and the Survey of Professional Forecasters.[7] If the objective is to use expectations data to predict personal consumption, expectations for business conditions should be relevant only to the extent that they are an input into formation of personal expectations. Hence, why not ask more questions that probe personal expectations directly and eliminate the questions on business conditions? The case for this change is especially strong if the month-to-month changes in the Index of Consumer Sentiment are being driven largely by spurious volatility in the responses to the national business conditions question BUS12.

We do think that consumers may usefully be queried about well-defined

---

[7] For discussion of the Livingston survey, see the website ⟨http://www.phil.frb.org/econ/liv/⟩ or Caskey (1985). For the Survey of Professional Forecasters, see ⟨http://www.phil.frb.org/econ/spf/index.html⟩ or Keane and Runkle (1990).

macroeconomic events that are directly relevant to their personal lives. The question eliciting expectations for growth in the value of a mutual fund investment exemplifies what we have in mind. One might similarly elicit expectations for aspects of government policy that directly affect consumer finances, like tax policy and Social Security policy.

Second, we think that the traditional qualitative questions of consumer confidence surveys should at least be complemented by, and perhaps replaced by, probabilistic questions inquiring about well-defined events. Economists had little experience with probabilistic questioning before the early 1990s, and skepticism about its feasibility was rampant. However, substantial experience has accumulated in the past ten years through the administration of probabilistic questions in the Survey of Economic Expectations and in major national surveys such as the Health and Retirement Study (Hurd and McGarry, 1995, 2002) and the National Longitudinal Study of Youth-1997 Cohort (Fischhoff et al., 2000; Dominitz, Manski and Fischhoff, 2001). This experience, plus the findings on the Survey of Consumers reported in this article, make plain that probabilistic questioning is feasible and yields richer information on consumer beliefs than is obtainable with traditional qualitative questions.

Third, we suggest that the producers of consumer confidence statistics prominently report their findings for separate questions and for different subgroups of the population. We do not go so far as to suggest a halt to reports of indices; simple summaries of masses of data often are a practical necessity. However, the responses to separate questions are much more readily interpretable than are monthly reports of an index constructed from disparate, noncommensurate elements. Moreover, it is important to understand how consumer confidence varies across persons with different socioeconomic and demographic characteristics.

■ *This research was supported in part by National Institute on Aging grant 2 P01 AG10179-04A1 and by a grant from the Searle Fund. Adeline Delavande provided excellent research assistance. We are grateful to the University of Michigan Survey Research Center's Committee for Research Initiatives in the Monthly Survey, which approved placement of the "percent chance" questions on the Survey of Consumers. We are also grateful to Richard Curtin, Principal Investigator of the Survey of Consumers, for his cooperation in this endeavor.*

References

Caskey, John. 1985. "Modeling the Formation of Price Expectations: A Bayesian Approach." *American Economic Review.* 75:4, pp. 768–76.

"Consumer Sentiment Hits 9-Year Low." 2003. *Reuters.* February 28.

Curtin, Richard. 1982. "Indicators of Consumer Behavior: The University of Michigan Surveys of Consumers." *Public Opinion Quarterly.* Fall, 46, pp. 340–52.

Dominitz, Jeff. 2001. "Estimation of Income Expectations Models Using Expectations and Realization Data." *Journal of Econometrics.* 102:2, pp. 165–95.

Dominitz, Jeff and Charles Manski. 1997a. "Using Expectations Data to Study Subjective Income Expectations." *Journal of the American Statistical Association.* 92:376, pp. 855–67.

Dominitz, Jeff and Charles Manski. 1997b. "Perceptions of Economic Insecurity: Evidence From the Survey of Economic Expectations." *Public Opinion Quarterly.* 61:2, pp. 261–87.

Dominitz, Jeff and Charles Manski. 2003. "How Should We Measure Consumer Confidence (Sentiment): Evidence from the Michigan Survey of Consumers." National Bureau of Economic Research Working Paper No. 9926.

Dominitz, Jeff, Charles Manski and Baruch Fischhoff. 2001. "Who are Youth At-Risk?: Expectations Evidence in the NLSY-97," in *Social Awakenings: Adolescents' Behavior as Adulthood Approaches.* Robert Michael, ed. New York: Russell Sage Foundation, pp. 230–57.

Federal Reserve Consultant Committee on Consumer Survey Statistics. 1955. "Smithies Committee Report in Reports of the Federal Reserve Consultant Committees on Economic Statistics." Hearings of the Subcommittee on Economic Statistics of the Joint Committee on the Economic Report, 84th U.S. Congress.

Fischhoff, Baruch, Andrew Parker, Wandi Bruine de Bruin, Julie Downs, Claire Palmgren, Robyn Dawes and Charles Manski. 2000. "Teen Expectations for Significant Life Events." *Public Opinion Quarterly.* 64:2, pp. 189–205.

Hurd, Michael and Kathleen McGarry. 1995. "Evaluation of the Subjective Probabilities of Survival in the Health and Retirement Study." *Journal of Human Resources.* 30:5, pp. S268–S292.

Hurd, Michael and Kathleen McGarry. 2002. "The Predictive Validity of Subjective Probabilities of Survival." *Economic Journal.* 112:482, pp. 966–85.

Juster, Thomas. 1964. *Anticipations and Purchases: An Analysis of Consumer Behavior.* Princeton: Princeton University Press.

Katona, George. 1957. "Federal Reserve Board Committee Reports on Consumer Expectations and Savings Statistics." *Review of Economics and Statistics.* 39:1, pp. 40–46.

Keane, Michael and David Runkle. 1990. "Testing the Rationality of Price Forecasts: New Evidence from Panel Data." *American Economic Review.* 80:4, pp. 714–34.

"The Kiss of Life." 2001. *Economist.* April 21, p. 23.

Leonhardt, David. 2001. "Confidence of Consumers at 8-Year Low." *New York Times.* April 13, Business Section.

Linden, Fabian. 1982. "The Consumer as Forecaster." *Public Opinion Quarterly.* 46:3, pp. 353–60.

Manski, Charles and John Straub. 2000. "Worker Perceptions of Job Insecurity in the Mid-1990s: Evidence from the Survey of Economic Expectations." *Journal of Human Resources.* 35:3, pp. 447–79.

Mueller, Eva. 1957. "Effects of Consumer Attitudes on Purchases." *American Economic Review.* 47:6, pp. 946–65.

National Bureau of Economic Research. 1960. *The Quality and Economic Significance of Anticipations Data.* Special Conference Series, Princeton: Princeton University Press.

Tobin, James. 1959. "On the Predictive Value of Consumer Intentions and Attitudes." *Review of Economics and Statistics.* 41:1, pp. 1–11.

Journal of Economic Perspectives—Volume 18, Number 2—Spring 2004—Pages 67–88

Latin America's Growth and Equity Frustrations During Structural Reforms

José Antonio Ocampo

T he debt crisis that the Latin American economies experienced during the 1980s led to a decline of 0.9 per year of per capita GDP, a "lost decade" in terms of economic growth. This experience shocked the region, as per capita GDP had increased by 2.7 percent annually from 1950 to 1980. This earlier growth had been based on development patterns characterized by high protection of domestic markets and strong state intervention. Despite rapid growth and industrialization, orthodox analysts considered these policies a source of inefficiencies, macroeconomic imbalances and a major cause of the debt crisis. With external pressure but also growing internal political support, Latin America embraced structural economic reform in the late 1980s and early 1990s aimed at reducing state intervention and exploiting the opportunities provided by international markets. Reforms had thus the dual objective of overcoming the "lost decade" and the patterns of development that had prevailed prior the debt crisis.

Structural economic reforms varied in intensity across sectors and countries. All countries in Latin America significantly liberalized international trade, external capital flows and the domestic financial sector. Policy decisions in these areas included reducing tariffs and their dispersion; dismantling nontariff barriers; eliminating most restrictions on foreign direct investment; phasing out many or most foreign exchange regulations; granting greater or total autonomy to central banks; dismantling regulations regarding interest rates and credit allocation; reducing reserve requirements on domestic deposits; and privatizing several state banks.

In the fiscal area, reforms strengthened the value added tax, reduced income tax rates and strengthened tax administration, though with only a limited effect on tax evasion. Social security systems were overhauled in several countries to allow for

■ *José Antonio Ocampo is Under-Secretary General of the United Nations for Economic and Social Affairs, New York City, New York. He was previously Executive Secretary, United Nations Economic Commission for Latin America and the Caribbean (ECLAC).*

the participation of private agents and a more clear balance between benefits and (employers' and workers') contributions.[1] Reforms were more limited in relation to privatization and labor markets. Despite the sale of many public-sector firms, most countries kept state enterprises accounting for large shares in GDP, particularly those operating in the mining and oil sectors, but also in public utilities and the financial sector. Also, although some labor contracts were made more flexible, liberalization of labor markets remained limited.

Aggressive reformers like Argentina, Bolivia, Chile and Peru carried out reforms in a short period of time, generally coupled with major macroeconomic stabilization packages, and were more ambitious in several areas, particularly in privatizations. Cautious reformers like Brazil, Costa Rica, Colombia, Jamaica and Mexico were more gradual and less ambitious (Stallings and Peres, 2000). However, even the aggressive reformers had major exceptions in some areas; for example, Chile, widely regarded as the most successful economic reformer, maintained state ownership of its copper and oil companies, as well as her commercial and development public-sector banks, and relied significantly upon capital account regulations throughout the 1990s.

Moderate rates of economic growth returned to Latin America in 1990 1997. Per capita GDP rose at an annual rate of 2.0 percent, generating positive evaluations of the reform effort (Edwards, 1995; IDB, 1997; World Bank, 1997). However, the region experienced a new "lost half-decade" in 1998–2002, when per capita GDP declined again by 0.3 percent per year, followed by a weak recovery in 2003. This grim return to stagnant growth brought an extensive reevaluation of the effects of structural reforms (ECLAC, 2003a; Kuczynski and Williamson, 2003).

It is obviously difficult to generalize about the effects of structural economic reform in a region as large and diverse as Latin America. Countries differ in how aggressively economic reforms were pursued; in their level of development, size, geographical proximity to the United States; in the magnitude of their external and fiscal debt overhangs; and in the strength or weakness of their economic, social and political institutions. However, a body of recent evidence suggests that the new development strategy has succeeded in some areas, but not in others.

In particular, the new development strategy has been effective in generating export dynamism, attracting foreign direct investment and increasing productivity in leading firms and sectors. In most countries, inflation trends and budget deficits were effectively brought under control, and confidence in the macroeconomic authorities (including newly independent central banks) increased. Reflecting the democratization wave that simultaneously swept over the region, social spending rose and innovations were introduced in the way social policy is undertaken. Nonetheless, economic growth remained frustratingly low and volatile, and domestic savings and investment remained depressed. Productivity growth has been poor, particularly when measured as output per worker, largely as a result of a growing

---

[1] Throughout the paper this term refers to the integral view of social security systems, which include not only old age pensions, but also health, insurance against work accident and death and, in a few countries, unemployment insurance.

underutilization of the available labor force. In turn, low economic and produc-tivity growth is associated with the fact that the reform process brought an increas-ing dualism, with the expansion of "world class" firms (many of them subsidiaries of multinationals) coinciding with increasing unemployment and growth of the informal labor employment. This dualism, together with other factors like the technological biases that led to an increase in the relative demand for skilled labor, generated adverse effects on an already poor income distribution record, weaken-ing the effects of growth on poverty reduction.

This paper evaluates the economic reform process in Latin America and how it affected economic and social outcomes. It is based on wide-ranging research undertaken by the United Nations Economic Commission for Latin America and the Caribbean (ECLAC) in recent years; a useful starting point to that research is ECLAC (2003a).[2]

Economic Performance

Macroeconomic Performance

The expectation of reformers was that structural economic reforms, coupled with improved fiscal and monetary management, would lead to low inflation, stable access to external capital flows, high investment rates and, particularly, strong productivity performance and economic growth. The reforms did bring low infla-tion, but the other gains failed to materialize.

The most salient macroeconomic advances in the 1990s were improvements in fiscal conditions and reductions in inflation rates. Average central-government budget deficits declined significantly in the second half of the 1980s, remained in an average range of between 1 and 2 percent of GDP through most of the 1990s, but increased to levels of around 3 percent since 1999. Government spending also increased from a simple average of 17.4 percent of GDP in 1990 to 21.1 percent in 2001, allowing in particular a strong expansion of social spending (see below), but government revenues increased enough to keep deficits under control. However, progress in the fiscal area has been uneven across the region, as reflected in the fiscal crises that several countries experienced in recent years. Particularly, the ability to avoid a skyrocketing public-sector debt dynamics during financial crises has been limited, as the reduction in tax revenues is matched during recessions by an increase in the debt service generated by high domestic interest rates and exchange rate depreciation. Progress against inflation has been more uniform and long lasting. Average inflation in Latin America fell steadily up to 2001, when it reached single digit levels in most countries. Setbacks in 2002, when average

---

[2] The overall assessment in ECLAC (2003a) can be complemented with the analysis of social trends in ECLAC (2000a, 2000b, 2001) and of issues associated with integration into the world economy in ECLAC (2002a, 2002b). The results of a long-term ECLAC project on the impact of structural reform in Latin America and the Caribbean are summarized in Stallings and Peres (2000), Moguillansky and Bielschowsky (2001), Katz (2001), Morley (2001) and Weller (2001).

Table 1
Latin America's Growth, 1950–2002

	1950–1980	*1980–1990*	*1990–1997*	*1997–2002*	*1990–2002*
GDP growth					
Weighted average	5.5	1.1	3.6	1.3	2.6
Simple average	4.8	1.0	3.9	1.7	2.9
GDP per capita					
Weighted average	2.7	−0.9	2.0	−0.3	1.0
Simple average	2.1	−1.2	1.9	−0.3	1.0
GDP per worker					
Weighted average	2.7	−1.7	1.0	−1.3	0.1
Simple average	2.4	−1.9	0.9	−1.2	0.0
Total Factor Productivity[a]					
Weighted average	2.1	−1.4	1.1	−1.1	0.2
Simple average	2.0	−1.4	1.9	−1.1	0.6

Source: Author calculations based on GDP series published in ECLAC *Statistical Yearbook for Latin America and the Caribbean,* and labor force series in ECLAC/CELADE *Demographic Bulletin,* various issues. TFP according to Hofman (2000) and updates facilitated by the author.

[a] Argentina, Bolivia, Brazil, Chile, Colombia, Costa Rica, Ecuador, Mexico, Peru and Venezuela.

inflation increased for the first time in a decade, were concentrated in a few countries and were followed by a renewed downward trend in 2003.

However, economic growth did not return to pre-1980 levels. Table 1 presents a variety of measures of annual growth, which include both simple averages across countries and weighted averages. The pattern is clear: Latin American economic growth in the 1990s has been frustratingly low. Even the acceleration of GDP growth to 3.6 percent in 1990–1997 does not look especially strong compared with the period 1950–1980. Contrasting GDP growth, rather than per capita GDP growth, makes some sense for this region because shifting age distributions can make comparisons of per capita GDP misleading. Indeed, Latin America's labor force grew in the 1990s at rates similar to those in 1950–1980. Thus, as Table 1 indicates, GDP per active worker grew at a slower rate in 1990–1997 than GDP per capita, reflecting a much poorer performance relative to the historical pattern before 1980. Furthermore, this growth recovery was followed by a sharp slowdown during the "lost half-decade" of 1998–2002, when GDP grew at a rate not unlike that in the 1980s. As a result, for the period 1990–2002 as a whole, the rate of growth of GDP and GDP per capita was less than half of those that characterized the three decades prior to the debt crisis.

These data are consistent with the record of poor productivity performance. Except for Chile and the Dominican Republic, average labor productivity—measured as the ratio of GDP to the labor force—stagnated in 1990–2002, a sharp contrast with an annual increase of 2.7 percent in 1950–1980. Rising unemployment and underemployment, largely due in both cases to poor overall economic growth, drove aggregate labor productivity. Total factor productivity also grew at a very slow rate for the period 1990–2002 as a whole and, for the weighted average, even during the years of faster economic growth, 1990–1997.

Figure 1
Net Resource Transfers

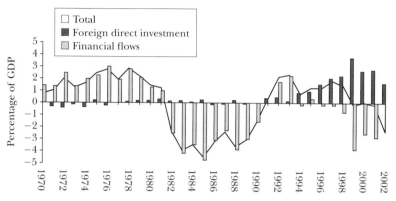

Source: ECLAC estimates, based on IMF, *International Financial Statistics.*

A major hope behind economic reforms was that they would lead to a steady inflow of external capital. Instead, fluctuations in the capital account became the major single determinant of the Latin American business cycle. Renewed access to international capital markets was evident in the early 1990s, as the sharp turn from negative to positive net resource transfers through the capital account in Figure 1 indicates. This pattern was the result of the low U.S. interest rates at the time and the 1989 Brady plan, which converted many bank loans to Latin America into securitized debt instruments, effectively creating a secondary market for Latin American securities. In the second half of the 1990s, foreign direct investment became the leading source of net resource flows to Latin America. After the east Asian financial crisis of 1997–1998, financial flows to Latin America turned negative again, and while foreign direct investment served as a compensatory factor up to 2001, its sharp fall in 2002 generated a large negative overall net resource transfer out of the region for the first time in more than a decade, which was followed by only a slight improvement in 2003.

The strong dependence of Latin America's economic growth on external capital flows operated in several ways. Since Latin America's domestic savings remained depressed in the 1990s, investment became highly dependent on external savings at the margin. Fixed investment rates (estimated at 1995 prices) experienced a partial recovery, to over 21 percent of GDP by 1997, but remained below the average 24.9 percent of GDP of the 1970s. Furthermore, this recovery was cut short by the interruption of capital flows since the east Asian crisis, which brought fixed investment to only 17.6 percent of GDP in 2003, a level lower than the worst annual records of the 1980s. Viewed from the point of view of balance of payments, there was deterioration in the trade balance/growth tradeoff (see below) that generated an increase in the demand for external funds to finance the current account deficit with the rest of the world.

The major links between capital flows and economic activity were associated, however, with the tendency to adopt procyclical fiscal and, particularly, monetary and credit policies, which made domestic macroeconomic policy a mechanism through which unstable capital flows were not only transmitted domestically but actually magnified. The result was lending booms facilitated by sharp drops in interest rates followed by crises characterized by marked monetary contraction and high interest rates. In addition, the strong bias in favor of currency appreciation that characterized the periods marked by an abundance of external financing was partly responsible for the adjustment problems faced by tradable sectors. Furthermore, the dependence on external finance created the risk of domestic financial crises when there was a sudden stop in capital flows. About half of the Latin American countries experienced domestic financial crises during the 1990s, absorbing considerable fiscal resources and affecting the functioning of financial systems (ECLAC, 2002b, 2003a, chapter 3; Ffrench-Davis, 2003; Ocampo, 2002b; Stiglitz, 2003).

Integration into the World Economy

Dynamic export growth and the surge of foreign direct investment are the clearest signs of how Latin American countries became more integrated into the world economy. From 1990 to 2000, the region posted the fastest growth of export volumes in history at close to 9 percent per year; the world economic slowdown of 2001–2002 led to a sharp drop in real export growth to 1.5 percent per year, with only a partial acceleration in 2003 to 4.4 percent. The strong growth of Mexican exports explains much of this strength in the 1990s. On the opposite side, up to 1999, Brazil experienced export growth below the regional average and her own historical performance since the 1960s. The performance of other countries fell in between but was generally dynamic.

Intraregional trade was also very dynamic, particularly among the two major South American economic integration processes: the Southern Common Market, or Mercosur, which includes Brazil, Argentina, Uruguay and Paraguay as full members with Bolivia and Chile as associate members, and the Andean Community, made up of Bolivia, Colombia, Ecuador, Peru and Venezuela. Trade growth within these two groups was very rapid in 1990–1997: 26 percent per year for Mercosur and 23 percent per year for the Andean Community. However, the expansion of trade within the two South American integration blocks was abruptly interrupted in 1998–2002, giving way to strong fluctuations in intraregional trade and a weakening commitment to regional integration.

As Table 2 indicates, export expansion has been generating two patterns of specialization, which approximately follow a regional "North-South" divide. The "Northern" pattern, shared by Mexico, several Central American and some Caribbean countries, is characterized by manufacturing exports with a high content of imported inputs, mainly geared towards the U.S. market. This pattern goes hand in hand with traditional agricultural exports and agricultural export diversification in Central America, as well as the growth of tourism in Mexico and the Caribbean. The "Southern" pattern, typical of South American countries, is characterized by the combination of extraregional exports of commodities and natural-resource-intensive (and in many cases, also capital-intensive) manufactures, and a diversified intraregional trade. A third pattern of specialization, found in Panama and some

Table 2

Composition of Latin American Exports

(*percentages of exports*)

	Primary Products		Manufactures Based on Natural Resources		Manufactures with Low Level of Technology		Manufactures with Middle Level of Technology		Manufactures with High Level of Technology		Nonclassified Products	
	1990	*2000*	*1990*	*2000*	*1990*	*2000*	*1990*	*2000*	*1990*	*2000*	*1990*	*2000*
Northern pattern												
Mexico	29.4	11.7	9.4	5.8	10.6	14.7	31.8	38.5	14.9	25.3	3.9	3.9
Central America	57.9	27.7	11.1	9.2	21.0	39.7	5.4	6.6	3.4	14.5	1.2	2.2
Southern pattern												
Mercosur	36.5	34.7	23.6	24.1	14.8	11.0	20.7	21.2	3.2	6.6	1.1	2.4
Andean Community	58.1	59.5	30.0	24.5	5.6	6.3	4.4	6.4	0.3	0.9	1.5	2.4
Chile	41.9	40.3	49.4	48.6	2.4	3.0	3.5	5.7	0.3	0.7	2.4	1.7
Latin America	39.3	27.3	22.6	17.0	11.5	14.0	18.7	24.6	5.7	14.0	2.2	3.1

Source: Author estimates based on ECLAC and World Bank (2002).

small economies in the Caribbean basin, is one in which service exports—like financial, tourism and transport services—predominate.

In general, and with major exceptions associated with intraregional trade, this pattern may seem to imply that Mexico and some Central American and Caribbean countries have been participating to a greater extent in the more dynamic world markets for manufactures, whereas South America has focused on the less dynamic commodity markets. Nonetheless, a more detailed breakdown indicates that most Latin American countries, whatever the region, tend to specialize in goods that are not playing a dynamic role in world trade (ECLAC, 2002a, 2002c).

Trade specialization and patterns of foreign direct investment have been closely linked. The "Northern" pattern has attracted multinationals actively involved in internationally integrated production systems. In South America, investment in services, natural resources and production for regional integration processes is more prevalent. The surge of foreign direct investment has included a large share of acquisitions of existing assets, initially through privatization but increasingly through private mergers and acquisitions. This pattern has led to a rapid increase in the share of foreign firms in sales—from 29.9 percent of the sales of the largest 1,000 firms operating in the region in 1990–1992 to 41.6 percent in 1998–2000—basically at the cost of public sector enterprises but also, in recent years, of large private domestic firms.

The contrast between the dynamic internationalization of the Latin American economies—increased trade and rising shares of foreign firms—and the weak GDP performance analyzed in the previous section is one of the paradoxical effects of structural reforms in the region. One explanation is that increasing international business connections have weakened or destroyed the previous links among domestic firms characteristic of the more protective environment of the past, leading in particular to a larger share of capital goods and intermediate goods bought in international markets. In addition, many internationalized sectors have an "en-

Figure 2
Trade Balance/Growth Tradeoff

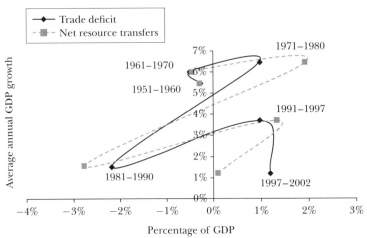

Source: Author calculations based on ECLAC *Statistical Yearbook for Latin America and the Caribbean* and IMF, *International Financial Statistics,* various issues.

clave" component: they participate actively in international transactions but much less in the generation of domestic value added. Indeed, the natural-resource-intensive sectors of the "Southern" pattern of specialization may ultimately provide more opportunities for the formation of domestic production and technological linkages than the assembly activities characteristic of the "Northern" pattern (ECLAC, 2003b, chapter 3; World Bank, 2002).

A traditional expectation has been that rapid economic growth may be accompanied by a larger trade deficit, because a rapidly growing economy draws in imports and financial capital more quickly that it can increase exports. Figure 2 shows that Latin America's rapid growth in 1971–1980 fits this pattern (in the figure, the trade deficit is measured as a positive number, representing a net inflow of resources). However, a similar trade deficit in 1991–1997 occurred at growth rates that were close to three percentage points below those registered in the 1970s.[3] This reflects the fact that the joint effects of the contraction of import-substitution sectors, the larger demand for imported intermediate and capital goods and the weakened domestic links of export sectors prevailed over the generation of new export capabilities.[4] As pointed out above, the macroeconomic bias toward currency appreciation during periods of booming capital inflows may have reinforced this trend. This process further worsened during 1998–2002, when the trade deficit remained stubbornly high in the face of slow economic growth.

[3] The analysis of UNCTAD (1999) indicates that a similar deterioration has occurred throughout the developing world in recent decades, except in China and some fast-growing Asian economies.
[4] An alternative way to look at this dynamics is to notice that the reduction in the technological gap vis-à-vis the world frontier was not enough to compensate for the extraordinary increase in the income elasticity of demand for imports and the consequent deterioration of the trade multiplier (the ratio of the technological gap to the income elasticity of the demand for imports), thus generating overall net adverse effects on growth (Cimoli and Correa, 2004).

Figure 3

Specialization Patterns, Export and GDP Growth, 1990–2000

A. Export and GDP growth

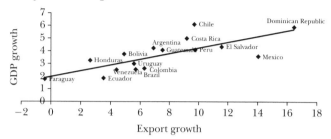

B. Change in the share of non-natural resource intensive exports and GDP growth

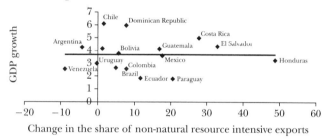

Source: Author calculations based on ECLAC *Statistical Yearbook for Latin America and the Caribbean,* various issues, and ECLAC and World Bank (2002).

Despite the weakened linkages between the internationally oriented activities and the domestic economy, export success has been a major determinant of overall national economic success during the 1990s, as the strong cross-country correlation between export and GDP growth in Figure 3a shows. However, GDP growth has not been associated with the extent to which a country shifted away from reliance on natural resource-intensive export patterns, as shown in Figure 3b. As indicated, the high import content of manufacturing exports and the tendency to specialize in technologically simpler tasks within internationally integrated production systems may, indeed, result in natural-resource-intensive exports generating more domestic value added and linkages than manufacturing exports.

Changing Sectoral and Productivity Patterns

The poor performance of aggregate production and productivity growth in Latin America reflects a diverse experience of some successful and some lagging sectors.[5]

One paradoxical effect of policies aimed at deeper integration into the world economy was the relative dynamism of nontradable sectors in many countries.

---

[5] The discussion of different sectors in this section draws upon ECLAC (2003a), chapters 4 and 5, Stallings and Peres (2000), Katz (2001), Moguillansky and Bielschowsky (2001) and, for agriculture, David (2000) and Ocampo (2000).

Transport, communications, energy and financial services, as well as construction, were dynamic, particularly during the expansionary phases of the regional business cycle in the early and mid-1990s. Some of these sectors like telecommunications, along with mining, most clearly demonstrate increases in productivity in the 1990s associated with the reform process as such—particularly the combination of privatizations, increasing involvement of multinational corporation participation and stronger protection of property rights. Mining has tended to grow rapidly, but extraction activities have grown more rapidly than those that generate more value added, like refining. Agriculture experienced significant divergence in performance across the region. Some of the most dynamic activities in this sector, like soybeans and poultry production, as well as their sustained increases in productivity, followed long-term trends largely unrelated to the reform process.

Among tradable sectors, economies specializing in manufacturing exports were characterized by the relative growth of manufacturing production, while the opposite was true of economies that specialized in natural-resource-intensive exports.[6] The manufacturing sectors that performed better include: *maquila* activities, in which inputs are shipped over the border into a special zone for processing and assembly before being shipped back, with no tariffs charged; the automobile industry, which is favored in Mexico by access to the U.S. market and in South America by special protection mechanisms; some natural-resource-processing industries; and, during periods of booming demand, activities geared toward the domestic market such as processed foods, beverages and construction materials. Some of the manufacturing industries that performed the worst in the 1990s include traditional, non-*maquila* labor-intensive industries like apparel, footwear and leather manufactures and furniture.

Productivity performance was to a large extent contrary to what traditional neoclassical analysis would suggest. Thus, productivity rose in Latin American manufacturing as a whole, but the gap with the industrialized economies, particularly the United States, widened in many sectors in the 1990s. Indeed, in many countries and manufacturing activities, the productivity gap in relation to the United States narrowed more quickly during the 1970s and 1980s than during the 1990s, reflecting in part the slower pace of technological change in U.S. manufacturing during those previous decades. At the sectoral level, the closing of the technology gap vis-à-vis the United States had more to do with the pace of economic growth in a particular sector and country than with patterns of technological catch-up induced by the reform process (Katz, 2001). For example, automobile production, for which selective instruments of protection were maintained, experienced productivity increases just as large as the natural-resource-intensive export activities, whereas import-competing sectors challenged by external competition did poorly in terms of productivity performance. Thus, the corresponding dynamics is closer to a Kaldorian pattern, in which growth determines productivity

---

[6] It is interesting to recall, in this regard, that the rising share of manufactures in GDP was a universal feature of Latin American countries in 1950–1980. During the reform period, this feature was found only in economies with a strong manufacturing export bias.

(Kaldor, 1978; Cripps and Tarling, 1973), rather than the opposite neoclassical causal link.

In more general terms, patterns of productivity performance highlight the increased diversity of production sectors and agents within each economy and, thus, the increasing dualism or "structural heterogeneity" that characterized the Latin American economies during the reform period. The expectations of economic reformers that rising productivity in internationalized sectors would spread throughout the economy, thereby leading to rapid overall economic growth, turned out to be overly optimistic. Productivity *did* increase in dynamic firms and sectors, and external competition, foreign direct investments and privatization played a role in that process. However, these positive productivity shocks did *not* spread out, but rather led to greater dispersion in relative productivity levels within the economies. The slow overall productivity performance in 1990–2002 reflects the fact that labor, capital, technological capacity and, sometimes, land that were displaced from sectors and firms undergoing productive restructuring were not adequately reallocated to dynamic sectors. This pattern also means that restructuring was not "neutral" in terms of its impact on different economic agents and sectors.

Summing up Economic Performance

In summary, the sluggishness of Latin America's economic growth in recent years is a sign of macroeconomic, mesoeconomic (sectoral and intersectoral) and microeconomic problems. Macroeconomic causes of sluggishness include a worsening of the relationship between economic growth and trade, an insufficient recovery of investment ratios, a propensity to procyclical macroeconomic policies that increase the sensitivity of economic activity to unstable external capital flows, and an associated propensity for financial crises. At a mesoeconomic level, it results from weak production and technological linkages from internationalized activities, the associated inability to transmit fully improved productivity in competitive sectors to other domestic economic activities, growing dualism and the associated underutilization of productive factors, including those displaced from uncompetitive activities. At a microeconomic level, it was the outcome of the fact that investors responded to the sharp changes in the rules to which business was subject and to uncertainty in growth prospects with "defensive" strategies that minimized fixed capital investment, rather than "offensive" strategies that would have combined restructuring efforts with substantial increases in investment in new equipment and technology.

These results are radically different from the expectations upon which the market-oriented structural reforms of the late 1980s and early 1990s were based. Thus, to what extent can we find a relation between these reforms and the patterns of GDP growth, either across time or across countries? This issue has been explored in the recent literature with no conclusive results. Although this article is not the place to review this literature in detail, some conclusions emerge.

It is clear that the reform period represented an improvement over the miserable growth record of the 1980s, but not a return to the strong performance

of 1950–1980, a period in which economic policy of Latin America was characterized by interventionist state-led industrialization,[7] not economic liberalization. By
itself, this pattern calls into question the association between reforms and improved
economic performance. Even some supporters of economic liberalization now
regard the period of state-led industrialization as a "golden age" and the growth
rates achieved during that period as a goal for future Latin American performance
(for example, Kuczynski and Williamson, 2003, pp. 305, 329).

Contradictory econometric results also lead to questions about the association
between reforms and economic growth. Evidence coming from ECLAC research
indicates that different components of the reform package probably had different
effects on economic growth, which tended to balance out to a statistically insignif-
icant overall net effect (Stallings and Peres, 2000; Escaith and Morley, 2001; Correa,
2002). Also, while the long-term effect of some reforms may have been neutral or
positive, their short-term impact was more commonly adverse. Among defenders of
the positive effects of reforms on growth, recent estimates indicate that those effects
were weaker and more temporary than originally estimated with earlier data
covering only the period of faster economic growth up to 1997 (compare, for
example, Lora and Panizza, 2002, with Lora and Barrera, 1998).

A typical confusion in the literature has been the tendency to mix the analysis
of the effects of *structural reforms* aimed at reducing the public sector's role in the
economy and liberalizing markets with those of *macroeconomic stabilization* policies.
Most aggressive reformers introduced liberalization together with major stabilization packages—for example, Chile in the mid-1970s, Bolivia in the mid-1980s and
Argentina and Peru in the early 1990s—but this pattern is far from universal.
Macroeconomic balances can be achieved with large differences in the degree of
economic liberalization and, conversely, liberalized economies can maintain significant macroeconomic imbalances. Whereas strong macroeconomic frameworks
are essential for growth, links between structural reforms and growth are at best
weak (Rodríguez and Rodrik, 2001).

There has also been a tendency in this literature to confuse structural *characteristics*
with structural *reforms*. For example, Loayza, Fajnzylber and Calderón (2002) claim, in
a recent paper, that reforms had significant effects on long-term growth, but they
actually show the effects of some structural *characteristics* like long-term effects of human
capital accumulation and infrastructure. They also show positive but somewhat weaker
impacts of effective trade openness and financial depth, but do *not* estimate those of
trade and domestic financial *reforms*. Indeed, structural characteristics that may have
positive effect on growth—like the accumulation of human capital, improved infrastructure, openness to trade and financial depth—can be achieved in a variety of ways,
with quite different degrees of public-sector involvement.

Thus, considerable work remains to be done on the determinants of economic
growth and the role played by the market-oriented economic reforms of the late
1980s and early 1990s. But, at least so far, research has failed to show the strong

---

[7] For reasons that are extensively discussed in Cárdenas, Ocampo and Thorp (2000, chapter 1), this term
is preferable to the widely used concept of "import substitution industrialization."

links between reforms and economic growth upon which the reform agenda was built.

Fragility of Social Trends

Social Spending and Restructuring of Social Services

The most positive feature of the 1990s in the social area of Latin America was the significant increase in spending in basic social services, social security and additional forms of social protection. This increase should be seen as a basic dividend of democracy that led, contrary to the initial expectations of some reformers, to an expansion of government spending.

Social sector government spending rose from 10.1 percent of GDP in 1990–1991 to 13.8 percent in 2000–2001, reaching the highest levels in the region's history (ECLAC, 2000a, 2000b, 2003c). Moreover, the increase was relatively faster in countries with lower per capita income, where social spending has been traditionally low. Uruguay and Brazil strengthened their relatively high levels of social spending, together with Costa Rica, Panama and, up to the recent crisis, Argentina. Colombia was the only country moving from a relatively low level of social spending to an average pattern given her per capita income levels. In any case, regional disparities remain large, and in several countries social spending continues to be clearly inadequate.

Increased social spending was accompanied by more selective allocation criteria (that is, better targeting), which account for differences in the distributive impact of different types of spending (ECLAC, 2000a, 2000b). Changes have also been made in the way public resources are allocated, basically through more deccntralized systems.

Rising social spending was reflected in improvements in education, health and other social standards, maintaining the long-term trend in the region toward improvements of living conditions as measured by indicators such as the Human Development Index—a feature even of the "lost decade." However, the only available long-term index of this type indicates that improvements over the 1990s tended to follow the slower pace of the 1980s rather than the more rapid betterment that characterized the period 1940–1980 (Astorga, Bergés and Fitzgerald, 2003).

Despite increasing attendance to secondary and university education, disparities in access between the top and the bottom quartiles/quintiles of the income distribution increased over the past decade (ECLAC, 2002a, chapter 10; World Bank, 2003, chapter 2). Also, the efficiency and quality of social services continued to be low, and social security coverage remained stagnant in most countries.

In some countries, increased spending led to the development of arrangements for private-sector participation in the provision of certain social services, particularly in the administration of social security pension plans and low-income housing. These arrangements may have brought progress in terms of efficiency, including the use of equivalence criteria for equating contributions paid into the social security system with benefits received from it, but strong evidence in this regard is not available. In some cases, however, private-sector provision has gone hand in hand with a concentration of providers in the higher-income, lower-risk sectors and a weakening of the principles of universality and solidarity that should be honored by social security systems (ECLAC, 2000a). It should be noted, however, that for the most part, these principles were not properly applied in the region in the past either, when a common pattern was incomplete and segmented social security coverage that included the proliferation of special arrangements that benefited certain social sectors.

Labor Market Weakness

The worst performance in the social area during the reform period was experienced in labor markets (ILO, 1999; ECLAC, 2002a, chapter 10; Weller, 2001). In Latin American economies, deterioration in this area should be measured both by rising unemployment and employment in low productivity activities (particularly in the informal sector), with the exact mixture in any country depending on the patterns of economic growth, labor market policies and international labor migration. Most countries experienced deterioration in either one of these indicators or in both of them. Despite faster economic growth since 1990 in relation to the "lost decade" of the 1980s, open unemployment in Latin America rose by almost three percentage points during the 1990s and shot up even higher in some countries, particularly during major external shocks. In turn, the share of urban informal-sector employment rose from 43.0 to 48.4 percent between 1990 and 1999, generating seven out of ten new jobs. The resulting deterioration in job quality is also evident in the relative increase in temporary employment, in reduced coverage of social security systems (particularly for workers in small enterprises) and in the rising number of individuals working without a written labor contract (Tokman and Martínez, 1999; ECLAC, 2002a, chapter 10).

One specific factor that played a significant role in labor markets was the pattern of international specialization (ECLAC, 2002a, chapter 10; Stallings and Weller, 2001). As Table 3 indicates, the "Northern" pattern of specialization in manufactures (and some services) proved much more effective in generating employment, particularly wage-labor employment in tradable sectors, than the "Southern" specialization in natural-resource-intensive goods. As employment did not follow specialization patterns in nontradable sectors (particularly in relation to wage employment), whereas in tradable sectors it did, the growth of employment was more dynamic in the Northern part of the region.

The considerable increase in the wage gap between skilled and unskilled workers—and, particularly, between college-educated workers and others—has been another widespread phenomenon (ECLAC, 1997 and 2002a, chapter 10; Morley, 2001). The widespread character of this trend indicates that divergent specialization patterns within the region are not part of the explanation; rather, technological change and the relative growth of sectors with high demands for human capital (particularly some services) seem to be the determining factors. According to a recent World Bank report, this trend may be associated also with the tensions that characterize middle-income countries in the current global order, as

Table 3

Patterns of Employment Generation, 1990–1999

(*annual average growth rates*)

	Total employment			Wage earner employment		
	Total	Tradable sectors[a]	Nontradable sectors[b]	Total	Tradable sectors[a]	Nontradable sectors[b]
Simple average						
Mexico and Central America	3.6	2.1	4.8	3.6	3.1	3.7
		(3.9)	(3.1)		(4.4)	(2.9)
South America	2.6	1.3	3.1	2.5	1.0	3.1
		(1.3)	(2.5)		(0.8)	(2.6)
Total	3.0	1.7	3.9	3.0	1.9	3.3
		(2.5)	(2.7)		(2.4)	(2.7)
Weighted average						
Mexico and Central America	3.2	1.8	4.1	2.8	2.0	2.7
		(4.1)	(4.3)		(3.6)	(3.6)
South America	1.8	0.2	2.6	1.8	0.1	2.5
		(0.2)	(2.5)		−(0.1)	(2.6)
Total	2.2	0.8	3.0	2.1	0.7	2.6
		(1.5)	(2.9)		(0.9)	(2.9)

Source: ECLAC (2002a), Table 10.8.

[a] The data between parentheses correspond to manufacturing sector.

[b] The data between parentheses correspond to government, social, community and personal services.

the wages of the more-skilled labor are being pushed up by the incomes they earn in the industrial world, whereas those of low-skilled labor are determined by competition in the international market for goods with lower-income countries, particularly China (World Bank, 2003, chapter 6). This explanation is consistent with Rodrik's (1998) view that globalization tends to benefit the more mobile factors like capital and skilled labor relative to the less mobile factors like unskilled labor. Given these adverse trends, the greater participation of women in labor markets is the most positive pattern found across the region. Also, in most countries the growing labor force participation of women has been accompanied by a reduction in the (still large) gender income gap.

Poverty and Income Distribution

Poverty rates shot up during the "lost decade," from 40.5 percent of the total population in 1980 to 48.3 percent in 1990, and fell as growth recovered, to 43.5 percent in 1997—although the absolute number of poor stagnated at roughly 200 million.[8] These positive trends were sharply interrupted during the "lost half-decade," causing an additional 20 million persons to fall below the poverty line.

---

[8] The poverty rates used here are those of ECLAC, estimated on the basis of a specific food consumption basket for each country. At the regional level, they differ in magnitude but not in the overall trend from those estimated by the World Bank on the basis of a poverty line estimated as $2 a day on the basis of purchasing power parities.

In this recent period, whereas per capita GDP has exceeded 1980 levels by some 6 percent, the poverty rate of 43.4 percent in 2002 remained three percentage points above the 1980 level.

Success in reducing poverty has varied across the region.[9] Figure 4 shows some differences in how growth affected poverty during the period of faster economic growth (1990–1997). Chile, which experienced the fastest economic growth, also had a strong performance in terms of poverty reduction. Costa Rica's good performance and the poor record of Honduras can be attributed to differences in the rates of economic growth. Nevertheless, other countries show significant divergence from the average pattern: Uruguay and Brazil did much better than expected given their rates of growth, whereas Argentina, Bolivia, Mexico and Venezuela did much worse. Specific policies can explain deviations from the pattern, including the extensive system of social protection in Uruguay and the targeted minimum pension policies in Brazil. The end of hyperinflation also had a positive effect in all countries that had gone through that traumatic experience, indicating that indexing of lower incomes was more imperfect than that of higher incomes during episodes of very high inflation. Also, there is evidence that minimum-wage policies also had a broadly positive effect in this regard.

Unlike poverty rates, income distribution trends have been uneven across the region but, on the whole, show a tendency to deteriorate. There are several countries where income distribution, measured by either the Gini coefficient or relative poverty,[10] displayed an adverse trend over the past decade and only a handful where the opposite is true. Deterioration was more common in South America,[11] indicating that there may be an association between the patterns of specialization and income distribution, probably through the divergent employment effects of different specialization patterns. Although comparing data on income distribution over long periods of time is a complex matter, there is probably no country in the region where inequalities have declined relative to what they were three decades ago and, on the contrary, many countries where inequality has increased.

Inequality of income is due to a combination of factors relating to education, demographics, employment and the distribution of wealth. As regards the first two,

---

[9] On the determinants of poverty and income distribution, see ECLAC (1997, 2000a, 2000b, 2001), IDB (1999), Morley (2001) and World Bank (2003).

[10] Relative poverty is estimated by ECLAC as the proportion of the population with an income below half of national per capita household income. This proportion tends to be higher when income is more unequally distributed and can thus be considered a measure of income distribution rather than poverty.

[11] This concentration of adverse distributive trends in South America is a conclusion of the recent report of the World Bank (2003, chapter 2) but is consistent with ECLAC estimates. There are, however, significant differences in individual calculations. The World Bank estimates an improvement in income distribution in Brazil over the 1990s, which is not confirmed by ECLAC. The opposite is true of Uruguay. Adjustments in the original household data explain the difference. Possible improvements in Brazil are the basic reason for the conclusion of the World Bank that regional income distribution, weighted by population, improved slightly in Latin America over the 1990s, a conclusion that is not confirmed with alternative data. However, both ECLAC and the World Bank agree that there was a deterioration of the average (unweighted) Gini coefficient.

Figure 4

Poverty Reduction and Per Capita GDP Growth, 1990–1997

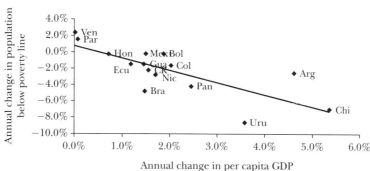

Source: Author calculations based on ECLAC *Statistical Yearbook for Latin America and the Caribbean* and ECLAC *Social Panorama of Latin America,* various issues.

some progress was made during the 1990s. Educational coverage improved, as noted, though there are signs of growing dispersion in that coverage and, probably, in the quality of education across social sectors. Reductions in birth rates generated a slower growth of the dependent youth population and facilitated a larger participation of women in the labor force. The combination of these two factors tended to reduce inequality, as the poorer households tend to be larger. These positive effects were, nonetheless, weaker than the negative shocks in the job front, which included rising unemployment and low-quality employment. Also, in some countries, there was a narrowing of disparities between the incomes of workers who have received only primary education and those who have some secondary education, but this has been overwhelmed by the growing income gap between college-educated and other workers, and by greater dispersion of incomes among college-educated workers (Morley, 2001; World Bank, 2003). Not much is known about what has happened in terms of wealth inequality, but it is likely that it became more unequal, as well.

There is considerable disagreement in the current literature as to why income distribution has tended to deteriorate (Altimir, 1997; Berry, 1998; Morley, 1995, 2001; IDB, 1997, 1999; ECLAC, 1997; World Bank, 2003). Some studies focus on factors specific to Latin America like the effects of the debt crisis of the 1980s or the structural reforms of the late 1980s and early 1990s. Other papers focus on more universal trends associated with technological and other factors influencing wage/skill differentials. Berry (1998) stands out for his early emphasis on the adverse distributive effects of structural reforms, a hypothesis that has received increasing support in later research. In the light of previous analysis, it seems that the increasing dualism generated by reforms, the patterns of specialization in manufactures versus natural-resource-intensive goods, and the worldwide factors generating adverse trends in the relative incomes of workers with higher skills also played a role.

In any case, adverse distributive patterns have long been evident in Latin America. Thus, the lack of equity is not just a characteristic of the recent reform

period, but a pre-existing condition that reflects serious problems of social strati-
fication and wealth inequality that have been handed down from generation to
generation (ECLAC, 2000a, 2000b).

The Way Forward

This paper has argued that the benefits of market-oriented economic reforms
that Latin America undertook since the mid-1980s were overstated and their risks
largely overlooked. Structural economic reforms, together with an increased monetary and fiscal discipline, were successful in many areas, particularly in bringing
down inflation, inducing export growth and diversification, and in attracting
foreign direct investment. But frustration also resulted from economic growth that
remained low and volatile, from increasing dualism of the economy and, particularly, from the disappointing social outcomes. Some basic assumptions of reformers
proved to be entirely wrong, particularly the assumptions that low inflation and
better control of budget deficits would ensure stable access to international capital
markets and dynamic economic growth, and that higher productivity in leading
firms and sectors would automatically spread throughout the economy, leading to
a broad acceleration of economic growth.

The interpretation of these poor outcomes of reforms remains highly controversial. One view explains these results as the effect of an insufficient commitment
to the original reform agenda and thus posits that the solution to the current
frustrations is even more liberalization. An alternative view, much in vogue recently,
argues that the agenda of market liberalization and strong macroeconomic frameworks was laudable but incomplete, and should now be complemented with a
"second generation" of reforms based on strengthening domestic institutions and
more active social policies (Birdsall, de la Torre and Menezes, 2001; Kuczynski and
Williamson, 2003). A third approach argues that some of the basic assumptions of
the liberalization process were in fact wrong and, thus, that the first generation of
reforms may have created some of the problems that Latin America is facing today
and that it is necessary, in some cases, to "reform the reforms" (Ffrench-Davis, 2000;
ECLAC, 2000a).

My own preferred alternative is to acknowledge that we must build upon the
positive aspects of the economic reform process, as well as the new agenda of
institutional and social reforms but also to correct the basic problems that the first
generation of reforms has evidenced. A view along these lines has been advocated
by Rodrik (1999, 2001a, 2001b), by ECLAC (2000a) and by this author (Ocampo,
2002a, 2002b, 2004), among others. This view implies that changes must be
introduced in three areas.

First, the view of macroeconomic stability needs to be expanded to include not
only low inflation rates and budget deficits, but also high and stable growth rates
and employment. For this purpose, it is essential to overcome the existing procyclical macroeconomic policies that heighten the effects of volatile external markets,
especially capital markets, and thus generate adverse effects on investment as well

as the latent risks of financial crises. The design of countercyclical macroeconomic fiscal and monetary policies is thus central to any alternative agenda. In view of the central role played by external capital flows in the determination of the Latin American business cycle, this policy may require an active regulation of external capital flows.

Second, the earlier reforms failed to realize that the emergence of dynamic economic activities is not necessarily a spontaneous outcome of liberalized, open economies. It requires adequate exchange rate management as well as active technology and domestic financial policies, to guarantee access to technology and long-term financing in domestic currencies to all firms; public-private partnerships to support the emergence of new economic activities (including, in some cases, the design of strategic, time-bound subsidies); and an active trade diplomacy. In the light of recent trends, two issues are particularly important. The first is to accept that production and technological linkages between dynamic firms and sectors and the rest of the economy do not occur automatically. Instead, special mechanisms must be designed to create such linkages, particularly through clearinghouse markets to facilitate local suppliers meeting with local demanders. The second is that active policies must be implemented to counteract dualism in productive structures, by strong policies of support to small-sector firms and their links with larger enterprises.

Third, the previous reforms failed to recognize that successful social outcomes are not just social but also *economic* objectives. The "residual" view of social policies, so common today, in which social policies are supposed to take care of those who are unable to adjust to more competitive markets, must be overcome. The accumulation of assets of the poor—including education, access to technology and credit markets, and to land—as well as the design of integral systems of social protection should be combined, under Latin American conditions, with explicitly redistributive policies. None of these conditions is likely to be satisfied without increasing progressive taxation and social spending and without improving efficiency in the delivery of social policy. Given the very serious deterioration that has characterized labor markets, a fresh social dialogue and series of interventions to improve employment generation must be added. But, beyond these interventions, it is essential that social objectives be mainstreamed into economic policy—that is, that the design of economic policy should consider social effects from its inception, thus abandoning the practice of assuming that social problems will be managed with residual social policies.

Reversing the errors of the macroeconomic and structural reforms of the 1980s and early 1990s does not mean returning to policies that Latin America adopted during its period of "state-led industrialization" from the 1940s to the 1970s. This article is not the place to debate the historical controversy about how much the policies of state-led industrialization contributed to the robust growth rate of growth of Latin American over that period (for a discussion along these lines, see Cárdenas, Ocampo and Thorp, 2000). Regardless of one's position in that debate, there is little reason to believe that the specific policies popular in Latin America at that time would produce the same growth rates in the very different global economic environment of today. But there is also little reason to believe that a policy focused on market liberalization, even if accompanied by stronger safety nets, will suffice to bring more rapid economic growth and improved social indicators, either. Furthermore, there are diverse solutions to the problems of economic and social development, and democracy must play an essential role in finding the appropriate policies for each particular context. No unique "recipe" for economic development will work for every country. The essence of democracy and institutional development is diversity and learning.

■ *This paper draws from a previous paper prepared for the Conference on Social and Economic Impacts of Liberalization and Globalization, organized by the Centre for International Studies of the University of Toronto, in honor of Professor Albert Berry, April 2002.*

References

Altimir, Oscar. 1997. "Desigualdad, Empleo y Pobreza en América Latina: Efectos del Ajuste y del Cambio en el Estilo de Desarrollo." *Desarrollo Economico.* 37:145, pp. 3–30.

Astorga, Pablo, Ame R. Bergés and Valpy Fitzgerald. 2003. "The Standard of Living in Latin America During the Twentieth Century." QEH Working Paper Series No. 103, March.

Berry, Albert. 1998. *Confronting the Income Distribution Threat in Latin America: Poverty, Economic Reforms, and Income Distribution in Latin America.* Boulder, Colo.: Lynne Rienner.

Birdsall, Nancy, Augusto de la Torre and Rachel Menezes. 2001. *Washington Contentious: Economic Policies for Social Equity in Latin America.* Washington, D.C.: Carnegie Endowment for International Peace and Inter-American Dialogue.

Cárdenas, Enrique, José Antonio Ocampo and Rosemary Thorp, eds. 2000. *Industrialisation and the State in Latin America: the Post War Years, An Economic History of Twentieth Century Latin America, Volume 3.* New York: Palgrave Press and St. Martins.

Cimoli, Mario and Nelson Correa. 2004. "Trade Openness and Technological Gaps in Latin America: A 'Low Growth Trap,'" in *Rethinking Development Challenges.* José Antonio Ocampo, ed. Santiago: ECLAC, forthcoming.

Correa, Rafael. 2002. "Reformas Estructurales y Crecimiento en América Latina: un Análisis de Sensibilidad." *ECLAC Review.* April, 76, pp. 89–107.

Cripps, T. Francis and Roger J. Tarling. 1973. "Growth in Advanced Capitalist Economies 1950–1970." Occasional Paper 40, University of Cambridge, Department of Applied Economics.

David, M. Beatriz. 2000. *Desarrollo Rural en América Latina y el Caribe: ¿La Construcción de un Nuevo Modelo?* Bogotá: ECLAC/Alfaomega.

ECLAC (Economic Commission for Latin America and the Caribbean). 1997. *The Equity Gap: Latin America, the Caribbean and the Social Summit.* Santiago: ECLAC.

ECLAC (Economic Commission for Latin America and the Caribbean). 1998. *Social Panorama of Latin America, 1997.* Santiago: ECLAC.

ECLAC (Economic Commission for Latin America and the Caribbean). 2000a. *Equity, Development and Citizenship.* Santiago: ECLAC.

ECLAC (Economic Commission for Latin America and the Caribbean). 2000b. *The Equity Gap, A Second Assessment.* Santiago: ECLAC.

ECLAC (Economic Commission for Latin America and the Caribbean). 2001. *Social Panorama of Latin America, 2000–2001.* Santiago: ECLAC.

ECLAC (Economic Commission for Latin America and the Caribbean). 2002a. *Globalization and Development.* Santiago: ECLAC.

ECLAC (Economic Commission for Latin America and the Caribbean). 2002b. *Growth with Stability: Financing for Development in the New International Context,* ECLAC Books, No. 67. Santiago: ECLAC.

ECLAC (Economic Commission for Latin America and the Caribbean). 2002c. *Latin America and the Caribbean in the World Economy. 2000–2001 Edition.* Santiago: ECLAC.

ECLAC (Economic Commission for Latin America and the Caribbean). 2003a. *A Decade of Light and Shadow: Latin America and the Caribbean in the1990s.* Santiago: ECLAC.

ECLAC (Economic Commission for Latin America and the Caribbean). 2003b. *Latin America and the Caribbean in the World Economy, 2001–2002 Edition.* Santiago: ECLAC.

ECLAC (Economic Commission for Latin America and the Caribbean). 2003c. *Social Panorama of Latin America, 2002-2003.* Santiago: ECLAC.

ECLAC (Economic Commission for Latin America and the Caribbean) and World Bank. 2002. *Database Software for a Competitive Analysis of Nations (TRADE CAN).* Washington, D.C.: World Bank.

Edwards, Sebastián. 1995. *Crisis and Reform in Latin America: From Despair to Hope.* Washington, D.C.: Oxford University Press.

Escaith, Hubert and Samuel Morley. 2001. "El Efecto de las Reformas Estructurales en el Crecimiento Económico de la América Latina y el Caribe. Una Estimación Empírica." *El Trimestre Económico.* October/December, 68:272, pp. 469–513.

Ffrench-Davis, Ricardo. 2000. *Reforming the Reforms in Latin America: Macroeconomics, Trade, Finance.* New York: St. Martin's Press.

Ffrench-Davis, Ricardo. 2003. "Financial Crises and National Policy Issues: An Overview," in *From Capital Surges to Drought: Seeking Stability for Emerging Markets.* R. Ffrench-Davis and S. Griffith-Jones, eds. London: Palgrave and Macmillan, Chapter 2.

Hofman, André. 2000. *The Economic Development of Latin America in the Twentieth Century.* Cheltenham, U.K.: Edward Elgar.

Inter-American Development Bank (IDB). 1997. *Latin America After a Decade of Reforms, Economic and Social Progress in Latin America 1997.* Washington, D.C.: Inter-American Development Bank.

Inter-American Development Bank (IDB). 1999. *Facing Up to Inequality in Latin America, Economic and Social Progress in Latin America 1998–1999.* Washington, D.C.: Inter-American Development Bank.

International Labour Organization (ILO). 1999. "Trabajo Decente y Protección para Todos. Prioridad de las Américas." Memoria del Director General, fourteenth Regional Meeting of the Americas, Lima, August 24–27.

Kaldor, Nicholas. 1978. *Further Essays on Economic Theory.* London: Duckworth.

Katz, Jorge. 2001. *Structural Reforms, Productivity and Technological Change in Latin America.* ECLAC Books, No. 64. Santiago: Economic Commission for Latin America and the Caribbean (ECLAC).

Kaufmann, Daniel, Aart Kraay and Massimo Mastruzzi. 2003. "Governance Matters III: Governance Indicators for 1996–2002." Mimeo, the World Bank.

Kuczynski, Pedro-Pablo and John Williamson, eds. 2003. *After the Washington Consensus: Restarting Growth and Reform in Latin America.* Washington, D.C.: Institute for International Economics, March.

Loayza, Norman, Pablo Fajnzylber and César Calderón. 2002. "Economic Growth in Latin America and the Caribbean: Stylized Facts, Explanations, and Forecasts." World Bank, June.

Lora, Eduardo and Felipe Barrera. 1998. "El Crecimiento Económico en América Latina Después de Una Década de Reformas Estructurales," in *Pensamiento Iberoamericano.* Madrid: Agencia Española de Cooperación Internacional, pp. 55–86.

Lora, Eduardo and Ugo Panizza. 2002. "Structural Reforms in Latin America Under Scrutiny." Background paper prepared for the seminar *Reforming Reforms,* Inter-American Development Bank Annual Meetings, Fortaleza, Brazil, March 11.

Moguillansky, Graciela and Ricardo Bielshowsky. 2001. *Investment and Economic Reform in Latin America.* ECLAC Books series, No. 63. Santiago: Economic Commission for Latin America and the Caribbean (ECLAC).

Morley, Samuel. 1995. *Poverty and Inequality in Latin America: the Impact of Adjustment and Recovery in the 1980s.* Baltimore: Johns Hopkins University Press.

Morley, Samuel. 2001. *The Income Distribution Problem in Latin America and the Caribbean.* ECLAC Books series, No. 65. Santiago: Economic Commission for Latin America and the Caribbean (ECLAC).

Ocampo, José Antonio. 2000. "Agricultura y Desarrollo Rural en América Latina: Tendencias, Estrategias, Hipótesis," in *El Impacto de las Reformas Estructurales y las Políticas Macroeconómicas Sobre el Sector Agropecuario de América Latina.* Bogotá: ECLAC/Alfaomega, pp. 55–93.

Ocampo, José Antonio. 2002a. "Rethinking the Development Agenda." *Cambridge Journal of Economics.* May, 26:3, pp. 393–407.

Ocampo, José Antonio. 2002b. "Developing Countries' Anti-Cyclical Policies in a Globalized World," in *Development Economics and Structuralist*

Macroeconomics: Essays in Honour of Lance Taylor.
Amitava Dutt and Jaime Ros, eds. Aldershot,
U.K.: Edward Elgar.

Ocampo, José Antonio. 2004. "Structural Dynamics and Economic Growth in Developing Countries," in *Rethinking Development Challenges.* José Antonio Ocampo, ed. Santiago: ECLAC, forthcoming.

Peres, Wilson, coord. 1998. *Grandes Empresas y Grupos Industriales Latinoamericanos. Expansión y Desafíos en la Era de la Apertura y la Globalización.* Mexico City: Siglo Veintiuno Editores.

Peres, Wilson and Giovanni Stumpo. 2000. "Small and Medium-Sized Manufacturing Enterprises in Latin America and the Caribbean Under the New Economic Model." *World Development.* September, 28:9, pp. 1643–655.

Rodríguez, Francisco and Dani Rodrik. 2001. "Trade Policy and Economic Growth: A Skeptic's Guide to the Cross-National Evidence," in *NBER Macroeconomics Annual 2000, Volume 15.* Ben S. Bernanke and Kenneth Rogoff, eds. Cambridge: MIT Press, pp. 261–325.

Rodrik, Dani. 1998. *Has Globalization Gone Too Far?* Washington, D.C.: Institute for International Economics.

Rodrik, Dani. 1999. *Making Openess Work: The New Global Economy and the Developing Countries.* Washington, D.C.: Overseas Development Council.

Rodrik, Dani. 2001a. "Why is There So Much Economic Insecurity in Latin America?" *CEPAL Review.* April, 73, pp. 7–31.

Rodrik, Dani. 2001b. "Development Strategies for the Next Century," in *Annual World Bank Conference on Development Economics 2000.* Boris Pleskovic and Nicholas Stern, eds. Oxford: World Bank, Oxford University Press.

Stallings, Barbara and Wilson Peres. 2000. *Growth, Employment and Equity: the Impact of the Economic Reforms in Latin America and the Caribbean.* Santiago, Chile: Brookings Institution /Economic Commission for Latin America and the Caribbean (ECLAC).

Stallings, Barbara and Jürgen Weller. 2001. "Employment in Latin America: Cornerstone of Social Policy." *CEPAL Review.* December, 75, pp. 181–200.

Stiglitz, Joseph A. 2003. "Whither Reform? Towards a New Agenda for Latin America." *CEPAL Review.* August, 80, pp. 7–40.

Tokman, Victor E. and Daniel Martínez, eds. 1999. *Flexibilización en el Margen: la Reforma del Contrato de Trabajo.* Lima: Regional Office for Latin America and the Caribbean, International Labour Organization (ILO).

United Nations Conference on Trade and Development (UNCTAD). 1999. *Trade and Development Report, 1999.* Geneva: United Nations Publication, Sales No. E.99.II.D.1.

Williamson, John. 1990. "What Washington Means by Policy Reform," in *Latin American Adjustment. How Much Has Happened?* J. Williamson, ed. Washington, D.C.: Institute for International Economics, Chapter 2.

Weller, Jürgen. 2001. *Economic Reforms, Growth and Employment: Labour Markets in Latin America and the Caribbean.* ECLAC Books Series, No. 66. Santiago: Economic Commission for Latin America and the Caribbean (ECLAC).

World Bank. 1997. *The Long March: A Reform Agenda for Latin America and the Caribbean in the Next Decade.* Shahid Javed Burki and Guillermo E. Perry, eds. Washington, D.C.: World Bank Latin American and Caribbean Studies Viewpoints.

World Bank. 2002. *From Natural Resources to the Knowledge Economy: Trade and Job Quality.* David De Ferranti, Guillermo E. Perry, Daniel Lederman, and William F. Maloney, eds. Washington, D.C.: World Bank Latin American and Caribbean Studies Viewpoints.

World Bank. 2003. *Inequality in Latin America and the Caribbean: Breaking with History?* David De Ferranti, Guillermo E. Perry, Francisco H. G. Ferreira and Michael Walton, eds. Washington, D.C.: Advanced Conference Edition.

Journal of Economic Perspectives—Volume 18, Number 2—Spring 2004—Pages 89–106

Latin America since the 1990s: Rising from the Sickbed?

Arminio Fraga

T he economic performance of Latin America was disastrous in the 1980s. In what is often called the "lost decade," the region's economy was disrupted by an international debt crisis and raging inflation. Per capita GDP declined at an average annual rate of 0.6 percent in the 1980s. Toward the end of the 1980s, the frustration with the performance led to a search for sound macro and structural policies. Thus, in the late 1980s and early 1990s, many countries in Latin America were receptive to a package of economic reforms that was dubbed the "Washington Consensus" (Williamson, 1990). The precise reforms varied from country to country, but in general they included some combination of fiscal and monetary tightness, greater openness to foreign trade (if not necessarily to foreign capital), privatization and deregulation. Yet the early 2000s have seen a disappointing economic performance in Latin America; for example, per capita GDP for the region contracted by 2.5 percent in 2002.

The long-time opponents of the Washington Consensus reforms are in full cry. Implicitly and explicitly, they make three broad claims. First, they argue that the economic performance of Latin America has not improved since the 1980s—and that on certain dimensions, like inequality, the economic performance of the region has worsened. Second, they claim that the application of the Washington Consensus reforms is the cause of this poor performance. Third, they hark back to the more rapid growth experienced by Latin America from the 1950s and 1970s, and they argue that economic policy in Latin America should return to government infrastructure investment and industrialization through protection and import substitution that were popular in some countries at that time.

■ *Arminio Fraga is Partner, Gávea Investimentos, Rio de Janeiro, Brazil. From March 1999 until December 2002, he served as President, Central Bank of Brazil. His e-mail address is ⟨arminiof@uol.com.br⟩.*

The first section of this paper compares Latin America's economic performance in the 1990s with the 1980s and finds definite macroeconomic and social progress during the decade. The following section considers the policy performance of the region during the 1990s and finds that, on a country-by-country basis, the nations of Latin America that were more active in carrying out Washington Consensus reforms also experienced better economic performance. The final section will argue that rather than seeking to reverse the economic reforms that have been carried out, Latin American nations should be thinking about how to extend and complement the existing reforms.

The Macroeconomic and Social Record in Latin America

Is it true that despite enacting a wide range of economic reforms in the late 1980s and early 1990s, the economies of Latin America made little gain in the years that followed? To measure the socioeconomic performance of Latin America over the last two decades, let us examine a number of economic and social indicators.

Table 1 gives a summary of the GDP per capita growth in the region over the last three decades. The seven countries included in the table represent 90 percent of the GDP of the Latin American region. During the 1980s, per capita income declined in five of the seven largest countries, the notable exceptions being Chile and Colombia—which were also the two countries that avoided a debt reduction exercise. Average GDP per capita growth in this sample declined by 0.7 percent per year and thus lagged the United States by 2.9 percent per year, a dramatic case of economic divergence.

In the 1990s, growth patterns in Latin America were mixed, with per capita growth ranging from Chile's stunning 4.9 percent to Venezuela's slightly negative performance. This high degree of dispersion makes it hard to speak categorically of "Latin America's growth performance in the 1990s." On the whole, however, performance did improve markedly, with average per capita growth increasing to 2.0 percent per year, the same as the United States and a reasonable number in absolute terms. But despite the overall improvement, in most countries a sense of frustration prevailed. This growth record was modest compared to that of Latin America in the 1970s and that of East Asia in the 1980 and 1990s.

While achieving higher growth during the 1990s, Latin America also managed to reduce inflation drastically. As shown in Table 2, rates of inflation varied considerably across these countries, but the average annual inflation rate (weighted by GDP) was 223 percent during the 1980s. Brazil was the last country in the region to lower inflation (with the *Plano Real* of 1994). In the second half of the 1990s, inflation in the region has averaged just 6.5 percent annually.

Another measure of improved financial stability is a reduction in the number of banking and currency crises, as shown in Table 3. Goldstein, Kaminsky and Reinhart (2000, pp. 19–20) define a banking crisis as one where there was a bank run followed by a closing, merger or government takeover of a bank (or when there

Table 1

Per Capita Growth: Annual Average per Decade

	Per capita growth				
	1970s	*1980s*	*1990s*	*Change 1970s–1980s*	*Change 1980s–1990s*
Argentina	1.5	−2.9	3.2	−4.4	6.1
Brazil	5.9	−0.4	1.3	−6.3	1.7
Chile	1.1	2.1	4.9	1.0	2.8
Colombia	3.3	1.3	0.8	−2.0	−0.5
Mexico	4.3	−0.3	1.8	−4.6	2.1
Peru	0.6	−2.9	2.1	−3.5	5.0
Venezuela	−0.4	−1.7	−0.1	−1.3	1.6
Average	2.3	−0.7	2.0	−3.0	2.7
Weighted Average	3.8	−0.6	1.7	−4.4	2.3
United States	1.7	2.2	2.0	0.5	−0.2

Source: World Bank and Pessoa (2003).

Table 2

Inflation Rate

	1980s	*1990s*	*1995–2000*
Argentina	437.6	14.9	−0.1
Brazil	336.3	199.9	3.7
Chile	20.3	9.4	2.5
Colombia	23.7	20.1	7.4
Mexico	65.1	18.3	9.1
Peru	332.1	38.1	3.4
Venezuela	23.2	43.3	19.3
Average	176.9	49.1	6.5
Weighted Average	223.3	92.3	5.5
United States	4.7	2.8	1.2

was no such run, all the above or a large-scale government assistance package for a large financial institution) and a currency crisis as a situation where a large loss in reserves or a sharp depreciation or both took place. Since crises can be of different magnitudes, from bad to truly terrible, not too much should be read into a simple total. But it is nonetheless striking that the number of crises in these seven large economies declined by about two-thirds between the 1980s and the 1990s.

On the social front, progress took place in many areas. Table 4 presents data on education and health that speak for themselves: despite the macroeconomic fiasco of the 1980s, significant progress took place during *both* decades. Over these 20 years, illiteracy rates were cut in half, life expectancy increased by six years and infant mortality declined from 50 to 23 deaths per 1,000 births. In Brazil, the most

Table 3
Number of Crises per Decade

Index	1980s	1990s
Argentina	7	0
Brazil	5	3
Chile	3	0
Colombia	3	1
Mexico	3	2
Peru	2	0
Venezuela	3	3

Note: The index is defined as the number of balance of payments and banking crises that occurred in each decade using the definition of Goldberg, Kaminsky and Reinhart (1998).

populous country on the continent, 20 percent of the children of school age were not attending school at the beginning of the 1980s. Now that figure has declined to 3 percent.

In short, Latin America's macroeconomic performance was indisputably better in the 1990s than the 1980s, even if considerable room remains for further improvement, and the region's performance in social indicators showed a continued pattern of improvement as well. But before closing this discussion we must examine two more issues: productivity growth and inequality.

Table 5 presents a measure of total factor productivity growth for the region. The estimates from Pessôa (2003) are based on data from the Penn World Tables, and they represent a residual after controlling for capital and education accumulation and labor force growth. The estimates are lower than the most frequently used productivity numbers, because those numbers typically do not account for investment in human capital. The results of this exercise are quite disturbing. It perhaps isn't surprising that average total factor productivity growth for the seven largest economies in Latin America was negative 2.28 percent per year in the macroeconomic turmoil of the 1980s. In the 1990s, total factor productivity growth moved into positive territory, although only slightly at 0.33 percent per year. One would expect or hope that over time, the standards of productivity in lower-income countries should converge to the levels of higher-income economies. But if one considers that the global productivity frontier was growing at perhaps 1.5 percent per year during the 1990s, we again see a picture of economic divergence for Latin American productivity.

However, the news on productivity, while poor overall, is at least somewhat mixed. Five of the seven countries do show important improvements in productivity from the 1980s to the 1990s, while Colombia and Venezuela show significant declines. If we exclude these two, the other five improved their productivity on average some 3.47 percent per year. In the 1970s, annual total factor productivity growth for Latin America averaged 0.27 percent. The only country that delivered

Table 4

Social Indicators

	Illiteracy rate[a]			Life expectancy at Birth			Infant Mortality rate[b]			Primary school Enrollment		
	1980	1990	2000	1980	1990	2000	1980	1990	2000	1985	1990	2000
Argentina	5.6	4.3	3.2	69.6	71.6	73.9	38.0	28.0	20.0	—	—	107.0
Brazil	24.0	18.0	13.1	62.6	65.6	68.1	70.0	50.0	32.0	81.2	86.4	97.0
Chile	8.6	6.0	4.2	69.3	73.7	75.6	31.7	16.0	10.1	—	87.7	88.8
Colombia	16.0	11.6	8.4	65.7	68.3	71.4	40.0	29.0	20.0	65.5	68.7	88.5
Mexico	18.7	12.7	8.8	66.8	70.8	73.1	56.0	37.0	25.0	99.6	100.3	103.4
Peru	20.6	14.5	10.1	60.4	65.8	69.3	81.0	58.0	31.0	95.9	—	—
Venezuela	16.1	11.1	7.5	68.3	71.2	73.3	34.0	23.0	20.0	83.7	88.1	88.0
Average	15.6	11.2	7.9	66.1	69.6	72.1	50.1	34.4	22.6	85.2	86.2	95.4

Notes: [a] percentage of people ages 15 and above; [b] per 1,000 live births.
Source: World Development Indicators—World Bank.

Table 5

Total Factor Productivity Growth: Average Growth per Decade

	Productivity				
	1970s	1980s	1990s	Change 1970s–1980s	Change 1980s–1990s
Argentina	0.08	−4.21	2.34	−4.29	6.55
Brazil	1.66	−2.62	0.37	4.28	2.99
Chile	0.50	0.02	1.65	−0.48	1.63
Colombia	0.75	−0.14	−2.78	−0.89	−2.64
Mexico	0.31	−2.98	0.24	−3.29	3.22
Peru	−0.75	−3.36	−0.82	−2.61	2.54
Venezuela	−6.15	−0.86	−1.77	5.29	−0.91
Average	−0.51	−2.02	−0.11	−1.51	1.91
Weighted Average	0.27	−2.28	0.33	−2.55	2.61
United States	0.10	0.47	0.58	1.28	0.11

positive total factor productivity growth during the three decades was Chile. Brazil posted high productivity growth during the miracle 1970s at a rate of 1.66 percent per year, but failed to continue this pace in the 1980s.

One aspect of performance in Latin America where little progress was made is in the distribution of income. Here the main indicators remained mostly stable at very unflattering levels, although there is some evidence from Ferranti, Ferreira, Perry and Walton (2003) that the income distribution for Latin America as a whole may have become slightly more equal in the 1990s thanks largely to greater equality in populous Brazil. The relative stability of inequality during the 1990s at a time of modest but sustained economic growth at least suggests that the gains from growth were being felt across the income distribution.

Policy Evaluation

To what extent did the policy reforms of the late 1980s and early 1990s lead to the improved macroeconomic performance of the 1990s? As a starting point, let's review the underlying causes of the negative growth, high inflation and balance of payments crises that Latin America faced in the 1980s. We will then discuss the macroeconomic and structural economic reforms that were carried out.

Causes of the "Lost Decade" in Latin America

The economies of Latin America experienced two destructive events in the 1980s. First, a combination of oil price and interest rate shocks rocked the global economy, but had especially difficult ramifications for Latin America. Second, the region experienced the exhaustion of a growth model that had been popular from the 1950s through the 1970s, in which economic policy focused on government-led investment and import substitution. Let's say a few more words about these events and why their combination was so economically destructive in the 1980s.

Global oil prices spiked upward in December 1973, and then again in 1979–1980.[1] Enormous quantities of dollar assets were transferred to oil-exporting nations, which in turn sought channels to invest their new wealth in a way that would bring a positive rate of return. International banks seeking to "recycle the petro-dollars" made substantial loans to Latin America. Because of the government-led economic policies of Latin America (discussed more in a moment), many of these loans were either made directly to government agencies or were guaranteed in some manner by government.

For some years in the 1970s, Latin America paid very low interest rates on these loans, as unexpectedly high rates of inflation held down real interest rates. For example, in 1974, the prime interest rate in the United States was 10.8 percent, and inflation as measured by the Consumer Price Index rose 11 percent; in 1975, the prime interest rate in the United States was 7.9 percent and the inflation rate was 9.1 percent. Thus, in the 1970s, the nations of Latin America that were oil-importers (that is, not Venezuela) suffered from higher oil prices, but experienced large inflows of foreign capital. In a way, the ample availability of foreign financing allowed these nations to postpone adjustment to the oil shock and, more importantly, to continue with the economic strategy of the previous decades. However, this development strategy also involved these economies taking the risk of accumulating large amounts of foreign debt.

In the early 1980s, the wheel turned. The international banks, in their reason-

---

[1] See Sachs (1989) for a good review of the causes of the Latin American debt crises of the 1980s.

able fear of being exposed to a risk of higher inflation, made most of the loans to Latin America at variable interest rates. In the early 1980s, nominal dollar interest rates climbed high under the pressure of Paul Volcker's Federal Reserve policy to reduce inflation, and inflation indeed diminished. In 1983, the dollar prime interest rate was 10.8 percent, while inflation was 3.2 percent. Not only were real interest rates sky-high, but also the terms of trade of Latin American oil-importing countries deteriorated, as oil prices remained high and the prices of the exports of most countries in the region declined. As a result, most Latin American countries were confronted with a substantial debt burden, and the region's oil-importing countries were faced with a much lower ability to pay their debts.

Brazil, the largest economy in Latin America, offers a good example of this pattern. In the aftermath of the oil shock of 1979, Brazil's initial policy response was to adjust the exchange rate and to tighten domestic demand so as to lower inflation and reduce the growing current account deficit. But soon these restrictive policies were abandoned in favor of encouraging a new inflow of foreign capital, at the cost of further accumulation of foreign debt, now mostly short-term, and inflation pressures. When the liquidity shocks of the early 1980s came, Brazil was vulnerable and ended up having to restructure its foreign debt. The rest of the decade was spent in a series of frustrated efforts to stabilize the economy, which included five failed heterodox anti-inflation plans (price controls, asset freezes and more) and two moratoria on foreign debt payments.

But the drastic growth slowdown was caused by more than the interest rate shocks of the early 1980s. The economies of Latin America experienced relatively rapid growth from the 1950s through the 1970s, and most countries had advocated a growth strategy led by policies of significant government investment and intervention and import substitution. How much credit these specific policies deserve for the growth record of the 1950s to 1970s is controversial. After all, the 1950s and 1960s were decades of rapid growth for the world economy as a whole, which surely buoyed growth in Latin America. It is analytically difficult to calculate what Latin America's path of accumulation of physical capital, human capital and technology would have been if the government in these years had followed policies in which the government moved toward freer trade and, except for investment in education and public goods infrastructure, left investment decisions to the private sector.

But even if one gives these policies of government investment and import substitution some credit for increasing Latin America's growth rates in the 1950s and 1960s, it was becoming apparent by the 1970s that this growth strategy was reaching its limits. Part of the reason was that even if import substitution policies had given a boost to certain industries in the 1950s and 1960s, these policies had largely congealed into protectionism that discouraged competition and technology transfer by the 1970s. During this period, in fact, trade openness (defined as the ratio of total trade to GDP) in the main countries declined or at best stayed stable. Even if government-led investment encouraged some additional investment in the 1950s and 1960s, it also encouraged widespread government ownership of industry, with reduced incentives for a culture of innovation and productivity growth.

As noted earlier, productivity growth in Latin America was very modest in the 1970s, which surely suggests that the growth agenda of government-led investment and import substitution was faltering before the "lost decade" of the 1980s. In the 1970s, growth remained possible in part because of an unsustainable increase in borrowed international capital, which in turn took place thanks to the low oil prices and interest rates that prevailed in the period.

When Latin America's debt crisis arrived in the 1980s, it took some time for a clear diagnosis to be achieved. For awhile, the beneficiaries of the economic strategy of the previous decades were able to block the reforms needed to move into a new growth model. Examples of this phenomenon include the industries that benefited from protection and government subsidies (and their labor unions), government employees and the middle class (by developed country standards). These groups often stood in the way of trade reform, privatization, pension reform and even education reform. But toward the end of the 1980s, if not sooner in some cases, it became clear that something had to be done to re-ignite growth and development in Latin America.

Macroeconomic Reforms

Here the set of economic reforms known as the "Washington Consensus" enters the stage. This list of reforms was originally proposed by John Williamson (1990; 2003) and consisted of ten economic policy recommendations: 1) fiscal discipline; 2) reordering public expenditures toward basic health care, education and infrastructure; 3) tax reform in the direction of a broader base with moderate rates; 4) liberalization of exchange rates; 5) a competitive exchange rate; 6) moving in the direction of trade liberalization; 7) liberalization of foreign direct investment, a recommendation that specifically did not include comprehensive liberalization of the capital account in a way that would also include portfolio capital; 8) privatization; 9) deregulation of barriers to entry and exit; and 10) improved property rights. It is worth emphasizing that Williamson did not offer this list as representing a complete agenda for economic health, only as a list of items on which he believed that a consensus existed at that time among Washington, D.C., policymakers with an interest in Latin America.

In discussing Latin America's actual economic reforms, it has become conventional to consider them in two broad categories: macroeconomic and structural. The macro portion of the consensus basically recommended fiscal prudence and monetary restraint (which does not appear on Williamson's list). The structural side recommended a focus on opening to trade and investment, tax reforms, privatization, deregulation, a certain degree of financial deregulation and improved property rights. Broadly speaking, the reforms sought to control the plague of inflation, to reduce the incidence of balance of payments crises and to move growth policy away from the closed-economy government-led strategies of the three decades that preceded the 1980s.

To what extent were economic reforms actually implemented and successful in Latin America? On the macro front, it would be extremely useful to compare data on the fiscal stance of government between the 1980s and 1990s, but good data here are simply nonexistent, especially for the 1980s, when fiscal behavior throughout the region is widely thought to have been extremely weak. Sizeable portions of spending controlled by the central government often occurred through government-owned companies or banks that did not appear in the national budget, and regional or provincial governments often incurred large liabilities that were poorly recorded, if at all, but were nonetheless eventually passed on the central government.

Perhaps the two clearest macroeconomic indicators are the dramatic reduction in the rate of inflation and the decline in the number of banking and balance of payments crises that took place in the 1990s, as documented earlier. These patterns clearly suggest that sound fiscal, monetary and exchange-rate policies became more prevalent in the 1990s.

But although Latin America's macroeconomy improved if judged by the dismal economic record of the 1980s, it was far from fully healthy. As Table 3 shows, even in the 1990s, Brazil and Venezuela have had three banking or balance of payments crises each, and Mexico had two. Argentina escaped the 1990s without such a crisis, but then experienced a severe crisis in 2001–2002.

This inability of Latin American countries to create a stable macro environment can be illustrated by the investment ratings in Table 6, which looks at the ratings of the main countries in Latin America and Asia from 1993 to 2003 (a decade chosen for the availability of ratings). Each entry in the table represents the number of years each country had an investment-grade rating (that is, a credit rating of BBB or higher) by Standard & Poor's. In Latin America, only Chile maintained an investment grade rating during this entire decade. Colombia also ran its macroeconomy competently in the early 1990s, but had to deal with huge political risk. Mexico had two years of an investment grade rating. The other countries did not have an investment grade rating in any year.

The experience of east Asian countries, shown for comparison in the table, suggests that it is difficult for an economy to stay on the development track, at least after reaching middle-income status, without maintaining an investment-grade rating. Growth cannot be sustained if a country is frequently running into macro crises. The crises in themselves typically represent a large, often dramatic detour from a path of growth. Moreover, crisis-prone countries have less access to capital and credit, and that at a higher cost.

Argentina and Brazil deserve a brief digression here, as the countries most recently affected by severe economic disruption. Brazil managed to end hyperinflation in 1994, but for the next four years, it had to cope with a fixed, and eventually overvalued, exchange rate and excessively loose fiscal policy. Moreover, Brazil's exchange rate and perceived risk suffered from contagion after the economic crises in east Asia in 1997–1998. Thus, Brazil ended the 1990s with a balance of payments crisis in 1998–1999. Brazil recovered well following the forced depreciation of its currency, the *real*, by promoting significant fiscal adjustment and reform and by adopting an inflation-targeting framework for the conduct of

Table 6
Ratings S&P Index

Asia	Grade	Latin America	Grade
China	10	Argentina	0
India	0	Brazil	0
Indonesia	4	Chile	10
Korea	9	Colombia	6
Malasya	10	Mexico	2
Singapore	10	Peru	0
Thailand	10	Venezuela	0

Note: Index is defined as the number of years each country was considered investment grade by S&P from mid-1993 to mid-2003.

monetary policy. But after a period of six quarters of growth at annual rates of 4 percent or higher, Brazil again had to face turbulent times: first in 2001, following the global bear market in stocks, contagion from the crisis in Argentina and a domestic power blackout, and then following the (fortunately unfounded) fears that a victory of Lula da Silva of the Workers Party in the presidential elections of late 2002 would lead to populist policies and economic and financial collapse. From a macroeconomic standpoint, the aftermath of Lula's election has proven to be quite encouraging, but Brazil still has to deepen further the credibility of the economic turnaround now underway.

In 1991, Argentina adopted a fixed exchange-rate policy that tied its peso to the U.S. dollar using a currency board approach. The country also implemented a wave of structural reforms. Argentina did manage to post good economic growth rates during the 1990s, second only to Chile. But during the end of the 1990s, Argentina's growth rate slowed down significantly as a consequence of a weakening fiscal stance and domestic inflation that, in combination with fixed exchange rate, led to an appreciation in real terms of the peso. The currency board arrangement collapsed in 2001. From 1999–2002, Argentina's GDP declined by approximately 20 percent! Recovery has now begun as the economy has rebounded back from the depths of this incredible collapse, but much remains to be done if Argentina is to go beyond the bounce.

Given that the Washington Consensus approach outlined by Williamson (1990, 2003) clearly calls for fiscal restraint and competitive exchange rates, it would be peculiar to blame those recommendations for the recent difficulties of Brazil or Argentina, which arose from a lack of fiscal restraint and persistently overvalued exchange rates. But setting aside the question of how to allocate blame, the question that follows is why does Latin America display a propensity for macroeconomic instability? Was the problem a lack of understanding of what needed to be done? Or poor implementation of the recommended policies? Or some political problem characteristic of Latin America that makes it difficult to enact such policies? I will return to this issue in the conclusion.

Structural Economic Reforms

On the microeconomic front, in addition to the progress in education and health mentioned above, significant structural reforms took place during the 1990s, as reviewed for instance by Edwards (1995). Eduardo Lora (2001) of the Inter-American Development Bank has collected information on the reforms that occurred, and I draw on his account here.

Substantial structural economic reform has occurred. In the area of foreign trade, tariffs for the 12 largest economies in Latin America dropped from an average rate of 49 percent in 1985 to less than 20 percent by 1994. Over a similar period, nontariff barriers affected 38 percent of imports in the mid-1980s, but only 6.3 percent of imports by the mid-1990s. In domestic financial markets, most countries have eliminated interest rate controls and substantially reduced the extent to which banks are required to make certain loans, although some mandated lending still exists in Colombia, Mexico and Venezuela, among others.

Many countries have reduced the high marginal tax rates that used to exist for personal income, along with lower taxes on corporate profits and the reduction in tariffs mentioned earlier. As a replacement, many Latin American countries have enacted value-added taxes, although the value-added tax is often applied with many exemptions and different rates.

Privatization has been substantial. In Brazil and Peru, cumulative privatizations between 1988 and 1999 exceeded 10 percent of GDP in 1999. In Argentina, Mexico, Venezuela and Colombia, cumulative privatizations over these years were 5 percent of GDP or more. Over half of all the privatizations by value in the developing countries of the world happened in Latin America. The privatizations in energy, telecommunications and finance have often brought with them an increase in foreign direct investment.

The specifics of how far these and other reforms reach on a country-by-country basis can certainly be explored in greater depth. There has been less deregulation of rules that may discourage hiring by restricting labor flexibility or by government imposition of large nonsalary costs for employee benefits. But overall, the depth and speed of these market-oriented structural reforms is impressive.

Lora (2001) calculates an overall index of structural reforms, which is admittedly pieced together based on the available evidence. For example, the trade component includes tariffs, but not nontariff barriers, since the evidence on nontariff barriers is shaky. The index, which appears in Table 7, is a simple average of reform indices in the areas of trade, financial system, labor, taxation and privatization. The numbers should be considered on a scale from 0 to 1,000, where zero consists of no reforms and 1,000 would be complete reform. The index shows a substantial degree of reform in the second half of the 1980s, with more reform in the 1990s.

The formal empirical evidence has not yet demonstrated a clear link from structural reforms to growth. In subsequent work, Lora and Panizza (2002) tried to identify which of the structural reforms had a greater impact on growth and productivity. Their panel and time series regressions fail to find a statistically

Table 7
Structural Reforms Index

	1985	1990	1999	Change 1980s	Change 1990s
Argentina	338	468	616	130	148
Brazil	259	430	610	171	180
Chile	488	570	606	82	36
Colombia	291	413	562	122	149
Mexico	290	424	511	134	87
Peru	279	335	659	56	324
Venezuela	284	343	514	59	171
Average	318	426	583	108	156

Note: Read the Index as a range 0–1,000, where 0 consists in no reforms as opposed to 1,000.
Source: Lora (2001).

significant impact of structural reforms on growth and productivity, with the exception of trade reform, where a significant link is found. One might surmise that the impact of macroeconomic crises remains large enough in the region that correlations between structural reforms and economic growth are difficult to discern. Still, the evidence on growth rates and, especially, the evidence on productivity gains in the 1990s relative to the 1980s presented in Table 1 do seem to suggest that the overall reform efforts initiated in the 1980s, including those on the education and health fronts, have had a positive impact.

Summing Up

The 1980s were indeed a lost decade for Latin America in terms of macro performance. Most countries in Latin America spent it trying to digest the aftermath of the debt and inflation crises of the early and middle years of the decade. Performance in the 1990s was significantly better than in the 1980s, with higher growth and lower inflation. Per capita growth averaged almost 2 percent in the 1990s, a reasonable but somewhat modest number when we consider that the United States grew at almost the exact same rate and east Asia grew a lot faster.

There was great variance in the growth and social records across countries in the region. Countries that got the macro right, like Chile and Mexico (after 1995), grew faster than the regional average. Structural reforms were implemented with varying degrees of commitment and success across the region. Thus far, and one must keep in mind that a decade of reforms is a short period of time by the standards of understanding trends in long-term growth, it has proven difficult to find ironclad evidence linking specific reforms to specific increases in growth. But total factor productivity growth moved into positive territory in the 1990s after averaging minus 2.28 percent per year in the 1980s. Finally, structural reforms alone did not guarantee success, as the case of Argentina illustrates.

Chile, the star performer in Latin America, both has the best macroeconomic policy performance and the best and earliest record in implementing structural reforms. One can reasonably argue that sound policies were applied and worked in Chile, and to some extent in Mexico, after 1995. In most other countries in the region, poor performance even after the reforms of the 1990s can be blamed on macroeconomic crises, often driven by loose fiscal policy and an overvalued exchange rate in an environment of large and volatile capital flows. On the whole, economic progress was achieved in Latin America in the 1990s. Still, one wonders why only Chile and Mexico have done well. The question is really one of political economy, to which I now turn.

Populism and Economic Reform

Populism has a long and disastrous history in Latin America (discussed in the essays collected in Dornbusch and Edwards, 1991). There are a number of definitions of populism for different times and places, but here is one useful definition aimed at the context of Latin American experience (Kaufman and Stallings, 1991, p. 16):

> [Populism] involves a set of *economic policies* designed to achieve specific political goals. Those political goals are: (1) mobilizing support within organized labor and lower-middle-class groups; (2) obtaining complementary backing from domestically oriented business; and (3) politically isolating the rural oligarchy, foreign enterprises, and large-scale domestic industrial elites. The economic policies to attain these goals include, but are not limited to: (1) budget deficits to stimulate domestic demand; (2) nominal wage increases plus price controls to effect income redistribution; and (3) exchange rate control or appreciation to cut inflation and to raise wages and profits in non-traded-goods sectors.

This definition of populism bears an intentionally close resemblance to Latin America's policies of import substitution and government-led industrialization that held sway from the 1950s to the 1970s. Import substitution helped gain support from organized labor while isolating foreign enterprises. Government-led investment was typically carried out through a combination of large fiscal and/or quasi-fiscal deficits and economic and financial controls.

Perhaps the main paradox of populist government in Latin America in the twentieth century is that even after decades of populist governments claiming to represent the interests of the poor and middle-class, the historically high levels of inequality in Latin America did not decline much, if at all. Indeed, even basic health and education services for the poor, which one might think would be a staple of "populism," were often neglected by populist governments. The populist economic formula was to assure highly visible benefits to key constituents just before elections, and then to pay for those benefits with macroeconomic crises and a lack of flexibility and productivity at other times. Yet many of those in the target audience for populism apparently believed, despite the continuing high levels of inequality, that their relative or absolute status would be even worse under the parties opposing the populist government (when alternative parties were available).

Since the late 1980s and early 1990s, many Latin American countries have tried to implement economic policies that are the opposite of those prevailing under populist governments: macro stability, structural reforms, institution building, a focus on health and education and so on. What has led some countries to persevere and succeed with sound policies, while others seem to experience repeated reversals? In other words, what made the more successful countries tick? The answers to these questions are not simple. I will first summarize some of the key political dynamics in the countries that have been the main focus of discussion here and then attempt to draw some general lessons.

The Political Dynamics of Reform by Country

Mexico is an example of a country where populist governments were often seen during the twentieth century. In fact, many times during the last several decades Mexico experienced economic crises at regular six-year electoral intervals, as the government overspent before the election to ensure popular support and then suffered inflation and in some cases debt defaults after the election. Mexico began some structural economic reforms in the 1980s, but it seems as if the nation's debt crisis of 1994–1995 finally led to deeper change. Mexico abandoned a managed exchange-rate regime that had played a recurrent key role in the financial crises of the past. Mexico took the giant step joining the United States and Canada in the North American Free Trade Agreement (NAFTA). Finally, in 2000, the PRI party lost the presidential elections for the first time in 70 years, but the transition took place smoothly. Not too long after, Mexico's debt became investment grade, and now prospects for sustained growth appear to have improved.

Brazil has been implementing a number of reforms that may allow it to follow a path similar to Mexico. Since the "lost decade" of the 1980s, Brazil has tamed inflation, managed a banking crisis in 1996–1997, improved health and education and instituted structural economic reforms. Perhaps most interesting, as already mentioned earlier, Brazil faced a financial crisis in 2002 driven primarily by the expectations that a victory by the opposition in the presidential elections would throw Brazil back to macro instability and populism. However, the new government of President Lula da Silva began its time in office by following sound macroeconomic policies. Thus, Brazil may have a fair shot at turning the page on two decades of slow growth.

Chile is the main economic success story of Latin America, with by far the highest rates of per capita GDP growth in both the 1980s and the 1990s. Chile suffered an economic crisis in 1972–1973 under the populist economic policies of the Allende government, which helped to drive the military takeover in 1973. However, the military dictatorship then experienced its own economic crisis in 1982–1983, which paved the way for what we now know turned out to be a permanent shift to sound macro and micro policies starting about 1985. Following

Chile's transition back to democracy in 1989, these sound macroeconomic policies were maintained and in many instances deepened. Within a few years, investment as a proportion of GDP jumped up by 6 percentage points and per capita GDP growth increased by almost 3 points, as usefully reviewed by Schmidt-Hebbel (1999). In the case of Chile, it seems likely that memories of the economic fiasco under Allende in the early 1970s were still fresh in the minds of the highly competent group that took over after the military.

Argentina was an eager economic reformer, willing even to enact a policy as strong as fixing its exchange rate to the U.S. dollar with a currency board. It was rewarded in the 1990s with by far the largest gain in per capita growth and in productivity compared with the 1980s—more than twice the change of any other country. But Argentina was unable to solve its persistent problem of government deficits. Eventually, these budget deficits, together with contagion from Brazil's 1998–1999 crisis, led to a loss of confidence in Argentina's currency peg. As Argentina's exchange rate mechanism fell apart in 2001–2002, the country suffered an extremely severe recession with GDP declining more than 20 percent from peak to trough over 1999 and 2002.

Of the six countries discussed here, the two that had the lowest growth rates of per capita GDP in the 1990s were Venezuela and Colombia. Venezuela is a country where the spirit of populism remains strong and that has also suffered considerable political instability in the last few years. Venezuela also had relatively high inflation into the late 1990s; it had as many financial crises in the 1990s as it did in the 1980s; and it ranks relatively low on the structural reform index. Colombia is the one large economy in Latin America where the growth rate was lower in the 1990s than in the 1980s, despite the country's relative macroeconomic stability (as certified by its investment-grade debt ratings for many years) and an average performance on structural reform. Presumably, the answer for Colombia's problems lies in its severe degree of political instability, which has verged on civil war in certain regions.

Popular Opposition to Populism?

The supply of populism is always abundant, all over the globe. But why has the demand for populism been so high over the years in Latin America? A full answer to this question is beyond the scope of this paper, but it does appear that the turnaround stories in the region were driven primarily by a decline in the demand for populism (and not by a decline in the supply).

Overcoming populism is not a politically easy task. The rhetoric of populism continues to have a strong appeal across much of Latin America. There is widespread nostalgia for the economic growth rates of the 1950s and 1960s and for the belief, widespread at the time, that Latin American countries could assure their own prosperity with somewhat *dirigiste* policies of government-led investment and import substitution. The fact that the success of these policies taken as a whole was questionable even in the short term, and that in the long term these policies were largely responsible for their own demise, seems to be overshadowed by the failure of other policies to guarantee glowing results.

Populist economic policies often deny that any tradeoffs are needed, at least for the vast majority of the population, while good economic policies often create a mix of losers and winners, whether real or perceived. Once threatened, special interest groups then gang up and obstruct the path of development-friendly reforms. The most important instance of such phenomena comes in the upfront sacrifice needed to eliminate budget deficits and to lower inflation. Latin America has seen a long history of weak fiscal and monetary practices and institutions, one weakness feeding the other down a vicious circle of macroeconomic instability.

The interaction between loose fiscal and monetary policy, inflation and exchange rates has been especially destructive. The cycle begins when populist fiscal policies increase government debt and, when accommodated by loose monetary policy, lead to inflation. One approach to fighting inflation that has been a constant feature of the Latin American scene over the years has been the use of the exchange rate as an anchor. While there is no known episode of hyperinflation that did not end with the help of an exchange rate anchor, it is also true that in most instances in Latin America the pegging of the exchange rate took place without the necessary fiscal discipline. The combination of a pegged or fixed nominal exchange rate with continuing domestic inflation invariably led to an appreciation of the real exchange rate, which in turn led to unsustainable current account deficits and subsequently, to a balance of payments crisis. Many if not most of the macroeconomic crises in Latin America in the last decade follow this general pattern: Mexico in 1994–1995, Brazil in 1998–1999, Argentina in 2001–2002.

If one looks at the experiences of a number of countries in Latin America and asks how the political pressure for populist economic policy was at some point interrupted, it seems that in most cases the situation got bad enough for people to realize that change was necessary and therefore had to be politically supported. These changing beliefs led to a collapse in the demand for populism and to a strong mandate for change. In Chile, the experience under Allende in the early 1970s seemed to generate this sort of consensus. In Mexico, the financial crisis following the election in 1994 seemed to be the final straw. There doesn't seem to be any general rule that causes people to believe that enough is enough. At least to this observer of policy cycles all over the developing world, there seems to be a fair amount of randomness involved in many of the episodes, whether they end in failure or success. In different situations, the key causes for the rejection or continued acceptance of populism may include external factors, such as whether the world economy seems welcoming and expanding, or internal factors such as the competence or charisma (or lack thereof) of the particular group running the country at a given moment.

In Chile in 1989, in Mexico in 2000 and so far in Brazil in 2003–2004, the new economic regime became more credible when political change took place and was followed by the continuation of sound economic policies. This point is quite important. Once a country proves that sound policies are no longer the preferred choice of a few enlightened technocrats or autocrats, or of a single political party that may soon be out of power, business and investor confidence increases, horizons are lengthened for both private and social investments, and the economy can move to a path of higher and sustained growth.

In all these cases, an important starting point of the economic change was the prominent role of sound macroeconomic policies in jumpstarting the process. Economies that suffer hyperinflation or frequent financial crises will find that other economic reforms have little traction. But when a reasonable degree of macroeconomic reform is in place, then structural and microeconomic reforms add to the credibility of the overall development program and also have a positive impact on growth via productivity gains. A reasonable degree of macroeconomic stability improves the odds that the package of economic change will be sustained, even if there is a turnover of political parties.

The economic record of the 1990s in Latin America shows improvement over the 1980s. The region displayed significant gains in per capita economic growth and in productivity. But so far, only Chile has reached the stage of per capita growth consistently strong enough to put that nation on a path toward convergence with high-income economies. Mexico and perhaps also Brazil appear to be on their way to demonstrating that the vicious circle of low growth caused by macro instability and micro inefficiency can be broken. However, a few years ago, Argentina would have been cited as a rising star among Latin American economies, only to take a dramatic step backward into macroeconomic crisis in the last few years. Meanwhile, Venezuela and Colombia are sunk deep in severe political discord that goes much beyond the choice between populism and the kinds of economic reforms discussed in this paper.

Given the somewhat modest growth performance of the 1990s, it is not surprising that one still finds on the discussion menu in most countries proposals to return to the closed-economy government-led development model of the 1950–1970 period, perhaps supplemented by better social policies. While the improvement of social policies is an essential part of any successful strategy, there are good reasons to be skeptical of this nostalgic return to 1950s economic policies. First, this approach in itself is not a substitute to sound macro and financial policies, as it is usually implied by most of those who support it in the real world. In fact, there is good reason to think that the 1950s approach tends to be associated with populism, nationalism and weak macro policies because of all the inconsistent demands it places on the state that cannot be met, at least in the short run. Second, these proposals ignore that the old model ran its course. As discussed above, it spun off the macro road and ran into greatly diminishing if not outright negative returns at the efficiency level. Lastly, in a world where the global growth frontier seems to have moved from physical capital accumulation to human capital development and technology improvement and where trade and financial integration places a premium on flexibility, sound macro and microeconomic policies are necessary so as to be able to deal with real shocks and with the financial booms and busts of this era.

The best course is to persevere with a sound agenda of reforms and to avoid the temptation of looking for shortcuts in the past. The path forward must surely include a sound macroeconomic framework, a focus on education and health, on microeconomic efficiency and flexibility, on building institutions, on creating a culture of trust and respect for the rule of law and so on. Each country will probably find a different way to reach these goals. This diversity of policies is the natural outcome of a constrained optimization exercise where the constraints are the country's history, culture and traditions, as well as the particular sequence of shocks, positive and negative, faced during different periods. Even when successful, the process takes time and requires a long view of things, something not always available because governments tend to be impatient. One can only hope that some learning will take place over time in Latin America and that the success stories of some countries inspire others to move in the right direction.

■ *I wish to thank Andrei Shleifer, Timothy Taylor and Michael Waldman for suggestions, editing and encouragement far beyond their formal role; Persio Arida, Amaury Bier, Pedro Bodin, Pedro C. Ferreira, Ilan Goldfajn, Peter Kenen, Samuel Pessôa, Pedro M. Salles and Sergio Werlang for comments on an earlier draft; and Igor Barenboim, Caio Megale and Tamara Wajnberg for superb research assistance.*

References

Dornbusch, Rudiger and Sebastian Edwards, eds. 1991. *The Macroeconomics of Populism in Latin America.* Chicago: University of Chicago Press.

Edwards, Sebastian. 1995. *Crisis and Economic Reform in Latin America.* New York: Oxford University Press.

Ferranti, David, Francisco Ferreira, Guillermo Perry and Michael Walton. 2003. "Inequality in Latin America and Caribbean. Breaking with History?" World Bank Report.

Goldstein, Morris, Graciela Kaminsky and Carmen Reinhart. 2000. *Assessing Financial Vulnerability.* Washington, D.C.: Institute for International Economics.

Kaufman, Robert R. and Barbara Stallings. 1991. "The Political Economy of Latin American Populism," in *The Macroeconomics of Populism in Latin America.* Rudiger Dornbusch and Sebastian Edwards, eds. Chicago: University of Chicago Press, pp. 15–43.

Lora, Eduardo. 2001. "Structural Reform in Latin America: What has been Reformed and How to Measure It." Research Department Working Paper No. 466, Inter-American Development Bank, Washington, D.C.

Lora, Eduardo and Ugo Panizza. 2002. "Structural Reforms in Latin America Under Scrutiny." Research Department Working Paper, Inter-American Development Bank, Washington, D.C.

Pessôa, Samuel de Abreu. 2003. "A Experiência de Crescimento das Economias de Mercado nos Últimos 40 Anos." Graduate School of Economics, Getúlio Vargas Foundation, Rio de Janeiro, Brazil.

Sachs, Jeffrey D., ed. 1989. *Developing Country Debt and the World Economy.* Chicago: University of Chicago Press.

Schmidt-Hebbel, Klaus. 1999. "Chile's Takeoff: Facts, Challenges, Lessons," in *Chile: Recent Policy Lessons and Emerging Challenges.* Danny Leipziger and Guillermo Perry, eds. WBI Development Studies, Washington, D.C.: The World Bank.

Williamson, John, ed. 1990. *Latin American Adjustment: How Much Has Happened?* Washington, D.C.: Institute for International Economics.

Williamson, John. 2003. "From Reform Agenda to Damaged Brand Name." *Finance and Development.* September, 40, pp. 10–13.

Journal of Economic Perspectives—Volume 18, Number 2—Spring 2004—Pages 107–126

Prediction Markets

Justin Wolfers and Eric Zitzewitz

I n July 2003, press reports began to surface of a project within the Defense Advanced Research Projects Agency (DARPA), a research think tank within the Department of Defense, to establish a Policy Analysis Market that would allow trading in various forms of geopolitical risk. Proposed contracts were based on indices of economic health, civil stability, military disposition, conflict indicators and potentially even specific events. For example, contracts might have been based on questions like "How fast will the non-oil output of Egypt grow next year?" or "Will the U.S. military withdraw from country A in two years or less?" Moreover, the exchange would have offered combinations of contracts, perhaps combining an economic event and a political event. The concept was to discover whether trading in such contracts could help to predict future events and how connections between events were perceived. However, a political uproar followed. Critics savaged DARPA for proposing "terrorism futures," and rather than spend political capital defending a tiny program, the proposal was dropped.[1]

Ironically, the aftermath of the DARPA controversy provided a vivid illustration of the power of markets to provide information about probabilities of future events. An offshore betting exchange, Tradesports.com, listed a new security that would pay $100 if the head of DARPA, Admiral John Poindexter, was ousted by the end

---

[1] Looney (2003) provides a useful summary of both the relevant proposal and its aftermath. Further, Robin Hanson has maintained a useful archive of related news stories and government documents at ⟨http://hanson.gmu.edu/policyanalysismarket.html⟩.

■ *Justin Wolfers and Eric Zitzewitz are both Assistant Professors of Business, Graduate School of Business, Stanford University, Stanford, California. Wolfers is also a Faculty Research Fellow, National Bureau of Economic Research, Cambridge, Massachusetts. Their webpages are ⟨http://faculty-gsb.stanford.edu/wolfers⟩ and ⟨http://faculty-gsb.stanford.edu/zitzewitz⟩, respectively.*

of August 2003. Early trading suggested a likelihood of resignation by the end of August of 40 percent, and price fluctuations reflected ongoing news developments. Around lunchtime on July 31, reports started citing credible Pentagon insiders who claimed knowledge of an impending resignation. Within minutes of this news first surfacing (and hours before it became widely known), the price spiked to around 80. These reports left the date of Poindexter's proposed departure uncertain, which explains the remaining risk. As August dragged on, the price slowly fell back toward 50. On August 12, Poindexter then issued a letter of resignation suggesting that he would resign on August 29. On the 12th, the market rose sharply, closing at a price of 96.

This anecdote describes a new—and emerging—form of financial market, often known as a prediction market, but also going by the name "information market" or "event futures." Analytically, these are markets where participants trade in contracts whose payoff depends on unknown future events. Much of the enthusiasm for prediction markets derives from the efficient markets hypothesis. In a truly efficient prediction market, the market price will be the best predictor of the event, and no combination of available polls or other information can be used to improve on the market-generated forecasts. This statement does not require that all individuals in a market be rational, as long as the marginal trade in the market is motivated by rational traders. Of course, it is unlikely that prediction markets are literally efficient, but a number of successes in these markets, both with regard to public events like presidential elections and within firms, have generated substantial interest.

Although markets designed specifically for information aggregation and revelation are our focus in this article, the line between these kinds of prediction markets and the full range of contingent commodities—from owning stock in your employer's company to betting on the Super Bowl—can become blurry. However, we will generally lean away from discussing markets where the primary focus is holding or trading risk that may be intrinsically enjoyable, as in sports betting and other gambling markets. We will also lean away from focusing on markets that are substantial enough in size to allow a significant extent of risk sharing and pooling by matching risky assets with risk-acceptant investors, like the major financial markets.[2] However, most contingent commodity markets involve some mix of risk sharing, fun and information transmission, so these distinctions are not impermeable.

We begin by describing the types of contracts that might be traded in prediction markets, before proceeding to survey several applications. We then draw together a rough and fairly optimistic description of what we have learned from early experiments, raise some market design issues, and conclude with some evidence on the limitations of prediction markets.

---

[2] For a vision of how prediction markets, if they develop sufficient liquidity, may also prove useful for those wishing to hedge against specific risks, see the discussions in Athanasoulis, Shiller and van Wincoop (1999) and Shiller (2003).

Types of Prediction Markets

In a prediction market, payoffs are tied to the outcomes of future events. The design of how the payoff is linked to the future event can elicit the market's expectations of a range of different parameters. We will speak as though the market is itself a representative "person" with a set of expectations. However, the reader should be warned that there are important but subtle differences between, say, the market's median expectation and the median expectation of market participants.

Table 1 summarizes the three main types of contracts. First, in a "winner-take-all" contract, the contract costs some amount $p and pays off, say, $1 if and only if a specific event occurs, like a particular candidate winning an election. The price on a winner-take-all market represents the market's expectation of the probability that an event will occur (assuming risk neutrality).[3]

Second, in an "index" contract, the amount that the contract pays varies in a continuous way based on a number that rises or falls, like the percentage of the vote received by a candidate. The price for such a contract represents the mean value that the market assigns to the outcome.

Finally, in "spread" betting, traders differentiate themselves by bidding on the cutoff that determines whether an event occurs, like whether a candidate receives more than a certain percentage of the popular vote. Another example of spread betting is point-spread betting in football, where the bet is either that one team will win by at least a certain number of points or not. In spread betting, the price of the bet is fixed, but the size of the spread can adjust. When spread betting is combined with an even-money bet (that is, winners double their money while losers receive zero), the outcome can yield the market's expectation of the median outcome, because this is only a fair bet if a payoff is as likely to occur as not.

The basic forms of these relevant contracts will reveal the market's expectation of a specific parameter: a probability, mean or median, respectively. But in addition, prediction markets can also be used to evaluate uncertainty about these expectations. For instance, consider a family of winner-take-all contracts that pay off if and only if the candidate earns 48 percent of the vote, 49 percent, 50 percent and so on. This family of winner-take-all contracts will then reveal almost the entire probability distribution of the market's expectations. A family of spread betting contracts can yield similar insights. An even-money bet in a spread contract will define the median, as explained above. But for similar reasons, a contract that costs $4 and pays $5 if $y > y^*$ will elicit a value of y^* that the market believes to be a four-fifths probability, thus identifying the 80th percentile of the distribution. As a final alternative, nonlinear index contracts can also reveal more information about

[3] The price of a winner-take-all security is essentially a state price, which will equal an estimate of the event's probability under the assumption of risk neutrality. The sums wagered in prediction markets are typically small enough that assuming that investors are not averse to the idiosyncratic risk involved seems reasonable. But if the event in question is correlated with investors' marginal utility of wealth, then probabilities and state prices can differ. In what follows, we leave this issue aside and use the term probability to refer to risk-neutral probability.

Table 1

Contract Types: Estimating Uncertain Quantities or Probabilities

Contract	Example	Details	Reveals market expectation of . . .
Winner-take-all	Event y: Al Gore wins the popular vote.	Contract costs $\$p$. Pays $1 if and only if event y occurs. Bid according to value of $\$p$.	Probability that event y occurs, $p(y)$.
Index	Contract pays $1 for every percentage point of the popular vote won by Al Gore.	Contract pays $\$y$.	Mean value of outcome y: $E[y]$.
Spread	Contract pays even money if Gore wins more than $y^*\%$ of the popular vote.	Contract costs $1. Pays $2 if $y > y^*$. Pays $0 otherwise. Bid according to the value of y^*.	Median value of y.

the underlying distribution. For instance, consider a market with two index contracts, one that pays in a standard linear form and another that pays according to the square of the index, y^2. Market prices will reveal the market's expectation of $E[y^2]$ and $E[y]$, which can be used to make an inference about the market's beliefs regarding the standard deviation of $E[y]$, more commonly known as the standard error. (Recall that the standard deviation can be expressed as $\sqrt{(E[y^2] - E[y]^2)}$, or the square root of the mean of the squares less the square of the means.) By the same logic, adding even more complicated index contracts can yield insight into higher-order moments of the distribution.

Applications and Evidence

Perhaps the best-known prediction market among economists is the Iowa Electronic Market, run by the University of Iowa. The original Iowa experiment, run in 1988, allowed trade in a contract that would pay 2 ½ cents for each percentage point of the popular vote in the presidential election won by Bush, Dukakis or others. More recently, it has run markets based on the 2003 California gubernatorial election, the 2004 presidential election, the 2004 Democratic presidential nomination and how the Federal Reserve will alter the federal funds interest rate. Universities in other countries have also started running event markets about their own elections, like the Austrian Electronic Market run by the Vienna University of Technology or the University of British Columbia Election Stock Market that focuses on Canadian elections.

There are a growing number of web-based event markets, often run by companies that provide a range of trading and gambling services. Some prominent examples include Tradesports.com and Betfair.com, and pseudomarkets (in which participants trade virtual currency) such as Newsfutures.com and Ideosphere.com.

Table 2
Prediction Markets

Market	Focus	Typical turnover on an event ($US)
Iowa Electronic Markets ⟨www.biz.iowa.edu/iem⟩ Run by University of Iowa	Small-scale election markets. Similar markets are run by UBC (Canada) ⟨www.esm.buc.ca⟩ and TUW (Austria) ⟨http://ebweb.tuwien.ac.at/apsm/⟩.	Tens of thousands of dollars (Traders limited to $500 positions.)
TradeSports ⟨www.tradesports.com⟩ For-profit company	Trade in a rich set of political futures, financial contracts, current events, sports and entertainment.	Hundreds of thousands of dollars
Economic Derivatives ⟨www.economicderivatives.com⟩ Run by Goldman Sachs and Deutsche Bank	Large-scale financial market trading in the likely outcome of future economic data releases.	Hundreds of millions
Newsfutures ⟨www.newsfutures.com⟩ For-profit company	Political, finance, current events and sports markets. Also technology and pharmaceutical futures for specific clients.	Virtual currency redeemable for monthly prizes (such as a television)
Foresight Exchange ⟨www.ideosphere.com⟩ Nonprofit research group	Political, finance, current events, science and technology events suggested by clients.	Virtual currency
Hollywood Stock Exchange ⟨www.hsx.com⟩ Owned by Cantor Fitzgerald	Success of movies, movie stars, awards, including a related set of complex derivatives and futures. Data used for market research.	Virtual currency

These websites often take the lead on defining a contract (as in the example of Poindexter's departure from DARPA described earlier), but then allow individuals to post their offers and to accept the offers of others.

Some prediction markets focus on economic statistics. The example of the Iowa market on the federal funds rate was mentioned earlier. More recently, Goldman Sachs and Deutsche Bank have launched markets on the likely outcome of future readings of economic statistics, including employment, retail sales, industrial production and business confidence. The Chicago Mercantile Exchange is planning to open a market in inflation futures. Some event markets also forecast private sector returns. The Hollywood Stock Exchange allows people to use virtual currency to speculate on movie-related questions like opening weekend performance, total box office returns and who will win Oscars. In several cases, private firms have found innovative ways to use prediction markets as a business forecasting tool.

Table 2 lists some of these prediction markets. Drawing on experiences with event markets, it is possible to start suggesting some generalizations about how prediction markets work, both in terms of their accuracy and whether arbitrage or market manipulation are possible.

Figure 1
Information Revelation Through Time

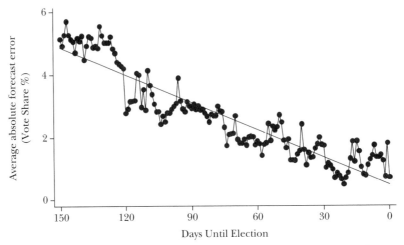

Source: Author's calculations based on data available at ⟨http://www.biz.uiowa.edu/iem⟩.

Accuracy of Prediction Markets

Arguably the most important issue with these markets is their performance as predictive tools. In the political domain, Berg, Forsythe, Nelson and Reitz (2001) summarize the evidence from the Iowa Electronic Markets, documenting that the market has both yielded very accurate predictions and also outperformed large-scale polling organizations. Figure 1 shows data from the past four U.S. presidential elections. The horizontal axis shows the number of days before the election. The vertical axis measures the average absolute deviation between the prices of index contracts linked to the two-party shares of the popular vote for each party and actual vote shares earned in the election. In the week leading up to the election, these markets have predicted vote shares for the Democratic and Republican candidates with an average absolute error of around 1.5 percentage points. By comparison, over the same four elections, the final Gallup poll yielded forecasts that erred by 2.1 percentage points. The graph also shows how the accuracy of the market prediction improves as information is revealed and absorbed as the election draws closer.

Perhaps more surprising in terms of how well prediction markets can aggregate information is the performance of markets at the level of the individual district. Typically, districts are sufficiently small that there is little interest (or funding) for local polling, yet when Australian bookmakers started betting on district-level races, Wolfers and Leigh (2002) report that they were extremely accurate.

That said, comparing the performance of markets with a mechanistic application of poll-based forecasting may not provide a particularly compelling comparison. A more relevant starting point might be to compare the predictions of markets with those of independent analysts. For an example along these lines, consider the "Saddam Security," which was a contract offered on TradeSports

Figure 2
The Saddam Security

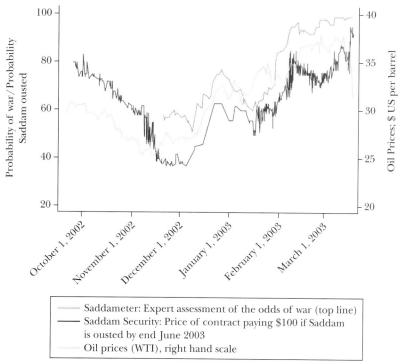

Sources: Trade-by-trade Saddam Security data provided by Tradesports.com; Saddameter from Will Saletan's daily column in Slate.com.

paying $100 if Saddam Hussein were ousted from power by the end of June 2003. Figure 2 shows that the price of this contract moved in lockstep with two other measures: expert opinion as shown by an expert journalist's estimate of the probability of the United States going to war with Iraq; and oil prices, an obvious barometer of political strife in the Middle East.

In a corporate context, the Hollywood Stock Exchange predicts opening weekend box office success, and Figure 3 shows that these predictions have been quite accurate. Further, this market has been about as accurate at forecasting Oscar winners as an expert panel (Pennock, Lawrence, Giles and Nielsen, 2001). Some firms have also begun to experiment with internal prediction markets. An internal market at Hewlett-Packard produced more accurate forecasts of printer sales than the firm's internal processes (Chen and Plott, 2002). Ortner (1998) described an experiment at Siemens in which an internal market predicted that the firm would definitely fail to deliver on a software project on time, even when traditional planning tools suggested that the deadline could be met. While the Hollywood markets have drawn many participants simply on the basis of their entertainment value, the HP and Siemens experiences suggested that motivating employees to trade was a major challenge. In each case, the firms ran real money exchanges, with only a relatively small trading population (20–60 people), and subsidized partici-

Figure 3
Predicting Movie Success

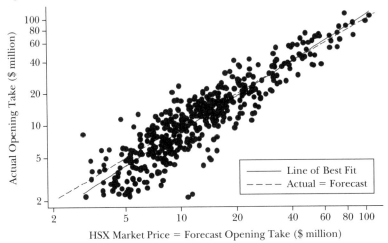

Source: Data from 489 movies, 2000–2003 (⟨http://www.hsx.com⟩).

pation in the market, by either endowing traders with a portfolio or matching initial deposits. The predictive performance of even these very thin markets was quite striking.

In another recent prediction market, traders in "Economic Derivatives" predict the likelihood that economic data released later in the week will take on specific values. The traditional approach to aggregating forecasts is simply to take an average or a "consensus estimate" from a survey of 50 or so professional forecasters. We now have data from the first year of operation of these markets. Table 3 analyzes these early outcomes, comparing average market and consensus forecasts of three variables: total nonfarm payrolls data released by the Bureau of Labor Statistics; retail trade data (excluding autos) released by the Bureau of the Census; and business confidence as measured by the Institute for Supply Management's survey of manufacturing purchasing managers. The market-based predictions of these economic indicators are always extremely close to the corresponding "consensus" forecast, and hence, the two estimates are highly correlated. There are no statistically (or economically) meaningful differences in forecast performance— measured as either the correlation with actual outcomes, or in terms of average absolute forecast errors. That said, this early sample is sufficiently small that precise conclusions are difficult to draw.

Interestingly, these markets yield not just a point estimate for each economic indicator, but involve a menu of ten to 20 winner-take-all contracts as to whether the indicator will take on specific values. This family of contracts reveals an approximation to the full probability distribution of market expectations. Consequently, we can calculate the level of uncertainty surrounding specific point estimates. One measure of uncertainty is the expected absolute forecast error (although calculations using standard deviation provide the same qualitative results). The market-based assessments of uncertainty are shown in the last line of panel B.

Table 3

Predicting Economic Outcomes: Comparing Market-Aggregated Forecasts with Consensus Surveys

	Nonfarm payrolls (monthly change, '000s)	Retail trade (ex autos) (monthly change, %)	ISM manufacturing purchasing managers' index
Panel A: Correlations			
Corr(Market, Consensus)	0.91	0.94	0.95
Corr(Consensus, Actual)	0.26	0.70	0.83
Corr(Market, Actual)	0.22	0.73	0.91
Panel B: Mean absolute error			
Consensus	71.1	0.45	1.10
Market (empirical)	72.2	0.46	1.07
Market (implied expectation)	65.7	0.34	1.58
Panel C: Standard deviation of forecast errors (Standard error of forecast)			
Consensus	99.2	0.55	1.12
Market (empirical)	97.3	0.58	1.20
Market (implied expectation)	81.1	0.42	1.96
Sample size	16	12	11

Notes: "Market" = market-implied mean forecast from ⟨http://www.economicderivatives.com⟩. "Consensus" = average of around 50 forecasters from ⟨http://www.briefing.com⟩. "Actual" = Preliminary estimates from original press releases (BLS, Census, ISM).

Comparing these implied expectations with outcomes in the first two rows of panel B suggests that the market-based assessments of uncertainty are of about the right magnitude. Finally, one can compare the implied standard errors of the forecasts with the reported standard errors of the statistics that the market is attempting to forecast. For instance, the Census Bureau reports that the change in retail trade is estimated with a standard error of around 0.5 percent, while the standard error implied by the prediction market is 0.42 percent. Taken literally, this suggests that the market believes that it is less uncertain about the Census Bureau estimate than the Census Bureau is.[4] Such results suggest either that the statistical agencies' errors are predictable, that their standard error estimates are (slightly) upwardly biased, or that traders are overconfident.

[4] A similar comparison can be made for nonfarm payrolls, although the inference is less direct. The U.S. Bureau of Labor Statistics estimates that their final estimate of the change in nonfarm payrolls has a standard error of around 64,000, while the preliminary estimate is more uncertain. The BLS has yet to estimate a standard error for their preliminary estimates, but the root mean squared error of the preliminary estimate relative to the final estimate is around 50,000. If the revision to the preliminary estimate and the subsequent error in the revised estimate were uncorrelated, this would imply a standard error for the preliminary estimate of about 81,500. Comparing these numbers with the average standard error of the market forecast of 81,100 suggests that the market is about as sure of the advance estimate as the BLS.

Figure 4
2003 California Gubernatorial Election

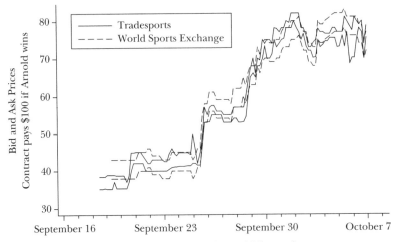

Source: Prices collected electronically every four hours by David Pennock.

Possibilities for Arbitrage

Prediction markets appear to present few opportunities for arbitrage. There are several ways of looking for arbitrage opportunities: whether prices for similar contracts can be arbitraged across different exchanges or different securities; whether predictable patterns in the movement of the prices allow for arbitrage; and whether arbitrageurs might be able to exploit predictable deviations from rationality.

Figure 4 shows the bid and ask prices on a contract that paid $100 if Schwarzenegger was elected California's governor in 2003, sampling data on bid and ask prices from two online exchanges every four hours. While both sets of data show substantial variation, they co-move very closely, and opportunities for arbitrage (when the bid price on one exchange is higher than the ask on another), are virtually absent.

The pricing of families of related securities tends to be internally consistent. For example, Figure 5 shows the prices of several securities launched by Tradesports that paid off if weapons of mass destruction were found in Iraq by May, June, July or September 2003. Their prices moved closely together in a way that suggested that the prices of each contract digested similar information at close to the same time.

In most cases, the time series of prices in these markets does not appear to follow a predictable path, and simple betting strategies based on past prices appear to yield no profit opportunities; for example, Leigh, Wolfers and Zitzewitz (2003) demonstrate this point for the aforementioned Tradesports "Saddam Security." However, there is also some evidence that this small-scale market responded to news about Iraq with a slight lag relative to deeper financial markets. Tetlock (2004) surveys a wide range of data from Tradesports, finding that their financial contracts are largely efficiently priced.

Figure 5

Will Weapons of Mass Destruction be Discovered in Iraq?

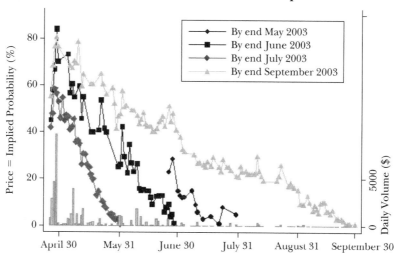

Source: Average daily price data provided by ⟨http://www.tradesports.com⟩.

Prediction markets do seem to display some of the deviations from perfect rationality that appear in other financial markets. There is substantial evidence from psychology and economics suggesting that people tend to overvalue small probabilities and undervalue near certainties. For example, there is a well-known "favorite–long shot bias" in horse races (for example, discussed in this journal by Thaler and Ziemba, 1988), in which bettors tend to overvalue extreme long shots and thus receive much lower returns for such bets, an effect that is offset by somewhat higher (albeit still negative) returns for betting on favorites. The "volatility smile" in options refers to a related pattern in financial markets (Bates, 1991; Rubenstein, 1994), which involves overpricing of strongly out-of-the-money options and underpricing of strongly in-the-money options (relative to their future values or their ex-ante values from the Black-Scholes option pricing formula).[5] These experiences suggest that prediction markets may perform poorly at predicting small probability events.

An example of this kind of miscalibration comes from financial variables that trade on Tradesports. Table 4 reports the bid and ask prices in the prediction market for a contract that will pay $100 if the Standard and Poor's 500 index finishes 2003 in a certain range. For comparison, one can look at the actual prices of December S&P options traded on the Chicago Mercantile Exchange. We used the method discussed in Leigh, Wolfers and Zitzewitz (2003) to translate the financial market prices into prices for a security comparable to the Tradesports contract. Comparing Tradesports prices with the actual option prices in Chicago suggests that the extremely unlikely (high and low) outcomes for the S&P 500 are

---

[5] Aït-Sahalia, Wang and Yared (2001) argue that the conclusion of miscalibration is less clear cut in this context, because these prices may be driven by small likelihoods of extreme price changes.

Table 4

Price of Standard and Poor's Future Price Securities on Tradesports versus Actual Prices from the Chicago Mercantile Exchange

(market close, July 23, 2003)

	Price on Tradesports		
S&P level on December 31, 2003	Bid	Ask	Estimated price from actual December S&P options
1200 and over	2	6	2.5
1100 to 1199	11	16	13.2
1000 to 1099	28	33	33.3
900 to 999	25	30	30.5
800 to 899	14	19	13
700 to 799	3	8	5
600 to 699	4	7	2
Under 600	5	8	1
S&P level on July 23, 2003		985	

Notes: Prices given in first two columns are for a security that pays $100 if S&P finishes 2003 in given range. Prices in third column are estimated from actual option settlement prices using the method in Leigh, Wolfers, and Zitzewitz (2003), adjusting for the 13-day difference in expiry date.

relatively overpriced on Tradesports. In fact, the price differences implied a (small) arbitrage opportunity that persisted for most of summer 2003 and has reappeared in 2004. Similar patterns existed for Tradesports securities on other financial variables like crude oil, gold prices and exchange rates. This finding is consistent with the long-shot bias being more pronounced on smaller-scale exchanges.

Another behavioral bias reflects the tendency of market participants to trade according to their desires, rather than objective probability assessments. Strumpf (2004) provides evidence that certain New York gamblers are more likely to bet the Yankees, while Forsythe, Reitz and Ross (1999) provide evidence that individual traders buy and sell in political markets in a manner correlated with their party identification. Even so, as long as marginal trades are motivated by profits rather than partisanship, prices will reflect the assessments of (unbiased) profit motive. Thus far, there is little evidence that these factors yield systematic unexploited profits.

A further possible limitation of prediction market pricing arises if speculative bubbles drive prices away from likely outcomes. Traditional markets may be subject to bubbles because of constraints on short selling and because investors will be reluctant to commit a large share of their wealth to an arbitrage opportunity, since if the mispricing does exist, it may grow worse before it gets better (Shleifer and Vishny, 1997). Since prediction markets typically impose no restrictions on short selling, and the markets are sufficiently small-scale that it is unlikely that informed investors will be capital constrained, the scope for bubbles might be more limited. It is impossible to make any serious attempt at describing the frequency of bubbles in the data we have so far. However, through September 2003, we suspected a bubble in the Tradesports security on whether Hillary Clinton would win the

Democratic nomination. Our suspicions were based on her public statements that she was not a candidate and the tenor of discussion among traders, which seemed to indicate that trading was being driven by expectations of future price movements rather than by fundamentals. Equally, these high prices may have reflected those with access to campaign insiders who knew more about her state of mind than we did.

Empirically, the best that we can say is that the performance of past markets at predicting the future has been, on average, pretty good, whether or not specific markets were in some cases distorted by biases or bubbles. Laboratory experiments hold out the possibility of learning more about bubbles, as it is possible for the experimenter to know the "true price" and, hence, to observe deviations. Plott and Sunder (1982, 1988) have set up extremely simple examples in which bubble-like behavior occurs in simple prediction markets. At the same time, bubbles in experimental markets often burst and give way to more rational pricing.

Can Event Markets Be Easily Manipulated?

The profit motive has usually proven sufficient to ensure that attempts at manipulating these markets were unsuccessful. There have been several known attempts at manipulation of these markets, but none of them had much of a discernible effect on prices, except during a short transition phase.[6] For example, Wolfers and Leigh (2002) report candidates betting on themselves at long odds to create a "buzz," while Strumpf (2004) placed random $500 bets on the Iowa Electronic Markets to trace their effect. In a similar vein, Camerer (1998) attempted with little effect to manipulate betting on horse races by canceling large wagers at the last moment. Clearly, the extent to which markets are manipulable depends—at least in part—on how thin the markets are.

It was feared that the DARPA markets would create the opportunity for a terrorist to profit from an act of terrorism or an assassination. With respect to the DARPA markets, this concern may have been misplaced, both because the proposed markets were unlikely to have included terrorism or assassination contracts in the first place, and because the small scale of these markets means that terrorists would not have been able to earn much relative to the presumed going rate for an assassination. An alternative view holds that such trade is actually a good thing to the extent that trading ultimately reveals previously secret information about the intentions of terrorist groups. That said, if terrorists are sophisticated enough to place bets in futures markets, surely they can do so with standard futures contracts on oil prices, by selling short stock in insurance companies or the entire stock market and the like. Indeed, rumors have circulated widely that there was unusual trading in options on United and American Airlines stock in the week prior to the attacks of September 11, 2001. A careful analysis by Poteshman (2004) found little evidence to support these rumors, suggesting that if terrorists did profit from their

---

[6] In their companion paper in this issue, Rhode and Strumpf document that attempts at manipulation in early twentieth-century political markets were typically unsuccessful.

actions, they neither left a noticeable footprint nor needed a prediction market to do so.

Market Design

The success of prediction markets, like any market, can depend on their design and implementation. Some of the key design issues include how buyers are matched to sellers, the specification of the contract, whether real money is used and whether a diversity of information exists in a way that provides a basis for trading. We consider these issues in turn.

In most prediction markets, the mechanism that matches buyers to sellers is a continuous double auction, with buyers submitting bids and sellers submitting asking prices, and with the mechanism executing a trade whenever the two sides of the market reach a mutually agreeable price. However, the new prediction markets in announcements of economic statistics operate more like the pari-mutuel systems that are common in horse-race betting. In a pari-mutuel system, all of the money that is bet goes into a common pot and is then divided among the winners (after subtracting transaction costs). Many prediction markets are also augmented by market makers who announce willingness to buy and sell at a certain range of prices; similarly, most sports bets are placed with bookmakers who post prices. Finally, while these mechanisms are relatively useful for simple markets, Hanson (2003) has proposed the use of market scoring rules to allow for simultaneous predictions over many combinations of outcomes. Instead of requiring separate markets for each combination of possible outcomes, traders effectively bet that the sum of their errors over all predictions will be lower.

For a prediction market to work well, contracts must be clear, easily understood and easily adjudicated. For example, we don't see contracts like "Weapons of Mass Destruction are not in Iraq," but rather contracts specifying whether such weapons will have been found by a certain date. This requirement for clarity can sometimes turn out to be complex. In the 1994 U.S. Senate elections, the Iowa markets proposed what looked to be a well-specified market, with contracts paying according to the number of seats won by each party. The day after the election (and while votes were still being counted in some jurisdictions), Senator Richard Shelby (D-Alabama) switched sides to become a Republican. As another example, in the course of Ortner's (1998) internal prediction market on whether a software project would be delivered to the client on schedule, the client changed the deadline.

One intriguing question is how much difference it makes whether prediction markets are run with real money or with some form of play money. Legal restrictions on gambling have led some groups like NewsFutures.com to adopt play money exchanges, with those who amass the largest play-fortunes eligible for prizes. Prices on play and real-money exchanges are not linked by arbitrage: in August 2003, for example, George W. Bush was a 67 percent favorite to win reelection on real-money exchanges, but was a 50-50 bet on NewsFutures. However, we do not yet have sufficient comparative data to know the extent to which money makes predictions more accurate. Indeed, it has been argued that the play money exchanges may even outperform real-money exchanges because "wealth" can only be accumulated through a history of accurate prediction. In a suggestive experiment, Servan-Schreiber, Wolfers, Pennock and Galebach (2004) compared the predictive power of the prices from real-money and play-money exchanges over the 2003 NFL football season, finding that both yielded predictions that were approximately equally accurate. Interestingly, both sets of prices also outperformed all but a dozen of 3,000 people in an online contest and also easily outperformed the average assessments of these "experts." One practical advantage of play money contracts is that they offer more freedom to experiment with different kinds of contracts. On "play money" exchanges, such as Foresight Exchange, one often sees quite loosely worded "contracts" such as that a "scientific study will conclude that astrology is a statistically significant predictive method to describe an individual's personality traits."

Even well-designed markets will fail unless a motivation to trade exists.[7] Most prediction markets are not large enough to allow hedging against specific risks. However, the "play money" exchanges and sports gambling industry both suggest that it may be possible to motivate (small-scale) trading simply through the thrill of pitting one's judgment against others, and being able to win a monetary prize may sharpen this motivation. Trade also requires some disagreement about likely outcomes. Disagreement is unlikely among fully rational traders with common priors. It is more likely when traders are overconfident in the quality of their private information or their ability to process public information or when they have priors that are sufficiently different to allow them to agree to disagree.

These insights suggest that some prediction markets will work better when they concern events that are widely discussed, since trading on such events will have higher entertainment value and there will be more information on whose interpretation traders can disagree. Ambiguous public information may be better in motivating trade than private information, especially if the private information is concentrated, since a cadre of highly informed traders can easily drive out the partly informed, repressing trade to the point that the market barely exists. Indeed, attempts to set up markets on topics where insiders are likely to possess substantial information advantages have typically failed. For instance, the Tradesports contracts on the next Supreme Court retirement or the future of the papacy have generated very little trade, despite the inherent interest in these questions. Trade can also be subsidized either directly or indirectly by adding noise trades into the market, which provides the potential to profit from trading.

Finally, the power of prediction markets derives from the fact that they provide incentives for *truthful revelation*, they provide incentives for research and *information discovery*, and the market provides an algorithm for *aggregating opinions*. As such, these markets are unlikely to perform well when there is little useful intelligence to aggregate or when public information is selective, inaccurate or misleading. Fur-

---

[7] The inflation futures market on the Coffee, Sugar, and Cocoa Exchange is a case in point; this market generated little volume, ultimately failing.

ther, the weights that markets give to different opinions may not be an improvement on alternative algorithms where the accuracy of pundits is directly observable. For example, the public information on the probability of weapons of mass destruction in Iraq appears to have been of dubious quality, so it is perhaps unsurprising that both the markets were as susceptible as general public opinion to being misled.

Making Inferences from Prediction Markets

How might economists use the results from prediction markets in subsequent analysis? The most direct form of inference involves using these predictions directly. For instance, in their experiments at Hewlett Packard, Chen and Plott (2002) elicited expectations of future printer sales, which were of direct interest for internal planning purposes.

Some analyses have tried to link the time series of expectations elicited in prediction markets with time series of other variables. For instance, in Leigh, Wolfers and Zitzewitz (2003), we interpreted movements in the Saddam Security as an index for the risk of war and interpreted the comovement with the oil price shown in Figure 2 as a causal relationship, concluding that war led to a $10 per barrel increase in oil prices. A similar analysis suggested that equity prices had built in a 15 percent war discount. Applying a similar methodology, Slemrod and Greimel (1999) linked the price of a Steve Forbes security in the 1996 Republican primary market with a rising interest rate premium on municipal bond prices, because Forbes's signature issue was a "flat tax" that would have eliminated the tax exemption for municipal bond interest. As with any regression context, one must be cautious before inferring that these correlations reflect causation and consider the issues of reverse causation, omitted variables, statistical significance, functional form and the like.

It seems quite possible to design prediction market contracts so that they would bring out the connection between an event and other variables. For instance, in 2002, we could have floated two securities, one paying P if Saddam were ousted in a year, where P is the future oil price, with the purchase price refunded otherwise, and another that paid P if Saddam remains in power, again refunding the purchase price. The difference in the equilibrium price of these two securities can be interpreted as the market's expectation of the effect of ousting Saddam on oil prices. This inference does not require researchers to wait until sufficient variation in the political situation has accrued for a regression to be estimated. Moreover, changes in the market's beliefs about how ousting Saddam would affect oil prices can be directly measured through such a conditional market.

Very few of these contingent markets have been constructed, although this year's Iowa Electronic Market on the 2004 presidential election is instructive. Table 5 shows the prices of a series of contracts that are standard index contracts that pay a penny for each percentage of the two-party popular vote won by each party, but are contingent in that the contract pays out only if the Democratic

Table 5

Contingent Markets: 2004 Presidential Election

(contracts pay according to vote share, conditional on the Democratic nominee)

Contract Pays Conditional on Specific Democratic Candidate	Democratic Candidate Vote Share (Contract Price, $) A	Republican Vote Share Against this Candidate (Contract Price, $) B	Implied Prob. this Candidate Wins Nomination C = A + B	Expected Share of Popular Vote if Nominated D = A/C
John Kerry	$0.344	$0.342	68.6%	50.1%
John Edwards	$0.082	$0.066	14.8%	55.4%
Howard Dean	$0.040	$0.047	8.7%	46.0%
Wesley Clark	$0.021	$0.025	4.6%	45.7%
Other Democrats	$0.015	$0.017	3.2%	46.9%

Notes: Columns A and B show the prices of contracts that pay a penny for each percentage of the two-party popular vote won by Democrats or Republicans respectively, conditional on picking the winner of the Democratic nomination. (Contracts pay $0 if the selected candidate does not win the Democratic nomination.)

Source: Closing prices January 29, 2004, Iowa electronic markets.

nominee is also successfully predicted. These contracts pay nothing if the nominee is not correctly predicted.

Because the Democratic and Republican shares of the two-party vote must sum to one, a portfolio containing contracts tied to both the Democratic and Republican vote shares, but conditional on Kerry winning the nomination, will definitely pay $1 if Kerry wins the primary and $0 otherwise. Implicitly then, this market embeds a winner-take-all market on the Democratic primary race, and adding the prices shown in columns A and B yields the prices of these synthetic securities that represent the probability that any specific candidate wins the Democratic nomination (shown in column C). The final column calculates the implied expected vote share for each candidate, if that candidate were to win the nomination, by deflating the cost of the Democratic vote share contract conditional on that candidate by the probability of that candidate actually winning the nomination. Hanson (1999) has called these contingent markets "decision markets," arguing that these expectations should be used to guide decision making. As such, delegates to the Democratic convention interested in selecting the strongest candidate would simply compare the ratios in the final column and, accordingly, vote for John Edwards. Berg and Reitz (2003) make a related argument using data from the 1996 Republican nomination race.

While we are optimistic that these data on contingent prediction markets can be used to inform decision making, some care is required. In making statements about the comovement of two variables, social scientists have long struggled to distinguish correlation from causation, and these decision markets do not resolve this issue. One could imagine that traders hold a frequentist view of probability and that they price the securities in Table 5 by simply inventing hundreds of possible scenarios, and prices simply reflect average outcomes across these scenarios. An econometrician running regressions based on these hundreds of scenarios would note a robust correlation between Edwards winning the nomination and the Democrats winning the presidency. But a careful econometrician would be reluctant to infer causation, noting that there are important "selection effects" at play, as the scenarios in which Edwards wins the nomination are not random. For example, the markets may believe that Edwards will not win the nomination unless Southern Democrats become energized, but if this does happen, it is likely that Edwards will win both the nomination and the presidency. Alternatively, with Kerry viewed as the likely nominee, Edwards may be perceived as a possible nominee only if he shows himself to be a politician of extraordinary ability, overcoming Kerry's early lead in the delegate count. If so, it also seems likely that a candidate of such extraordinary ability would win the general election. Or Edwards might be perceived as thin-skinned and likely to drop out of the race if it appears that the Democratic party is unlikely to win the White House. As such, the relatively high price of the Edwards-Democratic security may reflect either something about Edwards' ability or the selection effects that lead him to win the nomination.

Just as econometricians often deal with selection effects by adding another equation that explicitly models the selection process, there is a prediction market analog—floating another contract that prices the variables driving the selection of Democratic candidates. For example, adding a contract that pays off if a candidate drops out of the nomination race early would allow an assessment of the extent to which prices of contingent contracts are being driven by that specific selection mechanism, thereby yielding a more accurate indication of candidate ability. But since many key traits of candidates may be unobservable, or difficult to capture in a contract that would attract trading, it may be impossible to rely fully on contingent markets to guide voters to the candidate with the greatest vote-winning potential.[8]

These relatively simple contingent markets, as well as more complex combinatorial markets, are as yet virtually untested and a useful focus for further research. There may be important and interesting applications in domains where selection problems are minimal.

Innovative Future Applications?

Prediction markets are extremely useful for estimating the market's expectation of certain events: simple market designs can elicit expected means or probabilities, more complex markets can elicit variances, and contingent markets can be used to elicit the market's expectations of covariances and correlations, although as with any estimation context, further identifying assumptions are required before a causal interpretation can be made. The research agenda on these markets has reflected an interplay between theory, experiments and field research, drawing on

---

[8] Furthermore, it is worth noting that the incentives to manipulate a contract rise with its use in decision making, and the apparent failure of the past manipulation attempts mentioned above do not guarantee that it would fail in this context.

scholars from economics, finance, political science, psychology and computer science. This research program has established that prediction markets provide three important roles: 1) incentives to seek information; 2) incentives for truthful information revelation; and 3) an algorithm for aggregating diverse opinions. Current research is only starting to disentangle the extent to which the remarkable predictive power of markets derives from each of these forces.

Prediction markets doubtless have their limitations, but they may be useful as a supplement to the other relatively primitive mechanisms for predicting the future like opinion surveys, politically appointed panels of experts, hiring consultants or holding committee meetings. We are already seeing increasing interest in these markets in the private sector, with the experiments at Hewlett Packard now being supplemented with new markets on pharmaceuticals and the likely success of future technologies on NewsFutures.

DARPA's ill-fated attempt at establishing a Policy Analysis Market ultimately failed. However, it seems likely that private-sector firms will continue to innovate and to create new prediction markets, so policymakers will still be able to turn to prediction markets run by firms like Tradesports, Net Exchange, Incentive Markets and NewsFutures. It may be a sensible political outcome to have these event markets run by publicly regulated, private-sector firms. Nonetheless, to the extent that the valuable information generated by trade in these markets is not fully internalized into the profits earned by these private firms, prediction markets may be underprovided.

■ *The authors would like to thank David Pennock, Emile Servan-Schreiber of NewsFutures, David Dempsey and John Delaney of Tradesports, Alison Fealey and Oliver Frankel of Goldman Sachs and George Neumann of IEM for help with data. Thanks to Kay-Yut Chen, Robin Hanson, Andrew Leigh, Betsey Stevenson, Timothy Taylor, Hal Varian, Craig Yee and William Ziemba for stimulating discussions. Doug Geyser, Mike Goelzer, Chris Lion, Paul Reist, Erik Snowberg and Ravi Pillai provided outstanding research assistance.*

References

Aït-Sahalia, Yacine, Yubo Wang and Francis Yared. 2001. "Do Options Markets Correctly Price the Probabilities of Movement of the Underlying Asset?" *Journal of Econometrics.* 102:1, pp. 67–110.

Athanasoulis, Stefano, Robert Shiller and Eric van Wincoop. 1999. "Macro Markets and Financial Security." *Economic Policy Review.* 5:1, pp. 21–39.

Bates, David. 1991. "The Crash of '87: Was it Expected? The Evidence from Options Markets." *Journal of Finance.* 46:3, pp. 1009–044.

Berg, Joyce and Thomas Rietz. 2003. "Prediction Markets as Decision Support Systems." *Information Systems Frontiers.* 5:1, pp. 79–93.

Berg, Joyce, Robert Forsythe, Forrest Nelson and Thomas Rietz. 2001. "Results from a Dozen Years of Election Futures Markets Research," in *Handbook of Experimental Economic Results.* Charles Plott and Vernon Smith, eds. Amsterdam: Elsevier, forthcoming.

Camerer, Colin. 1998. "Can Asset Markets be Manipulated? A Field Experiment with Racetrack Betting." *Journal of Political Economy.* 106:3, pp. 457–82.

Chen, Kay-Yut and Charles Plott. 2002. "Information Aggregation Mechanisms: Concept, Design and Implementation for a Sales Forecasting Problem." California Institute of Technology Social Science Working Paper No. 1131, March.

Forsythe, Robert, Thomas Rietz and Thomas Ross. 1999. "Wishes, Expectations and Actions: Price Formation in Election Stock Markets." *Journal of Economic Behavior and Organization.* 39:1, pp. 83–110.

Hanson, Robin. 1999. "Decision Markets." *IEEE Intelligent Systems.* 14:3, pp. 16–19.

Hanson, Robin. 2003. "Combinatorial Information Market Design." *Information Systems Frontiers.* 5:1, pp. 105–19.

Heckman, James J. 1979. "Sample Selection Bias as a Specification Error." *Econometrica.* 47:1, pp. 153–61.

Leigh, Andrew, Justin Wolfers and Eric Zitzewitz. 2003. "What do Financial Markets Think of War in Iraq?" NBER Working Paper No. 9587.

Looney, Robert. 2003. "DARPA's Policy Analysis Market for Intelligence: Outside the Box or Off the Wall." *Strategic Insights.* September, 2:9; Available at ⟨http://www.ccc.nps.navy.mil/si/sept03/terrorism.asp⟩.

Ortner, Gerhard. 1998. "Forecasting Markets—An Industrial Application." Mimeo, Technical University of Vienna.

Pennock, David, Steve Lawrence, C. Lee Giles and Finn Arup Nielsen. 2001. "The Real Power of Artificial Markets." *Science.* 291:5506, pp. 987–88.

Plott, Charles and Shyam Sunder. 1982. "Efficiency of Experimental Security Markets with Insider Information: An Application of Rational-Expectations Models." *Journal of Political Economy.* 90:4, pp. 663–98.

Plott, Charles and Shyam Sunder. 1988. "Rational Expectations and The Aggregation of Diverse information in Laboratory Security Markets." *Econometrica.* 56:5, pp. 1085–118.

Poteshman, Allen. 2004. "Unusual Option Market Activity and the Terrorist Attacks of September 11, 2001." Mimeo, University of Illinois at Urbana-Champaign.

Rubenstein, Mark. 1994. "Implied Binomial Trees." *Journal of Finance.* 49:3, pp. 771–818.

Servan-Schreiber, Emile, Justin Wolfers, David Pennock and Brian Galebach. 2004. "Prediction Markets: Does Money Matter?" *Electronic Markets.* Forthcoming.

Shiller, Robert. 2003. *The New Financial Order: Risk in the Twenty-First Century.* Princeton, N.J.: Princeton University Press.

Shleifer, Andrei and Robert Vishny. 1997. "The Limits of Arbitrage." *Journal of Finance.* 52:1, pp. 35–55.

Slemrod, Joel and Timothy Greimel. 1999. "Did Steve Forbes Scare the Municipal Bond Market?" *Journal of Public Economics.* 74:1, pp. 81–96.

Spann, Martin and Bernd Skiera. 2003. "Internet-Based Virtual Stock Markets for Business Forecasting." *Management Science.* 49:10, pp. 1310–326.

Strumpf, Koleman. 2004. "Manipulating the Iowa Political Stock Market." Mimeo, University of North Carolina.

Tetlock, Paul. 2004. "How Efficient are Information Markets? Evidence from an Online Exchange." Mimeo, Harvard University.

Thaler, Richard H. and William T. Ziemba. 1988. "Anomalies: Parimutuel Betting Markets: Racetracks and Lotteries." *Journal of Economic Perspectives.* Spring, 2:2, pp. 161–74.

Wolfers, Justin and Andrew Leigh. 2002. "Three Tools for Forecasting Federal Elections: Lessons from 2001." *Australian Journal of Political Science.* 37:2, pp. 223–40.

Journal of Economic Perspectives—Volume 18, Number 2—Spring 2004—Pages 127–142

Historical Presidential Betting Markets

Paul W. Rhode and Koleman S. Strumpf

Wagering on political outcomes has a long history in the United States. As Henry David Thoreau (1848 [1967], p. 36) noted: "All voting is a sort of gaming, . . . and betting naturally accompanies it." This paper analyzes the large and often well-organized markets for betting on presidential elections that operated between 1868 and 1940. Over $165 million (in 2002 dollars) was wagered in one election, and betting activity at times dominated transactions in the stock exchanges on Wall Street.

Drawing on an investigation of several thousand newspaper articles, we develop and analyze data on betting volumes and prices to address four main points. First, we show that the market did a remarkable job forecasting elections in an era before scientific polling. In only one case did the candidate clearly favored in the betting a month before Election Day lose, and even state-specific forecasts were quite accurate. This performance compares favorably with that of the Iowa Electronic Market (currently the only legal venue for election betting in the United States). Second, the market was fairly efficient, despite the limited information of participants and attempts to manipulate the odds by political parties and newspapers. Third, we argue political betting markets disappeared largely because of the rise of scientific polls and the increasing availability of other forms of gambling. Finally, we discuss lessons this experience provides for the present.[1]

---

[1] Rhode and Strumpf (2004) provide a fuller analysis and a discussion of the data sources. This research has benefited from a recent innovation, the ability to search and access (via Proquest) machine-readable editions of historical newspapers including the *New York Times*, *Wall Street Journal* and *Washington Post*. Roughly one-half of our citations were found using old-fashioned microfilm and one-half using the new computer search engine. In alphabetical order, the newspapers that we searched as background for this article were the *Chicago Tribune*, *New York Sun*, *New York Times*, *New York Tribune*, *New York World*, *St. Louis Post-Dispatch*, *Wall Street Journal* and *Washington Post*.

■ *Paul W. Rhode is Professor of Economics and Koleman S. Strumpf is Associate Professor of Economics, both at the University of North Carolina, Chapel Hill, North Carolina. Rhode is also a Research Associate, National Bureau of Economic Research, Cambridge, Massachusetts. Their e-mail addresses are ⟨prhode@email.unc.edu⟩ and ⟨cigar@unc.edu⟩, respectively.*

Size and Scope of Historical Betting Markets

A large, active and highly public market for betting on elections existed over much of U.S. history before the Second World War.[2] Contemporaries noted this activity dated back to the election of Washington and existed in organized markets (such as financial exchanges and poolrooms) since the administration of Lincoln. Although election betting was often illegal, the activity was openly conducted by "betting commissioners" (essentially bookmakers) and employed standardized contracts that promised a fixed dollar payment if the designated candidate won office. The standard practice was for the betting commissioner to hold the stakes of both parties and charge a 5 percent commission on the winnings.

Although such markets emerged in most major cities, New York was the center of national betting activity. The scattered available evidence suggests that the New York market accounted for over one-half of the total election betting. The organization and location of the New York market evolved over time. In the 1880s, betting moved out of the poolrooms and became centered on the Curb Exchange (the informally organized predecessor to the AMEX) and the major Broadway hotels until the mid-1910s. In the 1920s and 1930s, specialist firms of betting commissioners, operating out of offices on Wall Street, took over the trade. In the 1890s and early 1910s, the names and relatively modest (four-figure) stakes of bettors filled the daily newspapers, but by the 1930s, most of the reported wagering involved large (six-figure) amounts advanced by unnamed leaders from the business or entertainment worlds.

The extent of activity in the presidential betting markets of this time was astonishingly large. For brief periods, betting on political outcomes at the Curb Exchange in New York would exceed trading in stocks and bonds. Crowds formed in the financial district—on the Curb or in the lobby of the New York Stock Exchange—and brokers would call out bid and ask odds as if trading securities. In presidential races such as 1896, 1900, 1904, 1916 and 1924, the *New York Times, Sun* and *World* provided nearly daily price quotations from early October until Election Day.

Table 1 assembles newspaper estimates, converted to 2002 dollars, of the sums wagered in the New York market in the presidential elections from 1884 to 1928. For context, the table also shows the total bets divided by the number of votes cast and by the total spending of the national presidential campaigns. The betting volume varied depending on the closeness of the races, enthusiasm for the candidates and the legal environment. The 1916 election was the high point, with some $165 million (in 2002 dollars) wagered in the organized New York markets. This amount was more than twice the total spending on the election campaigns that year. The average betting volume was over 200 times the maximum amount wagered in any election in the Iowa Electronic Market (Berg, Nelson and Rietz, 2003).

---

[2] For background on this description of the betting markets, see *New York Times*, November 10, 1906, p. 1; May 29, 1924, p. 21; November 4, 1924, p. 2; *Wall Street Journal*, September 29, 1924, p. 13.

Table 1
Election Betting Volume in New York

	2002 dollars (millions)	Dollars per votes cast	Dollars per campaign spending
1884	13.7	1.36	0.278
1888	37.6	3.30	0.907
1892	14.8	1.23	0.185
1896	10.7	0.77	0.124
1900	63.9	4.57	0.876
1904	50.3	3.72	0.894
1908	7.7	0.52	0.174
1912	4.6	0.30	0.087
1916	165.0	8.90	2.116
1920	44.9	1.68	0.726
1924	21.0	0.72	0.373
1928	10.5	0.29	0.086
Average	37.0	2.28	0.532

Notes: These figures report newspaper estimates of total bet volume over the course of the election cycle. See Rhode and Strumpf (2004) for details.

Predictive Power of the "Wall Street Betting Odds"

The New York betting markets were widely recognized for their remarkable ability to predict election outcomes. As the *New York Times* (September 28, 1924, p. E1) put it, the "old axiom in the financial district [is] that Wall Street betting odds are 'never wrong.'" As a basic, if unsophisticated, measure of the accuracy of the betting markets, the favorite almost always won, the only exception being in 1916 when betting initially favored the eventual loser (Hughes), but swung to even odds by the time the polls closed. In the 15 elections between 1884 and 1940, the mid-October betting favorite won 11 times (73 percent), and the underdog won only once (when in 1916, Wilson upset Hughes on the west coast). In the remaining three contests (1884–1992), the odds were essentially even throughout and the races very close. The capacity of the betting markets to aggregate information is all the more remarkable given the absence of scientific polls before the mid-1930s. The betting odds possessed much better predictive power than other generally available information. Moreover, the betting market was not succeeding by just picking one party or by picking incumbents. Over this period, Republicans won eight of the elections in the Electoral College and Democrats seven; the party in power won eight, the opposition seven.

Figure 1 offers a sense of how informative the betting odds were. The horizontal axis shows the Democratic margin in the popular vote. The vertical axis shows the Democratic "odds price," which is the price of a contract paying one dollar (before commissions) if the designated candidate wins. For example, a wager placing a $2 stake on a candidate's victory against a $1 stake on the candidate's loss is equivalent to a 0.667 odds price on the candidate. Each labeled point represents a single election and shows the average of the odds price over the relevant

Figure 1
Democratic Odds Price and Popular Vote Margin, 1884–1940

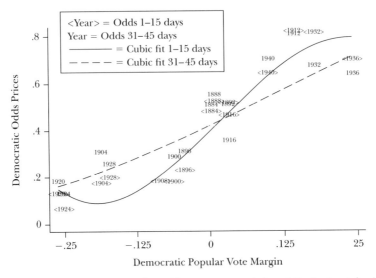

Notes: The vertical axis is the average market odds over some period, and the horizontal axis is the actual vote outcome. The regressions and averages are based on 417 observations of betting quotes for the period 1–15 days before the election and 65 observations for period 31–45 days before.

observation period. The solid line shows the best-fit cubic regression line using the outcome to "explain" the odds price 1–15 days before the election, while the dashed line shows the results for odds price 31–45 days prior. The relationship between odds prices and the eventual outcome was increasing over the 31–45 days period, indicating that market sentiment was reflecting the election probabilities. As Election Day approached, sentiment grew stronger in contests that would have a decisive outcome. That is, for the two weeks (1–15 days) just prior to the election, odds became much less favorable for the Democrat in elections he eventually lost by a significant margin and more favorable in those he won by a significant margin.

Another indication of the predictive power of the betting markets is that they were highly successful in identifying those elections—1884, 1888, 1892 and 1916— that would be very close (with vote margins of less than 3.5 percent). Figure 1 shows that the market odds correctly predicted these elections that would be tossups. In close elections where the final results were reported slowly—1876, 1884 and 1916—a vigorous postelection market emerged to allow further betting. Figure 2 presents daily odds price in 1916 from the New York market and the 2000 Iowa Electronic Markets Winner-Take-All contract, highlighting the postelection swings common to both of these two contests. (In the early morning following Election Day in 2000, the implicit odds on the Democrats fell to near zero in the Iowa Electronic Markets Winner-Take-All market. Because the Democrats won a plurality of the popular votes, which was the basis of the Iowa contract, the odds price rose to unity over the next day.)

When an election would be decided by a wide margin, the betting markets

Figure 2
Comparing 1916 and 2000 Elections

Panel A: New York Market for 1916 Election

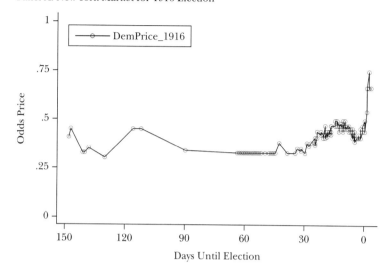

Panel B: Iowa Electronic Market Data for 2000 Election

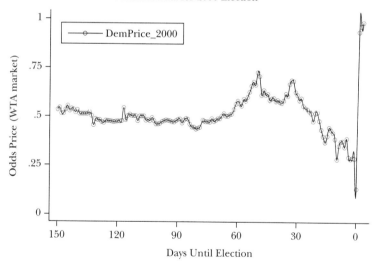

were generally successful in picking the winner early. Table 2 shows the dates when odds price permanently passed various thresholds for selected presidential races. In many elections decided by a wide margin, the odds price on the favorite started high and accelerated to still higher levels as Election Day approached. This pattern is illustrated in Figure 3, which compares the favorite's odds price in the 1924 New York betting market with those in the 1996 Iowa Electronic Markets Winner-Take-All contract.

Table 2
Date of Permanently Crossing Odds Price Thresholds in Selected Elections

Year	Candidate	Absolute popular vote margin	Days before election for odds prices:		
			0.66	*0.75*	*0.80*
1920	Harding	26.2%	125 days	49	43
1924	Coolidge	25.2	120	42	18
1936	F. Roosevelt	24.3	3	—	—
1904	T. Roosevelt	18.8	49	22	18
1932	F. Roosevelt	17.7	36	8	4
1928	Hoover	17.3	138	46	1
1912	Wilson	14.4	111	63	1
1900	McKinley	6.2	133	28	21
1908	Taft	8.4	115	115	6
1896	McKinley	4.4	97	7	1

Notes: The dates show when the odds price permanently passed various odds prices thresholds. In each case, the listed candidate won. The major party candidates in the races were as follows: 1920, Harding (R) vs. Cox (D); 1924, Coolidge (R) vs. Davis (D) and La Follette (Prog.); 1936, F. Roosevelt (D) vs. Landon (R); 1904, T. Roosevelt (R) vs. Parker (D); 1932, F. Roosevelt (D) vs. Hoover (R); 1928, Hoover (R) vs. Smith (D); 1912, Wilson (D) vs. Taft (R) and Roosevelt (Prog.); 1900, McKinley (R) vs. Bryan (D); 1908, Taft (R) vs. Bryan (D); 1896, McKinley (R) vs. Bryan (D). Source of Vote Margins is Historical Statistics, Y 79–83, pp. 1073–1074.

Betting Prices as Information

Covering developments in the Wall Street betting market was a staple of election reporting before World War II. Prior to the innovative polling efforts of Gallup, Roper and Crossley, the other information available about future election outcomes was limited to the results from early-season contests, overtly partisan canvasses and straw polls of unrepresentative and typically small samples. The largest and best-known nonscientific survey was the *Literary Digest* poll, which tabulated millions of returned postcard ballots that were mass mailed to a sample drawn from telephone directories and automobile registries. After predicting the presidential elections correctly from 1916 to 1932, the *Digest* famously called the 1936 contest for Landon in the election that F. Roosevelt won by the largest Electoral College landslide of all time. Notably, although the Democrat's odds prices were relatively low in 1936, the betting market did pick the winner correctly (see the third row of Table 2). The published price quotes allowed people who had not followed the election to catch up immediately. For example, when Andrew Carnegie returned in late October 1904 from his annual vacation to Scotland, he stated at his arrival press conference (*New York Times*, October 24, 1904, p. 1): "From what I see of the betting, . . . I do not think that Mr. Roosevelt will need my vote. I am sure of his election. . . ."

The betting quotes filled the demand for accurate odds from a public widely interested in wagering on elections. In this age before mass communication technologies reached into America's living rooms, election nights were highly social

Figure 3

Comparing the 1924 and 1996 Elections

Panel A: New York Market for 1924 Election

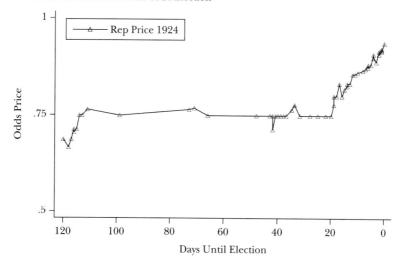

Panel B: Iowa Electronic Market Data for 1996 Election

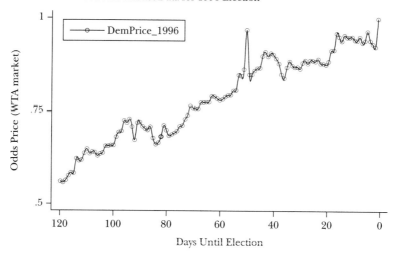

events, comparable to New Year's Eve or major football games. In large cities, crowds filled restaurants, hotels and sidewalks in downtown areas where newspapers and brokerage houses would publicize the latest returns and people with sporting inclinations would wager on the outcomes. Even for those who could not afford large stakes, betting in the run-up to elections was a cherished ritual. A widely held value was that one should be prepared to "back one's beliefs" either with money or more creative dares. Making freak bets—where the losing bettor literally ate crow, pushed the winner around in a wheelbarrow or engaged in similar public displays—was wildly popular. Gilliams (1901, p. 186) offered "a moderate estimate" that in the 1900 election "there were fully a half-million such [freak] bets—about one for every thirty voters." In this environment, it is hardly surprising that the leading newspapers kept their readership well informed about the latest market odds.

Markets versus Manipulation

Newspapers of this time couched their explanations of the accuracy of the Wall Street betting odds with analogies to stock prices. The *New York Times* wrote on October 7, 1924, (p. 18) "The Wall Street odds represent the consensus of a large body of extremely impartial opinion that talks with money and approaches Coolidge and Davis as dispassionately as it pronounces judgment on Anaconda and Bethlehem Steel." Similarly, a few days later another article in the *Times* explained (October 10, 1924, p. E9):

> Wall Street is always the place to which inside information comes on an election canvas . . . [and] it is a Wall Street habit, when risking a large amount of money, not to allow sentiment or partisanship to swerve judgments—an art learned in stock speculation; . . . any attempt to force odds in a direction unwarranted by the facts will always instantly attract money to the opposite side, precisely as overvaluation of a stock on the market will cause selling and its under-valuation will attract buying.

In the 1920s and 1930s, when betting activity moved toward specialist firms, the participants did not wait for political insiders to enter with private information, but instead began to conduct their own market analysis. According to a 1924 *Wall Street Journal* story (September 29, p. 13), the "betting firms maintain a statistical department for the benefit of their customers and also have a man present at the principal speeches made by the candidates. This man makes unbiased reports of the psychological reactions of the audiences." In 1936, according to the *Washington Post* (November 3, p. 16), upon becoming suspicious of the results of the *Literary Digest* canvas, Sam Boston, "American's most distinguished betting commissioner," began "conducting his own election poll."

At least two specific mechanisms could lead betting markets to aggregate information appropriately. The first case involves well-informed betting commissioners who serve as market makers and use their impartial beliefs to set the prices competitively. The commissioners have incentive to participate despite an absence of profit-making trades because they collect commissions. The second mechanism allows for partisan bettors lacking aggregate information. If each voter placed a one-dollar bet for his favorite candidate in a pari-mutuel, the betting totals would accurately pick the winner (though the price would not typically equal the probability of winning).

Working against the market forces leading to information aggregation were motivations to manipulate the odds for political gain. Given that the betting odds were taken as good indicators of the candidate's strength, the betting markets potentially provided a lever for influencing expectations. The newspapers periodically contained charges that partisans were manipulating the reported betting odds to create a bandwagon effect. This could happen if the reported betting was only a "wash sale" between confederates or it occurred outside the open market. Partisan newspapers also played a role through selective reporting. The most common thinking was that pushing up odds helped the preferred candidate by depressing the effort and turnout for the opposing candidate. If the marginal bettor was a partisan, was influenced by a manipulation or received information from a biased source, the markets would systematically err in their predictions.

The press did frequently refer to the betting activities of officials associated with the Republican and Democratic National Committees, with state party organizations from across the east and especially with Tammany Hall (the New York City Democratic machine). The newspapers recorded many betting and bluffing contests between Col. Thomas Swords, Sergeant of Arms of the National Republican Party, and Democratic betting agents representing Richard Croker, Boss of Tammany Hall, among others. In most but not all instances, these officials appear to bet in favor of their party's candidate; in the few cases where they took the other side, it was typically to hedge earlier bets.

However, there are only a few minor instances where market manipulation appears plausible. For example, in 1892, the Republican campaign managers went at midnight to the Hoffman House, the Democratic hangout, offering to bet large stakes at odds consistent with their candidate having a better than previously expected chance of winning. Only small fry were around, not the big Tammany money, so the offered large bets were not taken. The odds quoted in the newspapers made the Republican candidate appear stronger than he was (*New York Times*, November 8, 1892, p. 8).

Another barrier to accurate forecasts was the lack of national information sources. Over most of this period, news spread by telegraphs and was first made public in newspapers. As a result, news events might only slowly be reflected in prices. This effect might also dampen the odds price on favorites because there was always the possibility of latent bad news arriving. Also, since certain geographic areas received news later, a possibility existed of traders from information-rich areas earning excess returns, a topic we return to below.

One other potential friction did not prove to be problematic. The betting market repeatedly had to confront elections that were not decided until long after the polls closed. In the 1876 Hayes-Tilden race, the outcome was disputed for months after Election Day with the political parties charging each other with fraudulently manufacturing votes. A special Electoral Commission eventually resolved this hotly contested election on a strict party-line vote. The acrimony spilled over into the betting market, where John Morrissey, the leading New York poolseller (where the winners divide the total pool of money bet, minus the commission), opted to cancel the pools, returning the stakes minus his commission. This solution, while understandable, left many unsatisfied and contributed to the push in the next session of the New York legislature to outlaw pool-selling. In later years, betting commissioners handled contested elections by making the contracts contingent on whomever took office and by withholding payment until one candidate officially conceded. Indeed, they often kept the betting action alive. In the close 1884 election, betting lasted until the Friday after the election. In 1916, the leading betting commissioners did not settle up until November 23, almost two weeks after the polls closed. In the 1888 contest, when Harrison won the electoral college vote outright (233–168) and yet Cleveland very narrowly won the popular vote, settlement in favor of Harrison bettors occurred without a hitch.

Market Efficiency

In an efficient capital market, asset prices reflect all relevant information and thus provide the best prediction of future events given the current information (Roll, 1984). Because election bets are paid on victory (a binary event), efficient prices in this market should reflect the probabilities of the election outcomes. We now test whether the election betting market satisfies a standard set of efficiency conditions: arbitrage-free pricing, weak-, semistrong- and strong-form efficiency (Fama, 1970). Efficiency tests based on more structured models appear in Rhode and Strumpf (2004).

One of the weakest conditions for efficiency is arbitrage-free pricing, so that participants cannot instantly profit from simultaneously trading some set of contracts. In the context of election betting markets, the sum of the odds prices on all possible candidates cannot differ from a dollar by more than commission costs. For example, if the sum of prices on bets paying a dollar is strictly less than a dollar, then (abstracting from commissions) a trader can guarantee a profit by purchasing one share of each contract, since this ensures betting less than a dollar to win a dollar. We can evaluate this hypothesis in those elections when we observe the prices for all distinct contracts, as in 1912, 1916 and 1924. The arbitrage-free condition holds in most such cases, but it is violated for certain periods. For example, the Hughes and Wilson prices sum to less than a dollar during eight days in the beginning of September 1916, and the Wilson, Roosevelt and Taft prices sum to more than a dollar for the ten days just prior to the election in 1912. These differences are larger than the typical 5 percent commission rate, making arbitrage possible. Still, such violations are rare. In only 25 out of 807 observations are the sums far enough from one dollar to allow arbitrage. Moreover, it is unclear how many shares a participant could trade before altering the odds and eliminating the possibility of arbitrage.

A related arbitrage condition is the law of one price. This states that prices at different locations should be close enough, taking commission and transportation costs into account, that investors cannot simultaneously buy and sell contracts for a profit. The law of one price appears to hold for the various markets within New York City. Prices on a given contact usually differed by no more than a tick, and different newspapers reported that virtually the same odds were available on a given day (when listings are available from multiple newspapers, the correlation coefficient for the prices is 0.983 with $N = 344$). Cursory evidence indicates price variations across U. S. cities existed, but tended to be small.[3] We also know that investors actively worked to arbitrage pricing gaps and that at least one betting commissioner maintained offices in both New York and Chicago (*Washington Post*, November 1, 1932, p. 9).

A capital market is weak-form efficient if historical asset prices cannot be used to devise profitable trading rules. A loose implication of weak-form efficiency is that it is not possible to forecast prices using lagged price data, implying prices follow a random walk. Consistent with this, we find it is not possible to reject the hypothesis that daily odds prices follow a random walk in our 1884–1940 sample ($N = 236$).[4] Another test considers whether price changes can be forecast using historical data. When we regress the change in daily prices on its lags, the lagged prices do not have statistically significant effects ($N = 120$).[5] These simple tests are broadly consistent with weak-form efficiency and parallel results for the presidential betting markets in the Iowa Electronic Markets (Berg, Nelson and Reitz, 2003).

A capital market satisfies semistrong-form efficiency if an investor cannot expect to make excess returns based on publicly available information. A simple if low-powered test is to examine whether one could use generally available information to devise a betting rule that would yield profits above the commission costs. We experimented with three simple rules involving buying a single contract paying one dollar on 1) the Democrat; 2) the market favorite; or 3) the party in power. We also consider the alternative of betting one dollar (instead of buying one contract) on

---

[3] As examples, a 1888 *Chicago Tribune* survey of 10 major cities on election eve revealed the coefficient of variation of the odds prices was only 5.1 percent (November 6, 1888, p. 3), and a similar *New York World* survey of 13 cities in 1916 have a coefficient of variation of 4.6 percent (November 7, 1916, p. 1).

[4] We estimate the equation

$$\text{price}_{it} = \alpha + \beta \times \text{price}_{it-1} + u_{it}$$

where price_{it} is the price of some contract in election i occurring at day t and price_{it-1} is a lag of price. The estimated βs are 1.01, 1.01 and 0.99 for Democrat, Incumbent and Market Favorite party contracts, and these are statistically indistinguishable from unity (using classical or robust standard errors); the estimated αs are each indistinguishable from zero. We find similar results for an AR(2) process. Note this approach may be misspecified because efficiently priced options with termination dates can have a deterministic drift. Intuitively, as Election Day approaches, uncertainty about the outcome is likely to diminish because more voters make up their minds and there are fewer opportunities for an "October surprise." The favorite's probability of victory (and thus his market price) increases to one—as illustrated in Figure 3—while that of the underdog falls to zero. After accounting for these effects, we still cannot reject weak-form efficiency. See Rhode and Strumpf (2004) for a detailed theoretical and empirical treatment of this issue.

[5] The equation we estimate is

$$\Delta\text{price}_{it} = \beta_0 + \beta_1 \times \Delta\text{price}_{it-1} + \beta_2 \times \Delta\text{price}_{it-2} + u_{it},$$

where the variables are defined in the previous note. The estimated (β_1, β_2)s are $(-0.24, 0.14)$, $(-0.26, 0.12)$ and $(-0.20, 0.14)$ for Democrat, Incumbent and Market Favorite party contracts, and these are statistically indistinguishable from zero using robust standard errors. When just a single price lag is used, the estimated parameters are significantly negative. However, we find somewhat analogous results in analyzing the Democrat party contract for the Iowa Electronic Markets Winner-Take-All presidential market using daily price data from 1992, 1996 and 2000.

each of these choices, which places more weight on longshots. We found that buying one-dollar contracts on the Democrats, favorites and members of the incumbent party tended to be winning strategies over the 1884–1940 period.[6] However, the positive returns are not at all robust. The winning strategies typically yielded small net returns relative to their standard deviations. Moreover, strategies that made money in the first half of the time period (such as betting against the favorite) often lost in the second half of the time period. Some choices made money when the strategy was implemented in the form of betting one dollar, but not in the form of buying one contract, or vice versa. These results, as well as the more formal tests reported in Rhode and Strumpf (2004), suggest that it was difficult to use public information to construct a winning betting strategy. Again, the modern Iowa Electronic Market provides a useful benchmark. For the 1992–2000 period, we found that its Winner-Take-All bets allowed similar profitable opportunities—although this result should be viewed with caution given the small number of elections in the Iowa data.

Finally, we consider strong-form efficiency, which involves whether an investor can earn excess profits using private information. While this hypothesis is difficult to quantify, there are several reports of insiders profiting from superior information about specific states. In 1916, for example, some west coast investors wagered heavily on Wilson because they believed he would achieve an upset win in California, which he did (*Wall Street Journal,* October 31, 1916, p. 8). Leveraging on superior local information, several Ohioans fronted by the famous New York boxing promoter Tex Rickard (who was the main force behind the building of Madison Square Garden) placed a $60,000 wager on Wilson to win their state (*New York Times,* October 28, 1916, p. 1). These beliefs must have been strong ones, because the wager moved the odds price by nearly ten percentage points, and again the investors proved correct. It seems that insiders were able to profit from their information advantage, but rejections of strong efficiency are typical of most capital markets.

In conclusion, the historical betting markets do not meet all of the exacting conditions for efficiency, but the deviations were not usually large enough to generate consistently profitable betting strategies using public information.[7] The performance of the market was comparable to its modern counterparts and, given the barriers to efficiency discussed earlier, quite remarkable.

---

[6] The result for favorites is of interest since it suggests the possibility that markets did not place a high enough probability on the favorite, which is consistent with the favorite-long shot bias observed in racetrack betting (Thaler and Ziemba, 1988). One explanation for this finding is the role of commissions when one party is the heavy favorite. Suppose the Democrats are known to be more than 95 percent likely to win a contest. A bookmaker cannot offer these objective odds because the bettors will not be able to overcome the standard 5 percent commission. Hence, market odds must be biased down in such extreme election cases. The result concerning the underpricing of Democrats might reflect the influence of wealthier, partisan Republican bettors.

[7] The wager markets on state election outcomes over this time period more convincingly fail the efficiency conditions. Rhode and Strumpf (2004) devise various profitable betting strategies based on public information. This result is unsurprising given that the state markets were far thinner than the national market.

The Decline of Political Wagering

The newspapers reported substantially less betting activity in specific contests and especially after 1940. In part, this reduction in reporting reflected a growing reluctance of newspapers to give publicity to activities that many considered unethical. There were frequent complaints that election betting was immoral and contrary to republican values. Among the issues that critics raised were moral hazard, election tampering, information withholding and strategic manipulation.[8]

In response to such concerns, New York state laws did increasingly attempt to limit organized election betting. Casual bets between private individuals always remained legal in New York. However, even an otherwise legal private bet on elections technically disqualified the participants from voting—although this provision was rarely enforced—and the legal system also discouraged using the courts to collect gambling debts. Antigambling laws passed in New York during the late 1870s and the late 1900s appear to put a damper on election betting, but in both cases, the market bounced back after the energy of the moral reformers flagged. Ultimately, New York's legalization of pari-mutuel betting on horse races in 1939 may have done more to reduce election betting than any antigambling policing. With horseracing, individuals interested in gambling could wager on several contests promising immediate rewards each day, rather than waiting through one long political contest.

New York state was not alone in changing the legal and regulatory environment for election betting activity. The New York Stock Exchange and the Curb Market also periodically tried to crack down. The exchanges characteristically did not like the public to associate their socially productive risk-sharing and risk-taking functions with gambling on inherently zero-sum public or sporting events. In the 1910s and again after the mid-1920s, the stock exchanges passed regulations to reduce the public involvement of their members. In May 1924, for example, both the New York Stock Exchange and the Curb Market passed resolutions expressly barring their members from engaging in election gambling. After that, while betting activity continued to be reported in the newspapers, the articles rarely named the participants. During the 1930s, the press noted that securities of private electrical utilities had effectively become wagers on Roosevelt (on the grounds that New Deal policy initiatives such as the formation of the Securities and Exchange Commission and the Tennessee Valley Authority constrained the profits of existing private utilities).

A final force pushing election betting underground was the rise of scientific polling. For newspapers, one of the functions of reporting Wall Street betting odds had been to provide the best available aggregate information. Following the success of Gallup in predicting the 1936 election, many newspapers stopped lending credence to the *Literary Digest* poll. The scientific polls, available on a weekly basis,

---

[8] For selected historical criticisms of election betting, see *New York Tribune*, November 18, 1888, p. 6; *New York Times*, October 28, 1896, p. 1; November 3, 1896, p. 2; *Washington Post*, October 28, 1912, p. 2. For a recent discussion, see Hanson (2003).

provided the media with a ready substitute for the betting odds, one not subject to the moral objections against gambling. Our survey of the *Washington Post* and *New York Times* indicates that articles on the *Literary Digest* poll began to outnumber those on election betting in 1924 and 1928, respectively. Articles related to the Gallup poll began to appear in 1936 and to outnumber those in the other two categories by 1940. Whatever election betting continued to occur received far less media attention.

Lessons for the Future

Wagering on presidential elections has a long tradition in the United States, with large and often well-organized markets operating for over three-quarters of a century before World War II. The resulting betting odds proved remarkably prescient and almost always correctly predicted election outcomes well in advance, despite the absence of scientific polls. This historical experience suggests a promising role for other prediction markets. Our analysis complements a substantial body of experimental research that has hinted that asset markets can successfully aggregate information (Forsythe, Palfrey and Plott, 1982; Plott and Sunder, 1988). The informational efficiency of prediction markets has also been investigated in the field, such as Camerer's (1998) study of the difficulty of manipulating racetrack pari-mutuel betting and Leigh, Wolfers and Zitzewitz's (2003) study of futures markets on war probabilities.

However, recent experience indicates public skepticism about applying markets to novel situations. In summer 2003, word leaked out that the Department of Defense was considering setting up a Policy Analysis Market, somewhat similar to the Iowa Electronic Market, which would seek to provide a market consensus about the likelihood of international political developments, especially in the Middle East. Critics argued that this market was subject to manipulation by insiders and might allow extremists to profit financially from their actions. But these concerns were also evident in the historical wagering on presidential elections, with partisans serving as active participants and contemporary fears of election tampering. Although large sums of money were at stake in the historical presidential betting markets, we are not aware of any evidence that the political process was seriously corrupted by the presence of a wagering market. There are obviously important differences between the proposed Policy Analysis Market and the New York betting market, but the experience described in this paper suggests that many current concerns about the appropriateness of prediction markets are not well founded in the historical record.

■ *We thank Patrick Conway, Lee Craig, Thomas Geraghty, James Hines, Thomas Mroz, Mark Stegeman, Timothy Taylor, Michael Waldman and Justin Wolfers for comments and suggestions.*

References

Berg, Joyce, Forrest Nelson and Thomas Rietz. 2003. "Accuracy and Forecast Standard Error of Prediction Markets." Working paper, University of Iowa.

Camerer, Colin. 1998. "Can Asset Markets be Manipulated? A Field Experiment with Racetrack Betting." *Journal of Political Economy.* 106:3, pp. 457–82.

Fama, Eugene. 1970. "Efficient Capital Markets: A Review of Theory and Empirical Work." *Journal of Finance.* 25:2, pp. 383–417.

Forsythe, Robert, Thomas Palfrey and Charles Plott. 1982. "Asset Valuation in an Experimental Market." *Econometrica.* 50:3, pp. 537–68.

Gilliams, E. Leslie. 1901. "Election Bets in America." *Strand Magazine.* 21, pp. 185–91.

Hanson, Robin. 2003. "Shall We Vote on Values, But Bet on Beliefs?" Working paper, George Mason, September.

Leigh, Andrew, Justin Wolfers and Eric Zitzewitz. 2003. "What Do Financial Markets Think of War in Iraq?" NBER Working Paper No. 9587.

Plott, Charles and Shyam Sunder. 1988. "Rational Expectations and the Aggregation of Diverse Information in Laboratory Security Markets." *Econometrica.* 56:5, pp. 1085–118.

Rhode, Paul and Koleman Strumpf. 2004. "Historical Prediction Markets: Wagering on Presidential Elections." Working paper.

Roll, Richard. 1984. "Orange Juice and Weather." *American Economic Review.* 74:5, pp. 861–80.

Thaler, Richard and William Ziemba. 1988. "Parimutuel Betting Markets: Racetracks and Lotteries." *Journal of Economic Perspectives.* Spring, 2:2, pp. 161–74.

Thoreau, Henry David. 1848 [1967]. *The Variorum Civil Disobedience.* New York: Twayne.

Journal of Economic Perspectives—Volume 18, Number 2—Spring 2004—Pages 143–160

Making a Name: Women's Surnames at Marriage and Beyond

Claudia Goldin and Maria Shim

Throughout U.S. history, few women have deviated from the custom of taking their husband's name (Stannard, 1977). The earliest known instance of a U.S. woman who retained her surname upon marriage is Lucy Stone, the tireless antislavery and female suffrage crusader, who married in 1855. In the 1920s, a generation after her death in 1893, prominent feminists formed the Lucy Stone League to help married women preserve the identity of their own surnames. But until the late 1970s, almost all women, even the highly educated and eminent, assumed their husband's surname upon marriage. When prominent women who married before the 1970s wished to keep their maiden names as part of their professional image, they sometimes used their maiden names as their middle names, like the U.S. Supreme Court Justices Ruth Bader Ginsburg and Sandra Day O'Connor.

Ordinary observation suggests that during the past 25 to 30 years, the fraction of college graduate women retaining their surnames has greatly increased. But the basic facts concerning women's surnames as a social indicator have eluded investigation because none of the usual data sets contains the current married and maiden surnames of women. This article seeks to estimate the fraction of women who are "keepers" and the factors that have prompted women to retain their surnames.

We use three complementary sources—*New York Times* wedding announcements, Harvard alumni records and Massachusetts birth records—to examine patterns of surname retention. The *New York Times* and Harvard alumni records include college graduates almost exclusively. But because non-college graduate women retain their surnames with far less frequency than college graduate women

■ *Claudia Goldin is Henry Lee Professor of Economics, Harvard University, Cambridge, Massachusetts. She can be reached at ⟨cgoldin@harvard.edu⟩. Maria Shim graduated in the Harvard University class of 2001 and is currently working in San Francisco, California.*

(less than one-third as often, according to the birth record data), our concentration on the latter is deliberate. Each data set we use covers a select group of women and contains data on their surnames at particular life cycle moments. The *New York Times* gives surnames at the moment of marriage. The alumni records for Harvard undergraduates give surnames at marriage and beyond, while the Massachusetts birth records reveal a mother's surname at the moment of her child's birth. Thus, part of our task is to resolve differences in estimates from each of these sources and to extrapolate from these groups to all college graduate women.

A woman who keeps her name at marriage may not retain her name throughout her married life. The arrival of children, for example, might lead her to change her name to avoid the possible confusion of having two last names in one household. We have found, however, that among the Harvard class of 1980, in which 52 percent of women kept their names upon marriage, just 10 percent reverted to their husband's names subsequently. We discuss the details of this sample later.

We begin with a brief overview of the legal, social and economic changes that led more women to keep their surnames at marriage. We find that the fraction of all U.S. college graduate women who kept their surnames upon marriage rose from about 2 to 4 percent around 1975 to just below 20 percent in 2001. It seems likely that the fraction of women "keeping" their maiden name rose sharply in the 1970s and 1980s, but declined slightly in the 1990s.

Legal, Social and Economic Change in the 1970s

Custom was largely responsible for the preponderance of women who did not keep their surnames at marriage. But the legal, social and economic institutions supporting this custom began to shift in the 1970s: the laws that pressured women to take their husband's names changed; the appellation "Ms." became acceptable; the age at first marriage rose; and the number of advanced academic degrees received by women increased.

Under common law, a married woman is not compelled to take her husband's surname, yet the laws of various states have deprived women of rights, such as retaining their driver's license and voter registration, if they did not assume the surname of their husband. It was not until 1975, for example, that the Supreme Court of Tennessee in *Dunn v. Palermo* (522 S.W. 2d 679) struck down a law requiring that a married woman register to vote under her husband's surname. The court cited the state constitution's adoption of common law under which, with few exceptions, an individual can choose any name. By the mid-1970s, these legal restrictions were generally overturned or ignored (for example, Augustine-Adams, 1997).

Back in 1855, Lucy Stone bore the appellation "Miss," which was otherwise reserved for unmarried women. For many decades, most women who retained their maiden name also retained the title "Miss." The appellation "Ms." solved the obvious social problem of what to call a married woman who retained her surname. Although, according to the *Oxford English Dictionary*, the use of "Ms." dates from

1952, the term did not gain much notice until the appearance of *Ms. Magazine* in 1972. Usage spread rapidly, but there was initial resistance. In 1984, the *New York Times* (May 24, 1984, p. C10) reported of Gloria Steinem's fiftieth birthday party, "that proceeds from the . . . dinner will go to the Ms. Foundation . . . which publishes Ms. Magazine where Miss Steinem works as an editor."

Not until June 20, 1986, did the *New York Times* (p. B1) announce: "Beginning today, the *New York Times* will use 'Ms.' as an honorific in its news and editorial columns. Until now, 'Ms.' had not been used because of the belief that it had not passed sufficiently into the language to be accepted as common usage. The *Times* now believes that 'Ms.' has become a part of the language and is changing its policy. The *Times* will continue to use 'Miss' or 'Mrs.' when it knows the marital status of a woman in the news, unless she prefers 'Ms.' 'Ms.' will also be used when a woman's marital status is not known."

The age at first marriage among college graduate women increased substantially with cohorts born after 1950. Cohorts born from the 1930s to 1950 married within a year or two after college graduation. In the 1950 cohort, for example, more than 50 percent married before they turned 23 years old. But for those born in 1957, just 30 percent married before age 23 and less than half the cohort had married by the time they were 25 years old. Between the cohorts born from 1950 to 1957, the median age at first marriage among college graduate women increased by two years. The median college graduate woman born in 1950 married in 1973; the median college graduate woman born in 1957 married in 1982. Median age at first marriage for the 1965 birth cohort was about 26.5 years.[1]

At the same time that the age at first marriage rose, the fraction of college graduate women continuing their education in professional and Ph.D. programs began to soar. For example, in the mid-1960s, the ratio of first-year female law students to female B.A.'s was 0.5 percent. By 1980, it was 3.3 percent—a nearly seven-fold increase. In the field of medicine, the ratio of female first-year medical students to female B.A.'s was 0.4 percent in the mid-1960s; by the early 1980s, the figure had tripled to 1.2 percent (Goldin and Katz, 2002). Among Ph.D.'s granted (excluding those in education), the increase from 1970 to 1990 was about 1.7 times. For Ph.D. programs, the increase has continued beyond the early 1980s, whereas in law and medicine the ratio of female first-year students to female B.A.'s has remained at about the level achieved in 1980.[2]

The Pill—the female oral contraceptive—began to diffuse among young single women in the late 1960s and early 1970s, even though it had rapidly spread among *married* women within a few years after its federal approval in 1960. The reason for the later diffusion of the Pill among young unmarried women concerns a set of

[1] Estimates of age at first marriage are from the Current Population Survey, Fertility and Marital History Supplement, 1990 and 1995. See also Goldin and Katz (2002). The age at first marriage is from 1995 data, thus the fraction married is truncated at age 45 for the 1950 cohort and at age 38 for the 1957 cohort. The potential bias is to understate the median age at first marriage for the younger cohort.
[2] It should be noted that the fraction of (U.S. native-born) women who completed at least four years of college was fairly stable at 25 percent by age 35 for cohorts born from 1950 to 1960, after which it began a meteoric rise to today's level of around 35 percent (De Long, Goldin and Katz 2003).

restrictive laws and social norms, both of which changed in the late 1960s (Goldin and Katz, 2002).

Armed with the Pill, a young woman could minimize the unintended pregnancy consequences of sex and delay marriage. She could plan an independent existence at an early age—one not defined solely by marriage and motherhood. She could enter an advanced degree or professional program with far greater assurance that an active sexual life would not jeopardize her studies. By increasing the age at first marriage and allowing more women to continue with their studies, the Pill was one important cause of the increase in surname retention.

For all of these reasons, one would expect college graduate women to have retained their surnames to a far greater extent beginning sometime between the late 1970s and the early 1980s. Taken together, these factors suggest that more women found themselves in a situation where they had already "made a name" for themselves in a profession, business or among friends and colleagues before marriage. Like the brand names of consumer goods, women elected to keep their surnames to protect the value of their contacts, publications and professional goodwill. A greater number of women might also have kept their surnames as a means of preserving their personal identity (Akerlof and Kranton, 2000), along with their professional one. Davis and Robinson (1988) offer some supporting sociological evidence on how women versus men defined their identities within marriage across the 1970s and 1980s. Thus, there was both a greater incentive for women to keep their surnames and doing so became easier both legally and socially.

The social pressure for women to change their names upon marriage has lessened, but still exists. Yet the act of marriage is not enough to accomplish a name change. A certificate of marriage simply enables the woman to change her name without filing further legal documents. There is no single place in the U.S. government that stores your "legal" name. Rather, the new bride must write to various authorities to change her name on, for example, her driver's license, vehicle title, voter registration, U.S. passport, bank records, credit cards, medical records, insurance forms, wills, contracts and, most importantly, Social Security and Internal Revenue Service documents. To make the process less cumbersome, "bride name change kits" tailored for each state are sold on the Internet.

Levels and Trends in Surname Retention

The data sets we have compiled, when used in tandem, can reveal the levels and trends in surname retention from 1975 to the present. We first discuss data from wedding announcements in the *New York Times* from the mid-1970s to 2001; then data from Massachusetts birth records from 1990 to 2000; and finally data from the Harvard class of 1980. Each of these data sets presents the researcher with problems of selection and coverage, which we will discuss as they arise.

Evidence from the *New York Times*

Wedding announcements are typically submitted by the couple to the *New York Times* and then selected by the staff. The announcements generally provide information on the bride's and the groom's undergraduate colleges as well as their advanced degrees and schools, their occupations, parents' occupation(s), place of marriage and who officiated at the ceremony. Announcements in the *Times* are mainly about couples whose families reside in the greater New York City region and who are sufficiently prominent or newsworthy to merit inclusion. The *Times* sample is therefore skewed toward more prominent families independent of where the couple went to college.

The data come from the "society page" of the Sunday Style Section of the *Times*. We compiled two types of samples: a time-series sample containing data on surname retention from 1975 to 2001 and two cross-sections, containing all available information on every marriage announcement in 1991 and 2001. The time-series information was recorded from marriage (not engagement) announcements for eight weekends; specifically, every sixth weekend beginning with the first weekend in February and ending in December. (Beginning in 1995, marriage announcements appear only in the Sunday edition of the *Times*.) This procedure created a data set of 250 to 300 marriages per year and almost 7,000 for the 26-year period. For the cross-section data sets, we collected variables on announcement date, names and ages of bride and bridegroom, religious or civil nature of the ceremony and the place, occupations and education of bride and bridegroom and occupations of both sets of parents.

The reason for using 1991 and 2001 as the basis for the cross-section data is that it was not until 1989 that announcements routinely gave the age of the bride and groom, and age is an important factor in determining whether a woman will change her name. We stopped the data collection in 2001 because by 2002, the *Times* altered its coverage in ways that made comparability to previous years more difficult. For example, it expanded its coverage to include "commitment" ceremonies of single-sex couples, and over the late 1990s, it appears to have broadened the selected couples by race and ethnicity. More important for our coding, the announcements changed their format to one that is often more chatty and personal. A substantial fraction of them are now impossible to code with respect to surname retention by the bride, which is the main focus of our investigation.[3]

In writing an announcement, the editor uses information provided by the couple regarding education, occupation and type of ceremony. Other material, including the surname the bride will use after the wedding, is gathered by a *Times* fact-checker *after* the announcement is selected for inclusion. In our count, brides are coded as "keepers" if they stated they would retain their surnames socially and/or professionally. All others are deemed "changers"—those taking the groom's surname, those hyphenating their names and those for whom no information is given (they either chose not to provide the information or the writer

---

[3] For another article using the *Times* data to explore "nonconventional" names, see Scheuble, Klingemann and Johnson (2000).

chose not to include it). The "no information" category is often a large fraction of the total, and we have found that it almost always consists of women who changed their name.

Table 1 provides the categorization of name-keepers and changers from the *New York Times* data. The basic story is that the fraction keeping their surnames was 2 percent in 1975 and 4 percent in 1976, but increased to about 10 percent by 1980 and then to 20 percent by the mid-1980s. A plateau of around 20 percent was maintained for about ten years. The fraction increased once again after 1998, and the latest data show that about 33 percent of brides will keep their surnames. However, interpreting these data raises a number of questions.

We attempted to get a feel for how the *Times* collected this information and what changes have occurred over time by direct communication with Robert Woletz, the current Society News editor.[4] For example, Woletz said that beginning in 1999 *Times* fact-checkers explicitly asked the couple if the bride was keeping her surname for all functions or just "professionally." This change does not seem to have had much influence in our data, since the broad trends of "keepers" are given by those who keep their surname for all functions. Clearly, not too much should be made of year-to-year variation in this data, and even the broad trends must be interpreted with care.

Second, we classify those whose announcements did not reveal name change or retention information as "changers." The large variation over time in the fraction of announcements that gave no information on surname retention should not be too disturbing since writing styles differ among those crafting the announcements, and there is turnover in the position of "wedding announcement writer." It seems clear to us that the vast majority of those with no information given in the announcement were changers and this is probably true even for couples who did not offer such information to the fact-checker. In the late 1970s and early 1980s, the relatively small share of those who felt strongly enough to keep their surname seem unlikely to have held back from telling the *Times* about it. Also, we matched a few of the brides to our data from the Harvard class of 1980, and those whose announcements did not reveal anything about their surname after marriage were unanimously "changers."

Third, we are fairly confident that the rise in "keepers" from the mid-1970s to the mid-1980s and the flattening of that trend in the 1990s both reflect real phenomena; as we will see, it is confirmed by the other data sources. However, we

---

[4] According to Robert Woletz, Society News editor of the *New York Times* (personal correspondence with Goldin), inclusion in the *Times* reflects the "newsworthiness" of the wedding. Woletz also informed Goldin that the "fact checker" asks the couple if the bride will retain her maiden name socially or professionally or if the bride will change her name to that of her future husband or if the bride (and groom) will hyphenate their names. Some couples report to the fact checker that they have not thought seriously about the issue. In that case, the writer uses an oblique reference to "the bride" and "the groom." The information provided by Woletz is relevant to the *Times* in 2002 and for several years before. Woletz did not know what previous procedures had been. Woletz would not comment on the relative numbers of submitted and accepted announcements nor on the possibility that "newsworthiness" changed over time.

Table 1

Keepers and Changers in *New York Times* Sample: 1975 to 2001

	(1)	(2)	(3)	(4)	(5)	(6)	(7)	(8)
	Keeps surname			*Changes surname*				
Year	*For all functions*	*Only professionally*	*"Keepers" (1) + (2)*	*Hyphen surname*	*Take husband's surname*	*No information listed*	*"Changers" (4) + (5) + (6)*	*Number of observations*
1975	na	na	0.020	0.005	0.377	0.598	0.980	204
1976	na	na	0.040	0.023	0.364	0.572	0.960	173
1977	na	na	0.069	0.000	0.328	0.603	0.931	204
1978	na	na	0.098	0.000	0.392	0.510	0.902	153
1979	na	na	0.093	0.005	0.252	0.650	0.907	214
1980	0.078	0.012	0.090	0.000	0.213	0.697	0.910	244
1981	0.061	0.024	0.086	0.004	0.318	0.592	0.914	245
1982	0.074	0.026	0.100	0.000	0.258	0.642	0.900	229
1983	0.093	0.048	0.141	0.011	0.256	0.593	0.859	270
1984	0.122	0.057	0.179	0.022	0.367	0.432	0.821	229
1985	0.143	0.121	0.264	0.004	0.468	0.264	0.736	231
1986	0.108	0.118	0.226	0.018	0.570	0.186	0.774	279
1987	0.096	0.092	0.188	0.018	0.401	0.393	0.813	272
1988	0.105	0.119	0.224	0.018	0.412	0.347	0.776	277
1989	0.172	0.027	0.199	0.021	0.620	0.160	0.801	332
1990	0.208	0.003	0.211	0.032	0.668	0.090	0.789	379
1991	0.201	0.003	0.205	0.014	0.597	0.184	0.795	293
1992	0.190	0.004	0.194	0.061	0.706	0.039	0.806	279
1993	0.220	0.000	0.220	0.048	0.560	0.173	0.780	336
1994	0.167	0.009	0.176	0.027	0.421	0.376	0.824	330
1995	0.213	0.000	0.213	0.034	0.456	0.297	0.788	320
1996	0.177	0.000	0.177	0.038	0.550	0.235	0.823	260
1997	0.163	0.000	0.163	0.019	0.504	0.311	0.837	258
1998	0.184	0.000	0.184	0.041	0.461	0.314	0.816	245
1999	0.209	0.055	0.264	0.034	0.464	0.238	0.736	235
2000	0.259	0.079	0.339	0.017	0.456	0.188	0.661	239
2001	0.237	0.089	0.326	0.032	0.465	0.177	0.674	1315

Note: na = not available; the information on professional versus for all functions was not taken for those years because the fractions keeping were very small.
Source: New York Times Time-Series Data Set, 1975 to 2001, described in the text. The data sample is much larger in 2001 because all of the entries for the year were used, not just the sample of eight weekends used for the other years.

are less certain as to whether the increase in keeping starting around 1998 reflects a real phenomenon, rather than some change in how the *Times* was selecting the weddings that it would cover. We will return to this subject as we discuss the other data sources.

Finally, it is instructive to use the *Times* data to estimate the rate of keepers in the general population. After all, *Times* weddings are not representative of those of all college graduates. *Times* brides are older than the average college graduate bride and are disproportionately from the eastern United States, graduates of elite private colleges and universities and possessors of advanced degrees. Our approach here, using the detailed cross-section data for 2001, is to calculate an ordinary least squares linear probability regression in which the dependent variable is whether the woman kept her name. The independent variables are the bride's age, college characteristics and advanced degree, as shown in Table 2. The coefficients from the regression appear in column 1. When multiplied by the means of the *Times* 2001 data, given in column 2, they produce the results in column 4. The sum (given in the last row) is 0.323, meaning that about 32 percent of college-age women kept their surnames upon marriage in 2001 (about the same as the 2001 cell in column 3, Table 1). However, column 3 presents the independent variable means for the relevant U.S. population. Multiplying these means by the coefficients in column 1 has the effect of weighting the variables by the national averages. The resulting estimate, summed in the last row of column 5, is 0.185, meaning that 18.5 percent of college graduate women in the United States kept their names after marriage in 2001.

Looking more closely at the table, the most quantitatively important factor in the adjustment is age. Whereas 26 percent of all brides in 2001 were between 20 and 24 years, just 5 percent of those in the *Times* were. It is possible that the *Times* data are biased downward because of a selection on family background characteristics that are not observable to the researcher. It should be noted that we could not adjust for region since too few of the couples were from outside the east, and this bias could go in the opposite direction.

Evidence from Massachusetts Birth Records

Massachusetts is the only state (of which we are aware) that has publicly available birth records that include information on mother's surname, father's surname, parity (number of births to the mother) and mother's education and age, among other variables. Such data are available from Massachusetts since 1987. Various other states also have publicly available birth records, but do not have the actual surname of the mother and, instead, list only her "maiden" name. We use publicly available Massachusetts birth records for 1990, 1995 and 2000. We matched the parents' surnames (using, at most, the first five letters of each name) to determine whether the mother had a surname different from that of the father. All parents in the sample were legally married prior to the birth of the child. We looked only at first births.

An unmistakable aspect of the Massachusetts data, graphed in Figure 1, is the decrease in the fraction of "keepers" during the 1990s.[5] This finding holds for all college graduates and also for those who continued beyond their B.A. Whereas 21 percent of college, graduate (white, U.S.-born) women having their first child at 25 to 29 years were "keepers" in 1990, just 13 percent were in 2000. For those with more than four years of college, the decrease was from 29 percent to 20 percent.

A more detailed analysis of these data brings out some additional findings. At

---

[5] We have omitted mothers under 25 years old, because they were a small fraction of the college graduate group. For example, among white, U.S.-born, first-birth, college graduate women, 4.9 percent were under age 25 in 1990, 3.3 percent in 1995 and 2.1 percent in 2000.

Table 2

"Nationalizing" the *Times* 2001 Cross-Section

(Dependent Variable for Col. (1): Keeps surname at marriage)

Variables	(1) Coefficient	(2)	(3)	(4)	(5)
		Means of independent variables		Computation of predicted values	
		Times 2001	*U.S.*	*Times* 2001 (1) × (2)	*U.S.* (1) × (3)
Constant	0.450	1	1	0.450	0.450
Bride characteristics					
Ages 20 to 24	−0.492	0.0478	0.259	−0.0235	−0.127
Ages 25 to 29	−0.347	0.409	0.420	−0.1419	−0.146
Ages 30 to 34	−0.211	0.372	0.107	−0.0785	−0.0226
Ages 35 to 39	−0.0492	0.104	0.074	−0.0051	−0.0036
Ages 40 plus (omitted)	0	0.0672	0.043	0	0
Ivy league college	0.158	0.271	0.014	0.0428	0.0022
"Top 25" liberal arts college	0.145	0.0805	0.010	0.0117	0.0015
"Top 25" university	0.0924	0.128	0.0575	0.0118	0.0053
"Seven sisters" college	0.182	0.0414	0.003	0.0075	0.0005
M.A.	0.0422	0.296	0.35	0.0125	0.0148
M.B.A.	−0.0291	0.0821	0.05	−0.0024	−0.0015
J.D.	0.109	0.15	0.03	0.0164	0.0033
M.D., D.D.S., or D.V.M.	0.241	0.0606	0.015	0.0146	0.0036
Ph.D.	0.134	0.0566	0.03	0.0076	0.0043
Number of observations	1,255	1,255			
Predicted values, Σ (4) or (5)				0.323	0.185

Notes and Sources: The column (1) coefficients are from a standard OLS regression where the dependent variable is 0 or 1 depending on whether the woman kept her surname at marriage. Colleges are categorized using the 2001 *U.S. News and World Report* rankings, and the categories are unique; for example, the "top 25 universities" category omits the Ivy League institutions. The "top 25 universities" (minus the Ivies) are CalTech, Carnegie, Duke, Emory, Georgetown, Hopkins, MIT, Northwestern, Notre Dame, Rice, Stanford, UC Berkeley, UCLA, Virginia, Chicago, Michigan, North Carolina, Vanderbilt and Washington University. The top 25 liberal arts colleges (excluding the "seven sisters" that were in the top 25) are Amherst, Bates, Bowdoin, Carleton, Claremont-McKenna, Colby, Colgate, Davidson, Grinnell, Hamilton, Haverford, Middlebury, Oberlin, Pomona, Swarthmore, Trinity, University of the South, Washington and Lee, Wesleyan and Williams. The "seven sisters" school category includes Bryn Mawr, Mount Holyoke, Radcliffe, Sarah Lawrence, Smith, Wellesley and Vassar, although most are no longer single sex, and one (Radcliffe) merged with Harvard University in 1972. Professional and graduate degrees are not mutually exclusive; that is, a woman could list both an M.A. and a Ph.D. or an M.D. and a Ph.D., although it was usual for the bride to list her highest post-baccalaureate degree.

For the U.S. means in column (2), the age distribution for "married within the year" is derived from the percentage ever married in the Current Population Survey January 2002 for all college graduate (B.A. or more) women. The derivation implicitly assumes that the distribution of the age at first marriage does not change over the period considered. For the distribution of institutions we use data for 1997/1998, when there were about 1.184 million B.A.'s produced. The fraction in the "top 25" universities includes a somewhat wider group (it includes the top 30 in *U.S. News and World Report* excluding the Ivies) than that defined in the *Times* data set. The *Times* weddings are disproportionately those from the greater New York City area, and we could not, in coding the colleges and universities, include a broader list than the "top 25" including the Ivies. In creating a "nationalized" mean we have tried to include institutions that are similar in their student body to those we coded for the regressions. Data for advanced degrees come from the *Digest of Education Statistics, 2002,* on-line. Ph.D.'s and professional degrees issued to women in 2001 are divided by B.A.'s in 1995; M.A.'s issued to women in 2001 are divided by B.A.'s in 1998.

Figure 1

Fraction of Massachusetts Mothers Keeping their Surname at the Time of their First Birth: By Year, Age and Education

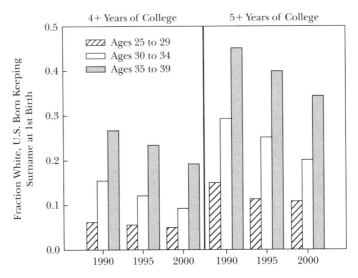

Source: Massachusetts birth records. See text.

the beginning, this article explained its focus on college graduates by stating that those who are not college graduates are more likely to be "changers." According to the Massachusetts birth data, college graduates, relative to those without college, were two to five times more likely (depending on age) to retain their surnames at the time of their first birth, although such estimates are biased downward because the college graduates have a higher fraction without first births, and those who married and never had a first birth were more likely to keep their surnames upon marriage.

An unexpected finding from the Massachusetts birth records concerns the surnames of (U.S.-born) African-American women. The (unadjusted) mean for married college graduate African-American women at the time of their first birth (at age 30 to 34 years) was about 34 percent in the late 1990s, or almost double the fraction for the comparable group of white women. Perhaps more surprising is that the fraction keeping their surnames at the time of their first birth was about the same for those with no college, whereas that figure is extremely low among white women. As in the case of white women, we limit these samples to women who have not had a previous birth to eliminate the possibility of prior children from another father and thus that the woman has a different surname from the current father, but the same surname as some of her children.

Although the Massachusetts birth records include all births that occurred within the state and to parents whose official residence is in the state, certain biases still exist when using these data to estimate surname retention. For example, some mothers elect to be known in the hospital by their husband's surname even if they use their own surname in both social and professional circumstances. While we have no estimate for how often this occurs, there are two other biases for which we can make a plausible adjustment. One issue in using birth records is that 18.6 percent of all ever-married college graduate (white) women who were age 38–43 years in 2000 had not had a first birth, according to the Current Population Survey Fertility Supplement 2000. If the fraction of "keepers" among these women was equal to that for women in the oldest age group of mothers, then the corrected fraction would add more weight to the oldest age group.[6] We also assume that 12 percent of "keepers" at marriage revert to their husband's name after having their first child, a finding from the Harvard class of 1980 study (see below). In this way we attempt to transform the fraction of women who retained their surname at their first birth into one at the time of marriage.

Using these two adjustments, the fraction of name-keepers among college graduates across all ages was 23 percent in 1990, 20 percent in 1995 and 17 percent in 2000. The fraction in 2000 is quite similar to the datum we computed from "nationalizing" the *New York Times* data. The decrease in surname retention in the 1990s found in the birth data differs from that revealed in the *Times* data. Data from Harvard Alumni Surveys confirms the decline and reinforces our sense that selection into the *Times* data changed in the 1990s.

Evidence from Harvard Alumni Surveys

Data for all women in the Harvard classes of 1980 and 1990 were collected from the Harvard archives. The classes of 1980 and 1990 were chosen because the majority of the members of the former married in the late 1980s and those of the latter married in the late 1990s, a decade of a high, but possibly declining, fraction of women who kept their surname. Both classes have sufficiently long histories to allow us to observe whether life cycle transitions, such as having children, affect the decision to retain one's name. Information from the five-year reunion class books of 1985, 1990, 1995 and 2000 was gathered for the class of 1980 and from the class books of 1995 and 2000 for the class of 1990. The class books are compiled by the Harvard Alumni Association, which sends questionnaires to graduates of the class, requesting information on their current name, address, occupation, graduate or professional degrees, spouse or partner name, date of marriage, occupation and education of spouse or partner and children with their dates of birth. When an individual did not respond to a questionnaire, information was imputed when such information was clearly factual. For example, if a woman stated in 1995 that she had been married in 1989 but did not respond to the 1990 questionnaire, we filled in that information. There were 603 graduates in the class of 1980 and 696 in the class of 1990. Across the entire two decades, 487 women of the 603 who graduated in 1980 responded to at least one of the five-year surveys.

Table 3 summarizes the results for the class of 1980. Of those who responded, 390 reported to have ever married, and of this total group, 52.3 percent did not

---

[6] The reweighting implicitly treats the cross-section of women who had a first birth in a year as if it were a cohort of women. Those who had never had a first birth by age 40 are added in, and the fraction of "keepers" among the women who delayed child bearing to 35 to 39 years is attributed to those who never had a first birth by age 40.

Table 3
Name Changing through the Life Cycle: Harvard Class of 1980

A. *Respondents who did not change surname at marriage*

Marriage interval	Percentage not changing in interval	Number married in interval	Number not changing in interval
Before 1985, after 1980	38.3	107	41
Before 1990, after 1985	58.2	153	89
Before 1995, after 1990	57.1	91	52
Before 2000, after 1995	56.4	39	22
All years, 1980 to 2000	52.3	390	204

B. *Surname change after marriage and after childbirth*

Marriage interval	(1) Number not changing after marriage	(2) Percentage changing later, among (1)	(3) Number with children, among (1)	(4) Percentage changing later, among (3)
1980 to 1995	182	10.4	142	12.0

Source: Harvard Class of 1980 Data Set. See Data Appendix.
Notes: Part A: The survey closest to the time of marriage was used for the surname information. The number of observations is the "flow" of individuals into the "ever-married" state. Part B: The marriage interval does not include the last survey so that those who retained their name at marriage could have time to alter that decision.

change their last name to that of their husband's in the alumni survey nearest their marriage year.[7] Those who married closest to college graduation had the lowest rate of surname retention: 38.3 percent of those marrying before 1985 did not change their surnames. For all subsequent survey years, the fraction keeping their names was about 57 percent.

The Harvard sample allows us to see the effects of life cycle transitions after marriage. The vast majority of women in the Harvard class of 1980 who retained their surname upon marriage continued to do so even after childbearing. Of those who did not change their surname upon marriage, about 10 percent changed subsequently (as shown in part B of Table 3). Within this group, 12 percent of those with children later changed their surname; just 5 percent did among those who did not list any children. Therefore, women with children have a higher tendency to take their husband's surname even if they did not do so at marriage. But the fraction that changed their surname after marriage is low, even among those with children.

Data from the Harvard Class of 1990 enables us to see if Harvard College women followed the downward trend in name retention that we found in the

---

[7] The marriage rate among the group is higher than these data would imply, $(390/487) = 80$ percent, because some women responded in 1985 but not after, and most who married did so after 1985. By using the data from the last alumni survey, we compute that the marriage rate to 2000 was about 85 percent, which makes it comparable with other populations of highly educated women.

Massachusetts birth data. Mean years from graduation to marriage for those who married up to ten years out for the Harvard class of 1980 was 4.81 and was 5.24 for the class of 1990—a modest increase. However, we find a large decrease in the fraction of women who retained their surname comparing the two classes. From those in the class of 1980 who reported being married by 1990, 44 percent retained their surname. In the 1990 sample, of those who reported being married by 2000, only 32 percent retained their surnames—a sharp reduction.

Correlates of Name Retention

What distinguishes women who retain their surnames from those who change? A major possibility concerns whether the woman has already "made a name" for herself. Women with advanced degrees, occupations in the arts and writing and longer careers before marriage would appear to be more likely to retain their names. More traditional individuals, perhaps as indicated by a religious ceremony, would be less likely to retain their surnames. Family expectations and peer effects might matter, as well. We will see that all of these reasons come into play. We emphasize that we are looking at the *correlates* of name change and that we are not claiming to identify a causal relationship.

The *New York Times* Cross-Section Data Sets: 1991 and 2001

To explore the correlates of name retention, information was collected from *all* marriage announcements in the *New York Times* in 1991 and 2001. As previously noted, the typical announcement contains education, occupation, age and family background information for both bride and groom and the religious nature of the ceremony. Across all weekends in 1991, there were 1,958 marriage announcements, of which 91 percent gave the bride's age; in 2001, there were 1,315 announcements, of which 95 percent gave the bride's age. (We do not know why the number of wedding announcements decreased during the 1990s and whether the *Times* published fewer announcements or fewer couples of the desired prominence submitted their announcement.)

Couples in these announcements form a distinctive stratum in society. Almost all graduated from college. In 1991, 49 percent of brides graduated from one of the top 25 universities or top 25 liberal arts colleges as ranked by the 2001 *U.S. News and World Report*, a figure that rose slightly to 52 percent in 2001. In 1991, 49 percent of the brides had a post-baccalaureate degree like an M.A., Ph.D., J.D., M.D. and M.B.A. or were pursuing one—a total rising to 65 percent by 2001. The median age of the bride (among first marriages) was 28 years in 1991, rising to 30 years in 2001. In 1991, first marriages were 97 (96 in 2001) percent of the total for brides and 91 (92 in 2001) percent for grooms. Religious ceremonies were performed for 92 (89 in 2001) percent of the weddings. About three-tenths of the religious ceremonies were Jewish and one-fifth were Catholic, higher than national averages, but not surprising given the location of the *New York Times*.

We have estimated an ordinary least squares linear probability regression where the dependent variable is whether the bride kept her surname.[8] Three groups of variables are included in Table 4—those concerning the bride, the groom and the ceremony.

Across the two years, 1991 and 2001, the fraction of women listed in the *Times* as keeping her surname at marriage increased (although, as we have noted, it probably did not increase in the nation as a whole). The age at first marriage rose considerably, and the fraction with advanced degrees also increased. But the changes in the observables are insufficient to explain the increase in "keeping."

A religious ceremony is associated with a lower probability of keeping one's surname. Relative to the base group (civil ceremony), a Catholic ceremony is associated with an 8.8 (14.3 in 2001) percentage point decrease in the probability of "keeping," and the effect is 8.5 (8.4) percentage points for a Jewish ceremony. Mixed religious ceremonies, as well as those for non-Western religions, had an equal effect as the base civil ceremony group in 1991, but were more like a Protestant ceremony in 2001.

Brides in their mid-twenties had a much lower probability of "keeping"—about 12 to 14 percentage points relative to brides older than about 30 years in 1991. The gradient of "keeping" with respect to age was greater in 2001 than in 1991 if one includes the youngest age group, which in 2001 was just 5 percent of the sample. Overall, a bride with an advanced degree had an increased probability of keeping her surname of about 14 percentage points in 1991.[9] An M.A. degree was associated with a 9 percentage point decrease in 1991, less in 2001. Interestingly, M.B.A. degrees were about equal to the base group of no advanced degree. Brides with occupations in the arts, writing and the media had an 18 percentage point increased probability of "keeping" in 1991 (10 percentage points in 2001). Each of the effects just mentioned is consistent with a desire to keep one's surname, once one has "made a name."

Graduation from an Ivy League school or a top-25 liberal arts college is associated with an 11 percentage point increase in 1991 and 14 percentage point increase in 2001 relative to any college or university ranked below number 25 in its class. Graduation from a "seven sisters" college is associated with an 8 percentage point increase in 1991 and a 16 percentage point increase in 2001. Graduation from other top universities has no effect relative to the base group.

Conditional on the bride's characteristics, few of the groom's observables like age, university or advanced degrees are associated with the bride's name retention, and we have included only those variables that were statistically and quantitatively

---

[8] The main results are robust to the estimation procedure and are almost identical to those from a "logit" regression.

[9] The increased coefficient on M.D., D.D.S. and D.V.M. is largely due to the inclusion of the group claiming to be keeping their surnames "professionally." The coefficients for the professional and Ph.D. degrees are all about 0.10 if one includes those "keeping" professionally as "changers."

Table 4

Correlates of Keeping One's Surname at Marriage: *New York Times:* **1991, 2001**

Variable	(1) 1991 Coeff.	S.e.	(2) 2001 Coeff.	S.e.	Means for cols. (1)	(2)
Dependent variable: Bride kept surname at marriage					0.190	0.324
Ceremony						
Catholic	−0.0879	(0.0377)	−0.143	(0.0478)	0.190	0.207
Jewish	−0.0851	(0.0353)	−0.0835	(0.0450)	0.306	0.298
Protestant	−0.0533	(0.0344)	−0.0992	(0.0452)	0.361	0.291
Other religion or mixed	−0.0284	(0.0463)	−0.0939	(0.0550)	0.0643	0.0996
Bride						
Ages 20 to 24	−0.129	(0.0572)	−0.413	(0.0759)	0.114	0.0478
Ages 25 to 29	−0.143	(0.0523)	−0.285	(0.0531)	0.559	0.409
Ages 30 to 34	−0.0244	(0.0537)	−0.169	(0.0528)	0.229	0.372
Ages 35 to 39	0.0362	(0.0606)	0.00178	(0.0618)	0.0671	0.104
Ivy league college	0.110	(0.0243)	0.136	(0.0307)	0.203	0.271
Top 25 university	−0.00353	(0.0299)	0.0844	(0.0390)	0.105	0.128
"Seven sisters" college	0.0754	(0.0311)	0.164	(0.0636)	0.0981	0.0414
Top 25 liberal arts college	0.114	(0.0336)	0.131	(0.0474)	0.0795	0.0805
J.D.	0.151	(0.0271)	0.115	(0.0365)	0.139	0.150
M.D., D.D.S., or D.V.M.	0.134	(0.0441)	0.229	(0.0541)	0.0446	0.0606
Ph.D.	0.147	(0.0506)	0.128	(0.0555)	0.0344	0.0566
M.A.	0.0912	(0.0240)	0.0330	(0.0286)	0.174	0.296
M.B.A.	0.0242	(0.0318)	−0.00984	(0.0472)	0.0948	0.0821
Bride occupation in arts[a]	0.180	(0.0265)	0.101	(0.0316)	0.136	0.190
Groom						
Ph.D.	0.196	(0.0416)	0.0258	(0.0559)	0.0513	0.0566
M.A.	0.0417	(0.0306)	0.123	(0.0329)	0.174	0.182
Uses patrimonial suffix	−0.0902	(0.0319)	−0.114	(0.0484)	0.0852	0.0725
Constant	0.232	(0.0589)	0.468	(0.0606)		
R^2	0.142		0.152			
Root mean squared error	0.365		0.435			
Number of observations	1,773		1,255		1,773	1,255

[a] "Occupation in the arts" includes artist, actress, dancer, also writer, editor, producer or director for some form of the media and architect.

Source: New York Times Cross-Section Data Sets: 1991 and 2001.

Notes: Omitted ceremony is "civil" and the omitted age group of 40 years plus. College categories are the same as in Table 2. "Uses patrimonial suffix" is a dummy variable equal to one if the groom was listed as a Jr., Sr. or with any Roman numerals following his name.

important. In 1991, a groom with a Ph.D. was more likely to marry a woman who retained her surname. Grooms with patrimonial suffixes like Jr., Sr. or III were about 10 percentage points less likely to marry a woman who retained her surname. In another regression we included information about the groom's father and found that having a prominent father-in-law diminished the probability of a bride's keeping her surname and that having a father-in-law in the arts or academia increased it. The effects just mentioned suggest that the bride's in-laws—the importance they place on names, their wealth and their nontraditional views—exert an independent impact.

Table 5

Correlates of Changing One's Surname: Harvard Class of 1980

Variables	Coefficient	S.e.	Means
Dependent variable: Woman changed surname after marriage			0.502
Woman's characteristics			
M.A.	0.0371	(0.0702)	0.253
M.B.A.	−0.160	(0.0900)	0.128
J.D.	−0.117	(0.0755)	0.223
M.D., D.D.S., D.V.M.	−0.234	(0.0843)	0.170
Ph.D.	−0.263	(0.0906)	0.115
Homemaker ever	0.190	(0.0935)	0.102
Arts/writing ever	−0.115	(0.0873)	0.121
Family characteristics			
Husband has Ph.D.	−0.204	(0.0765)	0.164
Children	0.212	(0.117)	0.820
Years to child/10	−0.127	(0.0896)	8.049
Years to marriage/10	−0.0977	(0.0715)	6.941
Constant	0.634	(0.0970)	
R^2	0.158		
Mean squared error	0.468		
Number of observations	305		

Source: Harvard class of 1980 data set.

Notes: Only women who were ever married and gave their year of marriage are included. Means for the years variables are not divided by 10. Advanced degrees refer to any and some women report more than one. "Children" is a dummy variable and indicates that at least one child is reported with a birth date, although the child could be a stepchild or an adopted child. "Years" means since graduation, June 1980. "Arts/writing" includes artists, photographers, writers, journalists, actresses, and so on. "Homemaker ever" and "Arts/writing ever" indicates that the woman listed one of these occupational groups during one of the four surveys. "S.e." is standard error.

Harvard Class of 1980 Data Set

We have also investigated the correlates of retaining one's surname using the Harvard class of 1980 data. The dependent variable here is a bit different from that in the *Times* data and is whether the woman *changed* her surname at marriage or any time thereafter, as reported in the reunion or class books from 1985 to 2000; that is, we include as "changers" women who kept their surname at marriage but subsequently changed it while married. In the sample given in Table 5, about 50 percent changed their name at some time after marriage. This sample includes only women who gave the date (or year) of their marriage. The women who did not give their date of marriage form a discernibly different group. A far lower fraction had children, and fewer earned advanced degrees. The correlates included are the presence of an advanced degree, whether the husband has a Ph.D., the presence of children, years from graduation to the first child's birth, years from graduation to marriage and if the woman was ever listed as a "homemaker" or in the "arts."

As in the *Times* data, the most important correlates concern the woman's characteristics: having an advanced degree and the time to marriage and to a first child. A Ph.D. or an M.D. is associated with a reduction of about 25 percentage points in the probability of changing one's name. Each year of marriage delay is related to a 1 percentage point decline, and each year of delay in having children is related to a 1.3 percentage point decline.

The husband's observable characteristics are not very important, with the exception that women who marry men with Ph.D.'s tend to retain their surnames, a finding that is similar to that from the *Times* 1991 data. However, in other regressions not shown here, using both the *Times* and the Harvard data, we found no meaningful interaction effect of bride-Ph.D. and groom-Ph.D. The effects, rather, are independent. Women with Ph.D.'s value the surnames under which they have published or were known, in a similar manner to writers and artists. But a groom with a Ph.D. may live in a place that is more accepting of a wife with a surname different from his.

Using the point estimates, the predicted probability that a woman from the Harvard class of 1980 would change her name after marriage if she did not have an advanced degree, married soon after college and had children a few years later was 0.846; the actual figure in the data is 0.79. At the other extreme, the predicted probability she would change her name after marriage if she had a Ph.D., married a Ph.D. ten years after graduation and had no children was 0.069; the actual figure in the data is 0.059. The quantitatively most important components in explaining these large differences are those concerning whether the woman "made a name" for herself before marriage.

Conclusion

A shift among college graduate women to keeping their surnames after marriage began sometime from the mid-1970s to early 1980s. The marriage announcements from the *New York Times* society page reveal a sharp increase in the fraction retaining their surnames from the early 1970s to the mid-1980s and then a plateau to the late 1990s. But although the *Times* data yield a further increase in name-keeping in the late 1990s, the two other data sets we use show an unambiguous decrease. Because one of those data sets—the Massachusetts birth records—contains the full population of women who had a birth in Massachusetts, we are fairly certain that no selection issues severely bias the trend. A comparison of the Harvard class of 1980 with that of 1990 reinforces the conclusion we reach from the Massachusetts birth records. The current share of college-educated women who keep their surnames at marriage appears to be a shade under 20 percent.

The reason for the decrease in surname-keeping in the 1990s is not clear. A number of correlates suggest that name-keeping should not have decreased; for example, the age at first marriage has not reversed its trend upward. We can only speculate about the social factors that have caused surname-keeping to decrease. Perhaps some women who "kept" their surnames in the 1980s, during the rapid increase in "keeping," did so because of peer pressure, and their counterparts today are freer to make their own choices. Perhaps surname-keeping seems less salient as a way of publicly supporting equality for women than it did in the late 1970s and 1980s. Perhaps a general drift to more conservative social values has made surname-keeping less attractive. The increase from the 1970s is far easier to explain: Women began to "make a name" for themselves and more often insisted upon retaining their name at marriage.

■ *This article began as Maria Shim's senior thesis at Harvard University, "What's In a Name? The Economic Value of Women's Names" (2001). The authors are grateful to Bert Huang for research assistance; Robert Woletz, editor, Society News, the* New York Times, *for information; and Charlene Zion of the Massachusetts Department of Public Health for performing the computer runs of the birth data. The authors thank Lawrence Katz, the participants in the NBER Labor Studies Summer Institute and the Yale University Labor and Economic History Workshops, especially Judy Chevalier, for comments and suggestions.*

References

Akerlof, George A. and Rachel E. Kranton. 2000. "Economics and Identity." *Quarterly Journal of Economics.* August, 115, pp. 715–53.

Augustine-Adams, Kif. 1997. "The Beginning of Wisdom is to Call Things by Their Right Names." *Southern California Review of Law and Women's Studies.* Fall, 7, pp. 1–35.

Davis, Nancy J. and Robert V. Robinson. 1988. "Class Identification of Men and Women in the 1970s and 1980s." *American Sociological Review.* February, 53, pp. 103–12.

De Long, J. Bradford, Claudia Goldin and Lawrence F. Katz. 2003. "Sustaining U.S. Economic Growth," in *Agenda for the Nation.* H.

Aaron, J. Lindsay and P. Nivola, eds. Washington, D.C.: Brookings Institution Press, pp. 17–60.

Goldin, Claudia and Lawrence F. Katz. 2002. "The Power of the Pill: Oral Contraceptives and Women's Career and Marriage Decisions." *Journal of Political Economy.* August, 110, pp. 730–70.

Scheuble, Laurie K., Katherine Klingemann and David R. Johnson. 2000. "Trends in Women's Marital Name Choices: 1966–1996." *Names: A Journal of Onomastics.* June, 48, pp. 105–14.

Stannard, Una. 1977. *Mrs. Man.* San Francisco, Calif.: Germainebooks.

Journal of Economic Perspectives—Volume 18, Number 2—Spring 2004—Pages 161–182

Manager-Investor Conflicts in Mutual Funds

Paul G. Mahoney

H alf of all of U.S. households own shares in one or more mutual funds, either directly or through personal or employer-sponsored retirement accounts. The growth in mutual fund investment has been dramatic. At the end of World War II, there were 73 mutual funds registered with the Securities and Exchange Commission holding $1.2 billion in assets (Investment Company Institute, 2003). By the end of 2002, over 8,000 mutual funds held more than $6 trillion in assets. Mutual funds own approximately 21 percent of the common equity and 11 percent of the debt securities of U.S. corporations (Federal Reserve, 2003). Table 1 shows the growth in the number and assets of mutual funds from 1992–2002.

The existing literature on mutual funds focuses primarily on whether fund managers' stock selection efforts generate excess returns that justify the associated fees and transaction costs (Daniel, Grinblatt, Titman and Wermers, 1997; Malkiel, 1995). In these studies, a mutual fund can be considered a black box that uses some strategy to convert investor cash into returns. But what happens inside the box has become front-page news. In July 2003, New York's Attorney General, Eliot Spitzer, notified a hedge fund, Canary Capital Partners, LLC, that it was the target of an investigation into mutual fund trading practices. In early September, Spitzer alleged various trading improprieties in a civil suit against Canary. Suits and criminal prosecutions against other mutual fund traders, brokers, mutual fund management companies and their respective executives followed at a breakneck pace over the following months.

Although the details of the alleged wrongdoings vary, the issues are all rooted

■ *Paul G. Mahoney is Brokaw Professor of Corporate Law and Albert C. BeVier Research Professor, University of Virginia School of Law, Charlottesville, Virginia. His e-mail address is ⟨pmahoney@virginia.edu⟩.*

Table 1

Mutual Fund Size and Household Ownership, 1992–2002

Year	Number of mutual funds	Mutual fund net assets ($ billions)	Long-term mutual fund net assets ($ billions)	U.S. households owning mutual funds (%)	Mutual fund investments as % of household financial assets
2002	8,256	6,391	4,119	49.6	17.8
2000	8,155	6,964	5,119	49.0	18.2
1998	7,314	5,525	4,173	44.0	16.2
1996	6,248	3,525	2,624	37.2	13.1
1994	5,325	2,155	1,544	30.7	10.5
1992	3,824	1,642	1,096	27.0	8.3

Source: Investment Company Institute (2003).
Notes: Long-term mutual funds exclude money market mutual funds. The 1992 figure under "U.S. households owning mutual funds" is not comparable to the rest of the column because it excludes ownership through employer-sponsored retirement plans.

in basic conflicts of interest between mutual fund investors and the companies and individuals that organize, sell and provide services to mutual funds.[1] This article describes the structure and regulation of mutual funds and the resulting incentives facing those who make decisions for the funds. After providing some basic institutional details, it focuses on the cash flows from mutual fund investors to fund managers, brokers and other third parties and the associated conflicts of interest. The article concludes with a summary of recent legal proceedings against mutual fund managers and brokers based on improper trading practices and regulatory proposals to curb those practices.

What Do Mutual Funds Do?

A mutual fund is "a low-cost way for the investor-in-the-street to own a stake in a portfolio of securities" ("Special Report: Mutual Funds," 2003). Some mutual funds, known as index funds, seek to replicate the average return on a wide and representative measure of the market, like the Standard and Poor's 500 or the Wilshire 5000. Most mutual funds, however, are actively managed, meaning that the fund managers chose securities that they believe are currently undervalued.

Mutual funds provide services in addition to diversification. They offer liquidity by standing ready to redeem their shares at net asset value, or the ratable value

---

[1] Discussions of specific individuals or entities in this article are taken from the allegations in civil and criminal complaints or administrative proceedings instituted by state or federal officials or investors. In most instances, the legal proceedings are ongoing or the defendants have settled without admitting the allegations. The author, the editors of the *Journal of Economic Perspectives* and the American Economic Association express no independent opinion on the truth of any such allegations.

of the fund's investment portfolio less any debts. Investment vehicles that continuously redeem shares in this way are called "open-end" funds, and this paper uses the term "mutual fund" to refer exclusively to publicly offered open-end funds.[2] Mutual funds also offer services such as check writing, record-keeping and telephone or Internet exchanges among funds in the same family.

Most mutual funds are created and managed by a mutual fund management company that is registered as an investment adviser with the Securities and Exchange Commission. The management company may be a subsidiary of a bank, a broker-dealer, an insurance company or a financial services firm that specializes in mutual fund management, such as Fidelity or Vanguard. The management company often manages a "complex" of funds with various investment objectives. As of January 2004, for example, Vanguard offered 98 different mutual funds to retail investors. Fund complexes that offer more choices and innovate by introducing new types of funds tend to gain market share. While the number of fund complexes has tripled over the past 20 years, the market share of the top five mutual fund complexes has remained steady at approximately one-third of total mutual fund assets (Khorana and Servaes, 2000).

The assets in any given mutual fund must be insulated from those of other mutual funds in the same complex and from the operations and associated risks of the management company and other firms that provide services to the fund. The simplest approach is to put each mutual fund's assets into a separate corporation, trust or other legal entity that engages in no activities other than acquiring, holding and selling investment assets and issuing and redeeming its own shares or other ownership interests.

The management company separately incorporates each mutual fund and provides a nominal start-up capital.[3] Before offering shares in the fund to the public, the management company selects an initial board of directors. Companies that manage a large fund complex frequently elect the same individuals to the boards of each of the funds. The board approves an advisory agreement between the fund and its investment advisor, which is usually the management company or an affiliate. After the mutual fund sells shares to the public, the management company retains only its nominal shareholding and formal control passes to the public investors, who periodically thereafter elect directors and approve significant policy changes.

Mutual funds must comply with securities laws that govern other publicly traded companies, which generally prohibit fraud and require various kinds of information disclosure. Mutual funds and other collective investment vehicles are

---

[2] So-called closed-end funds do not redeem shares continuously, but list their shares on an exchange to provide liquidity. Another investment vehicle, known as a unit trust, purchases a portfolio of assets but does not subsequently trade those assets. Mutual funds are substantially more popular in the United States than either closed-end funds or unit trusts, holding roughly 20 times the assets of the latter two categories combined.

[3] Mutual funds are organized either as corporations or business trusts. There are minor differences in governance between the two, but they are not substantively important.

also subject to a separate regulatory statute, the Investment Company Act of 1940, which requires mutual funds to register with the Securities and Exchange Commission and to comply with various disclosure, conflict of interest, capital structure and corporate governance rules. A fund's investment adviser is subject to registration and regulation under the Investment Advisers Act of 1940. Finally, the National Association of Securities Dealers prohibits dealers from selling mutual fund shares unless both the dealer and the fund itself meet certain requirements.

The Direct Costs of Mutual Funds

This section describes investor fees and annual costs of mutual funds. Some of the costs are paid directly by investors, others from the mutual fund's assets and still others by the management company. All costs represent income to the manager or to third parties the manager selects to provide services to the fund. The manager's income increases with the assets in the fund. The investor's objective is to maximize realized returns, not the size of the fund. This difference matters, particularly with regard to marketing expenses, which increase fund size but may reduce realized returns. After discussing the primary costs, I discuss whether competition among fund managers cures the manager-investor conflict. The next section discusses the potential for managers to extract hidden benefits from the mutual fund.

Marketing and Sales Costs

Mutual funds rely on one of two methods to sell shares to the public. Some sell exclusively through broker-dealers. Proprietary funds, such as the Merrill Lynch fund complex, are affiliated with a full-service broker-dealer that sells the fund's shares. Other "independent" fund complexes, such as Putnam, focus on mutual fund management and sell through unaffiliated brokers. Mutual funds sold through brokers often charge a sales load, or commission, that may be paid when the investor purchases shares (a "front-end" load) or sells the shares (a "back-end" load). Although the fund determines the amount of the load, it is retained by the selling broker and represents compensation for the broker's investment advice and ancillary services to the investor. Under the Investment Company Act, the selling broker may not increase or decrease the sales load by separate agreement with the customer.

Instead of or in addition to a sales load, a mutual fund may deduct an annual fee from the fund's assets that can be used to compensate selling brokers and for other marketing expenses. Section 12(b) of the Investment Company Act and the SEC's rule 12b-1 permit such payments only if they are approved by the fund's board and a majority of the board is independent of the management company. Fees deducted from the fund's assets to meet marketing expenses are therefore known as "12b-1 fees." Rules of the National Association of Securities Dealers limit

12b-1 fees to 1 percent of the mutual fund's assets annually. The majority of such fees are used to compensate selling brokers.[4]

Some mutual funds marketed through brokers offer multiple share classes representing ownership interests in the same portfolio, but using different fee structures. Each share class uses a different mix of front-end loads, back-end loads and 12b-1 fees to compensate selling brokers.

Other mutual funds are directly marketed to investors without the use of brokers. Investors purchase shares from the fund and pay no sales load. Alternatively, the investor may purchase through a "fund supermarket," such as Charles Schwab's OneSource. A fund supermarket is organized by a broker but does not solicit investors to purchase any particular fund. Instead, it offers (frequently at no fee to the investor) a menu of "participating" mutual funds. The advantage to the investor is that all of the investments purchased through the fund supermarket are held in one consolidated account, even though they may come from various mutual fund complexes.

A directly marketed fund may charge a 12b-1 fee and use it to pay for advertising and for "shelf space" at mutual fund supermarkets. For a fund to advertise itself as a "no-load" fund, however, the NASD requires that it charge no sales load and have a 12b-1 fee of no more than 25 basis points (that is, no more than 0.25 percent of net assets). Some directly marketed mutual funds, known as "pure" no-load funds, do not charge a sales load or deduct a 12b-1 fee from the fund's assets. Instead, the fund manager pays marketing expenses from its own resources.

The 12b-1 fees are controversial. The mutual fund industry argues that these fees are a means by which investors who purchase through brokers can spread out the broker's compensation over time rather than bear it all at once in the form of a sales load. Critics of 12b-1 fees note that they, unlike sales loads, are not paid directly by the investor in connection with a transaction, but deducted annually from the fund's assets. Thus, in effect, current shareholders bear the cost of attracting new shareholders. Because the manager has a greater interest in maximizing the size of the fund than do investors, the manager may spend more of the shareholders' money on marketing than the shareholders would prefer.

Any fund, whether indirectly or directly marketed and whether load or no-load, may charge the investor a small annual "account fee" covering the costs of account statements, postage and so on. In addition, a fund may charge a percentage fee for redemptions that follow within a short period (often 90 days) of the purchase in order to discourage frequent trading in the fund's shares. The fee is paid to the fund rather than the fund manager.

Table 2 provides the number and size distribution of mutual funds and share classes in September 2003, using the most recent available data from the Center for Research in Securities Prices mutual fund database maintained at the University of Chicago's business school. The 6,662 mutual funds for which the database includes

---

[4] According to the website of the Investment Company Institute, 63 percent of 12b-1 fees are paid to brokers. See ⟨http://www.ici.org/funds/abt/ref_12b1_fees.html⟩.

Table 2
Mutual Funds and Share Classes, September 2003

	Mutual funds	*Share classes*
N (asset size data)	6,662	16,018
Net assets ($ millions):		
Mean	941	391
Median	168	40
Maximum	82,215	66,719
75th percentile	565	181
25th percentile	49	7
Standard deviation	3,453	1,941
Expense and fee structures:		
Number charging a sales load		8,983
Number charging a 12b-1 fee		10,547
Number of "pure" no-load		5,148
Average expense ratio		1.37%

Notes: The table provides descriptive statistics on all mutual funds covered by the Center for Research in Securities Prices (CRSP) mutual fund database as of September 2003. A mutual fund may be divided into multiple share classes that represent ownership in the same portfolio of assets but that have different fee structures. CRSP treats each share class as a separate fund. For purposes of the table, therefore, each share class that has the same name except for a designator (such as "A," "B," "select," etc.) is taken to be part of the same mutual fund. See ⟨http://gsbwww.uchicago.edu/computing/research/unix/crspmutualfund.html⟩.

size data issued 16,018 different classes of shares in aggregate. Of those classes, 56 percent had a sales load, 66 percent had a 12b-1 fee and 32 percent had neither. Sales loads ranged from 0.1 percent to 10.5 percent of the amount invested, with a mean of 3.6 percent and a median of 4.5 percent. Although a majority of share classes assess a sales load and/or 12b-1 fee, the pure no-load classes have more assets in aggregate, accounting for 56 percent of the $6.3 trillion of total mutual fund net assets.

The Investment Company Institute (2004), the mutual fund industry's trade association, estimates the average sales loads paid by investors. Applying those estimates to the Investment Company Institute's (2003) annual sales figures suggests that investors paid approximately $2.5 billion in total loads in 2002. A more crude but commonly used procedure is to multiply each mutual fund's net assets by one-seventh of its total load, in effect assuming that investors hold mutual fund shares for seven years on average (Sirri and Tufano, 1998). That procedure generates an estimate of $2.8 billion in loads paid during 2003.[5]

---

[5] In calculating the dollar amounts of annual expenses, it is common to apply the relevant percentage fee to the average of net assets at the beginning and end of the year. Because the CRSP data do not yet

Estimating 12b-1 fees is simpler, as it is an annual expense and contained in the CRSP database. Investors paid approximately $9.5 billion in 12b-1 fees in 2003 in addition to sales loads. If my estimate of the latter is accurate, then investors paid approximately $12.3 billion in 2003 for marketing, distribution and account services provided by brokers.

Management and Administrative Expenses

A mutual fund's management company receives a management fee, paid from the fund's assets and calculated as a percentage of the net assets in the portfolio, as compensation for investment advice and administrative services provided to the fund. The fee is typically based only on assets under management, partly because the Investment Advisers Act and the SEC's rules limit a fund manager's ability to charge a performance-based fee (Das and Sundaram, 1998; Golec, 2003). Mutual funds also pay third parties for legal, accounting and administrative services.

The Securities and Exchange Commission requires that each mutual fund report an annual "expense ratio" consisting of the management fee, the 12b-1 fee (if any), all other asset-based fees and any other "annual" costs paid from the mutual fund's assets, including legal, accounting and other recurring expenses. The expense ratio is expressed as a percentage of net assets.

During 2003, the mutual funds included in the Center for Research in Securities Prices database incurred approximate annual expenses of $47.6 billion, or 0.76 percent of total net assets. The difference between that percentage and the average expense ratio of 1.37 percent shown in Table 2 reflects the fact that low-cost funds are larger on average than high-cost funds. Deducting the $9.5 billion in 12b-1 fees, operating expenses (management fees and legal, accounting and other administrative expenses) are approximately $38.1 billion.

Trading Costs

A mutual fund incurs trading costs, including brokerage commissions and bid-ask spreads, on portfolio transactions. These costs are not part of the expense ratio disclosed in the prospectus. Instead, the mutual fund reports total brokerage commissions to the Securities and Exchange Commission in a "Statement of Additional Information." The SEC (2000) explains this seeming anomaly by noting that there is no universally accepted means of measuring spread costs. Commissions can be measured easily, but if there is an inverse relationship between commissions and spread costs (perhaps because high-quality brokers charge higher commissions but obtain better trade execution), the disclosure of commissions alone might be misleading.

Using information for a sample of equity mutual funds, Livingston and O'Neal (1996) estimate average annual brokerage commissions at 28 basis points for the

include year-end figures for 2003, I used net assets at September 30, 2003 in place of that average for all of the 2003 expense calculations.

period 1989 to 1993. Chalmers, Edelen and Kadlec (1999) find that average annual brokerage commissions and spread costs for a sample of equity mutual funds were 31 and 47 basis points, respectively, over the period 1984–1991. They define "equity" mutual funds as those invested 50 percent or more in equities, and I use the same definition for purposes of the calculations described below.

Chalmers, Edelen and Kadlec (1999) find that both brokerage and spread costs are lower for mutual funds in the top size quartile (20 and 28 basis points, respectively). In their sample, the top quartile begins at $468 million in assets. As a rough way of taking account of mutual fund growth between their sample period and 2003, I arrange mutual funds into two groups based on whether the fund has more than $468 million in assets. I assume commissions and spread costs of 20 and 28 basis points, respectively, for the larger funds and 33 and 52 basis points, respectively, for the smaller. The resulting estimates for 2003 suggest that equity mutual funds likely paid approximately $6.5 billion in brokerage commissions and incurred $9.3 billion in spread costs. These estimates do not include trading costs for bond and money market funds.

Although some components of total costs are very rough estimates, it appears that investors paid approximately $66 billion to invest through mutual funds last year. The majority of those costs went to pay fund managers and brokers to devise and execute trading strategies. A substantial portion of the remainder went to pay marketing and distribution expenses, including payments to brokers who recommended that their clients purchase a particular mutual fund.

What Do Mutual Fund Expenses Buy?

The costs detailed above vary considerably among mutual funds. Are higher costs associated with higher investor utility? This question implies two subsidiary inquiries. Do investors who purchase through brokers receive value commensurate with the brokers' compensation? Does the level of operating expenses reveal information about value to investors?

The mutual fund industry has a large number of fund complexes and fairly low concentration. The natural starting assumption, then, is that competition will drive the price of services down to the marginal cost of providing those services—including personalized advice from the selling broker (if any), diversification, implementation of the fund manager's trading strategy, account statements, check writing privileges and other administrative services—and investors will purchase mutual fund shares only if those services add value in excess of their cost.

Economists have argued, however, that when consumers are boundedly rational, prices can exceed marginal cost even in the presence of competition (Gabaix and Laibson, 2003). This is especially true when the producer adopts a nonlinear pricing scheme like those seen in mobile telephone calling plans or health club memberships (Della Vigna and Malmendier, 2003). Mutual funds, particularly those sold through brokers, have complex pricing schemes. It is also worth noting the possibility that regulatory constraints make a first-best system of mutual fund pricing unachievable. Of course, neither point demonstrates that mutual fund services are inefficiently priced, but it does suggest that there is room for empirical inquiry into the relationship between costs and investor utility.

Such inquiries have produced a number of discomfiting results. Most notably, several studies conclude that investors' realized returns are negatively related to expense ratios (Elton, Gruber, Das and Hlavka, 1993; Malkiel, 1995; Carhart, 1997). Returns are also negatively related to estimates of trading costs (Livingston and O'Neal, 1996; Chalmers, Edelen and Kadlec, 1999). Investor returns net of sales loads are negatively related to the size of the load (Morey, 2002). Each of these results generates interesting interpretive questions.

It is well understood that tests of mutual fund performance are sensitive to the benchmarks used, and any test is accordingly a joint one of mutual fund performance and the underlying expected return model. Thus, Hortaçsu and Syverson (2003) approach the problem from a different angle by studying mutual funds whose expected returns are necessarily very similar. They limit their study to S&P 500 funds, which aim to track the return on the Standard and Poor's 500 index. For these funds, differences in expenses cannot convey information about the manager's stock-selection ability. Yet the authors find dramatic divergence in costs (measured as the expense ratio plus one-seventh of total loads). They interpret the results as suggesting the presence of two groups of investors—experienced investors who buy low-cost no-load funds and novice investors who rely on brokers and therefore purchase high-cost load funds.

As Hortaçsu and Syverson (2003) note, it is possible that a broker's advice is valuable to a customer even if it does not lead to the selection of mutual funds with superior risk-adjusted returns. Some investors may require guidance on issues unrelated to the return on a particular stock or mutual fund, such as the value of diversification, the differences among various categories of investments and their suitability given the investor's needs, and so on. The Investment Company Institute (2001) itself points out that many mutual fund purchasers are relatively inexperienced investors. Calculating the value of this advice is difficult. What would an unsophisticated investor have done absent the broker's advice? In any event, the value of generalized advice will not be reflected in superior returns on the investor's mutual fund investments.

This observation, however, raises an issue for the design of studies of the relationship between cost and performance. Starting with Jensen's (1967) pioneering study of mutual fund performance, researchers have often taken the expense ratio as a measure of the cost of the fund manager's investment advice *to the fund*, while the sales load, if any, is a measure of the cost of the selling broker's investment advice *to the investor*. Unfortunately, that connection has been weakened since 1980, when the Securities and Exchange Commission first permitted 12b-1 fees. Such fees are included in expense ratios, but are used principally to compensate selling brokers. Thus, the Investment Company Institute (2004) criticizes academic studies that use expense ratios as the measure of operating expenses, arguing that these studies should deduct 12b-1 fees from the expense ratio.

In light of the Investment Company Institute's criticism, I supplement

Table 3

Costs of Standard and Poor's 500 Index Funds Excluding Sales Loads and 12b-1 Fees

N	87
Cost in basis points (1 basis point = .01%):	
Mean	42.1
Median	40.0
Minimum	8.0
Maximum	85.0
75th percentile	55.0
25th percentile	28.5
Standard deviation	19.3

Source: Center for Research in Securities Prices mutual fund database. Standard and Poor's 500 Index funds are identified by name and through the IndexFunds.com website. The sample excludes funds designated as "enhanced" or "managed" and share classes available only to institutional investors or other special classes of investors.

Hortaçsu and Syverson's (2003) study by estimating the dispersion in operating expenses among S&P 500 funds. I calculate expense ratios minus 12b-1 fees for all retail S&P 500 funds included in the Center for Research in Securities Prices data.[6] Table 3 provides descriptive statistics. Even this narrow measure of operating expenses varies considerably, ranging from 8 to 85 basis points.

Economies of scale might explain some of the difference, with larger funds able to charge a lower management fee. In addition, load funds, which perhaps cater to less sophisticated investors, may charge higher management fees in addition to charging sales loads. I accordingly estimate the following regression for the mutual funds in my sample:

$$EXP_i = \beta_0 + \beta_1 * \log(TNA_i) + \beta_2 * LOAD_i,$$

where for mutual fund i, EXP_i is expenses (expense ratio minus 12b-1 fees), TNA_i is total net assets, and $LOAD_i$ equals one if the fund charges a load and zero otherwise.

Table 4 shows the regression results for two different specifications, one excluding the LOAD variable and the other including it. In both models, larger funds on average have lower expenses, although size variation alone explains only 16 percent of the variation in my expense measure. Funds with sales loads have, on average, expenses that are 15 basis points higher than those without, and the

[6] Like Hortaçsu and Syverson (2003), I treat each class of shares as a separate entity and exclude funds marketed only to institutional investors or other limited groups of investors, such as retirement plans. I also exclude funds designated as "enhanced" index funds, which are not entirely passive.

Table 4

Costs of Standard and Poor's 500 Index Funds versus Fund Characteristics

Variable	Model 1	Model 2
(Intercept)	57.7[a]	46.5[a]
	(4.22)	(4.69)
Log of net assets	−3.25[a]	−2.57[a]
	(0.785)	(0.736)
Indicator for load funds		15.0[a]
		(3.58)
Adjusted r-square	0.16	0.29

Notes: The dependent variable is the expense ratio minus 12b-1 fees (expressed in basis points) for each retail S&P 500 index fund contained in the Center for Research in Securities Prices data as of September 30, 2003. Standard errors are in parentheses.
[a] significant at $p < 1\%$.

inclusion of the LOAD variable substantially improves the predictive power of the model.

The results are what we would expect if mutual fund purchasers include a mix of sophisticated investors who are sensitive to costs and unsophisticated investors who purchase the mutual funds their broker recommends and are not sensitive to costs. The total investments of the former group appear to be much larger. Vanguard's S&P 500 index fund, a pure no-load fund with a cost of 18 basis points, is by far the dominant mutual fund in the category, holding 57 percent of the aggregate assets of the funds in my sample. A substantial majority of assets are held by the low-cost funds in the sample. Of course, index funds may be particularly attractive to sophisticated investors who suspect that active management does not add value.

So far, I have emphasized transactional or annual expenses that the investor or the mutual fund pays pursuant to explicit agreements with the fund manager or third parties. However, mutual fund managers may also be able to extract compensation from mutual fund assets that is not explicitly bargained for. This possibility underlies many of the recent legal proceedings concerning mutual fund management and is the focus of the next section.

Hidden Costs of Mutual Fund Investment

Although the brokerage fees and spread costs described in the prior section are paid to third parties, they have the potential to shift costs from the fund manager to the fund itself. In addition, the mechanics of setting the current net asset value of a mutual fund enable management companies to offer favored traders arbitrage profits in return for investments that increase the mutual fund's size and thus the manager's fees.

Directed Brokerage and Soft Dollar Commissions

A mutual fund pays brokers to execute portfolio transactions and to provide research, while the same brokers may recommend the mutual fund to their retail customers. When deciding which broker to use for portfolio transactions, some mutual funds take into account the broker's efforts to sell the fund's shares, a practice known as "directed brokerage." Directed brokerage creates two conflicts. Brokers may face a conflict between obtaining more brokerage business from the mutual fund and giving investors unbiased advice on which mutual fund is best suited to their needs. Fund managers may face a conflict between maximizing the sale of fund shares and obtaining brokerage services at the best quality and price available.

Brokers often provide research services to fund managers together with trade execution. Under so-called "soft dollar" arrangements, the cost of research services and execution may be bundled into the broker's commissions. The research services provided may include general-purpose items such as computer terminals and communications facilities. These arrangements give investment advisers a means of shifting costs that they would otherwise pay from their own resources to the mutual fund itself (Siggelkow, 1999).

Rules of the National Association of Securities Dealers forbid brokers to consider their receipt of commissions from a mutual fund's portfolio transactions when deciding whether to recommend that fund's shares to a client. The rules also require the broker to provide best execution to its mutual fund customers. Similarly, the Securities and Exchange Commission has provided interpretive guidance on when soft dollar practices are "reasonable." Nevertheless, the current rules may not be fully effective.

Livingston and O'Neal (1996) estimate that between 1989 and 1993, mutual funds paid an average brokerage commission of approximately 6 cents per share traded. During the same period, discount brokers offered commissions of 1 to 2 cents per share traded. There is accordingly reason to suspect that a substantial portion of commissions that mutual funds pay consist of soft money—perhaps $4 billion or more of the $6.5 billion I estimate for the most recent year. Chalmers, Edelen and Kadlec (1999) find that individual mutual funds' brokerage commissions and spread costs are positively correlated. If a fund paid higher commissions for superior trade execution, we would expect a negative correlation between commissions and spread costs. Again, the evidence is consistent with substantial use of soft dollars. Most importantly, trading costs are positively correlated with expense ratios. The theory under which soft dollars are permissible is that they reduce the manager's out-of-pocket expenses and the manager can then pass those savings along to the fund in the form of a lower management fee. The evidence, however, does not support the theory. The positive correlation again suggests that there are cost-sensitive and cost-insensitive mutual funds.

Stale-Price Arbitrage Losses

The price at which a mutual fund's shares trade does not arise through a minute-by-minute interaction of buy and sell orders, but through the fund's calculation of its net asset value. Mutual funds calculate their net asset value only once daily, generally at 4:00 p.m. Eastern time. The mutual fund then executes buy and sell orders placed that day at a price equal to net asset value. State and federal enforcement actions in late 2003 alleged that some brokers and fund managers permitted favored investors to trade at "stale" prices that did not reflect available information, thereby allowing a nearly risk-free profit. A description follows of the two principal forms of stale-price arbitrage, known as late trading and market timing.

"Late trading" occurs when a broker permits a customer to place orders after the close of trading, while still receiving a price based on that same day's net asset value. Investment Company Act Rule 22c-1 requires "forward pricing," that is, a fund must fill any orders it receives at the *next* calculated net asset value. Forward pricing prevents the risk-free arbitrage that would occur were an investor allowed to make a trade today using yesterday's price. Prior SEC guidance stated that an order is "received" when it is placed with a broker or other intermediary. Thus, an order placed with a broker at 3:00 p.m. and then transmitted as part of a batch of orders by the broker to the mutual fund at 5:00 p.m. could be filled at the same day's net asset value because the broker received the order before the 4:00 deadline.

This practice enables brokers to permit favored customers to submit orders after the 4:00 p.m. deadline but still receive the same day's net asset value. Canary's late trading in Bank of America mutual funds, as described in an SEC (2003a) enforcement release, provides an example. Bank of America owns a mutual fund management subsidiary and a broker-dealer subsidiary. An account executive at the broker-dealer permitted Canary to submit orders after 4:00 p.m. that were forwarded to Bank of America mutual funds as part of the broker's batch of orders. The account executive created a false audit trail making it appear that the Canary orders had been received prior to 4:00 p.m.

In return for the opportunity to late trade, Canary agreed to invest on a long-term basis in various Bank of America–sponsored investment vehicles and pay an annual "wrap fee" of 0.5 to 1.0 percent of all Canary investments made through Bank of America. The investments in Bank of America mutual funds and the wrap fee generated revenues for Bank of America's mutual fund management and brokerage subsidiaries. At the same time, the late trades diluted the value of other investors' shares. Canary was allowed to buy (or sell) at prices that were too low (or high) given information released after 4:00 p.m. In effect, then, the broker gave Canary free call and put options on the mutual fund shares at 4:00 p.m. prices, but expiring an hour or more after 4:00 p.m., with the cost of the options borne by the other mutual fund shareholders.

The "market timing" issue arises because in some cases, the prices of securities used to calculate net asset value are not current. The problem is most obvious when a mutual fund invests in non-U.S. stocks. The principal market for those stocks may have closed hours prior to the U.S. close. Even a domestic security may have last traded some time prior to the close. This is particularly true for less-liquid assets such as corporate bonds or small-capitalization stocks. The use of stale prices makes it possible for a trader to take advantage of information released after the last trade in foreign stocks or other assets, but prior to 4:00 Eastern time, based on information suggesting how the assets' price will change when trading reopens.

Unlike late trading, nothing marks an individual market timing trade as obviously improper. Any unsophisticated and uninformed investor could submit an order at an opportune time by chance and receive the benefit or suffer the loss from a stale price. The deliberate attempt to exploit stale prices, and not the occasional fortuity of benefiting from them, defines "improper" market timing.

Regulators have alleged that some mutual fund managers claimed to be taking aggressive steps to prevent deliberate market timing, but in fact permitted favored customers to engage in that activity. The essence of the claims, then, is that the fund managers misled shareholders into believing that market timing was not a problem.

The tell-tale sign of deliberate market timing is a high frequency of trades in and out of the fund. Frequent trades, whatever their motivation, create transaction costs for the mutual fund that are ultimately borne by long-term shareholders. No legal rule defines and prohibits excessive trading of mutual fund shares. In fact, a small number of mutual funds explicitly accommodate investors who wish to trade frequently. But mutual fund prospectuses usually state that the fund is intended for long-term investors and not in-and-out trading. Some funds charge a fee for redemptions that follow a purchase by less than a defined period (often 90 days). Other funds state that they limit the number of round-trip buying and selling transactions in a particular year. In addition, mutual fund prospectuses often reserve the right to refuse to execute individual trades if they are detrimental to long-term shareholders.

A mutual fund may also attempt to attack the problem of stale prices directly. Rule 2a-4 under the Investment Company Act of 1940 states that mutual funds should, where possible, use "current market value" to calculate net asset values. When current market value is unavailable, the fund should use the "fair value as determined in good faith by the board of directors." The SEC (2001) has expressed the view that a market value is not "current" when a "significant event" has occurred since the close of the principal market.

Fund managers may be able to estimate the current value of a foreign stock whose principal market is not open by reference to similar assets traded in the United States. For example, American Depositary Receipts (ADRs), which trade on U.S. stock markets, represent shares of specific foreign equities held on deposit by U.S. financial institutions. A mutual fund could base the value of its foreign stocks on the ADR closing prices, rather than the closing price in the home market. The fund could also estimate the value of a particular investment from futures prices or the prices of other traded assets.

However, the Securities and Exchange Commission has not explicitly approved any particular method of fair valuation. Moreover, departing from market prices requires the exercise of discretion by the fund's board, both to determine that the last-trade price is not "current" and that the methodology used to calculate "fair value" is appropriate. Mutual fund boards have apparently been reluctant to use fair valuation.

The market-timing enforcement actions in fall 2003 involved two basic patterns. In one, a would-be market timer used the services of an intermediary to camouflage its market-timing trades so that the target mutual funds were unaware of the market timer's presence. In the second pattern, a mutual fund management company deliberately permitted a large trader to time its funds in return for making long-term investments in the management company's other mutual funds or investment vehicles. In a variant on the latter pattern, some management companies permitted their own officers or employees to market-time their mutual funds.

Canary, which was allegedly set up primarily for the purpose of market timing, used both strategies. Canary entered into an arrangement with Security Trust Company (STC), which operates an electronic trading service for institutional clients. STC allows the manager of a pension plan, for example, to aggregate all its beneficiaries' transactions on a particular day in the mutual funds that are available under the plan and then to send a single net order to each of the relevant mutual funds. STC agreed to permit Canary to make trades that were transmitted as part of STC's net orders to the mutual funds, thus hiding Canary's orders in a larger flow and evading the funds' limits and fees on short-term transactions. Canary agreed to cease trading in a particular mutual fund if that fund complained to STC about the size and frequency of STC's orders. STC agreed not to provide similar accommodations to any other investor.

Canary also entered into arrangements with mutual fund management companies, including those affiliated with Bank of America, Bank One and Janus. In each case, the management company allowed Canary to make in-and-out trades in designated mutual funds, not to exceed specified amounts (often 0.5 or 1.0 percent of the fund's total assets) on any one day. The typical agreement provided that Canary would make its trades through exchanges to and from a money market fund in the same fund family. Canary agreed to invest on a long-term basis in other mutual funds or private investment vehicles managed by the same management company. Some of the management companies provided Canary with frequent updates on the composition of the target mutual fund's portfolio, which obviously facilitated Canary's attempts to profit from stale prices. Under SEC rules, mutual funds publicly disclose the make-up of their portfolios only semiannually (increasing to quarterly beginning in May 2004).

Shareholder Losses

How much did other mutual fund shareholders lose because of stale-price arbitrage? Zitzewitz (2003) estimates the losses from stale-price arbitrage in international funds. He compares daily net asset values with a hypothetical "fair value" net asset value that takes account of price changes in U.S. stocks and foreign equity futures occurring after the close of foreign markets. The paper multiplies the daily "error" in net asset value by total fund inflows or outflows, as relevant, to arrive at the dilution loss. Zitzewitz estimates that investors in international equity funds lost 56 basis points annually during the late 1990s.

Another estimate for a single mutual fund complex arose from New York state's suit against Invesco Funds Group. Invesco permitted favored customers to time its funds over the objections of its own individual fund managers, who complained that market timing harmed their funds' performance. In an internal memo that the attorney general's office obtained during its investigation, an Invesco employee analyzed the risk-adjusted performance of the target funds and argued to senior management that market timing was costing the target funds 75 to 100 basis points per year (*State of New York v. Invesco Funds Group*, 2003).

Manne (2004) questions the normative significance of these estimates. He argues that investors care about realized returns, which are made public, and should be indifferent to the precise means by which fund managers extract their compensation from the fund. Competition among funds and search by investors will assure that agency losses, like explicit management fees and other expenses, are minimized.

However, a wide range of legal rules governing fiduciaries limit compensation to what is agreed upon at the start of the transaction. Indeed, securities regulation originally developed in England and the United States as a means to ensure that all costs associated with the flotation of a new company were disclosed to investors prior to their purchases (Mahoney, 1995). Securities laws can improve welfare by providing a standard-form contract that specifies the ways in which corporate promoters may extract their compensation (La Porta, Lopez-de-Silanes and Shleifer, 2003). The legal proceedings against brokers, mutual fund management companies and their executives for "improper trading" are based principally on the extraction of non-bargained-for benefits. It is, however, an interesting research question whether investors' reduced demand for funds subject to market timing shifted part of the losses back to fund managers even before regulators intervened.

The Legal and Regulatory Response

Regulators have brought numerous civil and criminal proceedings against mutual fund managers, brokers and traders alleging improper trading in mutual fund shares. Meanwhile, the Securities and Exchange Commission, U.S. Congress and commentators have proposed a wide variety of regulatory changes. This section reviews these responses and identifies some underlying policy issues.

Legal Proceedings

Late trading and market timing schemes involved deceit against or by mutual fund managers and, in some cases, violations of explicit rules requiring forward pricing. Thus, assuming regulators can prove the relevant factual allegations, the traders, brokers or mutual fund managers who devised and benefited from these activities will likely be found to have engaged in securities fraud and other violations. In short, the late trading and market timing schemes described above were illegal under existing law.

The federal securities laws give the Securities and Exchange Commission ample remedies against violators. These are summarized in Table 5. The SEC can impose some of these sanctions on its own through administrative proceedings without going to court (although the defendant may appeal to the federal courts). Others require the SEC to bring suit in federal court. Federal prosecutors can also bring criminal charges against defendants who commit "knowing" violations of securities laws. When the defendant is an individual (such as a mutual fund or brokerage executive), the threat of jail time is a powerful bargaining chip for the government. Organizations, however, cannot be jailed, but only fined, so the difference between civil and criminal charges is less significant.

A regulator or prosecutor, through a settlement or plea bargain, may also fashion a remedy through negotiation with the defendant. Canary, for example, settled with New York without admitting or denying wrongdoing. The settlement required Canary to pay $40 million in restitution and cooperate with the state's investigation of various mutual fund complexes. In settling securities fraud charges brought by the state of New York, some mutual fund management companies have agreed to reduce their management fees going forward. A restriction on future management fees is a condition a court might have been reluctant to impose; indeed, the SEC declined to seek a similar agreement in its own settlement negotiations. However, these settlements were a brilliant public relations stroke for Spitzer, as they attacked the most visible deduction from investor returns.

Finally, federal and state securities laws give affected investors the right to sue those who commit securities fraud. Soon after the state of New York and the SEC began bringing suits against mutual fund management companies, private plaintiffs filed class action lawsuits. Many of these lawsuits name not only the mutual fund management companies, but also the mutual funds under their management, as defendants. Formally, a mutual fund is liable for misstatements in its prospectus. But the assets in the mutual fund are for practical purposes just a portfolio owned by current investors. Should the court permit *past* investors in Fund X to recover their losses from *present* investors in Fund X, the net effect will be a simple wealth transfer from one innocent group of investors to another innocent group of investors, plus their lawyers. If the courts allow suits to proceed against the mutual funds, the resulting losses to current investors could easily dwarf those from improper trades.

Proposed Rule Changes

Although existing laws should prove adequate to punish those who devised and benefited from improper trading practices, these practices nevertheless raise important policy questions. First, why didn't the Securities and Exchange Commission

Table 5

Remedies Available to the SEC in Civil Proceedings under Federal Securities Laws

Judicial remedies	
Monetary penalties	A court may assess penalties ranging from $5,000 to $100,000 for individuals and $50,000 to $500,000 for organizations for violations of the SEA, ICA or IAA. Alternatively, the penalty may equal the defendant's "gross pecuniary gain" from the violation. Penalties are paid to the U.S. Treasury except as noted below under "Disgorgement."
Injunction	A court may order the defendant to refrain from any "acts or practices" that violate the SEA, ICA or IAA. Failure to comply is punishable by fines and imprisonment.
Disgorgement	A court may order the defendant to forfeit any profit gained from the violation to the SEC, which distributes it to investors harmed by the violation. The Sarbanes-Oxley Act allows the SEC to supplement the disgorgement fund paid to investors with monetary penalties assessed for the same violation.
Prohibition on serving in specified capacities	A court may bar an individual defendant temporarily or permanently from serving in various capacities, including as a director or officer of a publicly traded company or mutual fund or as an investment adviser.
Administrative remedies	
Monetary penalties	The SEC has authority under the SEA, ICA and IAA to assess monetary penalties against certain regulated organizations and individuals, including broker-dealers and investment advisers and their professional employees, and mutual fund directors and officers. The penalties are generally of the same size available in judicial proceedings.
Cease and desist order	The SEC, after a hearing, may order any person who violates or causes a violation of the SEA, ICA or IAA to cease and desist from present and future violations. Failure to comply is punishable (through a court proceeding) by fines and imprisonment.
Disgorgement	In any proceeding under the SEA, ICA or IAA in which the SEC could impose a monetary penalty, it may also order disgorgement.
Prohibition on serving in specified capacities	The SEC may temporarily or permanently bar persons who engage in specified securities law violations from serving in various capacities, including as officers or directors of publicly traded companies or mutual funds, or as investment advisers.

Notes: The table lists the principal remedies available to the SEC in a civil suit brought in federal court or in an administrative proceeding under the Securities Exchange Act (SEA), Investment Company Act (ICA) or Investment Advisers Act (IAA). Special remedies related to insider trading are omitted entirely.

discover the late trading and market timing abuses until they had apparently become widespread? Second, although existing law will punish these improper trading practices after the fact, might different regulations have prevented these practices before the fact?

The Securities and Exchange Commission has proposed rule changes designed to resolve some mechanical pricing issues that made late trading possible. Other proposed rules will alter mutual fund corporate governance. One proposal is to require that orders be received by a mutual fund or its transfer agent, and not just a broker, by 4:00 p.m. to receive the current day's net asset value (SEC, 2003b). Another would require additional prospectus disclosures about the costs that frequent trading imposes on long-term investors and the steps the fund takes to limit such trading (SEC, 2003c). Another would require, with some exceptions, that mutual funds impose a 2 percent redemption fee on shares sold within five days of the purchase (SEC, 2004b). Yet another would require investment advisers to monitor their professional employees' trades (SEC, 2004c).

These reforms would address some of the manifestations of manager/shareholder conflicts that surfaced in 2003, but they do not alter the managers' incentives to find ways to increase their compensation. In keeping with its view that the board of directors is the principal means of dealing with these conflicts, the SEC (2004d) has proposed revisions of its board independence requirements. Independent directors of mutual funds would have to constitute at least 75 percent of the total and include the chairman. The independent directors would be entitled to their own staff to advise on corporate governance and conflict of interest issues. But outside the mutual fund context, there is at best mixed evidence that independent directors constrain management compensation or improve shareholder returns (Wan, 2003). In the case of mutual funds, it seems implausible that an independent director would have been able to see how management companies exploited details of price setting and order execution to extract additional compensation. In fact, many of the mutual funds affected by the scandals already had a majority of independent directors.

Other proposed reforms may offer more promising ways to reduce agency costs. The General Accounting Office has suggested that quarterly mutual fund account statements disclose the investors' pro rata dollar share of the fund's expenses (SEC, 2000). Thus, an account statement might note that the investor's shares increased in value by $120 for the quarter just ended and go on to note that the investor also bore $15 of management fees, 12b-1 fees and other expenses for the same period. The SEC (2004a), however, has rejected this proposal in favor of a new requirement that a mutual fund's semiannual shareholder report include a table showing the dollar amount of expenses incurred per $1,000 invested.

In the rush to adopt new rules, regulators have not asked whether existing investor protection rules unintentionally exacerbate manager-shareholder conflicts. The existing regulatory system encourages the segregation of sophisticated and unsophisticated investors into different investment vehicles with different compensation and governance arrangements. Because institutions and high-net-worth individuals are considered not to require the same protections as retail investors, they are permitted to invest in hedge funds, lightly regulated vehicles that typically use performance-based fees. Regulatory restrictions, by contrast, assure that the mutual funds offered to retail investors use asset-based compensation for fund managers. The compensation paid to brokers who sell mutual fund shares is set by the fund manager, rather than the brokers themselves. Mutual fund governance structures and contracts with fund managers and other service providers are regulated in detail. Although these restrictions were motivated by a desire to curb manager-shareholder conflicts, they may have institutionalized these conflicts by limiting a fund manager's ability to experiment with new compensation or governance practices and by reducing retail investors' opportunities to invest alongside institutions that would monitor and control fund managers.

One alternative policy response, then, would be to try to harness the monitoring efforts of institutional investors for the benefit of unsophisticated investors. Rather than relax regulatory restrictions for investment vehicles sold only to institutions and high-net-worth individuals, perhaps compensation and governance restrictions could be reduced for investment vehicles that include a mix of institutional and retail participation. Any rule changes, of course, may produce unintended consequences, such as introducing conflicts between the interests of institutional and retail investors. Given the potential benefits of greater monitoring, however, the idea may deserve consideration.

Finally, the SEC might pay greater attention to patterns of flows into and out of mutual funds, which may convey information about the manager's attempts to attract investors and about market timing. When a particular mutual fund experiences wide swings in daily inflows, the SEC might ask whether the fund manager's tactics for attracting inflows are consistent with the interests of long-run shareholders.

Conclusion

Mutual funds give investors the benefit of diversification and, if the fund is actively managed, professional money management. Many large, well-known mutual funds provide these services at low prices. But how can unsophisticated investors know whether they are paying a reasonable price? A premise of current mutual fund regulation is that the market should set fees, but those fees should be transparent. In the mutual fund scandals of 2003, mutual fund managers secretly obtained extra compensation by selling the right to trade at stale prices. But even before the scandals unfolded, some researchers were asking whether the size of management fees and other expenses in some mutual funds suggested that investors lacked the sophistication to take appropriate account of costs.

It appears politically inevitable that the policy response to the mutual fund scandals will include a large number of new rules. However, it would be a mistake for researchers and regulators to focus only on what could be done with new rules, to the exclusion of what might be done by relaxing or altering existing rules. Unlike most of securities regulation, mutual fund regulation is not focused principally on disclosure, but tightly constrains compensation and governance practices. Regulators should consider whether those constraints have frozen nonoptimal practices into place.

To the extent new rules are needed, the traditional focus on disclosure and transparency may work best. The Securities and Exchange Commission has tried to draw investor attention to fees and other expenses in mutual fund prospectuses and on its own website. It is therefore curious that the SEC has resisted calls for investor-specific disclosure of the dollar amount of fees and expenses in the quarterly account statements sent to investors. Given that industry-wide investor costs are measured in the tens of billions of dollars annually, even a modest increase in investors' sensitivity to costs could result in enormous aggregate savings.

■ *I am grateful to John Chalmers, John Harrison, James Hines, Gregory Kadlec, Julia Mahoney, Andrei Shleifer, Timothy Taylor, Craig Tyle and Michael Waldman for comments and suggestions.*

References

Carhart, Mark M. 1997. "On Persistence in Mutual Fund Performance." *Journal of Finance.* 52:1, pp. 57–82.

Chalmers, John M. R., Roger M. Edelen and Gregory B. Kadlec. 1999. "An Analysis of Mutual Fund Trading Costs." Working paper.

Daniel, Kent, Mark Grinblatt, Sheridan Titman and Russ Wermers. 1997. "Measuring Mutual fund Performance with Characteristic-Based Benchmarks." *Journal of Finance.* 52:3, pp. 1035–058.

Das, Sanjiv Ranjan and Rangarajan K. Sundaram. 1998. "On the Regulation of Fee Structures in Mutual Funds." NBER Working Paper No. 6639.

Della Vigna, Stefano and Ulrike Malmendier. 2003. "Contract Design and Self-Control: Theory and Evidence." Working paper.

Elton, Edwin J., Martin J. Gruber, Sanjiv Das and Matthew Hlavka. 1993. "Efficiency with Costly Information: A Reinterpretation of Evidence from Managed Portfolios." *Review of Financial Studies.* 6:1, pp. 1–22.

Federal Reserve. 2003. *Flow of Funds Accounts of the United States: Flows and Outstandings Fourth Quarter 2002.* Washington, D.C.: Board of Governors of the Federal Reserve System.

Gabaix, Xavier and David Laibson. 2003. "Some Industrial Organization with Boundedly Rational Consumers." Working paper.

Golec, Joseph. 2003. "Regulation and the Rise in Asset-Based Mutual Fund Management Fees." *Journal of Financial Research.* 26:1, pp. 19–30.

Hortaçsu, Ali and Chad Syverson. 2003. "Product Differentiation, Search Costs, and Competition in the Mutual Fund Industry: A Case Study of S&P 500 Index Funds." Working paper.

Investment Company Institute. 2001. *2001 Profile of Mutual Fund Shareholders.* Washington, D.C.: Investment Company Institute.

Investment Company Institute. 2003. *Mutual Fund Fact Book.* Washington, D.C.: Investment Company Institute.

Investment Company Institute. 2004. "The Cost of Buying and Owning Mutual Funds." *Fundamentals: Investment Company Institute Research in Brief.* 13:1, pp. 1–24.

Jensen, Michael C. 1967. "The Performance of Mutual Funds in the Period 1945–1964." *Journal of Finance.* 23:2, pp. 389–416.

Khorana, Ajay and Henri Servaes. 2000. "What Drives Market Share in the Mutual Fund Industry?" Working paper.

La Porta, Rafael, Florencio Lopez-de-Silanes and Andrei Shleifer. 2003. "What Works in Securities Laws?" Working paper.

Livingston, Miles and Edward S. O'Neal. 1996. "Mutual Fund Brokerage Commissions." *Journal of Financial Research.* 19:2, pp. 273–92.

Mahoney, Paul G. 1995. "Mandatory Disclosure as a Solution to Agency Problems." *University of Chicago Law Review.* 62:3, pp. 1047–112.

Malkiel, Burton G. 1995. "Returns from Investing in Equity Mutual Funds 1971 to 1991." *Journal of Finance.* 50:2, pp. 529–72.

Manne, Henry G. 2004. "What Mutual-Fund Scandal?" *Wall Street Journal.* January 8, p. A22.

Morey, Matthew R. 2002. "Should You Carry the Load? A Comprehensive Analysis of Load and No-Load Mutual Fund Out-of-Sample Performance." Working paper.

Securities and Exchange Commission (SEC). 2000. "Division of Investment Management: Report on Mutual Fund Fees and Expenses."

Securities and Exchange Commission (SEC). 2001. "Investment Company Institute." No-action letter, April 30.

Securities and Exchange Commission (SEC). 2003a. "In the Matter of Theodore Charles Sihpol III." Securities Act Release 8288, September 16.

Securities and Exchange Commission (SEC). 2003b. "Amendments to Rules Governing Pricing of Mutual Fund Shares." Investment Company Act Release No. 26288, December 17.

Securities and Exchange Commission (SEC). 2003c. "Disclosure Regarding Market Timing and Selective Disclosure of Portfolio Holdings." Securities Act Release No. 8343, December 11.

Securities and Exchange Commission (SEC). 2004a. "Shareholder Reports and Quarterly Portfolio Disclosure of Registered Management Investment Companies." Securities Act Release No. 8393, February 27.

Securities and Exchange Commission (SEC). 2004b. "Mandatory Redemption Fees for Redeemable Fund Securities." Investment Company Act Release No. 26375A, March 5.

Securities and Exchange Commission (SEC). 2004c. "Investment Advisor Codes of Ethics." Investment Advisers Act Release No. 2209, January 20.

Securities and Exchange Commission (SEC). 2004d. "Investment Company Governance." Investment Company Act Release No. 26323, January 15.

Siggelkow, Nickolaj. 1999. "Expense Shifting: An Empirical Study of Agency Costs in the Mutual Fund Industry." Working paper.

Sirri, Erik R. and Peter Tufano. 1998. "Costly Search and Mutual Fund Flows." *Journal of Finance.* 53:5, pp. 1589–622.

"Special Report, Mutual Funds: Perils in the Savings Pool." 2003. *Economist.* 369, pp. 65–67.

State of New York v. Invesco Fund Group. 2003. Civil Complaint, Supreme Court of the State of New York, County of New York, December 3; Available at ⟨http://www.oag.state.ny.us/press/2003/dec/dec02a_03.html⟩.

Wan, Kam-Ming. 2003. "Independent Directors, Executive Pay, and Firm Performance." Working paper.

Zitzewitz, Eric. 2003. "Who Cares About Shareholders? Arbitrage-Proofing Mutual Funds." *Journal of Law, Economics and Organization.* 19:2, pp. 245–80.

Asbestos and the Future of Mass Torts

Michelle J. White

L egal claims for injuries from asbestos involve more plaintiffs, more defendants and higher costs than any other type of personal injury litigation in U.S. history. As of the end of 2002, 730,000 individuals had filed lawsuits against more than 8,400 defendants, and the total amount that defendants and insurers had spent on resolving claims—including all legal costs—was estimated to be $70 billion (Carroll et al., 2004). Eighty-five corporations have filed for bankruptcy due to asbestos liabilities, and several insurance companies have either failed or are in financial distress (White, 2002b). Estimates of the total number of people who will eventually file claims range from 1.0 million to 3.0 million, and estimates of the eventual cost of asbestos litigation range from $200–$265 billion (Carroll et al., 2004).

Asbestos was once referred to as the "miracle mineral" for its ability to withstand heat. It was heavily used as a fireproofing and insulating material in ships, buildings and consumer products, including wallboard, roofing, flooring, cement, insulation, drinking water pipes, automobiles, clothing, paper, hair dryers, garden products, home appliances, artificial firelogs and children's toys. Estimates of the number of Americans exposed to asbestos range from 27 million to 100 million (Biggs et al., 2001).

But breathing asbestos fibers—which can be microscopic—causes a variety of diseases. Two of these diseases, asbestosis and mesothelioma, are uniquely associated with asbestos exposure. Asbestosis is scarring of the lungs that reduces breathing capacity; it can range from nondisabling to fatal. Mesothelioma is cancer of the pleural lining around the chest and abdomen and is quickly fatal. Other asbestos

■ *Michelle J. White is Professor of Economics, University of California at San Diego, La Jolla, California. She is also a Research Associate, National Bureau of Economic Research, Cambridge, Massachusetts. Her e-mail address is ⟨miwhite@ucsd.edu⟩.*

diseases such as lung cancer, gastrointestinal cancer and pleural plaque (thickening of the pleural lining that is nondisabling) can be caused either by asbestos exposure or by other factors, including smoking. Asbestos diseases have a long latency period: 20 to 40 years usually elapse between exposure and diagnosis. Longer and heavier exposure to asbestos increases the probability of developing asbestos diseases, but they can also occur in people who had only limited exposure (Carroll et al., 2004). A famous study of 370 insulation workers who were union members in 1942 illustrates the grim effects of asbestos: between 1963 and 1968, 113 of the workers died when 60 deaths would normally be expected. The deaths included 28 from lung cancer (2.5 would be normal) and eight from gastrointestinal cancer (two would be normal), plus 15 from asbestosis and 13 from mesothelioma (zero would be normal) (Brodeur, 1973, p. 29). Asbestos can also cause disease in workers' family members and bystanders, who are exposed to asbestos dust on workers' clothes or in the environment.

In this article, I first examine why regulation failed to prevent asbestos from becoming so widely used and how asbestos litigation widened from a trickle into a torrent. I also consider other countries' experience with asbestos and whether regulation or liability is more effective in deterring production of dangerous products. The article then asks how asbestos litigation differs from other mass torts: does asbestos litigation represent a "perfect storm" where many factors came together with disastrous results, or does it represent a path that is likely to be followed by other mass torts involving personal injury? Various ways in which the asbestos crisis might be resolved are considered, including bankruptcy, a class action settlement, legislation now pending in Congress to establish a national asbestos compensation fund and an alternative approach that would centralize asbestos lawsuits in a single federal court.

Liability versus Regulation of Asbestos Exposure

The Failure of Regulation

As early as the 1920s, physicians recognized that exposure to asbestos caused disease, and asbestosis was named and described in British medical journals. Around the same time, insurance companies in the United States and Canada stopped selling life insurance to asbestos workers. In 1931, the British government began regulating workplace safety in the asbestos industry, monitoring workers for asbestosis and providing worker's compensation to those who were disabled by it (Tweedale, 2000, p. 21). Safer substitutes for many uses of asbestos were known as early as the 1930s (Castleman, 1996, chapter 6). Nonetheless, U.S. consumption of asbestos increased from 100,000 metric tons in 1932 to 700,000 metric tons in 1951 and peaked at 750,000 metric tons in 1974. Thereafter, usage declined rapidly to about 25,000 metric tons in 1994 (Castleman, 1996, p. 788). That asbestos was so widely used from the 1950s to the 1980s suggests that multiple regulatory systems failed, including workers' compensation, workplace safety regulation, product safety regulation and liability law.

In the United States, many states set up workers' compensation programs in the 1930s. Under these programs, workers injured on the job or disabled by occupational diseases received compensation from a fund financed by experience-rated payments by employers. Asbestos producers favored the establishment of workers' compensation systems, but lobbied for low compensation levels and highly restrictive eligibility rules. Because asbestos diseases develop slowly and symptoms are easily mistaken for other diseases, workers often left their jobs without knowing that they had asbestos disease and therefore did not quality for compensation. Indeed, asbestos producers such as Johns-Manville conducted physical examinations of their workers, but did not inform them if they had asbestosis to hold down the number of compensation claims. Other workers were ineligible for compensation because of short statutes of limitations for filing claims (Castleman, 1996, pp. 194, pp. 238–242). Workers' compensation systems also benefited asbestos producers because they were workers' exclusive legal remedy against their employers—that is, if workers' compensation claims were denied, workers could not file lawsuits against their employers for damages. Because workers' compensation was so favorable to asbestos producers, producers did not face high costs, which would have given them an incentive to improve workplace safety.

As for regulation of workplace and product safety, there were scattered federal and state programs involving occupational safety in the 1950s and 1960s, but most were voluntary and, even when rules limiting asbestos exposure were adopted, they were not enforced (Sherrill, 1973; Brodeur, 1973). Moreover, some regulatory efforts actually increased exposure to asbestos, such as building codes that required use of asbestos insulation in the ventilation systems of commercial buildings. The insulation deteriorated as it aged, and then asbestos fibers were blown throughout the buildings.

In the early 1970s, efforts to regulate workplace and consumer product safety increased with the creation of the Occupational Health and Safety Administration (OSHA) in 1970, the Environmental Protection Agency (EPA) in 1970 and the Consumer Product Safety Commission (CPSC) in 1972. OSHA quickly adopted a maximum limit of five asbestos fibers per cubic centimeter of air, with the standard to fall to two fibers in 1976. Even the two-fiber standard was not very strict, since an exposed worker would breathe 10 million asbestos fibers in an eight-hour day. When unions and public interest groups petitioned OSHA to tighten the standard, it shortened the phase-in period for the two-fiber standard. But a few years later when studies indicated that the two-fiber limit was not strict enough to prevent asbestosis, OSHA had become more responsive to industry concerns, and it did not respond. Only in 1983 was the standard lowered again to 0.5 fibers (McCaffrey, 1982, chapters 5–6). In the late 1970s, the Consumer Product Safety Commission pressured manufacturers to remove asbestos voluntarily from products such as hair dryers and children's toys, but these efforts were halted in the 1980s under the Reagan administration. In 1989, the Environmental Protection Agency proposed a ban on asbestos use. But the ban was overturned by a federal circuit court in 1991 over technical issues, and since the EPA never appealed the decision to a higher court or resubmitted the proposal, it never went into effect (Bowker, 2003). As of 2004, the United States still has not banned asbestos.

Thus, because the large asbestos producers were able to capture the regulators, the government was very slow to limit asbestos exposure in the United States. Since regulation largely failed, what about legal liability?

A Short History of Asbestos Litigation

Workers who are harmed by asbestos products fall into two groups: those who produce the products and those who install or demolish them (such as shipyard and construction workers). While asbestos producers' liability to their own employees was limited by workers' compensation, their liability to non-employees who use their products was not.

The liability environment became less favorable for asbestos producers in the 1960s, for three reasons. First, a number of states changed their statutes of limitations for filing workers' compensation claims by starting them from the date of discovery of disease rather than the date of exposure, and this caused more workers to file claims. In 1969, Johns-Manville—the largest U.S. asbestos producer—paid nearly $1 million in workers' compensation to 285 of its employees who had severe asbestosis (Brodeur, 1973, p. 46). Second, a number of independent epidemiological studies were published in the 1960s that showed strong links between asbestos exposure and asbestosis, cancer and mesothelioma. Third, products liability law itself was changing. Before the 1960s, producers were liable for damage to users of their products only if producers were negligent. In practice, this standard was ineffective in deterring dangerous behavior because it was difficult for plaintiffs to prove negligence, regardless of how badly producers behaved. But during the 1960s, the law of product liability moved away from the negligence standard and toward making producers "strictly liable" for damages. Under the strict liability rule, producers are liable for damage to users regardless of whether they were negligent or not, as long as their products are "unreasonably dangerous" or users were not adequately warned of the danger. This change in the law made it easier for asbestos users to win lawsuits against the asbestos manufacturers, because asbestos products were extremely dangerous and rarely contained warnings. In response to the changed legal environment, asbestos producers began putting mild warnings on asbestos insulation starting in 1964 and on sacks of asbestos fiber in 1969 (Castleman, 1996, pp. 386–387). In theory, both the negligence and the strict liability rules can give producers economically efficient incentives to increase product safety (Shavell, 1987). But in practice, the move to strict liability rule gave producers a much stronger incentive to substitute safer materials for asbestos.

The first trial in which a user of asbestos products—an insulation worker—won damages from the large asbestos manufacturers was *Borel v. Fibreboard* (443 F.2nd 1076 [5th Cir. 1973]), which occurred in 1973. During the following decade, 25,000 additional products liability lawsuits were filed. These lawsuits gradually became more successful as plaintiffs' lawyers obtained evidence showing that the major producers had known the dangers of asbestos exposure for decades (Brodeur, 1985). One important piece of evidence was that, during the 1930s, the major producers commissioned research that demonstrated the health hazards of asbestos, but kept the results secret and did not warn either their workers or product users of the danger. Evidence of a cover-up, combined with defendants' failure to warn, frequently led juries to award punitive as well as compensatory damages. About one-sixth of all damage awards in asbestos trials from 1987–2002 included punitive damages—a high fraction compared to other types of litigation (White, 2002a). Because punitive damages are often uninsurable, many defendants shifted from a strategy of vigorously defending against all claims to a strategy of settling. But when defendants settle claims rather than going to trial, representing claimants becomes very profitable for plaintiffs' lawyers, since most of their costs are incurred at trial. Plaintiffs' lawyers therefore began seeking out additional claimants and the volume of asbestos litigation grew. The large number of plaintiffs is one distinguishing feature of asbestos litigation.

Plaintiffs' lawyers search for plaintiffs by screening large numbers of workers who might have been exposed to asbestos, such as textile factory workers. They file lawsuits on behalf of anyone whose x-rays show scarring or thickening of the pleural lining or the lungs. Few of these claimants have any asbestos-related impairment, but in many states they meet the legal standard for injury. Various studies have estimated that between two-thirds and nine-tenths of asbestos claimants are unimpaired and that many claims are fraudulent. But when lawsuits are settled rather than going to trial, plaintiffs' injury claims are never verified. The legal standards that allowed such a loose connection between being a plaintiff and having an actual asbestos-related disability are a second distinctive feature of asbestos litigation.

In asbestos lawsuits, plaintiffs may sue as many as 50 to 100 defendants, including all producers of products that the plaintiff might have been exposed to. Potential asbestos defendants include any firm that ever produced, installed or sold asbestos-related products, used some form of asbestos in its production process or in its products or owned a building that contained asbestos. Defendants include Sears (sold asbestos-containing products), Gerber Baby Food (owns factories that contained asbestos), Dow Jones & Co. (operates workplaces that contained asbestos), GM and Ford (vehicle brakes contained asbestos) and 3M (produced a respirator that did not protect users from asbestos). Plaintiffs' law firms have aggressively pursued litigation against insurers, too, and sometimes succeeded in collecting far more than the coverage limits of the original insurance policies. Recently, two separate insurers paid about $1 billion each to resolve liabilities based on small insurance policies that they issued many years ago to a former distributor of asbestos insulation (Oster, 2002; Treaster, 2003). Another insurer, MetLife, is currently being sued on the grounds that it was involved in research during the 1930s that showed the adverse health effects of asbestos, but failed to disclose the results (Oster, 2003). The extraordinarily high number of defendants is a third important factor that is distinctive about asbestos litigation.

Forum-shopping is also an important part of plaintiffs' success in asbestos litigation. During the 1980s, many asbestos claims were filed in federal courts. But federal courts rarely allowed punitive damages in asbestos trials, and starting in the 1990s, they began requiring that all asbestos claims be transferred to a single federal judge in Pennsylvania for pretrial discovery. This step substantially length-ened the litigation process, and in response, most plaintiffs' lawyers shifted to filing their asbestos claims in state courts. They particularly sought out states whose laws and legal procedures favor plaintiffs and jurisdictions within those states whose judges and juries are pro-plaintiff. They also seek out individual judges who pressure defendants to settle.

Favored locations have varied over time (Carroll et al., 2004). Texas was favored in the 1990s, until it adopted legislation that limited punitive damages and restricted the right of plaintiffs' lawyers to choose among jurisdictions (Glaberson, 1999). Currently favored locations include Madison County, Illinois, various coun-ties in West Virginia and especially Mississippi—where 20 percent of all asbestos claims are reportedly filed (Parloff, 2002). Mississippi courts favor asbestos plaintiffs in a number of ways. First, they have no limits on the size of punitive or compen-satory damage awards. Second, they allow plaintiffs' lawyers to join hundreds or thousands of asbestos claims from all over the country under a single docket number (at least one plaintiff must be a Mississippi resident). Joined claims differ from class actions in that, if they go to trial, the judge or jury decides each claim separately. But they are handled as a group for pretrial purposes, and, if a trial occurs, multiple claims from the group are tried together. This increases the degree of correlation of trial outcomes, which raises the risk of trial and encourages defendants to settle (White, 2002a). For example, a recent Mississippi trial involved 12 asbestos plaintiffs who were selected from a group of 1,738 joined claims. The 12 plaintiffs were awarded total damages of $48 million, with some receiving $2 million or more despite having no detectable asbestos disease. After the trial, the judge directed the parties to settle the remaining 1,726 claims and threatened that, otherwise, he would use the same jury for the remaining claims and would direct the jury to consider awarding punitive damages. In response, defendants settled all claims on what were reported to be very favorable terms for plaintiffs (Parloff, 2002). Third, Mississippi courts do not require judges to approve the terms of mass settlements, which means that plaintiffs' legal fees are not subject to judicial scrutiny. As a result, although plaintiffs' lawyers gain from economies of scale in litigating large numbers of joined claims, they can still charge plaintiffs the same high legal fees—25 to 40 percent of settlements or damage awards—that prevail in individual litigation. Fourth, in some Mississippi counties, courts do not allow defendants to verify disease claims by conducting medical exams of plaintiffs.

White (2002a) examined the effect of forum shopping on the value of asbestos claims, using a dataset of all asbestos trials since 1987. I found that the expected value of an asbestos claim at trial in favorable jurisdictions such as Mississippi, West Virginia and Houston, Texas, was $3 million higher than in other jurisdictions (in 2000 dollars). When asbestos claims went to trial in groups rather than individually, plaintiffs' expected gain from trial was about $600,000 higher. I also found that when defendants were found liable for punitive damages, their settlement costs increased sharply in later years and they attracted thousands of additional claims. Punitive damage awards signal that a defendant is a particularly vulnerable target.

Why are some states and jurisdictions so strongly pro-plaintiff? Since state court judges are elected, one answer is that plaintiffs' lawyers contribute generously to judges' re-election campaigns in jurisdictions where they frequently file claims. Plaintiffs' lawyers have an advantage over defendants' lawyers as contributors, since they choose where to file claims and tend to file in particular jurisdictions repeatedly. If judges do not treat them favorably, they can move their claims elsewhere. Another factor is that, for a small county seat, playing host to high-stakes trials that attract many out-of-state lawyers is a form of economic development, supporting local hotels and restaurants and increasing the number of jobs in the county courthouse. States also gain from having pro-plaintiff laws because some plaintiffs are state residents and litigation transfers resources to them from out-of-state defendants. State court judges sometimes encourage juries to award high damages in asbestos trials on the grounds that funds for damage awards are limited and will otherwise go to residents of other states. Plaintiffs' lawyers also sometimes arrange the terms of mass asbestos settlements to reward favorable states by paying higher damages to their residents. For example, one large asbestos settlement paid damages of $263,000 to plaintiffs who were residents of Mississippi, but only $14,000 to plaintiffs who had the same disease but were residents of Pennsylvania or Ohio (Rothstein, 2001). But there are also costs to attracting mass filings of asbestos and other tort claims—Texas changed its legal rules because of concern that excessive litigation was driving firms to leave the state (Glaberson, 1999).

Between 1982 and 2002, the total number of asbestos claimants grew from 1,000 to 730,000, the total number of firms that have been sued grew from 300 to 8,400, and the amount spent by defendants and insurers on asbestos litigation grew from $1 billion to $70 billion in nominal dollars. Because plaintiffs sue multiple defendants, the total number of asbestos claims—that is, the number of claims by individual plaintiffs against individual defendants—is in the millions. The number of new claims filed with the Manville Trust—which pays asbestos claims for the bankrupt asbestos producer Johns-Manville—increased from about 20,000 per year in the early 1990s to 101,000 in 2003. Average damage awards in asbestos trials rose from $675,000 in 1990–1991 to about $3 million in 2000–2003.[1]

The European Experience

Did European countries manage the asbestos problem better than the United States? No. Levels of asbestos exposure were even higher in Europe than in the United States, and consumption levels declined more slowly (see Table 1). Death

---

[1] All data are taken from Carroll et al. (2004), except for the number of Manville Trust claims, which comes from ⟨http://www.mantrust.org⟩, and the damage award figures, which are taken from White (2002a).

Table 1

Consumption of Asbestos in the United States versus Europe

(metric tons per million population)

	U.K.	Germany	France	U.S.	World
1970	6.69	3.91	5.32	3.46	0.92
1975	5.46	5.57	5.24	3.01	1.05
1980	3.07	4.07	3.42	1.53	1.05
1985	1.04	1.08	1.13	0.63	0.91
1990	0.92	0.58	3.40	0.20	0.80

Notes: Figures for the United Kingdom, France and Germany are calculated from the value of asbestos imports per million population, taken from the *NBER Trade Database*, Disk 2, *World Trade Flows*, 1970–1992. Import figures are converted to tons consumed using price data from the *Statistical Abstract of the U.S.*, various editions. (None of the three European countries produces raw asbestos.) Figures for the United States and the world are based on consumption of asbestos, taken from Castleman (1996, pp. 788, 838). Population figures are from the U.S. Census Bureau, International Data Base, ⟨http://www.census.gov/ipc/www/idbnew.html⟩.

rates from mesothelioma as of 1998 are higher in Europe than in the United States: 1.85 versus 1.0 per 100,000 people, respectively. Moreover, while the death rate from mesothelioma peaked in the 1990s and is starting to decline in the United States (National Cancer Institute, 2003, Table I-7), it is predicted to double over the next 20 years in six large European countries (Peto, Vecchia, Levi and Negri, 1999).

The European countries, like Britain, mandated compensation for workers who developed asbestos disease through their workers' compensation or national insurance systems. But because of industry pressure, few workers actually received compensation, so that there was little pressure on producers to reduce use of asbestos. In France, 500 new cases of mesothelioma occurred annually in the mid-1980s, but only 20–40 cases per year received compensation. Similarly in Italy, 400 new cases of mesothelioma occurred annually in the 1990s, but none received compensation between 1988 and 1995 (Castleman, 1996, p. 813). In both countries, long and complicated administrative procedures discouraged victims from filing claims. In Switzerland and the Netherlands, statutes of limitations that start from the date of exposure rather than the date of discovery of disease prevented many asbestos victims from receiving compensation. In the United Kingdom in 1986, there were four times the number of mesothelioma cases per capita as in the United States, but only one-fifth the number of asbestos-related legal claims (Kazan-Allen, 2000a). Asbestos victims in the United Kingdom were discouraged from filing lawsuits against either the workers' compensation system or asbestos producers, because contingency fees are not allowed and unsuccessful plaintiffs must pay the defendant's legal costs as well as their own. Also, British plaintiffs cannot collect punitive damages against producers and do not have the extensive rights of discovery that helped U.S. lawyers build strong cases against asbestos producers. In recent years, the situation in the United Kingdom has changed, with more asbestos claims being filed and more claimants obtaining compensation, although compensation levels remain modest by U.S. standards. Ironically, one of the largest asbestos producers in the United Kingdom, Turner and Newall Industries, went bankrupt because of the costs of paying asbestos claims by American plaintiffs who sued its U.S. subsidary.

As in the United States, regulation of asbestos in the European countries was weak because of regulatory capture. But, unlike the United States, liability did not emerge as a substitute for regulation, and as a result, European asbestos product makers were slower to reduce asbestos use than their U.S. counterparts. It was only when the European countries began to adopt bans on asbestos importation and use in the 1990s that asbestos exposure fell sharply. Switzerland banned use of asbestos in 1990, and ten other European countries adopted full or partial bans during the 1990s. The European Union adopted a ban on all types of asbestos in 1999, to take effect in 2005 (Kazan-Allen, 2000b).

The Effectiveness of Liability versus Regulation

Does the asbestos saga suggest any lessons concerning the effectiveness of liability versus regulation in controlling workplace and product dangers? For the United States, neither policy was effective until the early 1970s, when OSHA imposed new limits on workplace asbestos exposure and the *Borel* trial occurred. However, the regulatory efforts of OSHA, CPSC and EPA were quite ineffective throughout the 1970s, while the *Borel* trial was followed by a litigation explosion. By the late 1970s, the pressure of litigation caused U.S. producers to eliminate asbestos from most products, causing overall U.S. consumption to decline sharply. But, for Europe, neither liability nor regulation was effective until the 1990s.

The asbestos saga suggests that the worse the failure of regulation, the more likely that the courts will respond with high liability. This is because the callous behavior of producers in consciously exposing workers and product users to danger tends to make judges and juries very sympathetic to plaintiffs.

Is Asbestos Different from Other Mass Torts?

Several mass torts involving personal injury have been largely or fully resolved in recent years: for example, the Fen-Phen diet supplement litigation was resolved in 2000; a settlement of the tobacco claims involving the 50 states was reached in 1998; claims for harm due to breast implants were resolved in 1994; the Dalkon Shield (intrauterine contraceptive device) litigation was settled in 1988; and the Agent Orange litigation was settled in 1984. Along with asbestos, a number of other mass torts are still in litigation, including claims of harm due to lead exposure, firearms, fast food and individual claims involving harm from tobacco. Table 2 gives some characteristics of asbestos and other mass torts involving personal injury. In this section, I consider how asbestos differs from other mass torts and whether these differences offer some guidance as to how asbestos litigation might be resolved.

Table 2
Characteristics of Personal Injury Mass Torts

	Type of product	*Number of defendants*	*Number/type of plaintiffs*	*Amount of compensation fund*	*Year resolved*	*Type of resolution*
Asbestos	Insulation and other products	6,000 as of 2000	600,000 as of 2000			Individual defendant bankruptcies only
Agent Orange	Defoliant used in the Vietnam War	12	250,000	$180 million	1984	Class action settlement
Dalkon Shield	Defective I.U.D.	1	140,000	$2.3 billion	1988	Bankruptcy
Breast implants	Silicon gel breast implants	3	440,000	$4.2 billion	1994	Class action settlement (Later the main defendant filed for bankruptcy.)
Fen-Phen	Diet drugs	1	Filing period still open	$3.76 billion	2000	Class action settlement (nonmandatory)
Tobacco	Cigarettes	4	50 U.S. states	$246 billion	1998	Settlement between 50 states and the tobacco companies (Private lawsuits still pending.)
Lead	Leaded paint		State and local governments			None
Firearms	Guns		Cities, counties, U.S. government and private plaintiffs			None
Fast food	Hamburgers, etc.		Private plaintiffs			None

Sources: Mintz (1985) for Dalkon Shield; Schuck (1986) for Agent Orange; Tidmarsh (1998) and Rheingold (1996, p. 331) for breast implants; Dean (2001) and Butterfield (2003) for lead paint and firearms; Derthick (2002) for tobacco; Ives (2002) for fast food.

Number of Defendants and Plaintiffs

While 730,000 people have filed asbestos claims so far, other mass torts also have hundreds of thousands of claimants. The Agent Orange litigation eventually involved about 250,000 claimants, and the breast implant litigation involved 440,000. Tobacco and fast food litigation potentially involve many more plaintiffs than asbestos, since huge numbers of Americans smoked or are obese. But while many plaintiffs are necessary for a mass tort, they are not sufficient. There must also be funds to pay high damages.

Where asbestos differs strongly from other mass torts is in the number of defendants involved. About 8,400 defendants have been sued for asbestos damage, while no previous mass tort has had more than about a dozen. Because so many firms were involved with asbestos production, plaintiffs' lawyers have been able to substitute new defendants as old ones go bankrupt. Also, the large number of defendants means that many insurers have obligations to pay. As a result, even with hundreds of thousands of asbestos claims, there are enough deep pockets to keep the litigation going.

The Law is Different for Asbestos

Asbestos developed its own legal doctrines that differ from other areas of tort litigation. One difference is that the burden on asbestos claimants of proving causation is lower. Normally, plaintiffs must show that a particular defendant's product caused their harm. Providing this kind of evidence would be difficult for most asbestos plaintiffs, since they often were exposed to many different asbestos products and cannot establish that any particular product caused their harm. In response, courts loosened the rules of causation, so that asbestos plaintiffs were only required to present evidence that particular defendants' products were used at their workplaces. Co-workers' recollections of seeing a particular product in the workplace are usually allowed, even though this type of evidence would not normally be admitted in court (Brickman, 1992). Asbestos is not the first mass tort in which relaxed standards of causation have been used—an earlier example is litigation over the drug DES, which harmed the daughters of women who took it during pregnancy. Because multiple manufacturers produced DES and victims could not prove which manufacturer's DES harmed them, all were found liable for damages based on their market shares. But many mass torts remain small because plaintiffs cannot meet the burden of demonstrating causation. For example, in the lead paint litigation, plaintiffs generally lose lawsuits against paint manufacturers, because their homes have many layers of lead paint and they cannot show that any particular manufacturer's paint caused their harm (Dean, 2001; Cupp, 2000).

Another way that asbestos claims differ from other tort claims is in how claimants with no asbestos-related impairment are treated. Under normal tort law, their claims would not be allowed to proceed in the legal system, because they have not suffered any harm. Some state courts follow this general approach by putting these claims on an "inactive docket," which preserves plaintiffs' right to sue in the future if they develop a serious asbestos disease, but otherwise prevents their claims from proceeding. Other states allow these claimants to collect for "asbestos exposure" or for "fear of cancer." Still others allow them to collect twice, once for asbestos exposure and again for a disabling asbestos disease if one develops in the future. At trial, asbestos plaintiffs who have exposure only (for example, they have pleural plaque but are not disabled or injured) have been awarded damages as high as $5 million, and they have also received high settlements.

Other legal developments have expanded insurers' liability for asbestos claims. Suppose a plaintiff was exposed to asbestos in 1955 and diagnosed with asbestosis in 1985. Under the "triple trigger" doctrine that many states have adopted, inhaled asbestos fibers are treated as continuously injuring plaintiffs' lungs, so that a plaintiff can collect from the insurers that covered the firm in 1955, in 1985 or any date in between. By allowing a single plaintiff to claim under many insurance policies, the doctrine increases the amount of compensation that is available to victims generally. In addition, courts have reinterpreted many products liability insurance policies as "premises liability" policies. Products liability policies have an aggregate limit on coverage, but premises policies—which were intended for perils such as fire and hurricanes—have only a coverage limit for each occurrence. If each asbestos claim is treated as a separate occurrence, then insurers effectively have unlimited liability (Rheingold, 1996). The result of these changes in insurance law is to expand greatly insurers' liability for asbestos claims.

Why did tort law as applied to asbestos claims change so dramatically and in so many ways? One answer is that the policies were vague and judges applied a principle of insurance law that requires construing ambiguous insurance contracts against the interest of the insurer. Another answer is that judges' indignation at asbestos defendants' callous behavior sometimes led them to give juries instructions that favored plaintiffs. Of course, once plaintiffs win a case and the decision survives on appeal, the case becomes a precedent that increases plaintiffs' probably of winning later cases.

The Search for the "Next Asbestos"

Plaintiffs' lawyers have long been searching for the next big mass tort, but with the exception of tobacco, no other mass tort has achieved the same scale. Some mass torts, including the lead paint litigation, have remained small because plaintiffs have not been able to establish causation and the courts have not loosened the requirements, as they did for asbestos claimants. In other mass torts, causation can be established, but defendants have been found not liable because they provided adequate warnings of the danger of using their products or because the design of the product was not defective. Thus, in the firearms litigation, most lawsuits brought by gun victims have been dismissed on the grounds that guns cause injury because they are *not* defective, while manufacturers are only liable for harm when their products *are* defective (Kimball and Olson, 2000). In any case, firearms litigation will probably remain small, both because there are only a few gun manufacturers and because Congress may end the litigation by passing legislation to protect gun manufacturers from liability.

In the tobacco litigation, there is a long history of individual smokers losing lawsuits against cigarette manufacturers, because juries considered the congressionally mandated warnings on cigarette packages to be sufficient, and therefore smokers were held to have assumed the risks of smoking. Because individual plaintiffs were unsuccessful, several state attorneys-general decided in 1994 to bring suit against the tobacco companies. To keep the states' initial costs down, private law firms were hired to represent the states on a contingency fee basis—that is, the law firms would be paid a share of whatever damages the states received. After several false starts, the tobacco companies and all 50 states concluded settlements in 1997–1998 that required the tobacco industry to pay the states $246 billion (undiscounted) over 25 years (Derthick, 2002). The tobacco settlement did not bar individual plaintiffs from suing the tobacco companies, however, and in 2000, a jury in Florida awarded punitive damages of $145 billion to a class of 500,000 Florida smokers (Bragg, 2000). Thus, despite the settlement with the states, tobacco litigation still has the potential to grow.

Finally, fast food litigation is at an early stage. The first effort involved obese teenagers who sued McDonalds on the grounds that eating hamburgers made them fat. Their lawsuits were dismissed. But more limited claims have had greater success—McDonald's recently paid $12 million to settle a claim that it did not disclose the use of beef fat in its French fries, and the manufacturer of a cheese snack paid $4 million to settle claims that it understated the snack's fat content. Other lawsuits that are at an earlier stage allege deceptive marketing of unhealthy food products, particularly to children (Zernike, 2004). Whether this litigation will become "supersized" is still unclear.

High Legal Fees and Future Mass Torts

Asbestos litigation has generated a massive transfer to lawyers, far greater than any other mass tort. Of the $70 billion already spent on asbestos litigation, $21 billion went to defendants' lawyers and an additional $20 billion to plaintiffs' lawyers (Carroll et al., 2004). If asbestos legal costs continue to be the same proportion of total spending and if total spending on asbestos litigation eventually reaches $200 billion, then legal costs would grow from the current figure of $41 billion to $118 billion.

The $20 billion paid to plaintiffs' lawyers in asbestos litigation far exceeds even the enormous sums paid to lawyers in the tobacco settlement—lawyers for the 50 states earned a total of $13 billion (undiscounted) in the tobacco settlement, but the money is to be paid out over 25 years (Derthick, 2002).

High profits from asbestos litigation have changed the legal industry by encouraging more lawyers to enter the business of representing mass tort plaintiffs and providing start-up funds and expertise for new mass torts. The same plaintiffs' law firms that got their start representing asbestos claimants later represented the states in the tobacco litigation. They also initiated other mass torts including lead paint, firearms, Fen-phen, health care fraud and fast food, as well as representing victims in the Ford/Firestone defective tire litigation and the World Trade Center attacks. Many of the innovations that plaintiffs' lawyers developed in representing asbestos claimants—concentrating claims in favorable state courts, joining large numbers of claims together and suing insurers for funds well beyond the limits of their insurance policies—are likely to used in future mass torts. Plaintiffs' lawyers have also become large contributors to political campaigns of favorable candidates, including candidates for state judgeships, state attorneys-general and Congress. Several have run for Congress themselves (Derthick, 2002, p. 187). As a result of the growth of asbestos litigation, future mass torts are likely to be more numerous and more expensive and future legislation that plaintiffs' lawyers oppose is less likely to be passed.

Bankruptcies Resolve Other Mass Torts, But Not Asbestos

Bankruptcy proceedings are designed to resolve all claims against a bankrupt firm, including both current claims and claims that will come due in the future. As a result, they are one method of resolving mass torts. For example, in a Chapter 7 bankruptcy liquidation, the bankrupt company's assets are sold, either as a going concern or piecemeal, and the firm ceases to exist. The sale proceeds are used to pay all claims, including tort claims, according to a predetermined priority ordering. If the bankrupt company instead reorganizes under Chapter 11, it continues to operate rather than shutting down. Creditors then must approve a reorganization plan that provides for partial payment of all claims, with the funds coming mainly from the reorganized firm's future profits. This procedure preserves the company's going concern value by allowing it to emerge from Chapter 11 free of its tort and other prebankruptcy claims (White, 1989).

Most mass tort defendants that file for bankruptcy reorganize under Chapter 11. For bankrupt asbestos defendants, this choice makes sense because most of them no longer produce asbestos-containing products and would be profitable if not for their asbestos liabilities. The reorganization plan always involves setting up a compensation trust that takes over responsibility for paying present and future asbestos claims. The funding for the trust comes from the reorganized firm's future profits and from its insurers, who contribute money to the trust in return for a discharge from liability to the firm's tort claimants.[2]

Bankruptcy filings were used successfully to resolve the Dalkon Shield and breast implant mass torts. But while many asbestos producers have filed for bankruptcy, these bankruptcies have worsened the asbestos crisis rather than resolving it, by spreading the litigation to new defendants. The problem is that, when an asbestos defendant goes bankrupt, it stops paying claimants until its compensation trust begins to operate and even then, the value of payments will be low. As a result, plaintiffs' lawyers shift their litigation focus to nonbankrupt defendants, since the latter are more lucrative. In addition, many states have "joint and several liability," which means that each defendant found liable for a damage award is responsible for paying up to the entire amount if other defendants don't pay their shares. Therefore, when one defendant goes bankrupt, the liability of the remaining defendants increases. Similarly, if an insurer fails, some of its asbestos liabilities are transferred to other insurance companies, because multiple insurers are liable for the same claims under the triple trigger doctrine.

Thus, an important problem with bankruptcy is that it contains no mechanism

---

[2] In 1994, Congress adopted a set of amendments to the Bankruptcy Code that apply only to bankruptcies of firms with asbestos claims. The amendments require that a compensation trust be set up. They also specify special voting rules for adoption of reorganization plans—see below. White (2002b) discusses recent asbestos bankruptcies and reorganization plans.

for coordinating among multiple defendants that share liability for tort claims. As a result, bankruptcies by individual asbestos defendants shift liability to nonbankrupt defendants and spread the asbestos crisis rather than resolve it.

Bankruptcy filings by asbestos defendants also create additional distortions. For a bankrupt asbestos firm's reorganization plan to be adopted, 75 percent of current tort claimants must vote in favor of the plan, but future tort claimants do not have the right to vote at all. (The 75 percent approval requirement is higher than the normal standard for adopting reorganization plans.) As a result, asbestos reorganization plans overcompensate present claimants relative to future claimants. Another problem is that if asbestos producers expect to file for bankruptcy, their managers have an incentive to encourage the filing of claims by the unimpaired. After all, these claimants have an incentive to vote in favor of a reorganization plan even if it provides only low compensation, and because there are too few claimants with serious asbestos diseases to block adoption of the plan, those with serious diseases tend to be undercompensated (White, 2002b). Thus, the voting rules for adoption of asbestos firms' reorganization plans lead to overcompensation of unimpaired claimants and undercompensation of future claimants and those with serious asbestos diseases.

No Class Action Settlement of Asbestos Claims

Another method that the legal system has developed for resolving mass torts is the class action settlement, which was successfully used to resolve both the Agent Orange and Fen-Phen litigation. In a class action, a judge certifies a class consisting of all plaintiffs having a particular type of claim against one or more defendants that produced a harmful product. If the class action goes to trial, the judge or jury makes a single decision for each defendant—that is, all plaintiffs either win or lose against each defendant. But most class actions are resolved by settlements rather than trials, and class actions frequently are certified only after a settlement is reached. As in a bankruptcy, class action settlements often involve setting up a compensation trust to pay present and future tort claims, using assets provided by the defendant and its insurers.

Class action settlements can be used to resolve mass torts that involve multiple defendants. If multiple defendants produced a single dangerous product and individual plaintiffs cannot identify which defendant's product harmed them, a class action settlement can set up a single compensation trust to pay all plaintiffs' claims, with defendants and insurers agreeing on a formula for dividing the cost. Unlike bankruptcy filings by individual defendants, a class action settlement of this type prevents the mass tort from spreading. The settlement of the Agent Orange litigation followed this pattern—claims against all twelve producers of Agent Orange were resolved collectively by creating a single compensation trust.

During the mid-1990s, the asbestos mass tort seemed to be headed for resolution using this route. A large class action settlement was agreed on and certified that involved all of the tort claims against the Center for Claims Resolution, a consortium of 20 asbestos producers that were conducting their legal defenses jointly. But in *Amchem Products v. Windsor* (521 U.S. 591 [1997]), the Supreme Court overturned the class certification. Two years later in *Ortiz v. Fibreboard Corp.* (527 U.S. 815 [1999]), the Supreme Court overturned another asbestos class action certification that involved only a single large defendant. After the two decisions, defendants concluded that no class action settlement of asbestos claims would succeed, and 22 of them quickly filed for bankruptcy (Hensler, 2002).

Economists have strongly criticized the federal rules that determine when a class action can be certified, arguing that judges certify class actions too frequently. Their concern is that class actions are often certified even when plaintiffs' claims are very weak and they would lose in a trial. However, once a class is certified, defendants nearly always settle, since going to trial is too risky when losing could force the firm into bankruptcy (Priest, 1997). But economists have overlooked a benefit of certifying class actions in the mass tort context, which is that they can be used to resolve multidefendant mass torts collectively and can therefore stop the spread of mass torts to new defendants.

In the asbestos context, even if some U.S. Supreme Court justices changed their minds and the Court allowed a large class action of all asbestos claimants to be certified, it would probably be impossible for the parties to agree on a settlement. Plaintiffs and defendants would have to agree on how much is needed to compensate all present and future claimants, and defendants and insurers would have to agree on a formula for dividing the cost. The agreement concerning the cost allocation would have to be voluntary, since class action settlements have no mechanism for forcing dissenting defendants to agree (in contrast, dissenting plaintiffs can be forced to agree since only the judge must approve the settlement). While asbestos has 8,400 defendants, the largest number of defendants in a single mass tort class action settlement so far has only been a dozen—in the Agent Orange litigation. Schuck (1986) discusses how difficult it was for the twelve Agent Orange defendants to reach a settlement, even with an activist judge who forced them to bargain around the clock and refused to let them out until they reached an agreement.

While asbestos litigation shares many characteristics with other mass torts, it is the only mass tort that defies resolution within the court system. Collective solution mechanisms such as class action settlements and bankruptcy that worked for other mass torts do not work for asbestos. In addition, since most asbestos litigation occurs in state courts, tort reforms at the state level would be ineffective unless they were adopted simultaneously by a number of states.

Legislative Solutions to the Asbestos Crisis

In *Ortiz v. Fibreboard* (527 U.S.815 [1999]), Supreme Court Justice David Souter wrote that "the elephantine mass of asbestos cases . . . defies customary judicial administration and calls for national legislation." An ideal solution to the asbestos litigation mess would accomplish several goals: 1) compensate present and future claimants equitably based on their harm, but do not compensate those who are unimpaired; 2) reduce litigation costs; 3) resolve uncertainty for claimants, defendants and insurers; and 4) stop the spread of claims to new defendants that had little or no involvement in asbestos production.

Congress is now considering the "Fairness in Asbestos Injury Resolution Act of 2003" (S. 1125), which would resolve the asbestos crisis by establishing a privately funded, publicly run administrative procedure for compensating asbestos victims. Asbestos defendants and insurance companies would each pay a total of $52 billion to the fund over 27 years. An additional $10 billion in assets would be transferred to the fund from existing asbestos compensation trusts that were set up as part of asbestos bankruptcies, for a total of $114 billion. Defendants would be required to pay either a proportion of their revenues or a flat dollar amount to the fund each year, with the obligation depending on individual defendants' size and past asbestos liabilities. Small businesses and firms with no previous asbestos liabilities would be exempt. For insurers, a commission would be established to determine individual companies' assessments, which are to depend on past exposure to asbestos liabilities.

To receive compensation, claimants must provide evidence showing that they had particular levels of exposure to asbestos for at least a minimum number of years and must submit medical evidence to prove that they have a qualifying asbestos disease. (Specific requirements vary by disease.) Claimants are not required to show that they were harmed by particular asbestos products. The act specifies that independent medical experts will review all applications for compensation, and it also gives the fund authority to require that claimants submit to medical examinations and provide tissue biopsics.

Proposed compensation levels are shown in Table 3. Claimants with mesothelioma would receive $1 million, those with asbestos-related cancers would receive between $25,000 and $1 million (depending on disease and smoking behavior), and those with severe or disabling asbestosis would receive between $20,000 and $750,000 (depending on severity). Claimants with no impairment would receive free medical monitoring, but no cash. Compensation would be paid over three to four years, and future payments would be inflation adjusted. Table 3 also shows expected asbestos compensatory damage awards at trial since 1987 (punitive damage awards are excluded since payments by the fund are intended to be compensatory only). The comparison suggests that the act's proposed compensation levels for severe asbestos diseases are in the same range as compensatory damage awards at trial. But most tort claimants receive much less, since claims are generally settled out of court, and settlement levels are much lower than damage awards.[3] The act also includes a long-overdue ban on asbestos use.

---

[3] Data on settlement levels broken down by disease are not available. The average asbestos settlement level for all diseases is about $5,000 (in 2000 dollars), but claimants usually receive separate settlements from multiple defendants. Damage and settlement figures are calculated from data described in White (2002a).

Table 3

Proposed Compensation Levels under S. 1125 and Expected Compensatory Damage Awards in Asbestos Trials

	Proposed compensation under S. 1125	Expected compensatory damage awards, 1987–2002
Mesothelioma	$1,000,000	$2,340,000
Lung and other cancers	$25,000–$1,000,000	$760,000
Asbestosis	$20,000–$750,000	$460,000

Notes: Compensatory damage awards are in 2000 dollars and are calculated from data described in White (2002a). Punitive damage awards are excluded from the calculations. Damage awards take into account plaintiffs' probability of losing at trial, which is approximately one-third.

Is $114 billion likely to be adequate to compensate all present and future asbestos claimants? The Congressional Budget Office (2003) estimated that the proposed fund would in fact collect enough to cover the cost of paying claims. The CBO assumed that, during the first ten years, there would be 6,000 claims per year involving mesothelioma and other cancers and 63,000 claims per year involving asbestosis and other nonmalignant conditions. Of the latter, it assumed that only 15 percent of claimants would qualify for compensation, while the other 85 percent would received only medical monitoring. After the first ten years, the CBO assumed that the number of mesothelioma and cancer claims per year would fall in half, but the number of claims for nonmalignant conditions per year would double. The CBO cautioned that its estimates were extremely sensitive to the assumption concerning the proportion of asbestosis claims that would qualify for compensation as opposed to medical monitoring.

How well might a fund of this sort accomplish the four goals named at the beginning of this section? The total of $114 billion appears to be enough to compensate present and future claimants, but only if the fund is aggressive in weeding out claims by the unimpaired. To do so, the fund will have to spend substantial resources on auditing claims, conducting medical examinations and examining biopsies. Past experience by the Manville Trust suggests that, without careful auditing, claimants with pleural plaque will claim to have asbestosis, claimants with asbestosis who are unimpaired will claim to be disabled, and the number of claims will increase rapidly. These factors will quickly cause the fund to overrun its budget.

Will adoption of the fund reduce litigation costs relative to the current system? The answer is unclear, since the fund's own costs of auditing claims will be high, and the act does not specify limits on plaintiffs' attorneys' fees. Other asbestos compensation trusts, including the Manville Trust, often limit plaintiffs' attorneys' fees to 25 percent of compensation. But perhaps to reduce opposition by plaintiffs' lawyers, the act's drafters did not set any limits (although they specified that a legal assistance program for claimants be set up).

The fund would give greater certainty to all parties. Claimants would receive a uniform level of compensation by disease, in comparison to the tort system where they individually bear the risk of winning a multimillion dollar damage award at trial, losing at trial and receiving nothing or receiving much smaller settlements. Adoption of the fund also increases the probability that money will be available to compensate individuals who develop serious asbestos diseases in the future. Claimants would also receive their compensation more quickly than in the tort system, where lawsuits often take many years. The fund also eliminates defendants' uncertainty concerning their future asbestos liabilities and stops the spread of asbestos litigation to new defendants.

Whether the act will be adopted is unclear. The AFL-CIO announced in the fall of 2003 that $153 billion would be required to compensate all claimants, rather than $114 billion. Recently, the act's sponsors raised the proposed compensation levels by 10 to 300 percent and raised the required contributions from $114 to $118 billion. As a result of these changes, the CBO announced that the fund would not be able to pay all claims. Democrats in the Senate have consistently opposed the act, and they recently announced that they are preparing their own asbestos legislation.

An alternative approach for resolving the asbestos crisis would also require new legislation, but would be less complicated than the fund-based approach. It would require that all asbestos claims be filed in federal court and, moreover, that all asbestos claims be transferred to a single federal judge for pretrial discovery and trial. (Currently, many asbestos lawsuits are transferred to a particular federal judge for pretrial discovery, but they are returned to the jurisdiction where they were filed for trial.) Claims involving mesothelioma, asbestos-related cancers and severe asbestosis would be placed on an "active docket," while all other asbestos claims would be placed on an inactive docket. Only claims on the active docket would proceed. Congress would need to provide sufficient resources for the court to audit all claims for disease type and to process all claims on the active docket. Based on the CBO's claim estimates, there would be about 15,000 new active docket claims each year, which—given settlements—would require that several hundred trials be conducted each year. (These figures would be expected to decline over time.) By reducing the amount spent on compensating claimants with no asbestos-related disability, this approach would at least partially achieve the four goals specified above. It would also eliminate the need for agreement on how to pay for a compensation fund.

Conclusion

The asbestos litigation mess is a combination of a difficult situation and a series of unwise decisions. The difficult situation was that asbestos was widely used and demonstrably harmful to health and that a number of firms engaged in cover-ups and political pressure to hide their behavior. The bad decisions include preventing workers with asbestos-related diseases from collecting workers' compensation; not regulating asbestos until the 1970s; not banning asbestos in the early 1990s; allowing uninjured claimants to collect damages; allowing asbestos liability to spread to defendants with little asbestos involvement; and rewriting the meaning of past insurance policies to increase insurers' liability.

The asbestos situation suggests several lessons that may be applicable to other mass torts. First, because of capture by the large asbestos producers, regulation was ineffective in preventing large-scale asbestos exposure. However, the large producers were unable to capture the courts and liability was eventually effective in driving asbestos from the U.S. marketplace.

Second, regulation and liability are related in the sense that when producers knowingly expose large numbers of workers and consumers to highly dangerous products and attempt to cover up their behavior, judges and juries are likely to respond by punishing them with massive compensatory and punitive damages.

Third, asbestos is fairly unique as a mass tort because it was used in thousands of products, millions of plaintiffs were exposed, and thousands of defendants with deep pockets were potentially liable. This set of circumstances made it more likely that once the litigation got started, it would spiral out of control. But the same scenario seems unlikely to happen for other mass torts. After all, plaintiffs' lawyers have been searching for the next asbestos for years now, and, so far, they don't seem to have found it.

Fourth, the legal system has two methods to resolve mass torts collectively—bankruptcy and class action settlements—but neither of them worked for asbestos. Bankruptcy is effective in resolving a mass tort that involves only a single defendant. But bankruptcy has no mechanism for preventing the spread of liability from bankrupt to nonbankrupt defendants. A large class action settlement could potentially resolve mass torts involving multiple defendants, but the U.S. Supreme Court blocked this route for asbestos and, in any case, it would be nearly impossible to get thousands of defendants and hundreds of insurers to agree on a voluntary settlement. By a process of elimination, this argument suggests that Congress will eventually have to pass legislation to resolve the asbestos crisis. But, not surprisingly, the current bill in Congress is stalled over the same issue—how to decide on individual defendant's and insurer's contributions to the compensation fund.

Finally, while other mass torts are unlikely to replicate the size and scope of asbestos litigation, the legal techniques and precedents that lawyers developed for asbestos litigation are likely to be applied to other mass torts in the future. As a result, mass torts in the future will be more common and more expensive.

Will the asbestos mess at least have the beneficial effect of changing firms' attitudes toward the risks of using asbestos-like products in the future? Unfortunately, neither liability nor regulation works very well when the harm that results from exposure has a long latency period like that of asbestos. Because managers tend to discount the future heavily, if they can increase profits for 20 or more years by using dangerous substances, heavy institutional pressure will exist to ignore the high price that their firms and society will eventually pay.

■ *Michelle White is grateful to the National Science Foundation for research support under grant #0212444 and to Eli Berman, Roger Gordon, James Hines, Andrei Shleifer, Timothy Taylor and Michael Waldman for very helpful comments.*

References

Biggs, Jennifer L. et al. 2001. *Overview of Asbestos: Issues and Trends.* Report prepared by the American Academy of Actuaries Mass Torts Work Group; Available at ⟨http://www.actuary.org/pdf/casualty/mono_dec01asbestos.pdf⟩.

Bragg, Rick. 2000. "Juror Says a 'Sense of Mission' Led to Huge Tobacco Damages." *New York Times,* July 16, pp. A1, A16.

Bowker, Michael. 2003. *Fatal Deception: The Untold Story of Asbestos.* Emmaus, Pa.: Rodale.

Brickman, Lester. 1992. "The Asbestos Litigation Crisis: Is There a Need for an Administrative Alternative?" *Cardozo Law Review.* 13, pp. 1819, 1840–852.

Brodeur, Paul. 1985. *Outrageous Misconduct: The Asbestos Industry on Trial.* New York: Pantheon Books.

Brodeur, Paul. 1973. *Expendable Americans.* New York: Viking Press.

Carroll, S. J. et al. 2004. *Asbestos Litigation Costs and Compensation.* Santa Monica: RAND Corporation, DRR-3280-ICJ.

Castleman, Barry I. 1996. *Asbestos: Medical and Legal Aspects, 4th Edition.* Englewood Cliffs, N.J.: Aspen Law & Business.

Congressional Budget Office. 2003. "Cost Estimate, S. 1125, Fairness in Asbestos Injury Resolution Act of 2003." October 2.

Cupp, Richard L. Jr. 2000. "Beyond Tobacco Symposium: Tort Issues in Light of the Cigarette Litigation: State Medical Reimbursement Lawsuits after Tobacco: Is the Domino Effect for Lead Paint Manufacturers and Others Fair Game?" *Pepperdine Law Review.* 27, pp. 685–700.

Dean, Amber E. 2001. "Lead Paint Public Entity Lawsuits: Has the Broad Stroke of Tobacco and Firearms Litigation Painted a Troubling Picture for Lead Paint Manufacturers?" *Pepperdine Law Review.* 28, pp. 915–39.

Derthick, Martha A. 2002. *Up in Smoke: From Legislation to Litigation in Tobacco Politics.* Washington, D.C.: CQ Press.

Glaberson, William. 1999. "Some Plaintiffs Losing Out in Texas' War on Lawsuits." *New York Times,* June 7, p. A1.

Hensler, Deborah R. 2002. "As Time Goes By: Asbestos Litigation after Amchem and Ortiz." *Texas Law Review.* June, 80, pp. 1899–924.

Kazan-Allen, Laurie. 2000a. "Asbestos Compensation in Europe." *Newsletter.* International Ban Asbestos Secretariat, ⟨http://www.btinternet.com/~ibas/f_lka_eu_comp.htm⟩.

Kazan-Allen, Laurie. 2000b. "Europe Bans Asbestos." *Newsletter.* International Ban Asbestos Secretariat, ⟨www.btinternet.com/~ibas/f_lka_eu_comp.htm⟩.

Kimball, Anne G. and Sarah L. Olson. 2000. "Symposium: Municipal Firearm Litigation: Ill Conceived from Any Angle." *Connecticut Law Review.* 32:4, pp. 1296–301.

McCaffrey, David P. 1982. *OSHA and the Politics of Health Regulation.* New York: Plenum Press.

Mintz, Morton. 1985. *At Any Cost : Corporate Greed, Women, and the Dalkon Shield.* New York: Pantheon Books.

National Cancer Institute. 2003. *SEER Cancer Statistics Review 1975–2000.* Available at ⟨http://seer.cancer.gov/scr/1975-2000/results_single/sect_01-table.07.pdf⟩.

Oster, Christopher. 2002. "Chubb, Hartford Take Asbestos Hits." *Wall Street Journal.* October 31, p. A6.

Oster, Christopher. 2003. "MetLife Records Asbestos Charge Linked to Research." *Wall Street Journal.* February 11, p. C16.

Parloff, Roger. 2002. "Asbestos: The $200 Billion Miscarriage of Justice." *Fortune.* March 4, p. 155.

Peto, J., A. Decarli, C. La Vecchia, F. Levi and E. Negri. 1999. "The European Mesothelioma Epidemic." *British Journal of Cancer.* 79:3-4, pp. 666–72.

Priest, George. 1997. "Procedural versus Substantive Controls of Mass Tort Class Actions." *Journal of Legal Studies.* 26:2, Pt. 2, pp. 521–74.

Rheingold, Paul D. 1996. *Mass Tort Litigation.* Deerfield, Ill.: CBC.

Rothstein, Paul F. 2001. "What Courts Can Do in the Face of the Never-Ending Asbestos Crisis." *Mississippi Law Journal.* 71, pp. 1–34.

Schuck, Peter H. 1986. *Agent Orange on Trial: Mass Toxic Disasters in the Courts.* Cambridge, Mass.: Harvard University Press.

Shavell, Steven. 1987. *Economic Analysis of Accident Law.* Cambridge, Mass.: Harvard University Press.

Sherrill, Robert. 1973. "Asbestos, the Saver of Lives, Has a Deadly Side." *New York Times.* January 21, p. 256.

Tidmarsh, Jay. 1998. *Mass Tort Settlement Class Actions: Five Case Studies.* Washington, D.C.: Federal Judicial Center.

Treaster, Joseph B. 2003. "Hartford to Pay $1.5 Billion to Settle Asbestos Claims." *New York Times.* December 20, pg. C.4.

Tweedale, Geoffrey. 2000. *Magic Mineral to Killer Dust: Turner & Newall and the Asbestos Hazard.* Oxford: Oxford University Press.

White, Michelle J. 1989. "The Corporate Bankruptcy Decision." *Journal of Economic Perspectives.* Spring, 3:2, pp. 129–52.

White, Michelle J. 2002a. "Explaining the Flood of Asbestos Litigation: Consolidation, Bifurcation and Bouquet Trials." NBER Working Paper No. 9362, December.

White, Michelle J. 2002b. "Why the Asbestos Genie Won't Stay in the Bankruptcy Bottle." *University of Cincinnati Law Review.* 70:4, pp. 1319–340.

Zernike, Kate. 2004. "Lawyers Shift Focus from Big Tobacco to Big Food." *New York Times.* April 9, p. A15.

Journal of Economic Perspectives—Volume 18, Number 2—Spring 2004—Pages 205–226

State Budget Deficit Dynamics and the California Debacle

Steven M. Sheffrin

N ational recessions are bad news for state budgets. Virtually all states face some form of balanced budget requirement, which at a minimum requires that they adopt budget plans that avoid deficits in their general funds or basic operating budgets. With the onset of a recession, falling tax revenues and increasing transfer payments force governors and legislators to make difficult choices.

However, the recession of 2001 appeared to have created more than the usual chaos in state governments. Consider these examples reported in mid-2003. In Alabama, a Republican governor facing a $675 million budget deficit proposed a tax increase of $1.2 billion both to eradicate the deficit and to improve educational opportunities. Voters overwhelmingly rejected this proposal, resulting in sharp cuts in spending (Rawls, 2003). In Nevada, the state constitution requires both a two-thirds supermajority provision to raise taxes and also includes a requirement to provide adequate educational funding. The Republican governor brought a lawsuit to overturn the two-thirds majority and raise taxes for education, and the state Supreme Court agreed. Eventually, a tax increase was passed with a two-thirds vote, but irate voters initiated an (ultimately unsuccessful) recall attempt against the governor (Riley, 2003). Connecticut and Oregon both witnessed prolonged and bitter budgetary stalemates. Oregon broke its record for the length of the legislative session; Connecticut came within six days of breaking its record (Dixon, 2003; Har and Hogan, 2003). In New York, the legislature overrode a governor's veto of its spending plan for the first time in two decades. Also, it was the first time in memory that the legislature had enacted tax increases over a governor's veto (Baker, 2003).

■ *Steven M. Sheffrin is Dean of the Division of Social Sciences and Professor of Economics, University of California at Davis, Davis, California. His e-mail address is ⟨smsheffrin@ ucdavis.edu⟩.*

One episode in the saga of state budget problems was widely covered in the national and world media—the case of California. Not long after Governor Gray Davis signed a budget bill that featured a combination of tax increases, spending cuts and borrowing, enough signatures were gathered to place a recall of the governor on the ballot. In only the second successful gubernatorial recall in U.S. history—after North Dakota's recall of Governor Lynn J. Frazier in 1921—Davis was recalled and replaced by an Austrian-born bodybuilder, actor and political novice, Arnold Schwarzenegger.

These dramatic events for state budgets occurred in 2003, about 18 months after the recession's trough in November 2001. By postwar standards, the 2001 recession was relatively mild both in terms of its duration and depth—more like the mild recession of the early 1990s than the deep recessions of the early 1980s. The contrast between the extreme political and budgetary angst at the state level and the relatively mild national recession is striking.

This paper explores the dynamics of the recent state budget problems from several angles. We begin with a broad national look at recent state fiscal crises and contrast them to the experiences of the early 1990s, when the U.S. economy suffered its last recession. The initial magnitude of the decline in state budgetary fortunes was similar in these last two recessions, but the policy responses differed sharply. Policymakers throughout the states, and in California, initially responded much less aggressively to budgetary shortfalls in the 2001 recession than in 1990–1991. We then review the empirical and theoretical literature on the role that state institutions, such as differing balanced budget requirements, play in determining state responses to potential fiscal crises. Finally, we make an in-depth examination of California's experience as it coped with record budgetary shortfalls. Were California's fiscal difficulties just a larger version of the problems facing other states, or did California face unique factors not found elsewhere—like an interaction between California's large number of technology companies, income from stock options and the stock market decline that started in 2000? In California and elsewhere, postponement of hard choices and delays in budget information and analysis made difficult budget problems even worse.

The State Budget Experience in Perspective

All states except Vermont have some rules governing balances in their general fund accounts, but the rules differ (Bohn and Inman, 1996). The weakest rules require only that the governor submit a balanced budget plan or that the legislature pass a plan in which the budget is balanced. In these cases, the budget balance rules are *prospective* only; that is, there are no provisions that actual expenditures and revenues be balanced by the end of the appropriate fiscal year. States with such requirements include Illinois, Louisiana, Massachusetts, New Hampshire, New York and Nevada. The next category includes those states that may run a deficit at the end of the year, but must budget explicitly for the deficit in the next fiscal year. The states that can *carry over* deficits from one year to the next include Alaska, California, Connecticut, Maryland, Michigan, Pennsylvania and Wisconsin. The Advisory Commission on Intergovernmental Relations (ACIR, 1987) developed a numerical index of stringency of balanced budget requirements that distinguished between the prospective and carry-over states, with the latter being deemed to have more stringent rules. However, in practice, there is reason to doubt whether the budget differences in these systems will be large, since the prospective states will also typically incorporate current fiscal year deficits into planning for the next fiscal year. The remaining category is states that *cannot carry over* deficits from one fiscal year to the next. In these states, adjustments to taxes or spending must be made during the current fiscal year.

This section discusses the recent state budget experience from a number of different perspectives: the overall national trends in state budgets; the economic causes behind those budget trends in terms of taxes and spending; a disaggregated view looking at which states have the largest budget problems; and a discussion of how state budgets are affected by institutional factors like specific balanced budget requirements or political setting of the state government.

National Trends in Aggregate State Budgets

There are two traditional ways to measure the fiscal health of state, or state and local, governments. The most comprehensive method is the surplus/deficit measures of the National Income and Product Accounts (NIPA). The NIPA accounts include the state and local sector for the United States and also include depreciation of the existing stock of capital, although for present purposes we exclude balances in social insurance funds. The second traditional measure is produced by the National Conference of State Legislatures (NCSL) and the National Association of State Budget Officers (NASBO). These organizations measure the balances held by the states in their general funds, which are the states' core operating funds. Thus, the latter measure only applies to state governments—not local governments—and does not include "special accounts" like funds dedicated to transportation or other special purposes. General fund balances are probably most tied to traditional measures of fiscal distress; however, state governments can and do alter their net fiscal positions with respect to local governments and may sometimes be able (at least temporarily) to tap into special accounts.

Both data series tell approximately the same story. Figure 1 plots the NIPA surplus/deficit as a percentage of gross domestic product (GDP) from 1985:1 to 2003:1 on a quarterly basis. Figure 2 plots total general funds balances as a percentage of total state expenditures for fiscal year 1985 through fiscal year 2003. Both measures show a decrease during the recession of the early 1990s followed by sharp increases in the last part of the decade. Beginning in approximately 2000, both fiscal measures deteriorated. By 2003, general fund balances were 1.3 percent of expenditures, just slightly above the 1991 value of 1.1 percent. The deficit on the NIPA account in 2003 exceeded the deficit in the early 1990s. In 2003:1, the current balance reached −0.62 percent of GDP, whereas its previous low in the prior

Figure 1
Current Surplus or Deficit as Percentage of GDP

Note: Excludes social insurance funds.
Source: U.S. Bureau of Economic Analysis (2003).

Figure 2
Total General Funds Balances as Percentage of Total Expenditures

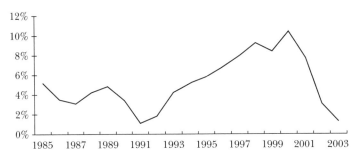

Source: National Association of State Budget Officers and National Governors Association (2003).

recession was −0.30 percent in 1991:1. The surplus of the late 1990s reached as high as 0.64 percent of GDP. While the precise numbers differ, the patterns look similar using either the NIPA or NCSL/NASBO measures.

Decomposing the Aggregate State Budget Numbers

What were the causes of the latest deterioration of the fiscal health of the states? Knight, Kusko and Rubin (2003) decompose movements in the NIPA measure of state budget balance into three components.

First, they use the high-employment budget concept, which estimates what the budget surplus would be if the economy were operating at full employment and, thus, effectively holds the business cycle constant.

Second, they use a capital gains component reflecting the collapse of the stock market and its effects on state revenues. Recent revisions of federal budget projections by the Congressional Budget Office reflect large "technical corrections" to their budget estimates, which is the CBO term for saying that the slowdown in the economy produced a larger-than-usual decline in tax revenue (Auerbach, 2003). In turn, these revisions appear to be connected to stock market related income. To address this issue, Knight, Kusko and Rubin include estimates of capital gains realizations at the national level as an independent factor in their analysis and calculate the implied state revenue changes using an average state capital gains rate. Other observers have also highlighted the relatively sharp decreases in revenues during the last recession and the key role that capital gains likely played in the decline. For example, Boyd and Jenny (2003) point out that the 7.4 percent decline in real per capita tax revenues in fiscal year 2002 was more than twice the size of the declines in the 1990–1991 recession (3.5 percent) and 1980–1982 recession (3.0 percent).

Third, Knight, Kusko and Rubin (2003) find a residual that they label as "policy and other" factors that measures actions taken (or not taken) by state and local governments with respect to spending and taxation as well as exogenous cost pressures from, for example, increases in the relative price of health care or from federal mandates.

Knight, Kusko and Rubin's (2003) decomposition of the sources of change in state budget balances is provocative. Looking first at the deficit in 2002, they conclude (p. 435) that "neither the cyclical weakness in the economy, nor the direct effects of capital gains realizations, when measured relative to their longer run trend, account for very much of the deficit in 2002. The implication is that the current deficit is largely structural . . . ." Cyclical weakness and capital gains do account for approximately one-third of the swing (or decline) in the current state budget balance from 1998 to 2002, but even by this accounting, the analysis implies that "policy and other related" factors were the principal causes of the most recent state fiscal crises.

Knight, Kusko and Rubin (2003) compare the most recent state fiscal crisis to the two prior crises during 1989–1991 and 1978–1982. In both the prior periods, cyclical factors dominated the causes of decline in state budget balances as measured by the National Income and Product Accounts. The 1980s recession had roughly the same impact on the state budget deficits as a percentage of GDP as the most recent recession. Policy and other changes accounted for only approximately 25 percent of the deterioration in the state and local fiscal position in the early 1980s, whereas they accounted for 75 percent during the most recent period.

What are some of the common state-level policy changes that can help to explain the deterioration of the states' underlying budget position from 1998 to 2002? First, many states cut taxes during the late 1990s. Second, states expanded eligibility for Medicaid at precisely the same time that they began facing increases in the relative price of health care. Third, state and local government spending generally increased. While state general fund spending increased in real terms by approximately 2.7 percent per year from fiscal years 1985–2003, it increased by

5.2 percent in 1999 and 4.0 percent in the three subsequent years (NASBO, 2003, p. 4).[1]

It also appears that state legislators were slower to respond to the fiscal stress of the early 2000s than they were during the previous recessions. Maag and Merriman (2003) use NASBO data on legislated state-level tax changes to examine the responses of policymakers during the last two economic downturns. They find that policymakers during the 1990 recession "quickly increased taxes to bring budgets into balance," but in the 2001 recession "shunned significant policy changes." In fiscal year 1991, state tax policy changes increased revenues by 3.43 percent, and for fiscal year 1992 revenues were increased by 4.62 percent. The largest tax increases stemmed from increases in personal income taxes. In contrast, for fiscal years 2002 and 2003, that revenue increased by only 0.2 percent and 1.64 percent, respectively. Maag and Merriman calculate that if states had been as aggressive in raising taxes during fiscal years 2003 and 2002 as they were during fiscal years 1991 and 1992, they would have raised an additional $33 billion in revenues and closed approximately two-thirds of the gaps in their fiscal 2003 budgets.

The National Association of State Budget Officers also provides data on budget cuts made during the current fiscal year. Measured as a percentage of expenditures, budget cuts during fiscal years 1991 and 1992 were 2.68 percent and 1.51 percent, respectively. In fiscal year 2001, the cuts were only 0.4 percent, although the cuts did increase to 2.68 percent in fiscal year 2002. These data also show that policymakers were less aggressive in making rapid adjustments to spending in the 2001 recession than in the 1990–1991 recession.

States that are not willing to raise taxes or reduce spending can use a variety of short-run strategies. One example was the frequent practice of securitizing revenues from the legal settlement that the tobacco companies made with the states in 1998; that is, states sold bonds based on the future revenues and used the proceeds to offset current budget shortfalls. Petersen (2003) provides a recent review of time-honored (and some relatively new) strategies that states can use to disguise or offset fiscal deficits. These methods include optimistic budget projections, sales of assets, capitalizing new income streams or even current costs, borrowing from other state funds, accelerating revenues and postponing spending without changing programs, or restructuring debt. Of course, strategies that provide temporary relief are not appropriate for structural problems in states' operating budgets and can exacerbate long-run problems.

Identifying the Worst State Budget Problems

The decline in measures of national fiscal health during recessionary periods is highly concentrated in a few states. Table 1 presents the percentage of total

---

[1] It is true that real state spending per capita grew more rapidly during the 1980s than the 1990s, but nonetheless, there was a clear escalation in spending growth during the last part of the 1990s (Snell, Eckl and Williams, 2003, p. 914).

Table 1

Top Five States With Declines in General Fund Balances

(in million $)

1990 State	*Change in balance*	*As % of total decline*	*1991* State	*Change in balance*	*As % of total decline*
Massachusetts	−837	26.9%	Connecticut	−809	12.9%
New Jersey	−410	13.2%	Pennsylvania	−715	11.4%
Michigan	−405	13.0%	Ohio	−373	5.9%
Georgia	−376	12.1%	California	−3,424	54.5%
California	−564	18.1%	Washington	−468	7.4%
Subtotal	−2,592	83.3%	Subtotal	−5,789	92.1%
Total balance change	−3,113		Total balance change	−6,284	

2001[a] State	*Change in balance*	*As % of total decline*	*2002*[a] State	*Change in balance*	*As % of total decline*
Indiana	−828	9.4%	Massachusetts	−1,880	8.7%
Wisconsin	−628	7.1%	New Jersey	−1,718	8.0%
Minnesota	−551	6.2%	Pennsylvania	−1,319	6.1%
Virginia	−512	5.8%	California	−5,170	24.0%
California	−6,102	69.0%	Oregon	−1,493	6.9%
Subtotal	−8,621	97.5%	Subtotal	−11,580	53.7%
Total balance change	−8,842		Total balance change	−21,553	

[a] Excludes Florida.

Source: Fiscal Survey of the States, Fall 1985 through Spring 2003, NASBO.

national decline in state general fund balances from the prior fiscal year accounted for by the five states with the largest declines for fiscal years ending in 1990, 1991, 2001 and 2002. The top five states accounted for over 80 percent of the decline in three of the four periods examined and over 50 percent in the other period. California is among the top five states in all four periods. It dominates the list in three of the four periods.

Boyd and Jenny (2003) point out that the decline in tax revenues varied across the states, with the west (dominated by California) facing the largest declines followed by New England. Aside from Alaska (a state in which revenue is tied closely to oil prices), the states with double-digit declines include California, Colorado, Connecticut, Massachusetts, New Jersey, New York, Oregon and Vermont. Boyd and Jenny (p. 4) characterize these states as "generally states with progressive income taxes and many taxpayers who were paying taxes on capital gains." These reasons help to explain why California's fiscal situation was particularly vulnerable.

As noted earlier, taxes that are related to the stock market fluctuations—like capital gains and stock options—played an important role in the state budget problems of the early 2000s. These issues loomed especially large in California. Using state-level data on capital gains from the *Statistics of Income* of the Internal

Revenue Service coupled with detailed data on state tax systems, Sjoquist and Wallace (2003) document that states differ widely in the importance that capital gains play in their tax bases. In general, capital gains are a more important source of revenues in states with higher per capita personal income, large numbers of retirees and higher tax rates on income from capital gains. For 1999, the following states had the highest concentration of capital gains as a fraction of income tax collection: Montana (27.2 percent), California (26.1 percent), Arizona (19.6 percent), New Jersey (19.4 percent), Nebraska (16.7 percent) and New York (16.2 percent). The interaction of capital gains income with state tax rates is important; Florida and Nevada have among the higher shares of capital gains as a percentage of federal adjusted gross income, but these states do not have personal income taxes.

In addition, the value of stock options is obviously related to stock prices. However, income from the exercise of "nonqualified" stock options (which in California accounted for 95 percent of option income) is reported as wage and salary income and taxed as ordinary income, not at a preferred capital gains rate.[2] Since this type of income is reported along with wage and salary income on income tax returns, it must be estimated based on deviations from past trends in wage and salary income for employers offering options. In California, firms in Silicon Valley offered stock options as a key component of employee compensation. The California Legislative Analyst's Office (2001, Chapter 3, p. 4) estimated that income from options accounted for between 35 and 40 percent of total stock market related income in fiscal year 2000. California's fiscal issues are discussed in greater detail below.

Changes in Legal and Political Constraints

A considerable literature has developed to discuss how legal and political factors affect state budget decisions. This literature has generally reached three conclusions. First, a state's constitutional or statutory constraints that affect spending, taxes or borrowing can definitely have an effect, especially when the balanced budget rules prohibit carrying over a deficit to the following year. Second, when political control is divided so that two houses of the state legislature are held by different parties or the state governor is from a different party than is the legislature, political adjustments to fiscal shocks will often take longer than if political control is unified in one party. For example, the two states mentioned in the introduction with especially protracted budget negotiations, Oregon and Connecticut, had governments where control of the two legislative chambers was split

---

[2] Phil Spilberg of the California Franchise Tax Board provided this estimate to me. A nonqualified stock option is treated as income to the recipient when the option is exercised, and it constitutes a compensation related deduction at that time to the company offering the option. The alternative is a "qualified stock option," also known as an "incentive stock option," which is not treated as income when the option is exercised, but is taxed as capital gains when eventually sold (if the stock is held for at least a minimum time). A company cannot deduct the gain on a qualified stock option as a compensation related expense.

between the parties. Third, state governments dominated by Democrats tend to spend more than state governments dominated by Republicans. For example, these three points sum up the general findings of Alt and Lowry. Alt and Lowry (1994) use data on total state government spending and taxes (not general fund data) from 1968 to 1997, and Alt and Lowry (2000) examine the effect of changes in state government for 33 states from 1952–1995 on real per capita general fund revenues.

Bohn and Inman (1996) use general fund budget data from 1970–1991 to examine the effects of balanced budget rules and alternative political configurations on the general fund surplus in a panel study of 47 states. While they generally confirm the Alt and Lowry (1994, 2000) findings, their work also raises two analytical issues that apply across this literature. One warning is that state balanced budget rules apply only to the general funds accounts of the states and not their total balances over all accounts, which leaves room for states to move funds between accounts. They find strong evidence that balanced budget rules matter, but *only* for the states with the strictest "no-carry-over" balanced budget provisions. A second warning is that it may be difficult to separate out the impact on spending of constitutional or statutory provisions from the political climate of a state itself. When Bohn and Inman included state fixed effects in their analysis, they did not find any response of general fund surpluses to government divided by party, but without the fixed effects they report results similar to Alt and Lowry.

Poterba (1994) tackled these issues using NASBO data on the actual revenues and expenditures from the prior year, forecasts of revenues and expenditures for the current fiscal year and any budget cuts or tax changes enacted during the fiscal year. He used this data to construct measures of *unexpected* fiscal deficits that transpired during the year, relative to the tax and expenditure system that was in effect at the beginning of the year. He then examined how states changed spending and taxes with respect to "fiscal news" and how institutional features affected these adjustments. Using this approach, Poterba finds for the period 1988–1992 that states with weak antideficit rules adjust spending less than states with strong antideficit rules, although he does not find similar effects for taxes. Poterba also finds that states with unified governments adjust to fiscal deficits more rapidly than states with divided government.[3]

Poterba and Rueben (2001) built on the measure of unexpected fiscal deficits from Poterba's earlier work and use it to explore the role of state institutions as

---

[3] Poterba's (1994) empirical work differs in several respects from other authors. First, because he looks at within-year adjustments, he excludes those states with two-year budgeting cycles. Second, his "weak antideficit rule" states include only those states with prospective balanced budget rules, and not those with carry-over rules. In a footnote in the paper, he indicates that the results are similar when he uses the Alt-Lowry classification. However, this finding stands contrary to results reported by other authors that only the no-carry-over deficit rules matter. At the minimum, this ambiguity puts large and important states such as California, Michigan, Maryland, Pennsylvania and Wisconsin into an empirical "fiscal limbo."

perceived through the bond market. For example, they find that unexpected deficits are associated with higher general obligation bond yields. Moreover, this effect, although small, is more pronounced in states with weak antideficit rules, which suggests that financial markets take fiscal institutions into account as they evaluate states' creditworthiness. Poterba and Rueben also find that other fiscal institutions matter, such as binding revenue limits or supermajority provisions for increasing taxes, which consistently exacerbate the effects of deficit shocks on bond yields. They also consider the effects of other fiscal institutions such as limits on the legislature's ability to issue long-term debt, binding expenditure limits, limits on local revenues (such as Proposition 13 in California) and supermajorities to pass local bonds. Fiscal institutions may also interact with each other in important ways. For example, limits on state revenues may not matter very much unless there are also local limits. If a state has supermajority provisions to pass a state budget, like California, then even if one party controls more than half of the legislature along with governorship, state government may not be "unified," in the sense that the majority party cannot pass a budget by itself.

Do changes in states' legal and political constraints over the decade of the 1990s help explain their markedly different responses to the fiscal crises at the close of the decade? Perhaps. Looking at Alt and Lowry's (1994, 2000) measures of divided government reveals no obvious explanatory factors. In fact, the number of unified state governments rose from 18 to 24 from 1989 to 2000, with a distinct trend toward unified Republican governments, from four in 1989 to 15 in 2000. Further, the number of split legislative states (potentially the most divisive political split) held constant at 12; while split branch governments declined from 19 to 13. On the other hand, legal constraints may provide a possible explanation for states' inability to close their budget deficits. Over the decade of the 1990s, nine states enacted or expanded measures that raise the requirements to pass taxes (Rafool, 1998; Ferrara, undated). Some enacted legislative supermajority requirements; others required voter approval of new taxes.

The increase in legal restraints to raise taxes, however, may also simply be a manifestation of the voting public's increasing reluctance to support tax increases. There certainly is a perception that raising taxes has become more costly for politicians in recent years, as exemplified by the defeat of politicians who raised taxes, such as Governor James Florio in New Jersey in 1994 and Governor Gray Davis in California in 2003. However, taxes have been a high-voltage political issue in U.S. states and in California for quite some time, and it is debatable whether it was politically harder to raise taxes in 2001 than in 1991 or in 1982.

It is difficult to study the impact of state fiscal institutions and political configurations on spending. Different rules and institutions interact with each other. They tend to exhibit only infrequent changes. It can be difficult to untangle the impact on spending and taxes of state fixed effects (which may reflect underlying political tastes for spending and taxation) from the institutional structures that are in place.[4] However, the evidence does suggest that rules creating a greater degree of inflexibility in state taxes, spending and borrowing may help to explain why state governments were slow to react to the budget trauma of the early 2000s.

Untangling California's Fiscal Crisis

California's fiscal crisis was a major part of the overall budget crisis of all 50 U.S. states in 2001–2002. On November 17, 2003, Governor Arnold Schwarzenegger was inaugurated in a modest ceremony in Sacramento. He came into power following the voters' recall of Governor Gray Davis. Governor Davis's reputation was already weakened by his delayed response to the electricity crisis in California,[5] but California's budget deficit and Davis's response were what fueled the recall. Governor Davis and the legislature passed a budget that the governor claimed closed a $38 billion dollar deficit. But closing the budget in one year was accomplished with over $16 billion in explicit borrowing, only $9.2 billion in program cuts and with the general knowledge that an $8 billion deficit would emerge at the beginning of the next fiscal year (Legislative Analyst's Office, 2003a, p. 5). Much to the voters' dismay, the budget also reversed prior reductions in the Vehicle License Fee, popularly known as the "car tax."

The financial markets made negative judgments on the final Gray Davis budget. In July 2003, Standard & Poor's downgraded California's bond ratings from A to BBB, the lowest of any state. Moody's followed in August with a downgrade in their rating. The state had already had to pay "credit enhancements" of $84 million to financial institutions to guarantee placements of an $11 billion bond sale in June. Following the downgrading in credit, the state had to pay an additional $34 million in credit enhancements—a cumulative total of over 1 percent of the face values of the bonds. The financial markets were pointing out that, whatever the wording of the state's constitution and laws, California did not in fact have "strong antideficit rules."

The Genesis of California's Crisis

How did the California's budget crisis originate? Contrary to one common belief, the 2001 electricity crisis was not the cause of California's fiscal difficulties. In 2001, the state of California did have to buy electricity on behalf of the public because the major utilities that customarily bought the electricity were bankrupt.[6] The state tapped into its general fund to pay these bills. However, the state then repaid the general fund after selling $6.2 billion in electricity bonds, which were

---

[4] Besley and Case (2003) provide an extensive review of the literature on political institutions and policy choices and present their own evidence, typically with state fixed effects, and often find a significant role for political factors in determining policy outcomes.

[5] For an analysis of the California electricity crisis in this journal, see Borenstein (2002).

[6] Sexton and Sheffrin (2002) provide an institutional perspective on the electricity crisis.

Figure 3
California General Fund and Total Spending from 1997–1998 to 2003–2004

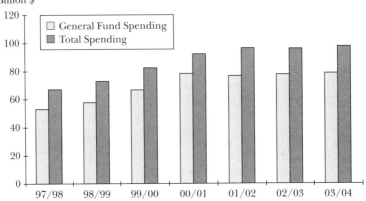

Note: Total spending in 2001–2002 was 7.08 percent of gross state product in 2001.
Source: Legislative Analyst's Office (2003d).

financed by ratepayers, not taxpayers. Thus, the electricity crisis in California only had a temporary effect on the state's general fund cash flow.

At the broadest level, the origins of California's fiscal problems are clear. Beginning in fiscal year 2000–2001, the state began to run an operating deficit, with revenues falling short of expenditures. The operating deficit widened and continued for the next three fiscal years, with the result that a budget surplus of approximately $7 billion at the beginning of 2000–2001 was transformed into a projected deficit of $38 billion at the beginning of fiscal year 2003–2004 (Legislative Analyst's Office, 2003a, p. 3). To put these numbers into some perspective, Figure 3 plots California's general fund and total spending for fiscal years 1997–1998 through 2003–2004.

How did the state create this multiyear operating deficit? Again, at a broad level the answer is straightforward. Starting in the late 1990s, general fund tax revenues began to grow sharply, particularly from the personal income tax. In fiscal year 1997–1998, total general fund revenues were $53.9 billion. By fiscal year 2000–2001, they had increased to $75.7 billion. Personal income tax revenues grew during that same period (with no changes in tax rates) from $27.9 billion to $44.6 billion, thus accounting for the lion's share of the rise in revenues. State spending grew in tandem with these revenue increases. But then revenues began to collapse. Personal income tax revenues fell back to $32.1 billion in 2002–2003, and total state revenues fell to $64.2 billion. Policymakers failed to adjust spending levels to these reduced revenues or to find significant sources of new revenue.

In retrospect, we now understand the genesis of the surge in revenue that began in the late 1990s. According to California's Legislative Analyst Office (2002b, p. 2), revenue from capital gains and stock options peaked in fiscal year 2000–2001 at $17 billion—or 38 percent of the revenue from the personal income tax. By the next fiscal year, following the stock market decline, these revenues were only $6 billion. Once the stock market bubble burst, this drop in tax collections became permanent. As a result, the earlier increase in spending was unsustainable, and the state began to face ongoing operating deficits.

This explanation of California's budget crisis raises several questions. What were the extra revenues spent on during the boom period? The answer to that question will help with the other natural question—why were policymakers slow to react to changing economic circumstances?

From fiscal year 1998–1999 to 2002–2003, general fund spending in California grew from $57.8 billion to $77.7 billion, a total increase of $19.9 billion. The governor and the legislature took advantage of what they deemed to be a new, expansive fiscal environment by creating new programs and increasing allocations to ongoing programs. The increase in total spending reflected the preferences of a Democratic governor and legislature consistent with the general pattern found by Alt and Lowry (1994) that showed that states controlled by Democrats had higher levels of spending.

Figure 4 shows a breakdown of the spending into some major categories: K–14 education, higher education, Medi-Cal (California's Medicaid program), other health and social services, "tax relief" (to be explained in a moment), youth and adult corrections and other (Legislative Analyst's Office, 2003b, p. 4). It also depicts the decomposition of the spending increases into increases attributable into case-load and inflation, new and expanded programs and other factors including federal mandates. Of the $19.9 billion dollar increase in spending, $8.9 can be accounted for by increased caseload and inflation, $3.4 billion by new and ex-panded programs and $7.6 billion in other increases including federal mandates.

Education accounted for $7.1 billion of the $19.9 billion total increase in spending over the four years leading up to 2002–2003. Over this time, total education spending increased by 23 percent. For example, in K–12 education, the state provided additional funds beyond constitutional mandates and added or supplemented new programs in child care, teacher recruitment and retention, testing, summer school and after-school programs. In 1997–1998, California ranked 30th in instructional spending in elementary-secondary public schools on a per pupil basis at $3,452 per pupil. By 2000–2001, instructional spending in elementary-secondary public schools had risen to $4,325 per pupil, with California's rank rising to 26th (U.S. Census Bureau, 2001, 2003). In higher education, the state provided increases in base support, offsets for fee increases, outreach to K–12 students and professional development funds for K–12 teachers.

Health and social services together also increased by $7.1 billion from 1998–1999 to 2002–2003, which was a 44 percent increase. Three-fourths of the $4.1 bil-lion increase in Medi-Cal was due to increased caseload and higher costs of service delivery, while one-fifth of the increase was a result of expanded program eligibility. Other health and social services programs increased by about $3 billion. California has a long history of providing one of the most generous Medicaid benefit packages of all the states, covering 32 of 34 categories of services deemed as optional by the

Figure 4
Where Did Increased California Spending Go?

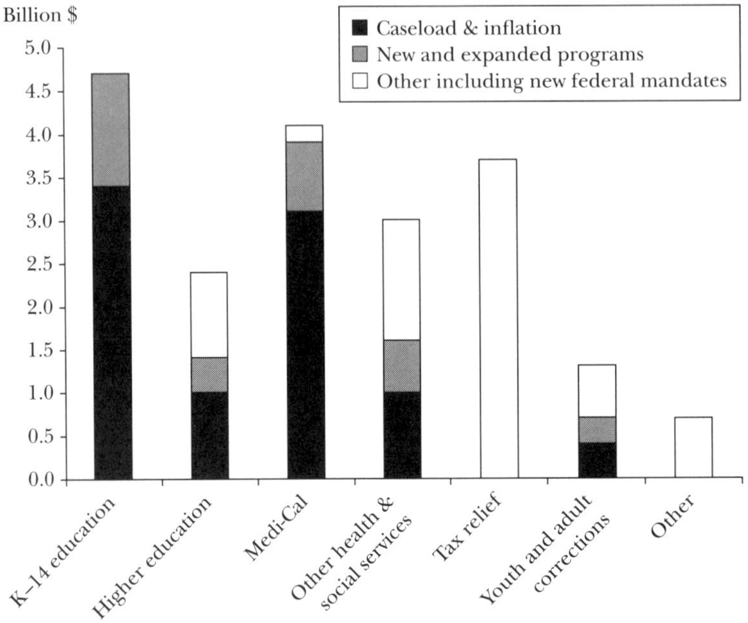

Source: Legislative Analyst's Office (2003b,c).

federal government. These optional services range from dental care and emergency services to chiropractic and personal care services. Governor Davis and the legislature also continued to expand health programs, including the popular Healthy Families program, even as the budget worsened. Healthy Families provides health, dental and vision benefits to children in low-income households. While the program is funded in part by federal funds, about half of the cost the program comes from state sources. In 2001–2002, Healthy Families expenditures totaled $556.3 million, with $55.3 million coming from state Tobacco Settlement funds and $148.7 from general funds (Legislative Analyst's Office, 2002c).

In the calculations of the Legislative Analyst's Office, the "tax relief" from the decrease in the Vehicle License Tax is also treated as a spending program. Since the proceeds of that tax had been allocated to local government, the state provided funds to local governments to offset the decrease in Vehicle License Tax revenues. This rise in state spending to compensate for the lower vehicle tax revenues shows up as "tax relief" on the spending side of the state budget. Tax relief increased by $3.7 billion from 1999–1999 to 2002–2003. Youth and adult corrections increased by $1.3 billion. This category included increased costs for providing health care to inmates (often court mandated) and overtime for prison workers. "Other" increases account for $700 million of the overall increase.

Most of California's increased spending went into broad areas that were generally viewed as providing positive value, such as increased funding for education and health care. Without detailed audits of these increased spending programs, it is impossible to say how much of the higher spending was a reasonable and well-targeted response to public policy problems by a state that found itself with more revenue and how much of the extra spending was dubious or wasteful. In some cases, the extra revenues made it easier to enact spending programs that almost certainly would not have been increased in this way in a time of tighter budget revenues. Here are some examples of what seem like excessive budgetary enthusiasm. Based on standardized tests scores in the 9th, 10th and 11th grades, students were eligible for up to $1,000 per year in college scholarships as Governor's Scholars. Students who scored very high on tests in mathematics and science were eligible for a $2,500 college scholarship. Neither of these programs was means tested. Teachers and schools were given cash awards ranging from $5,000 to $25,000 based on changes in school test scores. In September 2001, the legislature increased the maximum weekly benefit for unemployment insurance from $230 per week to $330 per week, with scheduled increases to $410 per week by 2004. As a final example, the state operated 12 foreign trade offices (expanding over time to include Johannesburg and Taipei) that traditionally were not subject to careful scrutiny.

In other cases, the spending increases crossed from the gray areas of being extravagant into waste or even fraud. A variety of such examples have been put forward from the Legislative Analyst's Office, newspapers, and taxpayer groups like the Citizens Against Government Waste and the Howard Jarvis Taxpayers Association. Here are a few examples, the first two drawn from the *Red Ink Diaries*— accounts of wasteful spending published by State Senator Ross Johnson, a Republican from Irvine—and the others drawn from newspaper accounts. Caltrans, the California transportation agency, proceeded with a costly plan to add numbers to freeway exit signs at a time when other transportation projects were being reduced. A state audit found that the Department of Motor Vehicles ordered $125,000 worth of teddy bears to induce people to fill out their census forms. Moreover, the teddies were ordered on a no-bid "emergency" contract because of a tight deadline. A "boot camp" for troubled youth, one of Governor Davis's pet projects, cost $12 million to run and housed only 25 students (St. John, 2002). A Low-Income Repair Assistance Program designed to help the poor cope with the California smog check program cost millions to run and served only 25 motorists (Willis, 1999). The *Piglet Book* published by the Howard Jarvis Taxpayers Association also highlights the ex-politicians and other political patrons who earn high salaries from government commissions, some which have relatively low workloads.

Of course, any state budget will have some examples of unjustified, wasteful or fraudulent spending, and it is impossible to draw general conclusions from a few anecdotes. But the sheer number and proliferation of anecdotes about wasteful spending in California in the late 1990s and early 2000s as its revenues and spending increased certainly suggests some reason for skepticism over whether the additional spending in big-ticket areas like health and education was all well targeted.

The Political Response to Budget Crisis: Davis versus Wilson

Why was California slow to respond to the emerging fiscal crisis? In general, as discussed earlier, states were more aggressive in closing budget gaps through changes in spending and taxes in the early 1990s than they were in the recent crisis. This pattern also holds in California if we compare the solutions adopted under Governor Davis with those adopted by Governor Pete Wilson in the early 1990s.

California first began to receive bad budgetary news during the passage of the 2001–2002 budget. By April 2001, it was clear that revenues were falling below projections, and the May Revision (the official time at which the state reassesses the budget) showed a deterioration of $5.7 billion from the January budget. The decisions made by Governor Davis at this time set the tone for future years. He adopted a budgetary strategy that relied heavily on one-time solutions, such as shifting funds from transportation accounts into the general fund. These one-time shifts were occurring as the budget continued to expand social programs, such as increased spending in K–12 and increased eligibility for health insurance.

By November 2001, the Legislative Analyst's Office forecast that the 2001–2002 budget would end with a $4.5 billion deficit, rather than the $2.6 billion reserve as originally projected. Moreover, they forecast a $12.4 billion deficit for the following fiscal year and an ongoing structural deficit. After the May Revision, Governor Davis faced a 2002–2003 budget deficit of $23.6 billion—and an upcoming fall election. After a record impasse of 67 days, the governor signed the budget on September 4, 2002. Of the $23.6 billion gap, only $7.5 billion was accounted for by program cuts and only $2.9 billion in revenue increases. The remaining $13.2 billion was comprised of borrowing, interfund shifts or loans, deferrals of expenditures and assumed increases in federal funding. As the Legislative Analyst's Office (2002a, p. 4) commented, "Because of the relatively limited amount of ongoing savings incorporated in the 2002–2003 budget package, the state will continue to face large multibillion shortfalls in 2003–2004 and beyond, absent corrective actions." This forecast proved accurate, so that Governor Davis then faced a disastrous budget deficit of $38 billion in 2003–2004.

Governor Pete Wilson reacted rather differently when he faced his first major fiscal crisis in developing the budget for fiscal year 1991–1992. After the May Revision, he projected a budget gap of $14.3 billion, approximately one-third of total general fund expenditures. He closed this gap with $8.4 billion in revenue increases, $3.4 billion in expenditure cuts and $2.5 billion in cost shifts, transfers from special funds or reductions in reserves. Therefore, 82 percent of the adjustment was made in changes in taxes and spending.

Governor Wilson then faced two more difficult budget years. For fiscal year 1992–1993, he closed an $11.2 billion dollar deficit by relatively large budget reductions ($5.1 billion), modest tax increases ($0.6 billion) and the remainder in cost deferrals and revenue accelerations ($1.9 billion), shifting costs to local government ($2.3 billion) and other actions. Finally, in fiscal year 1993–1994, he faced an $8.0 billion gap, which he closed with shifts to local government ($3.7 billion), deferral and revenue accelerations ($2.4 billion), program reductions ($1.1 billion) and modest revenue increases ($0.8 billion). Governor Wilson's aggressive initial response helped to limit the problems that emerged in the next two years.

What political factors can account for the much less aggressive stance that Governor Davis took to the California budget in the early 2000s than did Governor Wilson in the early 1990s? At first glance, we would expect, based on previously cited research, that Governor Davis would have the easier time making adjustments since California at that time had a unified government under the Democrats, while the Republican Governor Wilson faced a Democratic legislature. However, California is one of just three states that requires a supermajority (two-thirds) to pass a budget. Tax increases also require a supermajority. As all California governors discover, these restrictions sharply limit their apparent power and decrease the apparent advantage of a "unified government."

Political observers in California have pointed to three factors that made budget adjustments more difficult during this crisis. First, term limits for the legislature originally enacted in 1990 had taken full effect. When Governor Wilson was brokering his budget deals, he could rely on long-term Republican and Democratic legislators who were accustomed to negotiating with one another. During the recent crisis, fewer long term legislators remained, and animosity across the aisles was greater. A second factor was that the September 2001 legislative reapportionment reflected a deal struck by incumbents, which meant that most legislators had secure seats and decreased incentives to bargain. Finally, rather than trying to bargain with the Republicans, Governor Davis had previously put together governing majorities by enticing legislators to desert the Republicans through various perks, including the apparent promise of an appointment in his cabinet to a termed-out state senator.[7] Thus, when the Republicans were able to hold ranks during the budget negotiations, there was no history of past negotiations to build upon.

When Did They Know It?

During the 2003 recall vote on Governor Davis, one common accusation was that Davis had deliberately minimized the extent of California's budget problems when he was reelected in 2002. This accusation is at best only partly true, since even California's nonpartisan Legislative Analyst's Office underestimated the severity of the problems that Governor Davis would face.

Figure 5 plots the Legislative Analyst's Office forecasts for fiscal year 2003–2004 starting in November 1998 and ending in September 2003. As of November 2000, the official predictions did not show a bursting of the revenue bubble. A year later,

---

[7] Republican Senator Maurice Johannessen was appointed head of Veteran Affairs by Governor Davis in December 2002, after he sided with the Democrats in earlier budget negotiations.

Figure 5
Forecasts for 2003–2004 Fiscal Year

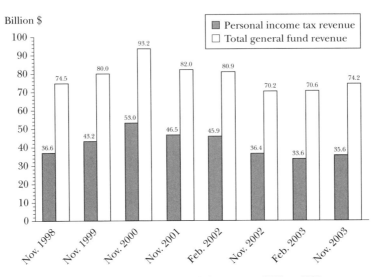

Source: Legislative Analyst's Office, various reports and documents, 1998 to 2003.

the Legislative Analyst's Office reduced its forecast. But even by February 2002, when Governor Davis had just announced his plans for the critical 2002–2003 budget, the Legislative Analyst forecasts still called for personal income tax revenue to be nearly $46 billion and total revenue $81 billion. In November 2002, the Legislative Analyst lowered its forecasts again, bringing personal income tax revenue down to $34 billion and total revenue to $71 billion. Clearly, there was a two-step drop in the forecasts, as new information changed the Legislative Analyst's Office assessment during 2002. This change complicated the underlying budget process during fiscal year 2002–2003 and exacerbated the budgetary woes caused by Governor Davis's reliance on borrowings and deferrals—a strategy that is predicated upon a recovering, not a declining, economy.

The Legislative Analyst's Office recognized that capital gains and stock options initially caused personal income tax revenues to increase above prevailing levels and discussed this point in their November 2001 *Fiscal Outlook.* Nonetheless, their forecasters were still hampered by a lack of full information. In November 2001, the Legislative Analyst's Office would have had access to state tax data for the 1999 calendar tax year, which would have details on capital gains.[8] Capital gains realizations are notoriously difficult to forecast in any case. Moreover, as we discussed above, options that accounted for between 35 and 40 percent of stock market related income in California in 2000 need to be estimated separately from payroll data from specific companies.

---

[8] Phil Spilberg of the Franchise Tax Board points out that tax returns for 1999 can be filed, with an extension, as late as October 15, 2000, and the FTB would conduct its analysis in April 2001.

In contrast, similar data from the early 1990s do *not* show a steep two-step drop in forecasted revenues. Adjusting for legislated tax changes, it appears that in the early 1990s, the bulk of California's bad fiscal news occurred all at once. Once the 1991–1992 budget was passed, revenue increases that were originally estimated to be $9.1 billion were later re-estimated to account for $7.5 billion, reflecting a mild deterioration in the economy. But this problem was relatively manageable. Governor Wilson faced the worst news in his first year, and the news did not get much worse over time.

In many ways, the California experience mirrored the experiences of other states during the most recent state fiscal crisis, but California's political environment was a fun-house mirror that exaggerated fiscal features. The surge in temporary capital gains revenue was spent, which is consistent with the literature on the "flypaper effect" that finds that lump sum grants (or their equivalent) are largely spent by state and local governments (Hines and Thaler, 1995). Like other states, California was slower to make permanent adjustments to alleviate its fiscal plight during the current crisis as compared to the earlier crisis. The drop in stock market related income caused additional difficulties, both because of its magnitude and the delay in information as to its full impact on revenues. A variety of political factors led California politicians to temporize and avoid difficult adjustments to taxes and spending. By postponing hard budget solutions, California became especially vulnerable to a second wave of bad news as the full impact of the stock market decline on tax revenues became evident.

After he was inaugurated, Governor Schwarzenegger fulfilled a campaign promise by reversing the increase in the car tax, which exacerbated the financial difficulties of the state. His January 2004 budget plan called for a public vote on a $15 billion dollar bond (slightly larger borrowing than what the legislature had passed) and relied substantially on program cuts, shifts in funding from local governments and one-time solutions. Although the Legislative Analyst Office (2004, p. 3) called the proposed budget a "solid starting point for budget deliberations," it would still leave an ongoing structural deficit of approximately $6 billion. Voters approved the bond in March 2004, but California's budget woes are still not over.

Conclusions

During the recent economic downturn, the reluctance of states to cut spending and raise taxes led to protracted fiscal difficulties. Politicians, responding to public sentiment that sought both to protect programs and avoid tax increases, were led to the increasing use of one-time solutions that postponed the resolution of their underlying fiscal problems. In many cases, they were constrained by legal or constitutional restrictions on tax increases, as well as court mandates that protected some spending programs. While restraints on taxation may be useful at some times, they do limit the ability of the political system to respond to fiscal shocks and raise borrowing costs. Moreover, restrictions on the ability to raise taxes may also make politicians less inclined to decrease them during boom times, leading to excessive state spending.

States clearly need to be more careful in assessing whether increases in tax revenue are permanent or temporary. The temporary bulge in tax revenues from stock market related income in California led to unsustainable spending increases in core programs, such as education and health care, as well as increases in a variety of other less essential spending. Cutting back on the latter is relatively easy, but cutting back on the former is more difficult politically and causes disruptions in expectations and program delivery.

Finally, as the California experience highlights, failure to come to grips early with budget difficulties sharply increases the risks of truly severe fiscal problems. Investors and financial institutions do give the states some leeway in finding their way through budget crises, but a prolonged failure to balance the budget may ultimately lead to a loss of state sovereignty to financial institutions.

■ *This work was supported by the Center for State and Local Taxation at UC Davis. I would like to thank Bei Li and Jean Stratford for their superb assistance in this research. Thanks to James Alt, Alan Auerbach, Therese McGuire, Jim Poterba, Kim Rueben, Phil Spilberg, Dave Vasche and Brad Williams for useful discussions on the issues addressed in this paper. James Hines, Andrei Shleifer, Timothy Taylor and Michael Waldman provided valuable comments on the initial draft of this paper.*

References

Advisory Commission on Intergovernmental Relations (ACIR). 1987. *Fiscal Discipline in the Federal System: National Reform and the Experience of the States.* Washington, D.C.: Advisory Commission on Intergovernmental Relations.

Alt, James E. and Robert C. Lowry. 1994. "Divided Government, Fiscal Institutions, and Budget Deficits: Evidence from the States." *American Political Science Review.* 88:4, pp. 811–28.

Alt, James E. and Robert C. Lowry. 2000. "A Dynamic Model of State Budget Outcomes under Divided Partisan Government." *Journal of Politics.* 62:4, pp. 1035–069.

Auerbach, Alan J. 2003. "Fiscal Policy, Past and Present." *Brookings Papers on Economic Activity.* 1, pp. 75–138.

Baker, Al. 2003. "Budgets in Crisis: State Legislature Overrides Pataki on Budget Vetoes." *New York Times.* May 16, p. A1.

Besley, Timothy and Anne Case. 2003. "Political Institutions and Policy Choices: Evidence from the United States." *Journal of Economic Literature.* 41:1, pp. 7–73.

Bohn, Henning and Robert P. Inman. 1996. "Balanced-Budget Rules and Public Deficits: Evidence from the U.S. States." *Carnegie-Rochester Series on Public Policy.* November, 45, pp. 13–76.

Borenstein, Severin. 2002. "The Trouble with Electricity Markets: Understanding California's Restructuring Disaster." *Journal of Economic Perspectives.* 16:1, pp. 191–212.

Boyd, Donald J. and Nicholas W. Jenny. 2003. "State Fiscal Crisis Far Worse than Economy Would Suggest." *Rockefeller Institute State Fiscal News.* 3:4, pp. 1–5; Available at ⟨http://stateandlocalgateway.rockinst.org⟩.

Citizens Against Government Waste and The Howard Jarvis Taxpayers Foundation. 2003.

2003 California Piglet Book. Washington, D.C. and Sacramento, Calif.: Citizens Against Government Waste and The Howard Jarvis Taxpayers Foundation; Available at ⟨http://www.hjta.org/pigletbook.htm⟩.

Council of State Governments. 1989. *State Elective Officials and the Legislatures.* Lexington, Ky.: Council of State Governments.

Council of State Governments. 1990, 2000. *Book of the States.* Lexington, Ky.: Council of State Governments.

Dixon, Ken. 2003. "Budget Done—Finally." *Connecticut Post.* August 18.

Ferrara, Peter J. Undated. "Supermajority Taxpayer Protection." *Americans for Tax Reform Policy Brief.* Available at ⟨http://www.atr.org⟩.

Har, Janie and Dave Hogan. 2003. "227 Days the House Wraps up the 2003–05 Budget." *The Oregonian.* August 28, p. A01.

Hines, James R. Jr. and Richard H. Thaler. 1995. "Anomalies: The Flypaper Effect." *Journal of Economic Perspectives.* 9:4, pp. 217–26.

Knight, Brian, Andrea Kusko and Laura Rubin. 2003. "Problems and Prospects for State and Local Governments." *State Tax Notes.* August 11, pp. 427–39; Available at ⟨http://www.taxpolicycenter.org/sfc2003⟩.

Legislative Analyst's Office. 2001. *California's Fiscal Outlook.* Sacramento, Calif.: Legislative Analyst's Office; Available at ⟨http://www.lao.ca.gov⟩.

Legislative Analyst's Office. 2002a. *California Spending Plan 2002–03.* Sacramento, Calif.: Legislative Analyst's Office; Available at ⟨http://www.lao.ca.gov⟩.

Legislative Analyst's Office. 2002b. *California's Fiscal Outlook.* Sacramento, Calif.: Legislative Analyst's Office; Available at ⟨http://www.lao.ca.gov⟩.

Legislative Analyst's Office. 2002c. *Analysis of the 2000–03 Budget Bill.* Sacramento, Calif.: Legislative Analyst's Office; Available at ⟨http://www.lao.ca.gov⟩.

Legislative Analyst's Office. 2003a. *California Spending Plan, 2003–04.* Sacramento, Calif.: Legislative Analyst's Office; Available at ⟨http://www.lao.ca.gov⟩.

Legislative Analyst's Office. 2003b. *State Expenditures: History and Forecast.* Sacramento, Calif.: Legislative Analyst's Office.

Legislative Analyst's Office. 2003c. *Sources of Spending Growth in Major State Programs.* Sacramento, Calif.: Legislative Analyst's Office.

Legislative Analyst's Office. 2003d. "Economics, Taxation and Fiscal Forecasting Data: Historical Data. Sacramento." Excel files available at ⟨http://www.lao.ca.gov/lao_menu_economics.asp⟩.

Legislative Analyst's Office. 2004. "2004-05: Overview of the Governor's Budget." Available at ⟨http://www.lao.ca.gov⟩.

Maag, Elaine and David Merriman. 2003. "Tax Policy Responses to Revenue Shortfalls." *State Tax Notes.* August 4, pp. 363–73; Available at ⟨http://www.taxpolicycenter.org/sfc2003⟩.

National Association of State Budget Officers and National Governors Association (NASBO). 2003. *The Fiscal Survey of the States.* Washington, D.C.: National Association of State Budget Officers and National Governors Association; Available at ⟨http://www.nasbo.org⟩.

National Association of State Budget Officers and National Governors Association (NASBO). Various issues; 1985–2003. *The Fiscal Survey of the States.* Washington, D.C.: National Association of State Budget Officers and National Governors Association.

Petersen, John E. 2003. "Changing Red to Black: Deficit Closing Alchemy." *National Tax Journal.* 56:3, pp. 567–78.

Poterba, James M. 1994. "State Responses to Fiscal Crises: The Effects of Budgetary Institutions and Politics." *Journal of Political Economy.* 102:4, pp. 799–821.

Poterba, James M. and Kim S. Rueben. 2001. "Fiscal News, State Budget Rules, and Tax-Exempt Bond Yields." *Journal of Urban Economics.* 50:37, pp. 537–62.

Rafool, Mandy. 1998. *Which States Require a Supermajority Vote to Raise Taxes?* Denver: National Conference of State Legislatures; Available at ⟨http://www.ncsl.org/programs/fiscal/suprmajr.html⟩.

Rawls, Philip. 2003. "Riley Reacts to Defeat By Planning Big Cuts." *Associated Press State and Local Wire.* September 10.

Red Ink Diaries. 2003. Issued by the Office of State Senator Ross Johnson, Sacramento, California.

Riley, Brendan. 2003. "Key Elements of Nevada Tax Plan Take Effect October 1." *Associated Press State and Local Wire.* September 25.

Sexton, Terri A. and Steven M. Sheffrin. 2002. "California's Energy Crisis: Implications for Public Finance and Taxation." *94th Annual Conference Proceedings of the National Tax Association.* pp. 27–32; Available at ⟨http://www.iga.ucdavis.edu/cec.pdf⟩.

Sjoquist, David and Sally Wallace. 2003. "Capital Gains: Its Recent, Varied and Growing (?) Impact on State Revenues." *State Tax Notes.* August 18, pp. 497–506; Available at ⟨http://www.taxpolicycenter.org/sfc2003⟩.

Snell, Ronald K., Corina Eckl and Graham Williams. 2003. "State Spending in the 1990s." *State Tax Notes.* September 29, pp. 913–20.

St. John, Kelly. 2002. "Governor's Costly Boot Camp for Teens." *San Francisco Chronicle.* June 7, p. A1.

U.S. Bureau of Economic Analysis. 2003. *National Income and Product Account Tables.* Washington, D.C.: U.S. Bureau of Economic Analysis; Available at ⟨http://www.bea.gov/bea/dn/nipaweb/SelectTable.asp⟩.

U.S. Census Bureau. 2001. *Public Elementary-Secondary Education Finances: 1997–98.* Washington, D.C.: U.S. Census Bureau; Available at ⟨http://www.census.gov⟩.

U.S. Census Bureau. 2003. *Public Education Finances: 2001.* Washington, D.C.: U.S. Census Bureau; Available at ⟨http://www.census.gov⟩.

Willis, Doug. 1999. "A Report from the Watchdogs Who Look for and Find Government Waste." *Associated Press State and Local Wire.* March 21.

Journal of Economic Perspectives—Volume 18, Number 2—Spring 2004—Pages 227–238

Prospects in the Academic Labor Market for Economists

Ronald G. Ehrenberg

A merican universities are currently graduating about 1,000 to 1,100 Ph.D.'s in economics, econometrics and agricultural economics each year. Combining these newly minted Ph.D.'s with those who are looking to make a change, several thousand economists are looking seriously for academic jobs. Recent years have not been good ones for job seekers; as an example, the number of new jobs listed in *Job Openings for Economists* declined from 2,650 in calendar year 2000 to 2,101 in calendar year 2003.[1] This decline was undoubtedly due to the decline in the stock market and the recession that took place during this period, both of which affected the finances of public and private higher education, as well the hiring of nonacademic employers.

Current Ph.D. students in economics, who will be looking for the positions in future years, should have some reasons for optimism. After all, American college faculty are aging and, in spite of some postponement of retirements due to the ending of mandatory retirement and the decline in the stock market at the start of the twenty-first century, one might expect that the replacement demand for faculty positions would be large. College enrollments are projected to increase substantially throughout the first decade of the twenty-first century, which might also be expected to lead to increased demand for faculty.

---

[1] New job listings in *Job Opportunities for Economists* are summarized annually in a report that appears in the May issue of the *American Economic Review*, where the data presented are for the previous calendar year. The 2003 data were provided by John Siegfried, Secretary-Treasurer of the American Economic Association.

■ *Ronald G. Ehrenberg is the Irving M. Ives Professor of Industrial and Labor Relations and Economics and Director of the Cornell Higher Education Research Institute (CHERI), both at Cornell University, Ithaca, New York, and Research Associate, National Bureau of Economic Research, Cambridge, Massachusetts. His e-mail address is ⟨rge2@cornell.edu⟩.*

However, the job picture ahead is far from sunny. American colleges and universities are increasingly substituting nontenure track full-time and part-time faculty for full-time tenured and tenure track faculty. Moreover, institutions of public higher education, where almost two-thirds of the full-time faculty members at four-year institutions are employed, are under severe financial pressure. The share of state budgets devoted to public higher education is declining. The salaries of economics department faculty members at public higher education institutions have fallen substantially relative to the salaries of their counterparts at private higher education institutions, and it is becoming increasingly difficult for the publics to compete for top faculty in economics. Moreover, it is at the economics departments in public institutions where the greatest increase in the usage of nontenure track faculty has also occurred.

This article begins by presenting levels of Ph.D. production, and then discusses factors determining demand for economics departments, differences between public and private universities, and the range of pay between departments within universities.

Ph.D. Production in Economics

The number of new economics Ph.D.'s granted by American universities in economics (including those granted in econometrics and agricultural economics) rose dramatically starting in the late 1960s, rising from just over 600 in 1966 to 1,100 by 1970. From that peak, as shown in Figure 1, the number of new economics Ph.D.'s hovered at just under 1,000 per year for most of the 1980s before rising to around 1,000 to 1,100 per year during the last few years.

However, this apparent stability in the number of new Ph.D.'s produced conceals a different underlying trend: the probability that an American college graduate goes on to receive a Ph.D. in economics has substantially declined. Between 1970–1971 and 2000–2001, the number of bachelor's degrees granted per year by American colleges and universities rose by about 50 percent from 840,000 to 1,244,000. On average, about 2 percent of all bachelor's degrees in the United States are granted annually to students majoring in economics, although there are cycles in the relative popularity of economics as an undergraduate major (Margo and Siegfried, 1996). Approximately three-quarters of all economics Ph.D.'s are granted to students who majored in economics as undergraduates (Siegfried and Stock, 2003). But despite the rise in the number of economics majors, traditionally the main feedstock of economics Ph.D.'s, the number of economic Ph.D.'s has not been rising.

While the chance that an economics major continuing on to a Ph.D. in economics has declined, the probabilities that an economics major goes on to receive either a law degree or a master's degree in business have risen substantially. From 1970–1971 and 2000–2001, the number of master's degrees granted in business administration almost tripled, growing from 42,000 to 116,000, and the

Figure 1

Number of New Economics Ph.D's Granted by American Universities

(academic years ending 1966–2002)

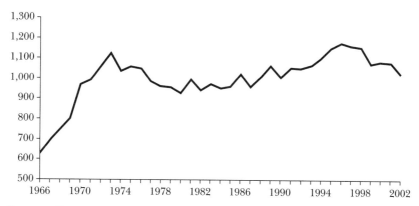

Source: Doctorate Records File. From Survey of Earned Doctorates via WebCASPAR (http://caspar.nsf.gov).

number of first professional degrees granted in law more than doubled, going from 17,000 to 38,000 (*Digest of Education Statistics 2002*, 2003, Tables 246, 253 and 259). Large and growing earnings differentials between academia and the professions have undoubtedly played a large role in these changes (Bok, 1993; Hamermesh, 1995).

In fact, the decline in the probability of American college graduates going on for Ph.D.'s in economics is even larger than that suggested by the relatively constant number of Ph.D.'s granted in economics at American colleges and universities, because the share of Ph.D.'s in economics granted to foreign students has dramatically increased. As Figure 2 indicates, the percentage of Ph.D.'s granted to foreign students has grown from a little over 20 percent in 1966 to about 56 percent in 2002. This growth in the share of Ph.D.'s granted to foreign students is not unique to economics; similar changes have occurred in many physical science and engineering fields.

Foreign Ph.D.'s in economics are less likely to stay in the United States and seek employment after graduation than are their American counterparts. In 2002, about 47.3 percent of temporary resident Ph.D.'s in economics found at least temporary employment in the United States. Furthermore, an increasing share of economics Ph.D.'s, including U.S.-born Ph.D.'s, are finding employment outside the academic sector (Siegfried and Stock, 2003). In recent years, only about half of all new economics Ph.D.'s who found employment in the United States did so in the academic sector; this is down from about 70 percent in 1991. As a result, American colleges and universities are increasingly turning to foreign Ph.D.'s to staff their economics faculties.

There has been some controversy over how this increase in foreign faculty has affected the quality of education. Faculty from other nations can enrich the

Figure 2
Share of New Economics Ph.D's Granted by American Universities to Temporary Residents
(1966–2002)

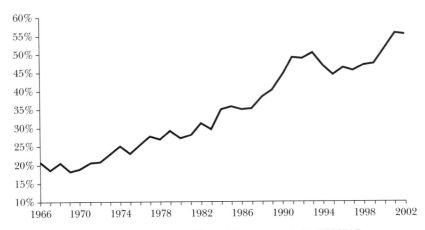

Source: Doctorate Records File. From Survey of Earned Doctorates via WebCASPAR (http://caspar.nsf.gov).
Note: Some new Ph.D.'s fail to report their citizenship status to the National Science Foundation each year (on average 4 percent of respondents per year). The computation of the percentage of new Ph.D.'s granted to foreign residents excludes these individuals from both the numerator and the denominator.

educational experience of American students by offering them perspectives from different cultures. However, some foreign Ph.D.'s (and foreign Ph.D. students in their role as teaching assistants) may lack command over the English language, may come from an educational background that does not encourage the questioning of professors by students or may come from a culture that undervalues the role of women. Hence, some foreign Ph.D.'s may be less effective undergraduate instructors than their American counterparts. Two recent studies have found conflicting evidence on the effectiveness of foreign-born teaching assistants in economics. Borjas (2000) found that undergraduate students with foreign-born teaching assistants at one major research university learned less in principles of economics classes than undergraduate students with American-born teaching assistants, but Fleisher, Hashimoto and Weinberg (2002), who studied another university, found no such evidence.

The Demand for Economics Professors

In 1996, about 14 percent of all four-year college faculty members were between the ages of 60 and 69, and this percentage, plus the percentage of faculty over age 69, are both likely to rise throughout most of the first decade of the twenty-first century (Ashenfelter and Card, 2002). Although the elimination of mandatory retirement has caused some faculty to postpone retirement at institutions with defined contribution pension plans, voluntary retirements of older faculty, coupled with increasing enrollments in higher education, might lead one to expect that the demand for faculty members in economics would grow in the years ahead.

Increasingly, however, colleges and universities are substituting relatively cheaper part-time and full-time nontenure track faculty members for full-time tenure and tenure track faculty.[2] Table 1 presents data from a survey of economics departments at four-year American colleges and universities that was undertaken by the Cornell Higher Education Research Institute (CHERI) during the spring and summer of 2003 that suggests that economics departments have not been immune to this type of substitution. Between 1982–1983 and 2002–2003, the share of economics department faculty members at survey respondents that were full-time tenure and tenure track faculty members fell from 75.2 percent to 57.6 percent. The decline was greater for public than private institutions, due in large part to the declining relative financial position at these institutions (Ehrenberg, 2003b). It was very pronounced at the large research universities—institutions at which many new Ph.D.'s in economics hope to find employment.[3] During the period, the share of full-time tenure and tenure track faculty at these departments fell from 72.3 percent to 54.5 percent.

One reason for this shift to part-time and nontenure positions is as a reaction to tight state finances. At private institutions, tuitions typically increase 2 ½ to 3 ½ percent above inflation each year, but state appropriations per full-time equivalent student at public institutions of higher education institutions are roughly the same in real terms in 2003–2004 as in the early 1990s. Other reasons relate to the fiscal strains that all academic institutions face from their need to finance student financial aid, library costs, renewal of aging facilities and rising health insurance costs.

Another reason is that economics and other departments face heightened competition for funds from science and engineering research. The costs of such research have increased substantially at many large universities in total and as a share of all educational and general operating expenditures. For example, between 1976–1977 and 1999–2000, research expenditures as a share of all educational and

[2] Ehrenberg (2003a, Table B) presents data on the dramatic growth of full-time lecturers and part-time faculty members at the State University of New York (SUNY) system during the 1985 to 2001 period. Ehrenberg and Klaff (2004) show that the substitution of full-time nontenure track faculty for tenured and tenure track faculty within the SUNY system was related to the declining relative cost of the former.
[3] We also asked the chairs to provide us with data on the share of undergraduate credit hours generated by tenure and tenure track faculty in their departments during 1992–1993 and 2002–2003. A smaller number of departments provided responses to these questions. However, the pattern of changes was very similar to those reported above with larger decreases in the shares being reported for publics than for privates and for research universities than for other institutions. The share of all students enrolled in economics classes being taught by tenure track faculty was 71.2 percent for all courses and 67.6 percent for principles classes in 2002–2003.

Table 1
Full-Time Tenured and Tenure Track Faculty Members as a Percentage of Total Economics Department Faculty Members

Year	All institutions	Public institutions	Private institutions	Research universities	Liberal arts colleges
2002–2003	57.6	51.7	65.4	54.5	70.3
1997–1998	68.6	67.0	70.9	62.1	75.1
1992–1993	70.8	68.9	73.3	64.0	77.2
1987–1988	74.8	73.4	76.5	71.0	79.9
1982–1983	75.2	74.8	75.8	72.3	78.4

Source: Cornell Higher Education Research Institute (CHERI) Survey of Economics Department Chairs at 799 American four-year colleges and universities undertaken during the spring and summer of 2003. The response rate to the survey was about one-half for the Research I and Research II institutions, but the overall survey response rate was about one-third. As a result, one should be cautious about generalizing its findings to the entire population of four-year American colleges and universities. A more complete summary of the survey findings is available on the web at ⟨http://www.ilr.cornell.edu/cheri⟩. Nationwide, in 1998 full-time faculty in public institutions represent about 66 percent of all full-time faculty employed at four-year institutions. The comparable percentage for research universities was about 42 percent and for liberal arts colleges about 11 percent (*Digest of Education Statistics*, 2002, 2003, Table 229).

general operating expenditures grew from 18.4 to 22.4 percent at public universities (*Digest of Education Statistics, 2002*, 2003, Table 350). Moreover, the share of research costs paid for by universities out of institutional funds (as opposed to external grants) has risen from 11 percent in the mid-1970s to over 21 percent by 2000 (Ehrenberg, Rizzo and Jakubson, 2003). Much of these costs come in the form of start-up costs for scientists and engineers that average $300,000 to $500,000 for new assistant professors in science and engineering fields at the major research universities—and are much higher for senior faculty members (Ehrenberg, Rizzo and Condie, 2003). Undergraduate students appear to be bearing part of these costs in the form of more lecturers and part-time faculty members.

To date, however, only few studies have addressed the impact, if any, on undergraduate students of being taught by a greater proportion of part-time and full-time nontenure track faculty members. Bettinger and Long (2004), using longitudinal student-record data from all public academic institutions in Ohio, find little evidence that part-time faculty adversely impact upon undergraduate students. However, in a work in progress, Liang Zhang and I are using panel data from College Board's *Annual Survey of Colleges* and are finding that increases in the shares of part-time faculty and nontenure track full-time at an institution are both associated with decreases in its six-year graduation rate.

Comparisons across Types of Institutions

Inequality in average faculty salaries across academic institutions has increased for at least the last two decades. Average salaries of professors at public doctoral universities, which stood at 91 percent of their private sector counterparts' average salaries in 1978–1979, declined relative to the average salaries of professors in private doctoral universities by about 14 percentage points between 1978–1979 and 2003–2004 (Ehrenberg, 2004): this widening gap makes it harder for the publics to attract and retain top faculty members. Data on continuation rates of associate professors collected annually by the American Association of University Professors shows that voluntary faculty turnover is higher at the publics than it is at the privates (Ehrenberg, 2003c). For example, the average turnover rate of associate professors at doctoral universities during the 1996–1997 to 2001–2002 period was about 9 percent, and during the period, the rate at public doctoral universities was about 2 percentage points higher than that at private doctoral universities.

Since the mid-1970s, the American Economic Association has collected data on the average salary of faculty in economics department annually in its Universal Academic Questionnaire. The departments that respond to the survey vary from year to year and, in recent years, some departments have reported their average assistant professor salaries but not their average full professor salaries. Figure 3 tracks, by rank, the ratio of the average salary of economists employed at public Ph.D. granting institutions to the average salary of economists at private Ph.D. granting institutions from 1975–1976 to 2001–2002.[4] To minimize problems relating to year-to-year changes in the sample, the ratios reported are three-year moving average of the annual ratios.

The pattern one observes for economists are similar to the patterns observed for all academics nationwide. At the full professor level, the average salary of economists in public Ph.D. granting institutions was about 96 percent of the average salary of economists at private Ph.D. granting institutions in 1975–1976. By 1993, this ratio had fallen to about 81 percent and, after rebounding during the middle and late 1990s (which were relatively good times for public higher education), it fell to about 83 percent in 2002–2003.[5] At the associate professor level, average salaries were roughly equal between the two sectors in 1975–1976; by 2002–2003, the ratio of average public to average private salaries was about 87 percent in 2002–2003. Finally, at the assistant professor level, the average salary of economists in economics departments at public universities was about 7 percent *higher* than those of their private counterparts in 1975–1976. However, by 2002–2003, their salaries were about 5 percent lower. So at all ranks, the average salaries of economists in departments at public universities have fallen relative to those of their counterparts at private universities. That the differential between private and public universities is largest at the full professor level is undoubtedly due to the fact

[4] I am grateful to John Siegfried, Secretary Treasurer of the American Economic Association for granting me access to these data and to Charles Scott of Loyola College (Maryland) for taking the time to provide me with the data.

[5] These data may understate the decline in the relative salaries of full professors in economics departments at public universities because it appears that the departments in private institutions that report assistant professor but not full professor average salaries in recent years are departments whose average full professor salaries were among the highest in the sample in years that they did report these data.

Figure 3

Public to Private Salary Ratios Across Ph.D. Economics Departments: Three-Year Averages

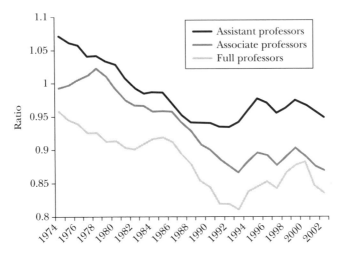

Note: Three-year averages centered on the year. The ratios for the first (1974) and last (2003) year are two-year averages.

that assistant professors are more mobile than full professors, and thus, entry level salaries must more closely reflect market conditions.

About two-thirds of all full-time faculty members (across all disciplines) at four-year institutions in the United States are employed at doctoral granting institutions, and it is reasonable to believe that the same percentage of academic economists is employed at them. But what about comparable salaries for economists who work at institutions that grant master's and bachelor's degrees? The American Economic Association collects average salary data by rank for these institutions, but the sample sizes are smaller and the data cover a smaller number of years, so I have not used these data in this paper. We do know, however, that nationally, the average salary of faculty across all fields at doctoral universities has grown relative to the average salary of faculty at master's and bachelor's degree granting institutions during the last 15 to 20 years. For example, in 1984–1985, the average salaries of full professors at doctoral universities was 18.8 percent higher than those at master's universities and 34.4 percent higher than those at bachelor's institutions; by 1999–2000, these differentials had grown to 29.9 percent and 50.0 percent, respectively (Bell, 2000, Table 5). Thus, it seems probable that the pay gap between economists at private doctoral granting universities and economists at institutions that grant master's and bachelor's degrees has also increased.

The decline in the average salaries of economists at public doctorate degree-granting universities relative to their private university counterparts leads to fears that it is becoming increasingly difficult for departments in public universities to attract and retain the very best faculty. When one regresses the change in an economics department's National Research Council faculty quality rating that took place between the 1980s (Jones, Lindzey and Cogshall, 1982) and the 1990s (Goldberger, Maher and Flattau, 1995) on the department's 1980s faculty quality rating and the percentage change in average full professor salary at the institution (across all fields) between 1982 and 1993, one finds that for departments ranked in the top half of all economics departments in the 1980s in terms of faculty quality, the association between average faculty salary changes and faculty quality rating changes is positive. Put another way, economics departments at universities in which average faculty salaries did not increase as much as their competitors' average faculty salaries experienced a decline in the ratings of their economics department faculty quality by the National Research Council.

Economics and Other Disciplines

How have academic economists' salaries fared relative to the salaries of their colleagues in other disciplines at the same universities? Each year the Office of Institutional Research and Information Management at Oklahoma State University conducts a survey of academic salaries by detailed field of study. These institutions are primarily public institutions, although a few privates that are land grant institutions, such as Cornell and MIT, also participate in the survey.

Figure 4 traces the ratio of the average salaries of full professors and new assistant professors in economics to the average salaries of their faculty counterparts in English literature at surveyed institutions from 1985–1986 to 2001–2002.[6] Again, because the institutions participating in the sample vary from year-to-year, all of the ratios are three-year moving averages. In 1985–1986, the average full professor in economics at these institutions earned 14 percent more than the average full professor in English. By 2001–2002, this advantage had risen to 28 percent. At the new assistant professor level, the comparable change was from 33 to 49 percent. Economists have done increasingly better relative to lower-paying humanities fields during the period, with the salary advantage being greatest at the entry level. The data in Figure 4, of course, relate only to salaries, there may also have been an increased divergence in the magnitudes of teaching loads, research accounts, summer salaries and other pecuniary and nonpecuniary types of compensation paid to faculty in the two disciplines.

National averages may give a very misleading impression, however, of how much higher economists' salaries are relative to another discipline's faculty salaries

[6] I am grateful to Lee Tarrant, Office of Institutional Research and Information Management at Oklahoma State University, for granting me access to the national average salary figures, which are published annually in their publication *Faculty Salary Survey by Discipline*, and for preparing special tabulations for me on the distribution of the ratio of economists to English faculty members' salaries across institutions.

Figure 4
Salary Ratio: Economics Professors to English Professors

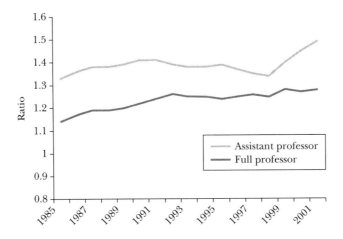

at different institutions. For example, suppose we order institutions in the survey by the magnitude of the percentage salary advantage that assistant professors in economics have over assistant professors in English in 2001–2002, with the institution with the smallest advantage being placed at the 1st percentile and the one with the largest advantage being placed at the 100th percentile. The data indicate that the advantage for new assistant professors in economics at the 25th percentile institution was 34 percent, while the advantage at the 75th percentile institution was 65 percent, a spread of 31 percentage points. Thus, there is no single salary advantage that economists automatically earn across institutions. Research has yet to be undertaken to explain why such a wide range of salary differentials between two disciplines exist, but at least five possible explanations exist: 1) perhaps the salary differential between the economics and English departments at a university will be larger when faculty in the two departments are employed in different colleges at the university, so that head-to-head comparisons are more difficult; 2) perhaps the range of differentials occurs because the rankings of the economics and English departments are similar at some schools but different at others; 3) perhaps the salary differential is larger at private universities in which individual salary information is more likely to be kept confidential; 4) perhaps the salary level differential is larger when there is a separate business school at the university that may put pressure on economists' salaries in the economics department; or 5) perhaps the salary differential is higher the lower the average salary level at the university, because economists have better nonacademic alternatives than English Ph.D.'s, and that puts a lower bound on the salaries that can be paid to economists.

Interestingly, the salaries of economists have declined relative to some of the higher-paying fields in academia, such as business. At the full professor level, economists' average salaries declined from 96 to 90 percent of business professors' salaries at surveyed institutions from 1985–1986 to 2001–2002. At the new assistant professor level, the salaries of economists as a share of the salaries of business professors declined from 83 to 74 percent. However, even if economists did not keep pace with business professors, the ability of at least some economists to consider offers from a business school probably helped to hold the pay of economists up relative to the pay of English literature professors and others who had no similar alternative career paths within academia.

Speculating About the Future

The increased use of low-wage part-time and full-time but nontenure track faculty in higher education is leading to growing pressure for collective bargaining coverage for these faculty members. Poorer job market prospects for graduate students have already led to increased collective bargaining coverage for graduate assistants in public higher education and the beginnings of coverage for graduate assistants in private higher education (Ehrenberg, Klaff, Kezsbom and Nagowski, 2004). To the extent that these movements succeed in improving the earnings of nontenure track faculty and the stipends of graduate teaching assistants, we may see a reduction in the substitution of these groups for tenure track faculty in the future. This step would lead to improved job market prospects for new economics Ph.D.'s and might help to stop the decline in the supply of U.S.-born Ph.D.'s in economics.

The job market for new economists also depends upon the ages at which senior faculty members retire. The decline in the stock market during the 2000–2002 period undoubtedly caused many faculty members in defined contribution retirement systems to postpone their retirements. If stock market prices increase in the future, so too may academic retirements in the years ahead, which would lead to improvements in the job market for new academic economists. Many institutions are also addressing whether, in response to the end of mandatory retirement, they need to alter their retirement policies to encourage faculty retirements (Ehrenberg, 2001), and these deliberations may affect the job market for new economists, as well.

Finally, we know surprisingly little about the effects on students' educational outcomes of substituting part-time and full-time nontenure track faculty these for full-time tenured and tenure track faculty. Much more research is needed on this topic to help frame the debate over the desirability of such substitutions at the institutional level and at the state government level, where decisions relating to the financing of public higher education institutions are made.

■ *I am grateful to the Andrew W. Mellon Foundation and the Atlantic Philanthropies (USA) Inc. for their financial support of CHERI; to Cornell students Albert Yung-Hsu Liu, Jesenka Mrdenovic, Matthew Nagowski and Andrew Nutting for their research assistance; and to Michael Rizzo, John Siegfried and the editors for their comments on earlier drafts.*

References

Ashenfelter, Orley and David Card. 2002. "Did the Elimination of Mandatory Retirement Affect Faculty Retirement?" *American Economic Review.* September, 92, pp. 957–80.

Bell, Linda. 2000. "More Good News, So Why the Blues?" *Academe.* March/April, 86, pp. 12–36.

Bettinger, Eric and Bridget Terry Long. 2004. "Do College Instructors Matter? The Effects of Adjuncts and Graduate Assistants on Student's Interest and Success." National Bureau of Economic Research Working Paper No. W10370, March.

Borjas, George. 2000. "Foreign Born Teaching Assistants and the Academic Performance of Undergraduates." *American Economic Review.* May, 90, pp. 355–59.

Bok, Derek. 1993. *The Cost of Talent.* New York, N.Y.: Free Press.

Digest of Education Statistics, 2002. 2003. Washington, D.C.: U.S Department of Education.

Ehrenberg, Ronald G. 2001. "Career's End: A Survey of Faculty Retirement Policies." *Academe.* July/August, 87, pp. 24–29.

Ehrenberg, Ronald G. 2003a. "Unequal Progress: The Annual Report on the Economic Status of the Profession 2002–2003." *Academe.* March/April, 89, pp. 22–33.

Ehrenberg, Ronald G. 2003b. "Financing Higher Education in the 21st Century." Cornell Higher Education Research Institute Working Paper WP32, March; Available at ⟨http://www.ilr.cornell.edu/cheri⟩.

Ehrenberg, Ronald G. 2003c. "Studying Ourselves: The Academic Labor Market." *Journal of Labor Economics.* April, 21, pp. 267–87.

Ehrenberg, Ronald G. 2004. "Don't Blame Faculty for Increases in Tuition: The Annual Report on the Economic Status of the Profession." *Academe.* March/April, 90, pp. 20–31.

Ehrenberg, Ronald G. and Daniel B. Klaff. 2004. "Changes in Faculty Composition Within the State University of New York System; 1985–2001." Cornell Higher Education Research Institute Working Paper No. 38; Available at ⟨http://www.ilr.cornell.edu/cheri⟩.

Ehrenberg, Ronald G., Michael J. Rizzo and Scott S. Condie. 2003. "Start Up Costs in American Research Universities." Cornell Higher Education Research Institute Working Paper WP33, March; Available at ⟨http://www.ilr.cornell.edu/cheri⟩.

Ehrenberg, Ronald G., Michael J. Rizzo and George H. Jakubson. 2003. "Who Bears the Growing Cost of Science at Universities." National Bureau of Economic Research Working Paper No. W9627, April.

Ehrenberg, Ronald G., Daniel B. Klaff, Adam T. Kezsbom and Matthew P. Nagowski. 2004. "Collective Bargaining in American Higher Education," in *Governing Academia: Who is in Charge at the Modern University?* Ronald G. Ehrenberg, ed. Ithaca, N.Y.: Cornell University Press, pp. 209–34.

Fleisher, Belton, Masanori Hashimoto and Bruce A. Weinberg. 2002. "Foreign GTAs can be Effective Teachers of Economics." *Journal of Economic Education.* Fall, 33,2, pp. 299–325.

Goldberger, Marvin L., Brendan A. Maher and Pamela Ebert Flattau, eds. 1995. *Research Doctorate Programs in the United States: Continuity and Change.* Washington, D.C.: National Academy Press.

Hamermesh, Daniel S. 1995. "A Ray of Sunshine." *Academia.* March/April, pp. 8–15.

Jones, Lyle V., Gardner Lindzey and Porter E. Cogshall, eds. 1982. *An Assessment of Research Doctorate Programs in the United States.* Washington, D.C.: National Academy Press.

Margo, Robert A. and John J. Siegfried. 1996. "Long Run Trends in Economics Bachelor's Degrees." *Journal of Economic Education.* Fall, 27, pp. 326–37.

Siegfried, John J. and Wendy A. Stock. 2003. "The Market for New Ph.D.'s in Economics." Preliminary draft of a paper to be presented at the January 2004 Allied Social Science Association Meetings, Vanderbilt Department of Economics.

Journal of Economic Perspectives—Volume 18, Number 2—Spring 2004—Pages 239–255

Policy Watch
Trade Adjustment Assistance

Katherine Baicker and M. Marit Rehavi

This feature contains short articles on topics that are currently on the agendas of policymakers, thus illustrating the role of economic analysis in illuminating current debates. Suggestions for future columns and comments on past ones should be sent to C. Eugene Steuerle, c/o *Journal of Economic Perspectives*, The Urban Institute, 2100 M Street NW, Washington, D.C. 20037.

The Evolution of Trade Adjustment Assistance

The Trade Adjustment Assistance Reform Act of 2002 profoundly changed the nature and scope of U.S. policy for addressing dislocations of workers caused by trade. First, the legislation will potentially double the number of TAA recipients and more than triple the total cost of the program to almost $2 billion annually, making it a much more important component of the patchwork of programs serving the unemployed (Congressional Budget Office, 2002). Second, it introduces new elements such as wage insurance and health credits into a program that had previously included primarily only training and cash benefits. The addition of these benefits creates both the opportunity for gains from greater coordination and the potential for costly distortions and serves as a testing ground for the broader use of such provisions. Although the program still covers only a small (and peculiarly

■ *Katherine Baicker is Assistant Professor of Economics, Dartmouth College, Hanover, New Hampshire, and Faculty Research Fellow, National Bureau of Economic Research, Cambridge, Massachusetts. M. Marit Rehavi is a Ph.D. student, London School of Economics, London, United Kingdom. Their e-mail addresses are ⟨kbaicker@dartmouth.edu⟩ and ⟨M.M.Rehavi@lse.ac.uk⟩, respectively.*

selected) fraction of the unemployed, these changes affect the incentives faced by many workers and may have far-reaching consequences in health and labor markets.

To put these changes in context, it is useful to begin with a brief history of trade adjustment assistance. Trade adjustment assistance (TAA) was formally introduced in the Trade Expansion Act of 1962 when it was used "to compensate workers for tariff cuts under the Kennedy Round of multilateral negotiations" (Feenstra and Lewis, 1994, p. 217) and other liberalizations. Similar provisions to compensate workers displaced by trade were also included in the Canadian-American Auto Agreement, the Manpower Development and Training Act of 1962 and the Economic Opportunity Act of 1964 (Richardson, 1982). TAA thus aimed to serve both economic and political goals, decreasing political resistance to new trade agreements and smoothing the cost of frictional unemployment by providing income support and retraining as workers moved from shrinking to growing sectors.

The 1962 version of trade adjustment assistance, however, had extremely limited eligibility and benefits; in the first seven years, no applicants were certified for benefits, and more than half of applicants were denied benefits in the early 1970s (Richardson, 1982). The Trade Act of 1974 increased the generosity of TAA benefits and expanded eligibility, and the Department of Labor loosened the criteria for the certification of firm eligibility, creating the modern TAA program. Workers laid off from firms certified by the Department of Labor to have been adversely affected by trade were eligible for retraining and for 52 weeks of cash assistance beyond that provided by the unemployment insurance program. In 1976, the first full year of operation under the new law, TAA covered 62,000 workers at a cost of $79 million.

By the early 1980s, concerns arose about the targeting and growing cost of the trade adjustment assistance program. A 1980 expansion had led to coverage of 532,000 workers at a cost of $1.6 billion (U.S. House of Representatives, 2003, Table 6-3). By this time, TAA provided more generous cash assistance than unemployment insurance: TAA provided 70 percent of workers' previous wages, compared with the 65 percent provided by unemployment insurance (Magee, 2001). Despite the perception that TAA recipients were particularly disadvantaged in the labor market, during the 1970s they did not appear to have more difficulty finding reemployment than other unemployed workers. In fact, Magee (2001, p. 109) cites studies showing that workers qualifying for TAA in this period were "more likely to be recalled to their old jobs, less likely to switch industries, and did not have longer unemployment spells than other displaced workers (Corson and Nicholson, 1981; Richardson, 1982)."

In 1981, a set of amendments to the Trade Act of 1974 reduced TAA cash benefits to the level of unemployment benefits and only provided cash assistance after unemployment benefits had been exhausted.[1] The incoming Reagan administration tightened enforcement of the eligibility rules. As a result, by 1982, total recipients of trade adjustment assistance dropped to 30,000 and costs dropped to $103 million (U.S. House of Representatives, 2003, Table 6-3). The number of recipients fell still lower as the economy expanded in the mid-1980s. A 1986 amendment added a job search requirement, and a 1988 amendment required workers to participate in training in order to receive cash benefits. These amendments suggested a shift toward retraining workers and facilitating structural adjustment. During this period, the characteristics of qualifying workers also changed. In contrast to research on the 1970s, Decker and Corson (1995) found that in the 1980s TAA recipients predominantly lost their jobs due to plant closings and were therefore not likely to be recalled by their previous employer. They also found that these workers had longer spells of unemployment and often had bigger drops in reemployment wages relative to their previous jobs than other workers who exhausted their unemployment insurance benefits.

In 1993, as part of the push to secure the passage of the North American Free Trade Agreement (NAFTA), Congress created NAFTA Transitional Adjustment Assistance (NAFTA-TAA), a separate trade adjustment assistance program for workers displaced by trade with or plant relocations to Canada or Mexico, and the Clinton administration committed to assisting secondary workers (upstream suppliers and downstream finishers) through dislocated worker programs in the Workforce Investment Act of 1998. Worker groups could simultaneously apply to both traditional TAA and this new program—and 75 percent of NAFTA-TAA certified workers were also included in TAA petitions (GAO, 2001)—although they could receive benefits through only one program. Two of the most important differences between TAA and NAFTA-TAA were that NAFTA-TAA covered secondary workers and did not require workers to prove that increases in imports caused their job loss if they were displaced when a plant moved to Canada or Mexico. Finally, the Secretary of Labor had discretion to waive training requirements in TAA, while such waivers were not allowed in NAFTA-TAA.

The workers eligible for modern trade adjustment assistance were not a representative cross-section of the labor force nor of the traded goods sector. Table 1 shows the distribution across industries of workers who were certified for assistance (but did not necessarily participate in the program) from 1975–2002, compared to the current distribution of all workers and of imported goods. Since 1975, for example, almost 30 percent of TAA workers had been employed in motor vehicles (although this fraction was much lower in the 1990s) and 20 percent in apparel and textiles (35 percent in the 1990s), but these groups together represented less than 2 percent of workers in 2001, and motor vehicles and apparel

---

[1] Before 1981, TAA supplemented unemployment insurance benefits (up to 75 percent of former wages) and provided income support of up to 65 percent of former wages after unemployment insurance benefits expired.

Table 1
Workers Certified by Industry

	Workers certified (1975–2002)	Fraction of total labor force working in industry (2001)	Fraction of value of U.S. imported goods coming from each industry (2002)
Total	3,316,000	132,213,000	$653,359 million
Motor vehicles	28.3%	1.3%	14.5%
Apparel	18.6%	0.4%	5.4%
Steel	6.7%	0.2%	1.1%
Footwear	4.4%	0.0%	1.4%
Electronics	10.4%	1.5%	5.4%
Oil and gas	5.7%	0.3%	9.1%
Fabricated metal products	2.8%	1.1%	
Textiles	3.6%	0.4%	1.4%
Other	19.5%	94.8%	

Note: Row category definitions vary slightly across columns.
Sources: Green Book (2003, Table 6-2); *Statistical Abstract of the U.S.* (2002, Table 603); BEA (⟨http://www.bea.doc.gov/bea/newsrel/trad0703.xls⟩).

represented only 20 percent of the value of imported goods in 2002. Table 2 shows that TAA recipients in 1990–2000 were disproportionately female, less educated and older, and Decker and Corson (1995) find that they were more highly paid than other unemployed workers. Magee (2001) finds that unionized workers and those displaced by trade from less-developed countries were more likely to have their TAA petitions approved. Rogers (1998) finds that 58 percent of all unemployment spells end in recall, while in contrast, Marcal (2001) shows that less than 12 percent of TAA recipients were working for their former employer three years after layoff. It is not clear, however, that TAA workers fare any worse than other unemployed workers with the same demographic characteristics and employment profiles (Irwin, 2002).

The primary focus of trade adjustment assistance has been on displaced workers, and we will focus on that component of TAA, as well. However, the program has also included small provisions for aiding firms and communities. The Trade Expansion Act of 1962 also created a firm-based component of the TAA program, designed to provide technical assistance and (until 1986) loans and loan guarantees to firms adversely affected by increased imports (EDA, 2003). The Department of Commerce established 12 regional TAA Centers in 1978 to help firms with their TAA petitions and to help them develop business plans for dealing with increased international competition. Firms whose business plans were approved were eligible for matching funds of up to $75,000 for technical assistance with implementation, including market research, information technology consulting, product development and quality programs. Firm TAA also included industry

Table 2

Worker Characteristics, 1999–2000

Characteristic	TAA and N-TAA participants	Unemployed or dislocated workers	Total U.S. workforce
Fraction male	36%[a]	52%[b]	53%[a]
Average age	43[a]	34[b]	39[c]
Limited English proficiency	12%[a]		8%[g]
Average hourly wage	$12.13 at separation $10.31 at reemployment[a]		$13.36 for production workers[a]
Median tenure	7 years at separation[a]	2 years at separation[e]	3.5 years[a]
Education			
Less than high school	25%[a]	23%[b]	10%[a]
High school graduate	55%[a]	29%[b]	32%[a]
Some post–high school	17%[a]	24%[b]	28%[a]
College graduate	4%[a]	16%[b]	30%[a]
Unionization (1989/90)	73%[d]	35%[d]	16%[f]

Sources: [a] GAO Report 01-988T (Table 1).
[b] Refers to unemployed workers. Statistical Abstract of the U.S. (2000, Tables 646, 674, 678).
[c] Statistical Abstract of the U.S. (2000, Tables 646, 712).
[d] Marcal (2001). Refers to 1988–1989 TAA recipients versus UI exhaustees.
[e] CPS, 2000, Dislocated Worker Supplement. Refers to workers dislocated in past 3 years (mean tenures is 4.9 years).
[f] Statistical Abstract of the U.S. (2002, Table 628, for 1990).
[g] CPS, 1995, Race and Ethnicity Supplement. Refers to fraction of employed workers reporting that they understand English "not well" or "not at all." Twelve percent of workers are immigrants.

grants, but no such grants have been given since 1995, and those allocated in the early 1990s comprised less than 5 percent of the firm program's budget (Congressional Research Service, 2000, Table 1). The 1993 NAFTA version of TAA also created the Community Adjustment and Investment Program, which was intended to provide assistance through grants and loan guarantees to communities significantly adversely affected by trade with Canada and Mexico and to firms providing new jobs in those communities. The initial CAIP appropriation was $22.5 million, with additional appropriations of $20 million. Only a handful of communities have received aid through CAIP.

2002 Reauthorization of Trade Adjustment Assistance

By the early 2000s, trade adjustment assistance had evolved into a program that provided generous support for a very limited number of workers. Worker groups of three or more or their representatives could apply to the Department of Labor to have workers in their firm certified as eligible for TAA benefits. Workers in certified firms could then apply to receive up to 52 weeks of cash assistance beyond that provided by unemployment insurance, but were required to participate in a training program to receive that support. Training was available for up to 104 weeks. The number of new workers receiving assistance varied from a low of 24,000 in 1998 to a high of 37,000 in 2002 (U.S. House of Representatives, 2003, Table 6-3). In 2001, roughly 145,000 workers were "certified" as potentially eligible for the program, and 33,000 took up benefits, which cost approximately $360 million (GAO, 2001). The average worker received $222 per week in cash benefits for 31 weeks and $2,900 in training (almost $4,000 per worker actually enrolled) (U.S. House of Representatives, 2003). Total spending on benefits for these workers was over $200 million, with some additional spending for job training and other programs.

In 2002, the political climate was ripe for a grand reworking of trade adjustment assistance. The Bush administration badly wanted congressional renewal of "trade promotion authority," which would require Congress to hold an up-or-down vote on new trade agreements without proposing amendments. However, the economy had gone through a recession in 2001, and job growth had remained stagnant in 2002. In exchange for trade promotion authority, Congress demanded substantial expansions of the trade adjustment assistance program, resulting in the Trade Adjustment Assistance Reform Act of 2002. Table 3 summarizes these expansions, which we discuss in turn. They have the potential to change the program from one designed primarily to provide political cover for trade agreements to one with much farther reaching effects.

Eligibility and Coverage

A much broader set of workers is now eligible for TAA. In the past, the main criteria for displaced worker eligibility were that "workers have been totally or partially laid off and that sales or productions have declined, and that increased imports have contributed importantly to worker layoffs" (U.S. Department of Labor, 2003a).[2] The 2002 act broadens this definition in two ways.

First, the 2002 act merges the trade adjustment assistance program with its previously separate cousin, the smaller NAFTA-TAA program, and uses the more expansive NAFTA-TAA basis for eligibility. Secondary workers at an affected firm's upstream suppliers and downstream customers who are indirectly affected by trade may now be eligible for TAA. The inclusion of these secondary workers in TAA is expected to increase the number of certified workers from 130,000 to 180,000 (Congressional Budget Office, 2002). The inclusion of workers laid off in plant relocations is expected to increase certifications by an additional 20,000 workers. To receive benefits, workers in certified firms must show a decline of at least

---

[2] In a 1988 amendment, Congress also extended eligibility to those who provided essential services to companies adversely affected by trade. However, this extension was not implemented because the import fee on which it was conditioned was never established (GAO/HRD-93-36 Dislocated Worker Assistance Program).

Table 3

Program Features over Time

	Trade Act of 1974	1981–2001	Trade Act of 2002
Eligibility		Workers who can demonstrate that "increased imports of articles like or directly competitive with articles produced by the firm . . . have 'contributed importantly' to both the layoffs and the decline of sales or production" (2000 Green Book). In 1988, Congress adds eligibility for natural gas and oil drilling and exploration workers. In 1993, NAFTA-TAA covers workers displaced by trade with Canada and Mexico, including secondary workers and workers affected by plant relocations.	Includes not only primary, but also upstream and downstream workers displaced by increased imports or due to a plant relocating overseas. Includes farmers who experience price declines due to imports.
Additional requirements for benefit receipt	None	Workers must actively participate in job search (1986) and complete authorized training unless specifically excused by the Secretary of Labor (1988). Training waivers are not possible in NAFTA-TAA.	Workers must participate in job search and training, but may receive a waiver for up to six months for the later if they meet one of six criteria (the Secretary of Labor has the discretion to issue longer waivers).
Duration of cash assistance (excludes weeks receiving unemployment insurance)	52 weeks	52 weeks (Workers participating in authorized training may receive an additional 26 weeks of cash assistance.)	78 weeks (Workers participating in remedial education are eligible for an additional 26 weeks of cash assistance.)
Training		Up to 104 weeks	Up to 104 weeks
Job search allowances		Grants not to exceed the lesser of 90 percent of costs or $800 per beneficiary (raised to $1,250 in the Trade Act of 2002). Recipients must apply within the later of one year of certification (or last complete layoff) or within six months of completing training.	
Relocation allowances		The lesser of 90 percent of relocation expenses and three times the worker's average weekly wage or $800 per beneficiary (raised to $1,250 in the Trade Act of 2002). Applicants must apply within 14 months of TAA certification (or last complete layoff) or within six months of completing training (whichever is later) and must have a job offer at the time of application.	
Health insurance	None	None	Refundable/advanceable tax credit for 65 percent of health insurance costs can be used to purchase COBRA, individual health insurance, coverage through a spouse's plan (if the employer subsidizes less than 50 percent of the cost) or a state insurance pool.
Additional programs		Supplemental Wage Allowance Demonstration (1988)	Alternative Trade Adjustment Assistance (five-year demonstration)

20 percent in wages or hours and must enroll in training. The Congressional Budget Office estimates that 30 percent of these certified workers will eventually draw TAA benefits. This represents a significant increase from the 23 percent seen in 2001, in part because of likely increases in take-up in response to the increased generosity of the program.

Second, for the first time farmers are now eligible for trade adjustment assistance. This part of the program, administered by the U.S. Department of Agriculture, is eligible for appropriations of up to $90 million per year. Farmers with average adjusted gross income less than $2.5 million are eligible for free technical assistance and for up to $10,000 of cash assistance (per year) when both the price of the commodity they produce is 20 percent less than the national average over the last five years and increases in imports contributed importantly to this decline (USDA, 2003).[3]

Cash Benefits

Benefits for TAA recipients have been expanded along many dimensions. First, workers may now receive cash benefits for up to 78 weeks if they continue to be enrolled in training, rather than 52, in addition to the 26 weeks of unemployment insurance they may receive. The size of the cash benefit remains the same as that under unemployment insurance. Those enrolled in remedial education can receive an additional 26 weeks of benefits, for a total of 130 weeks of cash assistance.

While workers are still required to receive training to receive cash assistance, it may now be easier to waive that requirement. Training costs for the program are capped at $220 million per year, double the previous combined TAA and NAFTA-TAA funding level.[4] Workers are eligible for higher job search allowances and relocation allowances, as well as the benefits available to other unemployed workers under the Workforce Investment Act of 1998.

Alternative Trade Adjustment Assistance for Older Workers: Wage Allowances

Typically, trade adjustment assistance cash payments end when workers take new jobs. As in unemployment insurance, the rationale for this structure of benefits is that workers need assistance only until they begin to earn wages again (insurance against unexpected loss in wages). One negative consequence of this insurance structure is that it dulls the incentive to find employment quickly or to accept a job with lower wages. In 1988, a supplemental wage demonstration project intended to add incentives for quick reemployment, even at lower wages, was authorized by

---

[3] Funds permitting, the USDA's Farm Service Agency will provide assistance "equal to the product of the amount of the commodity produced in the most recent marketing year multiplied by one-half the difference between an amount equal to 80 percent of the average of the national average prices of the commodity for the 5 marketing years preceding the most recent marketing year and the national average price of the commodity for the most recent marketing year" (USDA, 2003). However, the sum of counter cyclical payments and TAA payments may not exceed $65,000.

[4] Other government funds may be used for training when TAA's training funds are exhausted.

Congress as part of the amendments to trade adjustment assistance, although no states seem to have implemented the demonstration.

The 2002 act includes a provision for similar wage allowances. Certain workers age 50 or older are eligible for a new pilot program, Alternative Trade Adjustment Assistance (ATAA), that would provide them with cash benefits equal to 50 percent of the difference between their old salary and their new salary (capped at $10,000 total), health care assistance for up to two years and the standard relocation allowance (if applicable) in lieu of regular TAA benefits if they are reemployed within 26 weeks of separation at lower wages and earn less than $50,000 in their new job (U.S. Department of Labor, 2003b). The goal of this program is to insure workers against lower reemployment wages while encouraging them to find reemployment relatively quickly (within 26 weeks). A worker group must apply specifically for ATAA when filing its TAA petition. Some of the eligibility criteria include that the petitioning group have a "significant" number of workers over age 50, that the workers possess skills that are "not easily transferable" and that "competitive conditions within [the] industry are adverse" (Department of Labor, 2003c).[5] Once the U.S. Department of Labor certifies a group as eligible for TAA and ATAA, those eligible for ATAA have the option of applying for ATAA or TAA.

Health Insurance Credits

Recipients of trade adjustment assistance are eligible to receive an uncapped refundable advanceable tax credit to pay up to 65 percent of their health care premiums.[6] This tax credit is essentially a voucher for the purchase of health insurance (since, as described below, it does not depend on the amount of taxes owed and can be used to offset the cost of health insurance whenever it is purchased) and may be used in several ways. For example, under the Consolidated Omnibus Budget Reconciliation Act of 1985 (COBRA), workers leaving a job may continue to purchase their old employer-sponsored health insurance plan for up to 18 months, and the new credit can be used toward this purchase. The credit can also be used to continue individual insurance that the worker had had for more than 30 days before dislocation, to pay for coverage through a spouse or to participate in a state insurance pool. This provision represents a significant increase in the value of benefits available to workers. The average annual group health insurance premium for a family of four is around $5,500 (Gruber, 2000). The health credit thus represents more than 30 percent of the cash benefit the average

---

[5] The fact that such benefits are available only to older workers who work in firms with many other older workers makes an odd distinction between firms with heterogeneous workers and those with homogeneous workers. The Department of Labor is interpreting "a significant number of workers" as the lesser of 50 workers or 5 percent of the affected workers (in firms with fewer than 50 trade impacted workers at least three must be 50 or older), as explained in DOL (2003c).

[6] These provisions for assistance in purchasing health insurance will also apply to a broader set of workers, including some steel industry retirees and other Pension Benefit Guaranty Corporation recipients not eligible for Medicare.

TAA recipient would receive (65 percent of $5,500 per year is $70 per week, and the average cash benefit was $222 per week in 2001).

Trade Adjustment Assistance for Firms and Communities

Separate TAA benefits continue to be available for firms and communities, but these programs are small. The firm program for trade adjustment assistance is minimally funded, at $16 million annually (although this represents an increase from the $11 million budget for 1999). While the Community Adjustment and Investment Program continues to provide assistance based on previous awards, it has not accepted new grant applications since 2001, no new funds were appropriated in 2002, and the program was not included in the 2003 budget.

Preliminary Evidence and Expectations

Because workers have only been eligible for the new TAA benefits since November 2002 (and some benefits did not phase in until 2003) and because of the broad scope of the changes, there is little direct evidence on the effect of the recent program changes on take-up, duration of unemployment, reemployment wages, labor markets or health care markets. However, evidence from past studies of TAA and of unemployment insurance offer some evidence about what to expect.

Effects on Individual Unemployment Spells

Increasing the length of time that trade adjustment assistance benefits are available could increase the length of time that the average worker is unemployed. There is a well-documented spike in the likelihood of an unemployed worker becoming reemployed at 26 weeks—that is, when unemployment benefits expire (Katz and Meyer, 1990a). Card and Levine (2000) find that extending unemployment benefits by 13 weeks increases the average number of weeks of unemployment by one week, and others have found an even greater sensitivity (for example, Katz and Meyer, 1990a). With the Trade Adjustment Assistance Reform Act of 2002 extending benefits by 26 weeks, the duration of benefit receipt and unemployment spells may significantly rise for affected workers.[7]

Making benefits more generous may both increase take-up and increase the duration of unemployment. Anderson and Meyer (1997) find an elasticity of take-up with respect to benefit generosity of around 0.5 or higher in the unemployment insurance program. Estimates also suggest that more generous benefits lengthen unemployment spells, with a 10-percentage-point increase in generosity leading to an increase in duration of as much as one week or more (Meyer, 1996).

---

[7] Note that newly covered secondary workers were suddenly eligible for two years of benefits and thus faced a much larger change in incentives. For a small subset of recipients as discussed below, however, the ATAA experiment may provide modest incentives for faster reemployment.

Applying evidence from unemployed workers in general to workers receiving trade adjustment assistance is problematic, since TAA workers have different employment and demographic profiles from the average unemployed worker. Gibbons and Katz (1991) find that workers displaced by plant closings are less likely to face the same stigma as other unemployed workers, for example, so some trade adjustment assistance workers may fare better upon reemployment. In addition, TAA requires (most) workers to get training during this period, imposing a cost on continuing to get benefits that is not faced by most unemployment insurance recipients.[8] Despite these caveats, the increase in generosity of benefits for TAA recipients is so large that both take-up and duration seem bound to increase. Even if TAA recipients value the health insurance credit at only 50 percent of the actual expenditure on premiums, the credit alone could increase take-up by 10 percent and average duration by half a week. With 70,000 more workers potentially eligible for TAA, increases in take-up and duration make the program even costlier, as reflected in the Congressional Budget Office (2002) estimates.

Effects on Reemployment Wages

Are these potentially longer spells of unemployment helpful to workers, allowing them to wait for the best job match available, or are they detrimental, allowing skills to erode and reducing reemployment wages? The evidence suggests that a longer spell of unemployment does not lead to a better job match. For example, Meyer (1995) reviews a series of "reemployment bonus" experiments (in which workers were offered bonuses to find jobs more quickly) and finds that workers offered such bonuses did find jobs more quickly, but not at the expense of lower reemployment wages. Workers may also be harmed by long unemployment spells through stigmatization or through skill atrophy (Blanchard and Diamond, 1994; Pissarides, 1992). Addison and Portugal (1989) find that a 10 percent increase in the duration of unemployment may lower reemployment wages by 1 percent. Decker and Corson (1995) find that the training provided through trade adjustment assistance does not seem to increase reemployment wages. While Marcal (2001) also fails to find evidence that training increased reemployment wages, she finds some evidence that trainees had higher employment rates relative to recipients not in training and to those who have exhausted unemployment insurance benefits.[9]

Because of the new wage allowance program, older workers face a distinct set of incentives when choosing a new job. The new wage allowance program provides

---

[8] Black, Smith, Berger and Noel (2003) review the evidence on the effect of unemployment insurance "profiling," where the recipients of unemployment insurance who are projected to have the longest insured unemployment spells are required to get job search assistance. The threat of this requirement (rather than the services themselves) seems to reduce duration, suggesting that the training required of trade adjustment assistance recipients may serve to reduce their spells, as well.

[9] There is some limited evidence that older individuals' reemployment wages are higher because of unemployment insurance (Ehrenberg and Oaxaca, 1976).

lower benefits to workers whose new wages are higher, which works like a tax on seeking out the highest-paying job. Because the benefit is only available to workers reemployed within 26 weeks, it may encourage workers to become reemployed more quickly, but it also provides incentives only in a narrow band around week 26. It may also dull workers' incentives to seek out the highest-paying job available. The eligibility cutoff of reemployment wages of less than $50,000 creates enormous implicit tax rates in that region. For example, an ATAA-eligible worker who used to earn $60,000 but is reemployed at $40,000 would be eligible for $10,000 in wage insurance. The same worker reemployed at $50,000 would be eligible for nothing—a 100 percent tax rate from this program alone. A useful research project will be to study how older workers react to these incentives.

Effects on Firm Decisions

Firm decisions may also be affected by the expansion of the program. One well-documented problem with the unemployment insurance system is that firms may game the system through temporary layoff and recall of workers (Anderson, 1993). For example, firms may lay off workers seasonally and let unemployment insurance pay them for part of the year, because the unemployment insurance taxes paid by many firms are not adequately "experience rated"—these firms pay less in taxes than their workers receive in benefits for each of these layoffs. Katz and Meyer (1990b) find a spike in recalls at 26 weeks, suggesting that firms time recalls to correspond with workers' exhaustion of unemployment benefits. Imperfect experience rating may account for 20 to 50 percent of temporary layoffs (Topel, 1984; Card and Levine, 1994), with manufacturing receiving the biggest net unemployment insurance subsidies through temporary layoffs (Anderson and Meyer, 1993; Meyer and Rosenbaum, 1996).

Because trade adjustment assistance requires firms to demonstrate a decline in employment due to trade, it may be less subject to this kind of moral hazard. Also, as discussed above, TAA workers are less likely to be recalled to their original employers than are other unemployed workers. That said, firms may be less likely to offer generous severance packages (and workers may be less likely to flee declining industries) because of the increased generosity of TAA benefits.

Effects on Health Markets

The addition of the health care credit is perhaps the biggest structural change in the trade adjustment assistance program and could serve as a pilot program for health insurance tax credits for a broader segment of the population. Take-up of the health care credit is likely to be high, since it can be used for insurance from a wide variety of sources. The fact that it is "refundable" means that workers who owe no taxes will still be able to use the full credit amount (because if the credit amount is larger than a worker's tax bill, the difference is refunded for use toward insurance premiums), and the fact that it is "advanceable" means that workers will not have to wait until they file taxes to use the credit (since it can be used to pay an insurance premium at the time the insurance is purchased). While an advance-able credit alleviates concerns about unemployed workers' liquidity constraints, it also dramatically increases the complexity of administering the program. Overall, the credit is equivalent to a voucher for the purchase of health insurance.

This health insurance credit may affect other aspects of the health insurance market, including the individual health insurance market and the presence of state high-risk pools. The rationale for subsidizing the purchase of individual insurance only when such insurance had been purchased more than 30 days before the layoff occurred is to discourage firms (and workers) from discontinuing coverage imme-diately before layoffs and to discourage individuals from moving from employer-sponsored insurance to the individual health insurance market. That said, the ability to use the credit in the individual market seems likely to increase participa-tion. Subsidies to encourage people to join state insurance pools may help states establish such pools. Thirty states currently offer high-risk pools, designed to provide coverage to people with medical conditions that make private individual insurance particularly expensive for them. States that do not already have such pools for those without health insurance are being encouraged to create them through Department of Health and Human Services grants (and subsidies to offset partially the losses that the pools incur). The Congressional Budget Office (2002) expects that half of the states without high-risk pools will use this opportunity to establish them.

Discussion

Smoothing transitions for trade-displaced workers can help to make interna-tional trade closer to a true Pareto improvement. Moreover, trade adjustment assistance could facilitate the passage of international agreements to liberalize trade. Indeed, the small size of the program in the past—for example, trade adjustment assistance in 2000 covered less than 1 percent of the unemployed and had a budget less than 2 percent of the unemployment compensation program (U.S. Department of Commerce, 2002, Tables 416 and 593)—suggested that its role was more one of political expedience than of vital importance to structural adjust-ment. Like any program, trade adjustment assistance must face political realities. That said, the current incarnation of TAA falls short of the ideal program in several important ways, and the expansions of 2002 dramatically increase the program's potential to affect labor and health markets more broadly.

First and foremost, it is not clear why a program should single out workers adversely affected by international trade, rather than providing retraining and income support to all workers in shrinking sectors or even all unemployed workers. Increased import competition accounted for only 1.5 percent of separations due to mass layoffs in the late 1990s (Irwin, 2002, p. 100, from Bureau of Labor Statistics data). The expansion of TAA benefits in 2002 to upstream and downstream secondary workers highlights the inherent arbitrariness of drawing a sharp eligibility line based on something that has such diffuse effects as trade. In fact, policymakers on both sides of the aisle have proposed replacing trade adjustment assistance with a broader program (such as the dislocated worker program proposed in the 1994 Reemployment Act) or consolidating it with existing worker assistance programs (such as proposed inclusion in the 1998 Workforce Investment Act).

Second, the particular parameters of the program may not be desirable. Providing income support for unemployed workers for as long as two and a half years may decrease their work prospects more than the extra training they get increases them. Requiring all workers to receive training to receive income support may encourage workers to get training they do not need or value. The nonlinear structure built into the wage insurance option creates the kind of cliffs that are likely to induce significant distortions. The health insurance benefit exacerbates these incentive problems and presents serious administrative challenges.

We believe that a more flexible structural adjustment program would meet the economic goals of the current TAA program while minimizing the distortions that the program creates. The current program expansions have the laudable feature of addressing many different costs of dislocation in a coordinated framework, but the substantial constraints imposed by the structure of the benefits undermine the program's efficiency and undermine its potential to address structural adjustment costs more broadly. The ideal program would give workers more control over the resources available to them and make the size of those resources less dependent on extended unemployment spells. Making the program more flexible in this way could both reduce administrative costs and improve worker outcomes by mitigating adverse incentives and maximizing the program's impact.[10]

One way to create such flexibility would be to create "adjustment accounts" for workers, who could then allocate the funds as they saw fit between income support, job training, wage allowances, child care, health insurance and so on. These accounts could be available to all unemployed workers or to unemployed workers in shrinking sectors—not limited to those manufacturing workers categorized as adversely affected by trade. Imposing lifetime limits on the availability of the accounts to workers could minimize gaming by employers and workers. Workers could choose the combination of benefits best tailored to their circumstances. If policymakers are concerned that workers may spend down the accounts too quickly, relying on the availability of support from other government programs, withdrawals from the account could be limited in size and eligibility for other programs could be determined jointly. Allowing workers to make these decisions

---

[10] The Firm TAA program serves as example of the costliness of centralized decision making about the use of flexible funds. In its evaluation of the Firm TAA program, the Urban Institute (1998) found that only 55 percent of the program funds went to firm assistance, with much of the rest devoted to the very involved certification process.

would relieve the Department of Labor of its role in policing program recipients' participation in training and other requirements, while aligning recipients' incentives with the reemployment goals of the program. No doubt this would make the program more attractive to workers and would likely increase take-up. This increase in program size would have to be balanced against the increase in efficiency and the redistribution it would entail.

Choosing the right program parameters within this more flexible system requires estimates of several key elasticities, such as the effect of longer benefits on unemployment duration and reemployment wages for recipients of benefits, recipients' valuation of health insurance credits and so on. The Trade Adjustment Assistance Reform Act of 2002 will generate a substantial natural experiment, both because the changes in the program are substantial and because those already receiving such benefits before the legislative change must continue under the rules of the previous program for the next two years. The new elements of the program may serve as a trial for the broader use of wage insurance and health insurance tax credits. Studying this experience may provide information about how workers respond to adjustment assistance and may enable the creation of more efficient programs in the future.

■ *The authors thank Patty Anderson, Alan Durell, Doug Holtz-Eakin, Doug Irwin, Larry Katz and Michael Murray for numerous helpful comments and discussions. Baicker served as Senior Economist and Rehavi as Research Assistant at the Council of Economic Advisers in 2001–2002.*

References

Addison, John T. and Pedro Portugal. 1989. "Job Displacement, Relative Wage Changes, and Duration of Unemployment." *Journal of Labor Economics.* 7:3, pp. 281–302.

Anderson, Patricia M. 1993. "Linear Adjustment Costs and Seasonal Labor Demand: Evidence from Retail Trade Firms." *Quarterly Journal of Economics.* November, 108, pp. 1015–042.

Anderson, Patricia M. and Bruce D. Meyer. 1993. "The Unemployment Insurance Payroll Tax and Interindustry and Interfirm Subsidies," in *Tax Policy and the Economy, 7.* James Poterba, ed. Cambridge, Mass.: MIT Press, pp. 111–44.

Anderson, Patricia M. and Bruce D. Meyer. 1997. "Unemployment Insurance Take-Up Rates and the After-Tax Value of Benefits." *Quarterly Journal of Economics.* 112:3, pp. 913–37.

Black, D., J. Smith, M. Berger and B. Noel. 2003. "Is the Threat of Reemployment Services More Effective than the Services Themselves? Evidence from UI System Using Random Assignment." *American Economic Review.* September, 93:4, pp. 1313–327.

Blanchard, Olivier-Jean and Peter A. Diamond. 1994. "Ranking, Unemployment Duration, and Wages." *Review of Economic Studies.* 61:3, pp. 417–34.

Card, David and Phillip B. Levine. 1994. "Unemployment Insurance and Taxes and the Cyclical and Seasonal Properties of Unemployment." *Journal of Public Economics.* 53:1, pp. 1–29.

Card, David and Phillip B. Levine. 2000. "Extended Benefits and the Duration of UI Spells: Evidence from the New Jersey Extended Benefit Program." *Journal of Public Economics.* 78:1-2, pp. 107–38.

Corson, Walter and Walter Nicholson. 1981. "Trade Adjustment Assistance for Workers: Results of a Survey of Recipients Under the Trade Act of 1974," in *Research in Labor Economics, 4.* Ronald G. Ehrenberg, Farrell Bloch, Joseph Reid and Solomon W. Polachek, eds. Greenwich, Conn.: JAI Press, pp. 417–69.

Decker, Paul T. and Walter Corson. 1995. "International Trade and Worker Displacement: Evaluation of the Trade Adjustment Assistance Program." *Industrial and Labor Relations Review.* 48:4, pp. 758–74.

Ehrenberg, Ronald and Ronald Oaxaca. 1976. "Unemployment Insurance, Duration of Unemployment, and Subsequent Wage Gain." *American Economic Review.* 66:5, pp. 754–66.

Feenstra, Robert C. and Tracy R. Lewis. 1994. "Trade Adjustment Assistance and Pareto Gains from Trade." *Journal of International Economics.* 36:3-4, pp. 201–22.

Gibbons, Robert and Lawrence F. Katz. 1991. "Layoffs and Lemons." *Journal of Labor Economics.* 9:4, pp. 351–80.

Gruber, Jonathan. 2000. "Transitional Subsidies for Health Insurance Coverage." MIT and NBER, June.

Irwin, Douglas. 2002. *Free Trade Under Fire.* Princeton: Princeton University Press.

Katz, Lawrence F. and Bruce D. Meyer. 1990a. "The Impact of Potential Duration of Unemployment Benefits on the Duration of Unemployment." *Journal of Public Economics.* February, 41, pp. 45–72.

Katz, Lawrence F. and Bruce D. Meyer. 1990b. "Unemployment Insurance, Recall Expectations and Unemployment Outcomes." *Quarterly Journal of Economics.* 105:4, pp. 973–1002.

Magee, Christopher. 2001. "Administered Protection for Workers: An Analysis of the Trade Adjustment Assistance Program." *Journal of International Economics.* 53:1, pp. 105–25.

Marcal, Leah E. 2001. "Does Trade Adjustment Assistance Help Trade Displaced Workers?" *Contemporary Economic Policy.* 19:1, pp. 59–72.

Meyer, Bruce D. 1995. "Lessons from the U.S. Unemployment Insurance Experiments." *Journal of Economic Literature.* March, 33:1, pp. 91–131.

Meyer, Bruce D. 1996. "What Have We Learned from the Illinois Reemployment Bonus Experiment?" *Journal of Labor Economics.* 14:1, pp. 26–51.

Meyer, Bruce D. and Dan T. Rosenbaum. 1996. "Repeat Use of Unemployment Insurance." National Bureau of Economic Research No. 5423.

Pissarides, Chirstopher A. 1992. "Loss of Skill During Unemployment and the Persistence of Employment Shocks." *Quarterly Journal of Economics.* 107:4, pp. 1371–391.

Richardson, J. David. 1982. "Trade Adjustment Assistance under the U.S. Trade Act of 1974: An Analytical Examination and Worker Survey," in *Import Competition and Response.* Jagdish N. Bhagwati, ed. Chicago: University of Chicago Press, pp. 321–68.

Rogers, Cynthia L. 1998. "Expectations of Unemployment Insurance and Unemployment Duration." *Journal of Labor Economics.* 16:3, pp. 630–66.

The Economist. 2002. "A Step Forward; World Trade Talks." July 29.

Topel, Robert H. 1984. "Experience Rating of Unemployment Insurance and the Incidence of Unemployment." *Journal of Law and Economics.* 27:1, pp. 61–90.

Urban Institute. 1998. "Effective Aide to Trade-Impacted Manufacturers." Economic Development Administration, U.S. Department of Commerce.

U.S. Congress, Congressional Budget Office. 2002. *Pay-As-You-Go Estimate of H.R. 3009: Trade Act of 2002.* Washington, D.C., September 21.

U.S. Congress, Congressional Budget Office. 2003. *Economic and Budget Issue Brief.* Washington, D.C., May 12.

U.S. Congress, Congressional Research Service, J. F. Hornbeck. 2000. *RS20210 Trade Adjustment Assistance for Firms: Economic, Program, and Policy Issues.* Washington, D.C., February 1.

U.S. Congress, Congressional Research Service, James R. Storey. 2000. *IB98023 Trade Adjustment Assistance for Workers: Proposals for Renewal and Reform.* Washington, D.C., October 3.

U.S. Congress, General Accounting Office, Loren Yager, Director International Affairs and Trade. 2001. "Trade Adjustment Assistance: Improvements Necessary, but Programs Cannot Solve Communities' Long-Term Problems." Testimony before the U.S. Senate Committee on Finance, Subcommittee on International Trade, Washington, D.C., July 20.

U.S. Department of Agriculture, Foreign Ag-

riculture Service. 2003. "Trade Adjustment Assistance for Farmers: Trade Act of 2002, FAQs." Washington, D.C.; Available at ⟨http://www.fas.usda.gov/itp/taa/taafaq.htm⟩.

U.S. Department of Commerce. 2002. *Statistical Abstract of the United States: 2000*. Washington, D.C.

U.S. Department of Commerce, Bureau of Economic Analysis. 2003. "U.S. International Trade in Goods and Services News Release." Washington, D.C., September; Available at ⟨http://www.bea.doc.gov/bea/newsrel/trad0703.xls⟩.

U.S. Department of Commerce, Economic Development Administration. 2003. "Trade Adjustment Assistance." Washington, D.C.; Available at ⟨http://12.39.209.165/xp/EDAPublic/Research/TradeAdj.xml⟩.

U.S. Department of Labor, Bureau of Labor Statistics. 2002. *The Employment Situation: May 2002*. Washington, D.C.

U.S. Department of Labor, Employment & Training Administration. 2003a. "Trade Adjust-

ment Assistance." Washington, D.C.; Available at ⟨http://www.doleta.gov/programs/factsht/taa.asp⟩.

U.S. Department of Labor, Employment & Training Administration. 2003b. "Trade Adjustment Assistance Reform Act of 2002." Washington, D.C.; Available at ⟨http://www.doleta.gov/tradeact/2002act_summary.asp⟩.

U.S. Department of Labor, Employment & Training Administration. 2003c. "Interim Operating Instruction for Implementing Alternate Trade Adjustment Assistance for Older Workers." Washington, D.C.; Available at ⟨http://www.doleta.gov/tradeact/directives/teg12-03.cfm⟩.

U.S. House of Representative, Committee on Ways and Means. 2000. "2000 Greenbook." Washington, D.C.

U.S. House of Representatives, Ways and Means Committee. 2003. "2003 Green Book." Available at ⟨http://waysandmeans.house.gov/Documents.asp?section=813⟩.

Journal of Economic Perspectives—Volume 18, Number 2—Spring 2004—Pages 257–261

Retrospectives
How Joan Robinson and B. L. Hallward Named Monopsony

Robert J. Thornton

This feature addresses the history of economic words and ideas. The hope is to deepen the workaday dialogue of economists, while perhaps also casting new light on ongoing questions. If you have suggestions for future topics or authors, please write to Joseph Persky, c/o *Journal of Economic Perspectives*, Department of Economics (M/C 144), University of Illinois at Chicago, 601 South Morgan Street, Room 2103, Chicago, Illinois 60607-7121.

Introduction

As every economist knows, the word "monopsony" refers to a single buyer of a good or service and is the counterpart of "monopoly," which refers to a single seller. Both terms are derived from classical Greek. However, monopoly is a much older term. According to the *Oxford English Dictionary* (volume 6, p. 624), the earliest written record of the word monopoly in English occurred in 1534 in Thomas More's *Treatise upon the Passion*.

Monopsony is a considerably more recent term. The OED attributes it to Joan Robinson of Cambridge in her 1932 classic *The Economics of Imperfect Competition*. At the time, the common term for a single buyer was "monopoly buyer." Robinson recognized that this term was "illogical," since it means literally "a single seller-buyer." She then argues (p. 215): "It is necessary to find a name for the individual buyer which will correspond to the name *monopolist* for the individual seller. In the following pages an individual buyer is referred to as a *monopsonist*." In an accompanying footnote, she credits classics

■ *Robert J. Thornton is MacFarlane Professor of Economics, Lehigh University, Bethlehem, Pennsylvania. His e-mail address is ⟨rjt1@lehigh.edu⟩.*

scholar B. L. Hallward of Cambridge for the new term, which is derived from the Greek verb *opsonein* (ὀψωνειν), which she says means "to go marketing." However, the word *opsonein* is not in fact the most appropriate Greek word for making purchases in a market or buying. In this paper, I discuss the etymology of the word monopsony and describe in some detail how the term came into being. I then examine several other more appropriate terms for "a single buyer" that may have come within a whisker of entering the economist's lexicon.

Monopsony Means What?

The word "monopoly" is formed from the Greek adjective *monos* (μονος) meaning "alone, only, one" and from the verb *polein* (πωλειν) meaning "to sell." Both Greek words are perfectly appropriate as the bases for the derived word monopoly. Indeed, the combined word *monopolia* (μονοπωλια) was actually used by Aristotle to indicate "an exclusive sale" (*An Intermediate Greek-English Lexicon,* p. 518.) The suffix "y" (and its equivalent "ia") means "the state of " or "the quality of."

However, the stem of monopsony, *opsonein* (ὀψωνειν), has a meaning that is more idiosyncratic than just "to go marketing," the translation given by Joan Robinson. In classical Greek, the word *opson* (ὀψον) means "fish" (or "cooked meat"). And the verb *opsonein* (ὀψωνειν) that Robinson refers to actually means "to buy *fish*," making the literal meaning of monopsony a market situation with "a single buyer of *fish*."[1]

There are at least two other more general Greek words for "buy" that one could think of as more appropriate stems for constructing a word for "a single buyer." Perhaps the most obvious choice is *oneomai* (ὠνεομαι), but one might also turn to *priamai* (πριαμαι), both commonly translated as "I buy." Why weren't these other words used to construct the term for "one buyer"?

Recently Professor David Card shared with me handwritten personal communication that he received in 1995 from B. L. Hallward, the classicist whom Mrs. Robinson credits with coining the term monopony. In the letter to Card, Hallward writes:

> It was at tea with Austin and Joan [Robinson] in their home that Joan suddenly turned to me and asked me to make up a word parallel to MONOPOLY but with the emphasis on BUYING rather than SELLING. A classical scholar at once thinks of ονεομαι but it is a deponent verb and

---

[1] Those who wish to check these translations might begin with Henry George Liddell and Robert Scott, *A Greek-English Lexicon* (p. 1283), or *An Intermediate Greek-English Lexicon* (p. 582). In the light of the other meaning of *opson* (ὀψον) as "cooked meat," it is ironic that the term monopsony has most often been applied to certain low-wage labor markets, which are sometimes derogatorily called "meat markets."

MONO prefixed does not produce an attractive (in rhythm or sound) word MONON—A new word if coined must have coinage sound and sense. OPSONEIN was a common classical Greek word "to make . . . purchases often of dried fish." It is used by Aristophanes twice in the *Wasps*, [by] Plutarch, and also it is common in the New Testament. MONOPSONY as parallel to MONOPOLY at once sounded good and has won acceptance by economists.[2]

Are Hallward's reasons for selecting monopsony as the appropriate term convincing? The "deponent" nature of the verb would not really be a problem. A deponent verb is passive voice in form (such as in the sentence "we were beaten") but active voice in meaning ("we lost"). Both the Latin and Greek languages contain many deponent verbs, though there are no deponent verbs in English. The point here, though, is that many English words have been constructed from deponent Latin and Greek verbs: for example, dynasty, mortuary and arbitration.

What about Hallward's other claim, that the use of (ὠνεομαι) would have resulted in a word that was not "attractive in rhythm or sound"? Prefixing mono (μονο) to *oneomai* (ὠνεομαι) could have produced the word "monoöny," where the two dots over the last "o" (a "diaresis") indicate that the "o" is sounded separately as in "cooperative." Thus, this term would sound like a Cockney pronunciation of monotony, with no "t" sound. More likely, though, one of the double "o" sounds would have been dropped (as Hallward seems to imply in his letter), thus producing the word "mónony," which would rhyme with "hominy."

In a one-page 1939 communication in the *American Economic Review*, Vanderveer Custis and J. Clyde Murley suggest that monony would be their preferred term. Their objection to the term monopsony is similar to that expressed here—namely that it is "unsuitable for the [general] use for which it is intended . . . [such as] . . . the situation in which there was a sole employer of a certain type of labor in one of our industrial towns" (p. 348). This short note from 65 years ago appears to be the only previous objection to the term monopsony on etymological grounds, and it seems to have been ignored and forgotten.

The second Greek word for "I buy," as mentioned above, is *priamai* (πριαμαι). If the stem of this verb ("pria") were to be coupled with "mono" as its prefix, the resulting word for "a single buyer" would be *monópria*. Just as the early form *monopolia* became Anglicized to monopoly, *monopria* might have become monopry.

[2] Liddell and Scott's *Greek-English Lexicon* spells the word with an initial long o (ω, omega) rather than with a short o (o, omicron), as does Hallward.

Which Sounds Better?

Whether monopsony is a word that is really more "attractive" sounding than monoöny, monony, monopria or monopry is ultimately a matter of opinion. Those who would argue that Hallward surely made the right choice might well reflect on the reactions (smiles, chuckles, surprised looks?) that instructors often receive from students when they hear monopsony (or oligopsony) for the first time.[3] It is likely that professional economists have simply become accustomed to the word, as they would have become accustomed to whatever term became conventionally used.

The term oligopsony was not coined by Hallward, however. In his book *Monopsony in Motion* (2003, p. 2), Allan Manning credits the invention of the word oligopsony to E. Ronald Walker (1943), who wrote (p. 61): "It is surely only a matter of time before No. 23 [a market situation with two or more large buyers] is christened 'oligopsony.' " Manning remarks that this "matter of time" turned out to be "the time necessary for [Walker] to finish writing the sentence"! However, there are mentions of oligopsony in the economics literature that predate Walker's use of the term by several years: Martin Bronfenbrenner (1940) and Benjamin Higgins (1939), for example.

B. L. Hallward went on to pursue an interesting career after composing the term monopsony for Joan Robinson, as discussed in the biography by Winterbottom (1995). He established his reputation as a classicist principally by his several chapters (including "The Fall of Carthage") in the 12-volume *Cambridge Ancient History* series. He was an acquaintance of A. C. Pigou and often accompanied Pigou on climbing expeditions in the Swiss Alps. In Oscar Wilde's *Picture of Dorian Gray*, the artist who painted the picture that grows old and monstrous was also named Hallward, after a cousin of B. L. Hallward who was a friend of Wilde. In 1948, Hallward became vice-chancellor (executive head) of the University of Nottingham, where he served until 1965. The B. L. Hallward Library at Nottingham bears his name. The father of the term monopsony celebrated his 102nd birthday in May 2003.

■ *The author wishes to thank David Card (for sharing his earlier correspondence with B. L. Hallward), Barbara Pavlock, Nicholas Balabkins, Bryan Arkins and Jeffrey Syracuse. All errors remain the responsibility of the author.*

---

[3] For a time in the 1930s and 1940s, the economics profession seemed to have an obsession for using Greek to coin new terms for various market structures, some of which have faded from the economist's lexicon. Among them would be "polypoly," or many sellers. (The first "poly" means "many" [from πολυς] and is unrelated to the second "poly," which again is from the word "to sell.") The list would also include "pliopoly," by Fritz Machlup (1942), to indicate "more sellers" (newcomers), as well as "heteropoly" and "homeopoly." See Machlup (1952).

References

Bronfenbrenner, Martin. 1940. "Applications of the Discontinuous Oligopoly Demand Curve." *Journal of Political Economy.* June, 48:3, pp. 420–27.

Custis, Vanderveer and J. Clyde Murley. 1939. "Monony or Monopsony?" *American Economic Review.* June, 29:2, p. 348.

Higgins, Benjamin. 1939. "Elements of Indeterminacy in the Theory of Non-Perfect Competition." *American Economic Review.* September, 29:3, pp. 468–79.

An Intermediate Greek-English Lexicon. 2002. Oxford: Oxford University Press.

Liddell, Henry George and Robert Scott. 1968. *A Greek-English Lexicon.* Oxford: Clarendon Press.

Machlup, Fritz. 1942. "Competition, Pliopoly, and Profit." *Economica.* February, 9:33, pp. 1–23.

Machlup, Fritz. 1952. *The Economics of Sellers' Competition.* Baltimore: Johns Hopkins Press.

Manning, Alan. 2003. *Monopsony in Motion.* Princeton: Princeton University Press.

The Oxford English Dictionary, Volume VI. Oxford: Clarendon Press.

Robinson, Joan. 1932. *The Economics of Imperfect Competition.* London: Macmillan.

Walker, E. Ronald. 1943. *From Economic Theory to Policy.* Chicago: University of Chicago Press.

Winterbottom, Derek. 1995. *Bertrand Hallward: First Vice Chancellor of the University of Nottingham, 1948–1965.* Nottingham, U.K.: University of Nottingham Press.

Journal of Economic Perspectives—Volume 18, Number 2—Spring 2004—Pages 263–270

Recommendations for Further Reading

Bernard Saffran

This section will list readings that may be especially useful to teachers of undergraduate economics, as well as other articles that are of broader cultural interest. In general, the articles chosen will be expository or integrative and not focus on original research. If you write or read an appropriate article, please send a copy of the article (and possibly a few sentences describing it) to Bernard Saffran, c/o *Journal of Economic Perspectives*, Department of Economics, Swarthmore College, Swarthmore, PA 19081.

Smorgasbord

Thomas C. Leonard has published a fascinating article, "'More Merciful and Not Less Effective': Eugenics and American Economics in the Progressive Era." He includes an argument for the minimum wage that is new to me. "More surprising than Progressive support for legal minimum wages was the fact that Progressive economists, like their marginalist interlocutors, believed that binding minimum wages would result in job losses. What distinguished supporters of minimum wages from their marginalist opponents was how they regarded minimum-wage-induced job loss. . . . . [M]inimum-wage advocates regarded minimum-wage-induced disemployment as a social *benefit—a eugenic virtue of legal minimum wages.*" Leonard also includes a coda about Gunnar Myrdal, a Nobel-winning economist, "both Myrdal and his wife Alva were themselves eugenicists who promoted an expansion of Swedish-coercive sterilization laws during World War II. More than 60,000 Swedes, over 90% of them women, were sterilized from 1941 to 1975. The Myrdals' eugenics

■ *Bernard Saffran is the Franklin and Betty Barr Professor of Economics, Swarthmore College, Swarthmore, Pennsylvania. His e-mail address is ⟨bsaffra1@swarthmore.edu⟩.*

was not racist. They saw forced sterilization of the unfit, says Daniel Kevles, 'as part of the scientifically oriented planning of the new welfare state.'" *History of Political Economy*, 2003, 35:4, 687–712.

"Explaining Happiness" by Richard A. Easterlin is his "Inaugural Article" as a new member of the National Academy of Sciences. Easterlin concludes, "Economic policy proposals to improve well-being are typically directed toward altering the socioeconomic environment, but not to changing individual preferences. Viewed in terms of the present analysis policies to improve health or facilitate more time with one's family are consistent with greater happiness. But the present analysis implies that preferences too are an appropriate policy concern. The reason preferences are excluded from policy consideration by mainstream economics is because each individual is assumed to be the best judge of his or her own interests. But if individuals are making decisions in ignorance of the effect that hedonic adaptation and social comparison will have on their aspirations, this assumption no longer holds. . . . It is, perhaps, time to recognize that serious attention is needed to devising measures that may contribute to more informed preferences." PNAS (Proceedings of the National Academy of Sciences), September 16, 2003, 11176–11183.

Gilles Saint-Paul writes on "Economic aspects of human cloning and reprogenetics." He points out: "While most discussions of human cloning start and end with ethics, this paper analyzes the economics on human cloning. I analyze the incentives for cloning and its implications for the long-run distribution of skills and income . . . . An important consequence of these models is that cloning will act as a form of what might be called 'unnatural selection', assuming that ability is genetically determined and cloners prefer to make high-ability clones." The issue also includes some discussion of these arguments. *Economic Policy*, April 2003, 74–122.

In his Presidential Address to the American Economics Association delivered in San Diego, which appears in the March 2004 issue of the *American Economic Review*, Peter A. Diamond delivered a spirited defense of the current structure of social security. In a recent book with Peter R. Orszag, he presents his plan for *Saving Social Security*, subtitled "A Balanced Approach." After presenting their plan, they conclude, "The long-term deficit projected in Social Security should not serve as an excuse for destroying the program's social insurance structure. Nor should it be 'fixed' with accounting or other gimmicks that promise to erase the deficit without any pain—eventually the bill for those gimmicks will come due." The book also has a useful question and answer section on the details of the plan. ISBN 0-8157-1838-1.

Games and Economic Behavior contains some of the papers given at the first World Congress of the Game Theory Society held in Bilbao, Spain, in July 2003. Kenneth Arrow offered some "Introductory remarks on the history of game theory": "What really made game theory a working tool was the growing interest on the one hand among economists in asymmetric information and on the other hand in games of incomplete information. Here the fit of tool and subject was exemplary. We have had, then, a conjunction of indirections: ideas, both in mathematics and in economics whose implications and fruitfulness were not understood, dramatizations of concepts for the wrong reasons, and fruits in applications not originally considered. I suppose that history is fairly usual among scientific developments." 2003, 45, 15–18.

From the abstract of "Energy Resources and Global Development" by Jeffrey Chow, Raymond J. Kopp and Paul R. Portney: "In order to address the economic and environmental consequences of our global energy system, we consider the availability and consumption of energy resources. Problems arise from our dependence on combustible fuels, the environmental risks associated with their extraction, and the environmental damage caused by their emissions. Yet no primary energy source, be it renewable or nonrenewable, is free of environmental or economic limitations." *Science*, November 28, 2003, 1528–1531.

The "post-autistic economics network" publishes an online review and other news at ⟨http://www.paecon.net/⟩. It challenges mainstream economics, especially its mathematization. I found some of the sociology of economics especially interesting, including the beginnings of the post-autistic movement in France and the recent Harvard controversies on the teaching of Ec.1.

The "open courseware" at MIT is now up and running. From the website ⟨http://ocw.mit.edu/index.html⟩, you can go to the courses of any department. The website takes some exploring. Not all courses are on the website, and even some courses on the website may offer only a syllabus. For an example that includes a syllabus, readings, problem sets and brief lecture notes, see Frank Levy's course on "Information Technology and the Labor Market" at ⟨http://ocw.mit.edu/OcwWeb/Urban-Studies-and-Planning/11-128Information-Technology-and-the-Labor-MarketSpring2003/CourseHome/index.htm⟩.

From the Federal Reserve

Michael R. Pakko and Patricia S. Pollard discuss, "Burgernomics: A Big Mac™ Guide to Purchasing Power Parity." For some years, the *Economist* magazine has published a guide to whether exchange rates are overvalued or undervalued by comparing the market exchange rate to the local cost of a Big Mac sandwich at McDonald's. The authors write: "It is interesting to find that the simple collection of items comprising the Big Mac sandwich does just as well (or just as poorly) at demonstrating the principles and pitfalls of PPP as do more sophisticated measures." Along the way we learn: "The price of a Big Mac in 2003 ranged from $2.03 in Miami to $3.04 in New York." Also, it took 11 minutes of work to buy a Big Mac in the United States and 112 minutes in the Philippines. *Review:* Federal Reserve Bank of St. Louis, November/December 2003, 9–28.

Douglas Clement has written, "European Vacation," subtitled "There's a simple reason Americans work longer hours than Europeans, says economist Ed Prescott. And it isn't what you think." "The average American worked 1,815 hours in 2002, well above the comparable figures for France (1,545) and Germany

(1,444), for example . . . . According to Prescott, the reason for these large differences in labor supply is not culture. 'French, Japanese, and U.S. workers all have similar preferences,' he writes. 'The French are not better at enjoying leisure. The Japanese are not compulsive savers.' The reason for the wide range in working hours is, in a word, taxes." *Region,* Federal Reserve Bank of Minneapolis, December 2003, 8–11.

The Federal Reserve Bank of New York's *Economic Policy Review* has selected papers from a conference on "Economic Statistics: New Needs for the Twenty-First Century." In "Price Hedonics: A Critical Review," Charles R. Hulten writes: "Changes in official statistical policy therefore should be conservative and credible, and the research agenda must include a component aimed at building confidence that the benefits of change outweigh the costs. Accordingly, the National Research Council panel is right to insist on a conservative approach to the increased use of price hedonics in the CPI [Consumer Price Index]. However, the research community is also right to insist that this technique is the most promising way to account for changes in product quality in official price statistics." Readers will also find an interesting analysis in the article by Jack E. Triplett and Barry P. Bosworth titled "Productivity Measurement Issues in Service Industries: 'Baumol's Disease' Has Been Cured." September 2003, 5–15, 23–33.

Inspiring Classroom Debates

Frank R. Lichtenberg asks, "Are modern pharmaceuticals worth the price?" His answer: "On the basis of years of intensive research, I believe the answer is a resounding 'yes.' For not only is there strong evidence that the benefits from new pharmaceuticals in terms of longer life and better health in old age far exceed the costs, it appears that drug innovation also saves money by reducing demands for other forms of medical care." "The Value of New Drugs" subtitled, "The Good News in Capsule Form." *Milken Review,* Fourth Quarter 2003, 17–25.

Gordon C. Winston's "Point of View" column is entitled, "$50,000 for Your Thoughts: Why Colleges Pay Wages to Their Students." He begins: "College students influence not only one another's clothes, vocabulary, and mating rituals, but also their academic performance. Students educate students, and some do it better than others. Students will learn more, think more carefully, and perform better by associating with academically strong fellow students. We call such influences 'peer effects.'" Winston concludes, "Recognizing the role of peer effects is starting to change our understanding of higher education. It helps answer some previously nagging economic questions, like: Why don't colleges expand to meet excess demand? Why do they often engage in aggressive price discounting even when they can fill their classrooms and dorms? Why do the most expensive colleges have the longest queues of students trying to get in? None of this makes sense in a normal, familiar business environment, but all of it, and more, is motivated by the role of peer effects in producing high-quality education. What remains to be seen is, in the rush to compete for students offering peer quality, will colleges freeze out growing numbers of students with far greater financial needs." *Chronicle of Higher Education*, November 28, 2003.

In his "Economic Scene" column in *The New York Times* on January 8, 2004, Alan B. Krueger asks and answers the question, "After 40 years, what are some results and lessons of America's war on poverty?"

Science discusses "The State of the Planet," starting with an overview by the demographer Joel E. Cohen on "Human Population: The Next Half Century." Cohen begins, "It is a convenient but potentially dangerous fiction to treat population projections as exogenous inputs to economic, environmental, cultural, and political scenarios, as if population processes were autonomous." From the summary, "By 2050, the human population will probably be larger by 2 to 4 billion people, more slowly growing (declining in the more developed regions), more urban, especially in less developed regions, and older than in the 20th century. Two major demographic uncertainties in the next 50 years concern international migration and the structure of families. Economies, nonhuman environments, and cultures (including values, religions, and politics) strongly influence demographic changes. Hence, human choices, individual and collective, will have demographic effects, intentional or otherwise." November 14, 2003, 1172–1175. This paper offers a useful complement to the article by Ronald Lee, "The Demographic Transition: Three Centuries of Fundamental Change," in the Fall 2003 issue of this journal.

Jonathan B. Wight has written, "Teaching the Ethical Foundations of Economics," which is subtitled, "It is time for moral inquiry to be included as part of economics education—or, more accurately, to be reintroduced." Wight begins, "Some economists consider their discipline a science, and thereby divorced from messy ethical details, the normative passions of right and wrong. They teach in a moral vacuum, perhaps even advocating economic agents' operating independently and avariciously, asserting that this magically produces the greatest good for society. Never mind that such a view woefully misinterprets Adam Smith's 'invisible hand'; it also belies economists' own instinctive experience, even if we do not often preach it, of the role of morals and virtue in our scholarly endeavors. . . . Ethical inquiry is an essential component of my economics courses, and it doesn't take much class time because it is integrated into other work. I use a variety of methods, including a scarcity game, public-policy essays, and novels and movies; some of my colleagues add service learning." *The Chronicle Review* of *The Chronicle of Higher Education*, August 15, 2003, B7–B9.

"Jaw-Boning Business Ethics," subtitled "You can lead a shark to water . . ." offers a different perspective. Richard B. McKenzie and Tibor R. Mahan begin, "In the wake of every wave of corporate scandals—many apparently orchestrated by executives with MBAs from elite schools-pundits and academics alike have decried the detachment of modern business education from ethical considerations." They conclude, "You may be tempted to conclude that we oppose any and all training in business ethics. Not so. What we do oppose is the simplistic view that mandated ethics courses will improve business conduct." *Milken Institute Review,* Third Quarter 2003, 42–49.

About Economists

Willem H. Buiter has written "James Tobin: An Appreciation of His Contribution to Economics." "Jim Tobin, who died on March 11, 2002 at the age of 84, was one of the giants of economics of the second half of the twentieth century and the greatest macroeconomist of his generation. Tobin's influence on macroeconomic theory is so pervasive—so much a part of our professional 'acquis,' that many younger economists often are not even aware that it is his ideas they are elaborating, testing, criticizing, refuting or re-inventing." He concludes, "The two economists Tobin admired most were John Maynard Keynes and Irving Fisher. This is not surprising, as he combined in himself the best of both. Tobin had Fisher's analytical skills, insistence on clarity and rigour and attention to relevant detail. He had Keynes's talent for identifying the key economic issues of the time and for cutting through irrelevant detail to address the core analytical and policy issues." Buiter also reminds me of Tobin's review of Milton Friedman's *A Theory of the Consumption Function.* It "ends with the (rhetorical) question: 'It is certainly better to be simple than complicated. But is it better to be simple than right?'" *Economic Journal,* November 2003, F585–F631.

The *Eastern Economic Journal* has a symposium on James Tobin that includes an article from Robert S. Goldfarb, "Remembering James Tobin: Stories mostly from his students." Robert Summers tells the following tale from when he was "a young, struggling ABD instructor." Summers was having some difficulty with his thesis and then hit on a topic involving simulations that Tobin felt was "a good idea." "Because Yale at that time didn't have the computer capability to carry this out, I had to commute to the better-equipped Columbia. Entirely unexpectedly, Jim—who was a colleague and mentor, but not a close friend—came to me in November to say 'Look, Bob, you haven't taught the stat course before . . . and it will take a *lot* of your time. You're spending three days a week in New York, and you have a baby at home. I've taught the course three times, so the cost would be low for me to teach it again. I'm going to teach it for you.' I protested some, but he did it. His compensation was my gratitude! I'm sure he thought it's what a good academic citizen does." Fall 2003, 499–518.

In "Edith Penrose: A Feminist Economist?" Michael H. Best and Jane Humphries argue: "*The Theory of the Growth of the Firm* provides an approach to industrial organization that is not only consistent with feminist economics but can be read as a methodological and expositional exemplar." They also "believe Edith Penrose was a 'feminist economist.' She would not have so defined herself. However, unlike many successful women of her generation, Penrose was not hostile to or dismissive of feminism. Indeed, she was increasingly intrigued by ideas about women's subordination and its causes and consequences. . . . But Penrose did not crusade for women's rights, and she did not work on women's issues. Ironically, her bailiwick within economics was the High Sierra of technology, patents, multinational enterprise, and petroleum economics. How, then, can anyone consider her a feminist economist?" *Feminist Economics*, 2003, 9:1, 47–73.

Anil K. Bera provides "The ET Interview: Professor C.R. Rao," which offers a lot of interesting information about Dr. Rao, of Cramer-Rao inequality fame, and also about the development of statistics in India. For example, the interviewer asks why there are not many brilliant Indian econometricians. Rao is also asked to elucidate on a comment he made in an earlier interview, "I don't think we were very successful with statistical methods in psychology or even in economics. Possibly what is wrong with the economists is that they are not trying to refine their measurements or trying to measure new variables which cause economic changes." *Econometric Theory*, 2003, 19, 331–400.

Hamid Hosseini has written "The arrival of behavioral economics: from Michigan, or the Carnegie School in the 1950s and the early 1960s?" He argues that the roots of behavioral economics go back to George Katona's work on consumer sentiments at Michigan and Herbert Simon's work on bounded rationality at Carnegie. He also offers a quotation that explodes a myth that John Muth developed the rational expectations hypothesis as response to a challenge from Simon. "According to Muth, the assertion that 'Herbert Simon challenged me to come up with a theory of information as rational as the theory economists use to explain the allocation of other resources is definitely not true. There was never such a challenge. The only thing even remotely resembling that is when Franco Modigliani assigned a problem in class to explain executive salaries. Herb Simon presented a model to explain that phenomenon. As a member of Modigliani's class, I tried to develop one too, but it wasn't very good.'" *Journal of Socio-Economics*, 2003, 32:4, 391–409.

David Warsh's "Economic Principals" column for November 16, 2003, is titled "The Man Who Became Keynes." "In the late 70s, when the global economy seemed out of control, and the need for a figure of commanding authority to point the way was widely felt, the plaint was sometimes heard among economists and in the press, 'We need a new Keynes!' From the distance of 25 years, it is clear that even then we were in the process of acquiring just such an economic prophet, albeit from a somewhat unexpected quarter. His name was Milton Friedman." Warsh concludes, "Milton Friedman's nemesis was the clinician Keynes, the trickster who wrote *The General Theory*. It is to Keynes that the author of *Capitalism and Freedom* eventually will be compared." Available at ⟨http://www.economicprincipals.com⟩.

"The father of fractals" is subtitled, "Benoit Mandelbrot's unusual multidisciplinary approach led him to an extraordinary discovery. He worries that modern science is now becoming too specialized." The profile in *The Economist* concludes, "The long saga of fractals, says Dr. Mandelbrot, can be perceived as a ring from art through mathematics, finance, many corners of science and engineering, and finally back to art. Within this smooth ring, Dr. Mandelbrot has pursued his unusual and rough-edged career path. With its many unpredictable twists and turns, but governed by an unseen logic, it is tempting—not to mention fitting—to liken the course of his life to a fractal." December 6, 2003. Available at ⟨http://www.economist.com/science/tq/displayStory.cfm?story_id=2246127⟩.

Asimina Caminis interviews Esther Duflo in "Putting Economic Policy to the Test," subtitled "An economist's real-life experiments yield surprising results." Duflo is described as "part of a rising group of young economists who are questioning traditional development strategies." The article concludes, "What does she hope to accomplish through her work? She answers without hesitation. 'I would like us to know more about what we can do. When someone of good will comes and wants to do something to affect education or the role of women or local governments, I want them to have a menu of things they can experiment with. In the medium term, I want to persuade other people to spend more energy working on that, maybe financing fewer programs, but evaluating the ones they do seriously, using randomized evaluations.' Will she continue with her 'micro' approach? 'For the time being, this is where I am.'" *Finance and Development,* September 2003, 4–7.

"The Economist as Affable Provocateur" is subtitled, "MIT's Sendhil Mullainathan uses interdisciplinary methods to study issues like cigarette taxes and racial bias in hiring." David Glenn writes, "A hallmark of Mr. Mullainathan's work is the use of 'natural variance'—real-world variations that cast light on economic hypotheses." The article concludes, "'The more I got to know economics,' says Mr. Mullainathan, 'I kind of started to feel like—it didn't seem that the highest returns are in mathematical models of one thing or another. Little by little I was led to empirical work. . . . I'm not that motivated by theoretical questions. Usually I'm just motivated by real stuff. And if something theoretical comes of it, that's great.'" *Chronicle of Higher Education,* December 5, 2003.

■ *I would like to thank Joshua Hausman, Robert Kilpatrick, Timothy Taylor and Larry Willmore.*

Journal of Economic Perspectives—Volume 18, Number 2—Spring 2004—Pages 271–276

Comments

To be considered for publication in the Comments section, letters should be relatively short—generally fewer than 1,000 words—and should be sent to the journal offices at the address appearing inside the front cover. The editors will choose which letters will be published. All published letters will be subject to editing for style and length.

Inequality and Poverty

In "Halving Global Poverty," Tim Besley and Robin Burgess (Summer 2003, pp. 3–22) note that, conditional on mean real per capita national income, higher inequality (as measured by the standard deviation of income) is correlated across countries with higher absolute poverty as measured by the headcount of those with less than $1 a day (see their Table 3). This result is not surprising. Indeed, as stated, the observation might be little more than tautological. After all, the more of total national income is taken by the rich and mean income is held constant, then the less is available for the rest, and as such there are likely to be more absolutely poor people.

Is there more to the inequality-poverty link than this tautology? In fact, there is. Consider a regression in which the poverty headcount is the dependent variable, and the two explanatory variables are the mean income of the lower 90 percent of the income distribution and the share of income going to the top decile. One might expect that after taking into account the mean income of the bottom 90 percent of the income distribution, the share of income going to the top percentile should not affect the poverty headcount.

However, when I carried out this regression for using data for 89 countries and territories—that is, all for which these variables are available using the World Bank GPID database

and World Development Indicators—I found that the share of income going to the top decile is large and statistically significant. In an ordinary least squares regression, if the share of income going to the decile rises by 1 percentage point, the percentage of the population below the $1 per day poverty line rises by about half a percentage point, after including the mean income level of the bottom 90 percent as another explanatory variable and adding a constant term. This finding survives inclusion of other variables such as financial depth, and measures of institutional quality (Honohan, 2004). Almost equivalent results are obtained by substituting the mean income of the top decile for their share in total income. These results can be found at ⟨http://econ.worldbank.org/programs/finance/library/⟩.

It is by no means clear why making some rich people richer should increase the number of absolutely poor people: as an empirical fact, this is rather startling. Admittedly, it is consistent with most of the functional forms that are used to fit the statistical distribution of incomes in any country. Two-parameter functional forms for income distribution (such as the log-normal) almost necessarily imply such a relationship, in the sense that mean-preserving parameter changes for any given functional form will send the share of the top decile and the poverty headcount in the same direction. Even a more flexible functional form such as the widely favored three-parameter Singh-Maddala (McDonald, 1984) tends to predict the positive association in this sense. However, this insight only pushes the question back one further step inasmuch as these statistical models lack any serious economic rationale. Besides, the empirical fit of these curves near the ends of the distribution have traditionally been their weak point; thus, there was no *a priori* assurance that this prediction would have been empirically robust.

Of course, there is no surprise that increasing mean national income reduces the poverty headcount. But what is it about societies where the rich are rich that tends to result in more people falling into poverty? This appears to remain something of an unresolved puzzle.

Patrick Honohan
The World Bank
Washington, D.C.

■ *Without implicating him, I am grateful to Aart Kraay for helpful suggestions. This note reflects the views of the author alone and not those of the World Bank.*

References

Honohan, Patrick. 2004. "Financial Development, Growth and Poverty: How Close are the Links," in *Financial Development and Economic Growth: Explaining the Links.* Charles Goodhart, ed. London: Palgrave, forthcoming.

McDonald, James B. 1984. "Some Generalized Functions for the Size Distribution of Income." *Econometrica.* 53:3, pp. 647–63.

Fuel Economy Standards

In their article "The Economics of Fuel Economy Standards," Paul Portney, Ian W.H. Parry, Howard K. Gruenspecht and Winston Harrington (Fall 2003, pp. 203–217) note that engineering studies suggest a substantial opportunity to improve the energy efficiency of new vehicles using demonstrated, cost-effective technologies and that the failure of markets to exploit this potential is difficult to reconcile with economic theory. Given the gap between evidence and theory, the authors express skepticism about the evidence; that is, they criticize the use of engineering studies in justifying more stringent fuel economy standards. The authors do not, however, note that important econometric evidence also points to significant inefficiencies in markets for energy-using equipment.

In a seminal paper on home appliance purchases, Hausman (1979) found that consumers employ an implicit discount rate of 25 percent per year in evaluating the net benefits of improved energy efficiency. A subsequent literature found discount rates ranging from 25 percent to 300 percent in markets for refrigerators, heating and cooling systems, building shell improvements and a variety of other technologies (Frederick et al., 2002). These anomalously high discount rates provide reason to reject the hypothesis that markets for energy-using equipment are characterized by substantive rationality and efficient resource allocation. In a study that is directly relevant to the fuel economy debate, Dreyfus and Viscusi (1995) undertook a hedonic price analysis of the U.S. automobile market to assess consumers' willingness to pay for improved safety and energy efficiency. On the assumption that consumers use a common discount rate in evaluating both safety and fuel economy, the study calculates an implicit discount rate that ranges from 11 to 17 percent in alternative specifications. More tellingly, Dreyfus and Viscusi conclude that only 35 percent of the present-value cost savings provided by improved energy efficiency is capitalized in the purchase price of vehicles.

Attempts to interpret the so-called "energy efficiency gap"—the failure of real-world markets to implement energy-efficient technologies that are cost-effective at prevailing energy prices—have focused mainly on issues of information asymmetries (Howarth and Andersson, 1993), bounded rationality (Conlisk, 1996) and inefficiencies in the structure of large organizations (DeCanio, 1993). These explanations are consistent with empirical work in behavioral economics, which finds that a wedge often exists between observed behavior and the model of substantive rationality in the context of intertemporal decisions (Loewenstein and Thaler, 1989). A contrasting approach is taken by Hassett and Metcalf (1993), who seek to explain the use of high discount rates as a rational response to issues of risk and irreversibility. Sanstad et al. (1995), however, show that these effects are too small to account for the empirical magnitude of the efficiency gap.

Although Portney and his co-authors reason that car buyers are well-informed about fuel economy tradeoffs by the energy labels required for new vehicles, behavioral studies suggest that providing consumers with technically accurate information often has little influence on their decision making (Gardner and Stern, 2002, chapter 4). This observation does not imply that consumers are fundamentally irrational. As Conlisk notes, limitations on people's cognitive capabilities imply that (boundedly) rational agents must rely on simple decision heuristics that are subject to systematic bias. In the context of automobile purchase decisions, energy costs (a) constitute only a small fraction of the total cost of owning and operating a vehicle; and (b) are not tangibly apparent to consumers at the point of decision. These conditions match the circumstances under which bounded rationality most typically prevails, explaining why consumers fail to optimize fuel economy choices as they would given perfect information and infinite cognitive capabilities (Kempton and Layne, 1994).

Portney, Parry, Gruenspecht and Harrington are on firm ground when they note the importance of taxing gasoline to reflect the social costs of fuel consumption. The imperfections that appear to exist in vehicle markets, however, weaken the force of the authors' critique of enhanced fuel economy standards. As the authors note, the National Research Council (2002) found that strengthening the Corporate Average Fuel Economy (CAFE) standards could substantially raise the energy efficiency of new vehicles while maintaining or enhancing consumer welfare. Although this conclusion seems difficult to reconcile with the traditional theory of efficient markets, it is arguably consistent with recent developments in information and behavioral economics.

Richard B. Howarth
Dartmouth College
Hanover, New Hampshire

References

Conlisk, John. 1996. "Why Bounded Rationality?" *Journal of Economic Literature*. June, 34, pp. 669–700.

DeCanio, Stephen J. 1993. "Barriers within Firms to Energy-Efficient Investments." *Energy Policy*. September, 21, pp. 906–14.

Dreyfus, Mark K. and W. Kip Viscusi. 1995. "Rates of Time Preference and Consumer Valuations of Automobile Safety and Fuel Efficiency." *Journal of Law and Economics*. 38:1, pp. 79–98.

Frederick, Shane, George Loewenstein and Ted O'Donoghue. 2002. "Time Discounting and Time Preference: A Critical Review." *Journal of Economic Literature*. 40:2, pp. 351–401.

Gardner, Gerald T. and Paul C. Stern. 2002. *Environmental Problems and Juman Behavior*. Boston: Pearson Custom Publishing.

Hassett, Kevin A. and Gilbert Metcalf. 1993. "Energy Conservation Investment: Do Consumers Discount the Future Correctly?" *Energy Policy*. 21:4, pp. 710–16.

Hausman, Jerry. 1979. "Individual Discount Rates and the Purchase and Utilization of Energy-Using Durables." *Bell Journal of Economics*. 10:1, pp. 33–54.

Howarth, R. B. and B. Andersson. 1993. "Market Barriers to Energy Efficiency." *Energy Economics*. 15:4, pp. 262–72.

Kempton, Willett and Linda Layne. 1994. "The Consumer's Energy Analysis Environment." *Energy Policy*. 22:10, pp. 857–66.

Loewenstein, George and Richard H. Thaler. 1989. "Anomalies: Intertemporal Choice." *Journal of Economic Perspectives*. 3:4, pp. 181–93.

National Research Council. 2002. *Effectiveness and Impacts of Corporate Average Fuel Economy (CAFE) Standards*. Washington: National Academy Press.

Sanstad, Alan H., Carl Blumstein and Steven E. Stoft. 1995. "How High are Options Values in Energy-Efficiency Investments?" *Energy Policy*. 23:9, pp. 739–43.

Reply from Paul Portney, Ian Parry and Winston Harrington

Unfortunately, one of the most crucial issues in assessing the economic merit of tighter fuel economy standards is also one of the most contentious. A number of engineering studies suggest that there is a wide range of fuel-saving technologies that could be adopted by auto manufacturers for which the discounted fuel saving benefits over the vehicle lifetime would exceed the costs of vehicle production—see in particular NRC (2002). If so, tightening Corporate Average Fuel Economy (CAFE) standards on new passenger vehicles can easily be welfare-improving overall; if not, tightening CAFE could be welfare-reducing, due to its perverse effects on increasing the incentive to drive and on compounding distortions from pre-existing fuel taxes (Parry, 2004).

Is there a market failure that prevents auto manufacturers from installing fuel-saving technologies that consumers should be willing to pay for? The most common hypothesis is that auto buyers have very high discount rates and undervalue the true social benefits from future fuel savings. Richard Howarth draws our attention to a number of econometric studies suggesting that consumers may in fact discount future fuel costs at high rates. Howarth's underlying explanation is that when fuel costs are a small portion of total vehicle owning and operating costs and are not tangibly apparent to consumers at the point of purchase, then "...[boundedly rational] consumers fail to optimize fuel economy choices as they would given perfect information and infinite cognitive capabilities."

Maybe. But some of the evidence Howarth cites relates to energy savings from home appliances, and it is not necessarily clear that discount rates from these studies are applicable to automobiles, largely because the energy savings are so difficult for consumers to observe. Of most relevance is the Dreyfus and Viscusi (1995) hedonic analysis of car purchases, which finds a discount rate of 11 to 17 percent. The discount rate used in the NRC (2002) report is 14 percent—exactly the midpoint of this range.

Perhaps it is not that consumers misperceive or overly discount fuel-saving benefits, but rather that engineering studies underestimate the true economic costs of actually adopting fuel-saving technologies. The true economic cost is probably larger than the engineering cost estimates used by the NRC for two reasons. First, it ignores the possible opportunity cost of not using fuel saving technologies for other vehicle enhancements. That is, by forcing automakers to apply their technical expertise to more fuel-efficient engines, tighter CAFE standards could mean fewer of the improvements to which consumers have responded enthusiastically in the past—including such things as enhanced acceleration, towing capacity and so on. It is the implicit values of these foregone improvements that ought to be compared with the fuel economy savings that tighter CAFE standards would bring. A second point is that engineering studies may exclude various sosts of actually implementing a new technology that are difficult to observe—for example, marketing, consumer unfamiliarity and retraining of mechanics.

While it would be extreme to assume all manufacturers incorporate fuel saving technologies that pay for themselves the instant they become available, basing the case for substantially tightening fuel economy standards purely on results from engineering studies is also on rather shaky ground. Until a greater consensus emerges on the extent to which the true economic costs of tightening fuel economy standards differ from engineering costs, policymakers would be well advised to focus on other initiatives that are on firmer ground. We would advocate a moderate (economy-wide) carbon tax to reduce greenhouse gases, a broad oil tax (of perhaps $3 per barrel) to help reduce the economy's dependence on imported oil, encouragement of per-mile insurance (rather than annual lump-sum payments) to reduce driving and reforming the CAFE program by allowing manufacturers to trade fuel economy credits.

References

Dreyfus, Mark K. and W. Kip Viscusi. 1995. "Rates of Time Preference and Consumer Valuations of Automobile Safety and Fuel Efficiency." *Journal of Law and Economics.* 38:1, pp. 79–98.

National Research Council. 2002. *Effectiveness and Impact of Corporate Average Fuel Economy (CAFE) Standards.* Washington, D.C.: National Academy Press.

Parry, Ian W. H. 2004. "Welfare Effects of Tightening the Corporate Average Fuel Economy (CAFE) Standards." Discussion paper, Resouces for the Future, Washington, D.C.

Exchange Rate Regimes

Guillermo Calvo and Frederic S. Mishkin's article "The Mirage of Exchange Rate Regimes for Emerging Market Countries" (Fall 2003, pp. 99–118) illustrates a problem that has plagued discussion of exchange rate regimes: lack of precision, especially regarding fixed exchange rates. Like many other economists, Calvo and Mishkin use the terms "fixed" and "pegged" interchangeably. It is confusing to have two terms for the same thing.

Their definition of one type of fixed exchange rate, a currency board, is vague in a key respect. Calvo and Mishkin (p. 100) say only that a currency board has "enough" reserves "to exchange domestically issued notes for the foreign [anchor] currency on demand." A currency board does not hold just any amount of foreign reserves that may be "enough." Rather, it holds net foreign reserves equal to 100 percent of the monetary base. A currency board does not let its reserves fall below 100 percent, nor does it accumulate excess reserves beyond at most an additional 10 percent. The excess reserves, if any, serve as a cushion against possible losses in the capital value of assets, not as a source of funds for discretionary monetary policy. A currency board holds no significant financial assets other than its foreign reserves, hence it does not hold domestic financial assets.

Their vague definition leads Calvo and Mishkin to say that Argentina's monetary system of April 1991 to January 2002, known locally as "convertibility," was a currency board. However, the central bank held large amounts of domestic financial assets, and over the life of the convertibility system, the ratio of net foreign assets to the monetary base was often quite far above or below 100 percent. It is more accurate to view the convertibility system as the latest of Argentina's many attempts to combine a hard pegged exchange rate with central banking.

Calvo and Mishkin claim that the choice of exchange rate regime "is likely to be of second order importance" in developing good overall economic policies (p. 115). Here again, I think it is possible to be more precise, in a way that is useful for economic policy. Even the best exchange rate regime (whatever you may consider that to be in a particular case) is not enough by itself to ensure economic growth, but a very bad regime is enough by itself to reverse growth. A good exchange rate regime enlarges the potential scope for mutually beneficial trades, but high tax rates, insecure property rights or other factors may still discourage people from actually making the trades. A very bad regime shrinks the scope for mutually beneficial trades, in extreme cases making barter more attractive than monetary exchange. The difference between a good exchange rate regime and the best regime may be small in terms of its effect on economic growth, but there is abundant evidence that the difference between a good regime and a very bad regime is large.

Kurt Schuler
Senior Economist to the Vice Chairman
Joint Economic Committee, U.S. Congress
Washington, D.C.

■ *The views expressed here are the personal views of the author, not necessarily the views of the Joint Economic Committee.*

School Accountability

In their excellent article on "The Promise and Pitfalls of Using Imprecise School Accountability Measures" (Fall 2002, pp. 91–114), Thomas J. Kane and Douglas O. Staiger point out that many accountability systems treat small schools in a capricious fashion. Because a small school has greater sampling variation, its average scores, or average gains, are likely to be volatile and occasionally extreme, even if the school itself is steady and average. Quite ordinary schools, if they are small, are likely to be praised in some years and censured in others.

To address this problem, Kane and Staiger suggest setting "different thresholds for schools of different sizes. For example, grouping schools according to size . . . and giving awards to the top 5 percent in each size class." This proposal solves the problem of comparing small schools to large schools, but it does not change the fact that, within the small school group, schools in the top 5 percent are likely to be there because of luck. Kane and Staiger's other suggestion— lowering the threshold so that more schools win rewards—has the same problem.

What Kane and Staiger overlook is that at least one government recognizes the small-school problem and has taken steps to avoid it. The danger is addressed by Sanders's influential value-added methodology, which is a mixed model focused on year-to-year gains. In Tennessee and other systems that have adopted Sanders's suggestions, school effects are treated as random and estimated using a "shrinkage" estimator known as the empirical Bayes (EB) residual or the best linear unbiased predictor (BLUP). This estimator "shrinks" school averages toward the system mean, with greater shrinkage for schools with smaller enrollments (Sanders, Saxton and Horn, 1996; Robinson, 1991; Raudenbush and Bryk, 2002). Kane and Staiger (2001) allude to empirical Bayes methods in describing their complex "filtered" estimates of school effects, but do not mention that empirical Bayes methods, with their shrinkage properties, are already part of the simpler accountability system in Tennessee.

Shrinkage ensures that a small school is unlikely to have a large estimated effect. For example, suppose that sampling variation made average scores 75 percent reliable for large schools, but only 50 percent reliable for small schools. If both a small school and a large school reported average scores that were two standard deviations above the mean, the large school's estimate would be shrunk to 2×75 percent $= 1.5$ standard deviations, while the small school's estimate would be shrunk to $2 \div 50$ percent $= 1$ standard deviation above the mean. The small school is shrunk more, because a smaller sample provides weaker evidence of extraordinary achievement.

A drawback of this approach is that shrinkage makes it hard for an exceptional small school to get much attention (Raudenbush and Bryk, 2002). From a policy perspective, however, it may be appropriate to focus attention on large schools, since large schools impact more students. In short, one of the pitfalls that Kane and Staiger have identified is something that certain governments have learned to sidestep. These governments should be commended, and others should be encouraged to follow their example.

Paul T. von Hippel
Department of Sociology and Initiative in
  Population Research
Ohio State University
Columbus, Ohio

References

Kane, Thomas J. and Douglas O. Staiger. 2001. "Improving School Accountability Measures." NBER Working Paper No. 8156; Available at ⟨http://www.nber.org/papers/w8156⟩.

Raudenbush, Stephen W. and Anthony S. Bryk. 2002. *Hierarchical Linear Models.* Thousand Oaks, Calif.: Sage.

Robinson, G. K. 1991. "That BLUP is a Good Thing: The Estimation of Random Effects." *Statistical Science.* 6:1, pp. 15–32.

Sanders, William L., Arnold M. Saxton and Sandra P. Horn. 1997. "The Tennessee Value-Added Assessment System: A Quantitative, Outcomes-Based Approach to Educational Assessment," in *Grading Teachers, Grading Schools: Is Student Achievement a Valid Evaluation Measure?* Jason Millman, ed. Thousand Oaks, Calif.: Corwin Press, pp. 137–62.

Notes

2005 Nominating Committee of AEA. In accordance with Article IV, Section 2 of the Bylaws of the American Economic Association, President-elect Daniel McFadden has appointed a Nominating Committee for 2005 consisting of Robert Lucas, chair, Marianne Baxter, Donald Brown, Angus Deaton, Edward Glaeser, Paul Jaskow, Rosa Matzkin and Janet Yellen.

Attention of members is called to the part of the bylaw reading, "In addition to appointees chosen by the President-elect, the Committee shall include any other member of the Association nominated by petition including signatures and addresses of not less than two percent of the members of the Association, delivered to the Secretary before December 1. No member of the Association may validly petition for more than one nominee for the Committee. The names of the Committee shall be announced to the Membership immediately following its appointment and the membership invited to suggest nominees for various offices to the Committee.

Nominations for AEA Officers: 2005. The slate of nominees for Association officers is available on the AEA Web Page, ⟨http://www.vanderbilt.edu/AEA⟩. If you do not have Internet access, you may request this information by e-mail at ⟨aeainfo@vanderbilt.edu⟩, by fax (615-343-7590) or by mail (American Economic Association, 2014 Broadway, Suite 305, Nashville, TN 37203).

Call for abstracts. The Committee on the Status of Women in the Economics Profession (CSWEP) of the American Economic Association will sponsor sessions at the January 2006 American Economic Association meetings in Boston. We will be organizing three sessions on gender-related topics and three sessions on non-gender-related topics. For the gender-related sessions, we are particularly interested in receiving proposals on the under-representation of women in undergraduate economics majors, on the gender implications of increasing global economic integration, and on gender and immigration. However, anyone doing research with gender implications is encouraged to submit an abstract. The three sessions on nongender-related topics will focus on industrial organization. Abstracts are particularly encouraged in the areas of regulation, deregulation and the performance of sectors with significant governmental involvement. Send a cover letter (specifying to which set of sessions the paper is being submitted) and three copies of a one- to two-page abstract (250–1000 words), clearly labeled with the paper title, authors' names and contact information for all the authors, by January 11, 2005, to Francine Blau, CSWEP Chair. We strongly encourage e-mail submissions to ⟨CSWEP@cornell.edu⟩. Hard copy submissions may be sent to Francine Blau, CSWEP Chair, School of Industrial and Labor Relations, 265 Ives Hall, Cornell University, Ithaca, NY 14853-3901 (please note on envelope "CSWEP Abstract").

The **Sixth Annual Economics and the Classroom Conference** will be held September 16–18, 2004, at Jackson Lake Lodge, Grand Teton National Park, Wyoming. Idaho State University, Aplia, Inc., Pearson Addison Wesley and Worth Publishing are sponsoring this event. Scheduled keynote speakers are Paul Krugman and Michael Parkin. Conference information can be obtained from Tesa Stegner, Chair, Department of Economics, Idaho State University; tel.: (208) 282-2346; e-mail: ⟨stegtesa@isu.edu⟩; URL: ⟨http://www.isu.edu/departments/econ⟩.

Call for papers. The Kentucky Economic Association recently changed the name of its journal to the *Journal of Applied Economics and Policy* from the *Kentucky Journal of Economics and Business.* The *Journal* will now be an electronic journal that will publish manuscripts from all *JEL* classifications. All manuscripts will be reviewed by at least two referees. Authors should send three copies of their manuscript and a check for $20 to Thomas G. Watkins, Editor, *Journal of Applied Economics and Policy,* Department of Economics, Eastern Kentucky University, 521 Lancaster Ave., Richmond, KY 40475.

Call for papers. The **69th Annual Meeting of the Midwest Economics Association** will be held March 11–13, 2005, in Milwaukee, Wisconsin. The MEA invites papers and organized sessions in all areas of economics. To submit a paper, send two copies of a one-page abstract indicating appropriate *JEL* classification along with the appropriate submission fee to Professor Greg Duncan, President, Midwest Economics Association, PO Box 467, Cameron, MO 64429. Submissions may also be faxed to 816-632-7820 or sent electronically to ⟨MEA@grinnell.edu⟩. If you would like to submit an organized session, please contact Professor Duncan by September 9, 2004. See the MEA website at ⟨http://web.grinnell.edu/MEA/⟩ for additional guidelines. Deadline for abstract submissions is October 3, 2004. Submission fee for MEA members is $15 per paper. Membership dues are $10 for the 2004–2005 year and may be paid with the paper fee. If you decline to join the MEA at this time, the submission fee is $30 per paper.

Call for papers. *Economic Development and Cultural Change,* now under the editorial leadership of John Strauss, Professor of Economics at Michigan State University, invites new submissions. *EDCC* is a venue to explore what economic and other social sciences reveal about a policy issue. Articles with new insights as well as carefully executed replications that explore robustness of results to different data, different model specifications, or ways of estimation will be entertained. Papers that focus on data quality—for instance, carefully comparing the results of different ways of collecting the same data or comparing the impacts of different definition—will also be considered. For more information visit *EDCC* online: ⟨http://www.journals.uchicago.edu/EDCC⟩.

Call for abstracts, papers and participants. The **2005 Academy of Economics and Finance**

Meetings will be held February 9–12, 2005, in Myrtle Beach, South Carolina. You may participate as a panel organizer, presenter, chair, moderator, discussant or observer. The deadline for submissions is November 1, 2004. All accepted paper may submitted for inclusion in the proceedings. For more information, please contact Graham Mitenko, Program Chair, University of Nebraska, Omaha, 402-554-2532; or e-mail ⟨Gmitenko@unomaha.edu⟩ or AEF at ⟨www.economics-finance.org⟩.

Submissions are invited for a special issue of *Advances in Financial Economics* (Volume 10) on corporate governance broadly defined as the system of controls that helps corporations and other organizations effectively manage, administer and direct economic resources. The deadline is September 1, 2004. Contact Anil Makhija, Ohio State University, 700 E. Fisher Hall, 2100 Neil Avenue, Fisher College of Business, Columbus, OH 43210; e-mail: ⟨makhija_1@osu.edu⟩; tel.: (614) 292-1899; or Mark Hirschey, University of Kansas, 1300 Sunnyside Avenue, School of Business, Lawrence, KS 66045; e-mail: ⟨mhirschey@ku.edu⟩; tel: (785) 864-7563.

Call for papers. The *Indian Journal of Economics and Business* is an international journal that aims at dissemination and advancement of research in all areas of economics and business. The journal welcomes submissions in all areas related to economics and business fields. Each manuscript must include a 200-word abstract. Refer to the "Guidelines for Manuscript Submission" on the website. Submit submission fee, three copies and a diskette to Prof. Kirshore G. Kulkarni, Editor, *Indian Journal of Economics and Business,* Campus Box 77, PO Box 173362, Metropolitan State College of Denver, Denver, CO 80217-3362; tel.: (303) 556-2675; fax: (303) 556-3966; e-mail: ⟨kulkarnk@mscd.edu⟩; URL: ⟨www.ijeb.com⟩.

The *Global Business & Economics Review* (*GBER*) is an international refereed journal, published semiannually (June and December) by the Business & Economics Society International, for the presentation, discussion and analysis of advanced concepts, initial treatments and fundamental research in all fields of Business and Economics. Priority is given to insightful policy oriented articles that deal with the implications of the increasingly global business activity, especially written for the educated layperson.

The *GBER* welcomes contributions from academicians, corporate executives, staff members of research institutions, international organizations and government officials. Interested authors should submit four copies of original manuscripts in English, with authorship identified on a removable cover page, accompanied by a submission fee of $30 payable to B&ESI. Manuscripts and editorial correspondence should be directed to Editor, *GBER*, 64 Holden Street, Worcester, MA 01605-3109, USA.

The **American Academy of Political and Social Science** (AAPSS) recognized its new group of Fellows for 2004. Among the group of nine Fellows are economists Nancy Folbre, University of Massachusetts, and Alan B. Krueger, Princeton University. The academy designates a group of Fellows each year in order to recognize and honor individual social scientists for their distinguished scholarship in the social sciences, sustained efforts to communicate that scholarship to audiences beyond their own discipline, and professional activities that promise to continue to promote the progress of the social sciences. AAPS also designated 27 Graduate Fellows in this first year of the program as well as 157 Junior Fellows of the Academy for a second year. For further information, contact Robert W. Pearson, AAPSS Executive Director; tel.: (215) 746-6500; e-mail: ⟨rwpearso@sas.upenn.edu⟩; url: ⟨http://www.aapss.org⟩.

The **American Institute of Indian Studies** invites applications from scholars from all disciplines who wish to conduct their research in India. Junior fellowships are given to doctoral candidates to conduct research for their dissertations in India for up to eleven months. Senior long-term (six to nine months) and short-term (four months or less) fellowships are available for scholars who hold the Ph.D. degree. Scholarly/Professional development fellowships are available to scholars and professionals who have not previously worked in India. Eligible applicants include 1) U.S. citizens; and 2) citizens of other countries who are students or faculty

members at U.S. colleges and universities (this rule does not apply to U.S. citizens). For applications please contact the American Institute of Indian Studies, 1130 E. 59th Street, Chicago, IL 60637; tel: 773-702-8638; e-mail: ⟨aiis@uchicago.edu⟩; website: ⟨www.indiastudies.org⟩. Application deadline is July 1, 2004.

Call for papers. The 2004 meetings of the **New York State Economics Association** will be held at Ithaca College in Ithaca, New York, October 15–16, 2004. Papers on all topics in economics, business and related social sciences are welcome. Student papers, both graduate and undergraduate, are welcome as well. For more information, including registration forms and submission guidelines, visit the NYSEA website at ⟨http://www.nysea.org⟩, or contact Elia Kacapyr, Department of Economics, Ithaca College, Ithaca, New York; e-mail: ⟨kacapyr@ithaca.edu⟩.

Call for papers. The **Euro-American Association of Economic Development Studies** welcomes proposals of articles for the its journals *Applied Econometrics and International Development*, and *Regional and Sectoral Economic Studies*. These journals select articles with main emphasis on Applied Economics and with quantitative contents. Comparisons among different countries or regions are specially interesting. Both journals occupy top positions at international level by the number of downloads per item. More information and some free downloadable articles at our website: ⟨http://www.usc.es/economet/eaa.htm⟩.

Call for papers. The **National Business and Economics Society** announces a call for papers for our March 10–13, 2005, conference in Key West, Florida. The National Business and Economics Society is a multidisciplinary academic association that focuses on promoting interdisciplinary research of both a theoretical and practical nature. See our website at ⟨www.nbesonline.com⟩. Submission requirement: One page abstract of the research paper in Word e-mailed to ⟨info@nbesonline.com⟩. Submission deadline is July 1, 2004.

To Department Representatives and Executive Officers

When submitting information for inclusion in *Notes*, please observe the following guidelines: Calls for papers, notices of professional meetings, and other announcements of interest to economists should be submitted in one paragraph that contains all relevant information.

News of individual members should be labeled as to category: (1) deaths; (2) retirements; (3)

leaves for special appointments. Give individual's name, present place of employment and relevant dates.

Deadlines for each issue are Spring (May), December 15; Summer (August), March 15; Fall (November), June 15; Winter (February), September 15.

Please send all information to the *Journal of Economic Perspectives,* Macalester College, 1600 Grand Avenue, Saint Paul, Minnesota, 55105. Alternatively, send the information by e-mail to ⟨jep@macalester.edu⟩. We reserve the right to edit material received. The *Notes* are also available at the web site of the American Economic Association: ⟨http://www.vanderbilt.edu/AEA⟩.

New from The MIT Press

The Coming Generational Storm

What You Need to Know About America's Economic Future

Laurence J. Kotlikoff and Scott Burns

"[Kotlikoff's] unfuzzy arithmetic decisively rebuts the Bush tax cuts, which are based on the delusion that 5 - 4 = 6, not 1. Read and judge for yourself the specter of our future: too many retirees dependent on too few working-age people. Fiscal imprudence now mandates broken promises later."
— Paul A. Samuelson, MIT, Nobel Laureate in Economic Sciences (1970)
328 pp. $27.95

Inequality in America

What Role for Human Capital Policies?

James J. Heckman and Alan B. Krueger
edited and with an introduction by Benjamin M. Friedman

"Critical reading for anyone who wants to understand the debate over policy choices to combat widening inequality in the U.S."
— David Card, University of California, Berkeley
The Alvin Hansen Symposium on Public Policy at Harvard University
384 pp., 42 illus. $35

Public Policy and the Economics of Entrepreneurship

edited by Douglas Holtz-Eakin and Harvey S. Rosen

"Anyone interested in the success and failure of entrepreneurs and their organizations, from drug companies to charities to minority-owned firms, will find this book invaluable." — Bruce Meyer, Northwestern University
232 pp., 29 illus. $30

To order call **800-405-1619**.
Prices subject to change without notice.

http://mitpress.mit.edu

Labor Economics

Pierre Cahuc and André Zylberberg

"Offers a uniquely comprehensive, technically in-depth, and up-to-date treatment of modern labor economics."
— David H. Autor, MIT
872 pp., 127 illus. $90

Comparative Economics in a Transforming World Economy

Second Edition

J. Barkley Rosser, Jr., and Marina V. Rosser

"I highly recommend this book for undergraduate and graduate courses in comparative economic systems and political economy."
— Peter J. Boettke, George Mason University
672 pp., 160 illus. $52 paper

India's Emerging Economy

Performance and Prospects in the 1990s and Beyond

edited by Kaushik Basu

"A valuable collection of articles on India's economic performance in the 1990s. This is essential reading for the development scholar; indeed, I would recommend it to anyone with a serious interest in contemporary India."
— Debraj Ray, New York University
328 pp., 17 illus. $42

now in paperback

Our Modern Times

The New Nature of Capitalism in the Information Age

Daniel Cohen

"Explaining capitalism in a scant 124 pages is a daunting task, but Cohen cuts to the quick—the battle over commodities, whether it be gold or labor." — *Wired*
136 pp. $14.95 paper

Water, Race, and Disease

Werner Troesken

"This book will be required reading for anyone interested in public health, political economy, demography, and the history of race relations." — Dora Costa, MIT
NBER Series on Long-Term Factors in Economic Development
288 pp., 43 illus. $35

Life Under Pressure

Mortality and Living Standards in Europe and Asia, 1700-1900

Tommy Bengtsson, Cameron Campbell, James Z. Lee et al.

"This is the richest and most important work in population history In many years."
— Ronald Lee, University of California, Berkeley
Eurasian Population and Family History Series
544 pp., 29 illus. $45

The Economics of Knowledge

Dominique Foray

"Foray has put together a masterly and much-needed book on the economics of knowledge that brings in ideas from law, management, and sociology. The result is a definitive and overarching statement of what we know and where we next need to go."
— Danny Quah, London School of Economics and Political Science
288 pp., 12 illus. $35

now in paperback

Social Dynamics

edited by Steven N. Durlauf and H. Peyton Young

The essays in this book, by some of the creators of the field, provide an overview of social economics.
Economic Learning and Social Evolution series • 256 pp., 21 illus. $18 paper

NORTHWESTERN
UNIVERSITY

THE ERWIN PLEIN
NEMMERS PRIZE
IN ECONOMICS

$150,000 AWARD
PRESENTED BY
NORTHWESTERN
UNIVERSITY

Previous recipients:

2002
EDWARD C. PRESCOTT

2000
DANIEL L. MCFADDEN

1998
ROBERT J. AUMANN

1996
THOMAS J. SARGENT

1994
PETER A. DIAMOND

NEMMERS
PRIZES

2004 RECIPIENT

ERWIN PLEIN
NEMMERS PRIZE
IN ECONOMICS

ARIEL
RUBINSTEIN
*Tel Aviv University
New York University*

*"for a broad series of highly
original contributions to game
theory ranging from analyses
of bargaining and repeated
games to models of bounded
rationality"*

THE SEVENTH
NEMMERS PRIZE IN
ECONOMICS WILL BE
AWARDED IN 2006
WITH NOMINATIONS
DUE BY DECEMBER 1,
2005. FOR FURTHER
INFORMATION,
CONTACT:

nemmers@northwestern.edu

OR

SECRETARY
NEMMERS PRIZES
SELECTION COMMITTEE
OFFICE OF THE PROVOST
NORTHWESTERN
UNIVERSITY
633 CLARK STREET
EVANSTON, ILLINOIS
60208-1119
U.S.A.

www.northwestern.edu/provost/awards/nemmers

CALL FOR PROPOSALS
FOR
POSTER SESSION
ASSA JANUARY 2005

The Committee on Economic Education will sponsor a poster session at the 2005 ASSA Meetings in Philadelphia devoted to active learning strategies across the economics curriculum. Instead of papers, session presenters will prepare large visual summaries of their work mounted in an exhibition room to allow presenters to talk directly with participants. Although we encourage presenters to include evidence that their strategy enhances learning, we do not require quantifiable evidence. We suggest that presenters emphasize the originality of their strategy and provide sufficient information so that participants may apply the technique in their own classrooms.

Proposals should describe the teaching strategy and explain how it will be described in the poster.

Proposals are limited to two pages and due by 1 June 2004.

Please send proposals to:

> Rae Jean B. Goodman
> Economics Department
> U.S. Naval Academy
> 589 McNair Road
> Annapolis, MD 21402-5030
> Phone: 410-293-6891
> Fax: 410-293-6899
> E-mail: Goodman@usna.edu

AMERICAN ECONOMIC ASSOCIATION
COMMITTEE ON THE STATUS OF WOMEN
IN THE ECONOMICS PROFESSION

CSWEP is a committee of the American Economics Association (AEA) established in 1971 to address the need to improve the status of women in the economics profession.

Why support CSWEP?
CSWEP represents women's points of view in the committee work of the AEA, monitors the progress of women within the economics profession, and promotes the advancement of women in the profession. CSWEP represents women in academia, government and business.

CSWEP organizes sessions at the annual meetings of the AEA and the regional economics associations. The Committee also holds social events where women economists can meet and exchange information.

CSWEP publishes a thrice-yearly newsletter containing information that will keep you up-to-date about what is happening in the economics profession and providing useful tips for professional advancement. You will receive the Newsletter when you become a CSWEP Associate.

How do I become a CSWEP Associate?
To become an associate of CSWEP and receive the newsletter, fill out the application below. Students may become CSWEP Associates at no cost. You will still receive the newsletter. We also encourage men to join.

CSWEP MEMBERSHIP FORM

NAME: _____

MAILING ADDRESS: _____

CITY, STATE, ZIP: _____

E-MAIL ADDRESS: _____

☐ check here if currently an AEA member

☐ check here if currently a student   Institute name: _____
                                            Expected Graduation Date: ____

Paying by: ☐ check
                              ☐ credit card (MasterCard/Visa/Amex)

Credit card Number: _____

Expiration Date: _____ Authorizing Signature: _____

If paying by check please send $25.00 to CSWEP, c/o Joan Haworth, Ph.D.; 4901 Tower Court; Tallahassee, FL 32303 (Please make check payable to CSWEP). If paying by credit card, you may fax your membership form to (850) 562-3838.

Please mention THE JOURNAL OF ECONOMIC PERSPECTIVES *When Writing to Advertisers*

Subscribe to the AEA e-Journals!

Electronic access to the AEA journals for libraries, institutions, and firms!

Site licenses to issues of the *American Economic Review, Journal of Economic Literature,* and *Journal of Economic Perspectives* are now online at **www.ingentaselect.com**. Site license access includes reference links (updated daily) to full-text articles through CrossRef and Ingenta, links to full-text articles citing AEA articles, table of contents alerts, and searchable full-text.

An electronic site license to the *AER, JEL,* and *JEP* beginning in 2002 is available only in conjunction with a print or CD-ROM subscription. Site licenses and print subscriptions run concurrently—if you add a site license, it must be renewed when your current print or subscription expires. Please see **www.aeaweb.org/ subscribe.html** for terms and conditions as well as site license usage guidelines.

Send in this form or contact your subscription agent to add an electronic site license to the AEA journals today!

Library/Institution subscriber number (on your mailing label)_____

Site License price as of 1/1/2004 (includes all 3 AEA online journals)...........................$240.00

Company Name_____

Email Address_____
Email address is required for online site licenses

Address Line 1 _____

Address Line 2 _____

City_____ State/Country _____ Zip/Postal Code _____

Advance payment required.
Canadian and foreign payments must be in the form of a check drawn on a United States (U.S.) bank payable in U.S. dollars and must contain proper coding to allow processing through the normal U.S. banking system.

Send with payment to:
American Economic Association, 2014 Broadway, Suite 305, Nashville, TN 37203

Questions?
aeainfo@vanderbilt.edu or phone 615-322-2595

MAILING LIST CORRECTIONS

Information as it currently appears (attach mailing label if available).
PLEASE PRINT.

_____   _____
FIRST NAME AND INITIAL   LAST NAME

_____
ADDRESS LINE 1

_____
ADDRESS LINE 2

_____
ADDRESS LINE 3

_____   _____   _____
CITY   STATE OR COUNTRY   ZIP/POSTAL CODE

Please **PRINT** your **NEW** address and numbers here.

_____   _____
FIRST NAME AND INITIAL   LAST NAME

_____
ADDRESS LINE 1

_____
ADDRESS LINE 2

_____
ADDRES LINE 3

_____   _____   _____
CITY   STATE OR COUNTRY   ZIP/POSTAL CODE

_____   _____
TELEPHONE   FAX

_____
E-Mail ADDRESS

A change of address must be received at least six weeks prior to publication month to ensure uninterrupted delivery of your journals. We charge $4.00 to replace each regular issue not delivered because of an incorrect address. This helps cover the cost of handling and postage. Undelivered journals are not returned to us.

Send to:

AMERICAN ECONOMIC ASSOCIATION
2014 Broadway, Suite 305
Nashville, TN 37203
Fax 615 343.7590

AMERICAN ECONOMIC ASSOCIATION

MEMBERSHIP INFORMATION

Membership includes **three quarterly publication/journals**, plus the *Papers and Proceedings*. Members may access the journals and Directory online, participate in and vote at the annual business meeting, and vote in the election of officers.

Publications/Journals:

American Economic Review (AER), four regular issues published in March, June, September, and December plus the *Papers and Proceedings (P&P)* of the annual meeting published in May. The regular and *P&P* are now available on CD-ROM. *The Survey of Members* is now published electronically.

Journal of Economic Literature (JEL), four issues published in March, June, September, and December. JEL has been available on CD-ROM since 1994; the CD is cumulative (December 1994 through the current issue). JEL switched from print to electronic media for disseminating bibliographic information. This information is available on the CD and online (see URL below).

Journal of Economic Perspectives (JEP), four issues published in February, May, August, and November. Issues are available on CD-ROM.

Journal delete option: You may choose not to receive one journal and deduct $9.00 from your dues.

Membership records are updated monthly: posting date determines journal start date. Membership may not be backdated. Access to online journals is available after records are updated. Journals are mailed second class; please allow 6 to 8 weeks for arrival of journals shipped outside the U.S. Second Class mail service is unusually slow in December; allow 12 weeks for delivery. CDs are mailed First Class.

Regular Membership dues are based on annual income. **Junior Membership** is available to registered students for up to five years. Your faculty advisor or school registrar must certify student status. **Family Membership**, persons living at the same address as a regular member, is an additional membership without publications in print or on CD. A family member can obtain access to AEA journals online.

Membership dues may be paid for a maximum of three years at one time. Payments are not acknowledged at this time; keep a copy of your application for reference. Duplicate payments extend your membership. Payments may be made by check in U.S. dollars drawn on a U.S. bank and must contain proper coding to allow processing through the normal U.S. banking system. Complete all of the information on the application form including the "TOTAL PAID." You may also pay by credit card. Please check your card number. You may fax the application OR mail it; do not do both. The card companies do not allow us to accept payments by telephone or e-mail. It is the Association's policy NOT TO REFUND dues.

All three AEA journals are available online for personal use at no additional charge AEA members (access available after records have been updated). For an additional $15.00 per year, you also may access JSTOR for online back copies of all three journals.

All three journals are available on CD-ROM. You may elect to receive a journal in print format **OR** CD at no additional charge. You may choose to receive any of the journals in print **AND** on CD for an additional $15.00 per journal.

It is **very important** to include your e-mail address and to keep it up to date. It often is used for verification of services. In addition, we plan to notify you of new services by e-mail.

AEA Headquarters:
http://www.vanderbilt.edu/AEA

AEA Publications:
Home Page: http://www.aeaweb.org

American Economic Association
2014 Broadway, Suite 305
Nashville, TN 37203
Telephone: (615) 322.2595 Fax: (615) 343.7590
E-mail: aeainfo@vanderbilt.edu

Journal Access for Members:
Http://www.aeaweb.org/e-pubs

User ID_____(create by accessing e-pubs)
Research: http://www.aeaweb.org/RFE

American Economic Association Application for Membership 2004

Federal I.D. No. 36-2166945

☐ Applying for a new membership ☐ Renewing my membership; membership number (if known)_____

First Name and Initial_____ Last Name_____

Address Line 1_____

Address Line 2_____

Address Line 3_____

City_____ State/Country_____ Zip/Postal Code_____

Telephone_____ Fax No._____

E-mail Address_____ ☐ Do not post e-mail address on Internet.

Fields of Specialization (list 2 only): Primary Field (ED1)_____ Secondary Field (ED2)_____

Include my name on e-mail list to receive: ☐ Announcements ☐ Survey ☐ Commercial Advertising

Membership Dues—Dues include three journals: AER, JEL, & JEP. Journals available in print form and/or CD-ROM. Also available online for personal use. Sign up at http://www.aeaweb.org/e-pubs. It is the Association's policy <u>not to refund dues</u>.

Regular Member
(With annual income of:)
☐ $41,000 or less (08) $64
☐ $41,000-54,000 (09) $77
☐ Above $54,000 (10) $90

☐ Junior Member (06), registered
  student with verification $32

☐ Foreign Postage $30
  (Country other than U.S.A.)

☐ Family Members (03) $13
(Additional membership,
  no publications)

Journal delete option; may
select only 1: *AER* O *JEL* O
JEP O OR *All three* O
         ☐ Deduct   ($9)

Access to JSTOR through
e-PUBS for personal use (EK-J)
         ☐ Add $15

Amounts Paid:
Regular/Junior Dues $___
Family member   ___
Foreign Postage   ___
Less (1) journal delete(___)
Access to JSTOR   ___
Print + CD____
  @ $15 each   ___
TOTAL PAID $___

MULTIPLE YEAR OPTION
Pay for two years $___
Pay for three years $___

Please circle journal format desired (F0). Print only requires no entry.

Journal	Print	CD only	Print + CD	Print + CD add $15 ea.
AER	A	B	C	$15
JEL	D	E	F	$15
JEP	G	H	I	$15

IMPORTANT: Allow time for processing of your membership. Immediate access to online journals is not available. Online access is restricted to your personal use.

Checks must be in US dollars drawn on a US bank and must contain proper coding to allow processing through the normal US banking system. Send checks to: **American Economic Association**
2014 Broadway, Ste 305
Nashville, TN 37203

Charge to: MasterCard ☐   Visa ☐   American Express ☐

Card Number_____ *CSC Code_____ Expire Date_____

*The CSC Code is a 3 or 4 digit number, which is not part of the credit card number. The CSC number is usually found on the back of the card in the Signature area.

Fax #_____ Telephone #_____

Signature_____

Type cardholder's name if different from member's_____

Credit card payments may be faxed to 1-615-343-7590. Fax OR mail. Please do not do both.

Please mention THE JOURNAL OF ECONOMIC PERSPECTIVES *When Writing to Advertisers*